Praise for *Suppressing Dissent*

"There is perhaps no more important way of expressing disagreement, disappointment, insight, the experience of pain, and calling for justice than through dissent. This is how political systems are corrected. This is how oppressed communities are heard and eventually liberated. Unfortunately, this is also why those who engage in dissent are targeted, harassed, and killed. The path to freedom and an improvement of the human condition sits at the intersection of dissent and repression. Nowhere is this more important to explore than in Palestine–Israel and *Suppressing Dissent* is a much-needed reflection on how neglected forms of repression, which target individuals and organizations throughout the world, operate. The book clearly reveals that to understand struggles and counter-struggles within individual nation-states one must understand struggles and counter-struggles throughout the world."
  Christian Davenport, Mary Ann and Charles R. Walgreen Professor for the Study of Human Understanding, University of Michigan

"Democracy is under threat around the world, as illiberal governments cooperate to develop and refine their tools of repression. This incredibly timely book sounds the alarm about efforts by the Israeli government to export its repression of Palestinian rights to the United States, with implications for political dissent and activism globally. Anyone who cares about the future of democracy should pay attention."
  Matt Duss, Executive Vice President, Center for International Policy, former foreign policy advisor to Senator Bernie Sanders

"No issue since the Cold War has tested our society's commitment to free expression like the Palestine–Israel conflict. This timely anthology – examining censorship campaigns against dissidents and civil society groups in the United States, Israel, and Palestine, and the Arab world – is essential reading for anyone who wants to understand how the tactics of McCarthyism have been refurbished for the globalized twenty-first century."
  Brian Hauss, Senior Staff Attorney, ACLU Speech, Privacy, and Technology Project

"This comprehensive collection unpacks how policy on an issue ever more central to US and global security has often been precooked by the delimiting and even criminalization of open discourse and debate. For anyone trying to figure out the appalling policy outcomes and American complicity in war crimes, this collection is a good place to start."
>   Daniel Levy, President, U.S. / Middle East Project, former Israeli negotiator under prime ministers Yitzhak Rabin and Ehud Barak

"An urgent and compelling read, this collection of essays dismantles the false promise that repression can ever guarantee safety. A must-read that envisions a future grounded in the self-determination and human rights of both Palestinians and Israelis."
>   Tess McEnery, Executive Director, Middle East Democracy Center, former director for Democracy and Human Rights at the White House National Security Council

"Repressing speech is never the end of a problem, but rather the beginning of a bigger one. This volume clearly shows that creation of a bigger problem for Israel and Palestine, a region desperately in need of dialogue not imposed silence. *Suppressing Dissent* fills a gap in the policy community's understanding of how shutting down discussion only fuels anger, limits cooperation, and undermines possibilities for peace."
>   Sarah Yager, Washington Director, Human Rights Watch

SUPPRESSING DISSENT

*Shrinking Civic Space,
Transnational Repression
and Palestine–Israel*

EDITED BY
ZAHA HASSAN AND
H.A. HELLYER

Oneworld Academic

An imprint of Oneworld Publications Ltd

First published by Oneworld Academic in 2024

Cover image © Alamy
Copyright © Zaha Hassan and H.A. Hellyer, 2024

All rights reserved
Copyright under Berne Convention
A CIP record for this title is available from the British Library

*Suppressing Dissent: Shrinking Civic Space,
Transnational Repression and Palestine–Israel* © 2024
by H.A. Hellyer and Zaha Hassan (eds.) is licensed under
Creative Commons Attribution 4.0 International. To view a copy of
this license, visit https://creativecommons.org/licenses/by/4.0/

ISBN 978-0-86154-940-5
eISBN 978-0-86154-913-9

Typeset by Geethik Technologies

Oneworld Publications Ltd
10 Bloomsbury Street
London WC1B 3SR
England

Stay up to date with the latest books,
special offers, and exclusive content from
Oneworld with our newsletter

Sign up on our website
oneworld-publications.com

Contents

Introduction: Palestine, Israel, and the Battle for Hearts and Minds – and the Levers of Policy   1
Zaha Hassan

PART ONE: CIVIL SOCIETY IN PALESTINE AND ISRAEL

1. Palestinian Civil Society in the Shadow of a One-State Reality: Managing the Terms of Subjugation After the Oslo Accords ... Resentfully and Ineffectively   21
   Nathan J. Brown

2. The Oslo Framework and Palestinian Authoritarianism   35
   Dana El Kurd

3. Between a Rock and a Hard Place: The Impact of Israel's Occupation and Palestinian Authoritarianism on Community Organizing and NGOs   48
   Zaha Hassan and Layla Gantus

4. The Rise, Weakening, and Resurgence of Civil Society in Israel   63
   Dahlia Scheindlin

5. Neo-Kahanism: The Growing Influence of a Violent, Jewish Supremacist Ideology   79
   Jessica Buxbaum and Katherine Wilkens

PART TWO: MECHANISMS TO REPRESS SPEECH, ACTIVISM, AND AGENCY

6. US Counterterrorism Law and Policy: Its Role in Shutting Down Palestinian Activism and Agency   95
   Nour Soubani and Diala Shamas

7 Israeli Mechanisms to Restrict Civic Space: From Surveillance and Repression in the Occupied West Bank to Policing Israelis Writ Large   110
   Yael Berda

8 Made in Palestine: Repackaging Apartheid as "Smart" Cities   123
   Matt Mahmoudi

9 Digital Repression: How Palestinian Voices are Censored, Surveilled, and Threatened Online   135
   Marwa Fatafta

10 The How-to of Shutting Down Pro-Palestinian Speech and Protest in the US   151
   Lara Friedman

11 Restrictions on Financial Services and Banking and their Impacts on Palestinian NGOs   167
   Ashleigh Subramanian-Montgomery and Paul Carroll

PART THREE: TRANSNATIONAL REPRESSION AND THE IMPACT ON ARAB CONSTITUENCIES IN THE US AND ABROAD

12 Closing Spaces Beyond Borders: Israel's Transnational Repression Network   187
   Yousef Munayyer

13 From Exclusion to Erasure: The Attempt to Silence Arab Americans on Palestine   206
   Maya Berry

14 Shrinking Civic Space in the Arab World and its Relationship to Palestine/Israel   218
   Marwan Muasher and Rafiah Al Talei

Conclusion: Rules, Dissent, and National Security   239
   H.A. Hellyer

List of Contributors   244
Acknowledgements   252
Notes   254

Introduction

Palestine, Israel, and the Battle for Hearts and Minds – and the Levers of Policy

Zaha Hassan

Before October 7, 2023, a discussion about free speech, foreign policy, and social justice activism on American college campuses might have conjured up images of the anti-apartheid protests of the 1980s and the call at that time for universities to divest holdings from companies profiting from South Africa's racist regime. After October 7, the focus is squarely on Palestine/Israel, and not since the violent repression of students opposing the Vietnam War at the University of California, Berkeley, and Kent State University in the 1960s and 1970s has the United States witnessed a foreign policy issue causing such popular unrest and domestic blowback. Not only have the protests calling for a ceasefire in Gaza generated high-voltage debate and controversy, but the sweeping nature of the mobilizations across the country and around the world, and their persistence in the face of public and private efforts[1] to quash them, have exposed Palestine as the defining human rights and social justice issue of our time – something the late Nelson Mandela had recognized decades earlier.[2] To some extent, the student demonstrations should be unsurprising. Israel's regime over Palestinians has been compared to apartheid South Africa for some time,[3] and this perspective is increasingly voiced in the cultural mainstream.[4] In line with this analysis, the tactics students have deployed mirror those of the anti-apartheid campaigners of yore: sit-ins, consumer and cultural boycotts, and divestment campaigns. However, the virulent backlash against pro-Palestinian activists surpasses anything that those calling for an end to South Africa's apartheid were subject to.

What has that backlash looked like? Some university administrators are opposing the right of faculty and students to engage in protest, even preemptively rewriting institutional policy to allow for harsher measures to be taken against them. Donors and lawmakers are threatening to pull funding from universities if administrators do not act against their own students. Afraid of losing donor and federal funding, administrators have called in police in riot gear to arrest students engaged largely in peaceful sit-ins or those who have set up protest encampments – but only after suspending students first so they could be arrested for trespass on their own campus.[5] Some students have been expelled or banned from their colleges, while others face civil litigation for material support for terrorism. A valedictorian at one major university had her speech canceled because administrators claimed it might pose a security risk[6] before administrators decided to cancel the ceremony entirely. External actors have launched online smear campaigns or purchased mobile ads to impugn students as racists, a practice known as doxing.[7] One law school professor even penned an op-ed asking prospective employers not to offer jobs to some of his students, due to their campaign to prevent supporters of Israel from speaking at events hosted by student societies.[8]

Some characterize the crackdown on college campuses as the new McCarthyism,[9] while others say it is justified in order to deal with the disruption to academic life and the threat of property damage. Some Jewish students report feeling uncomfortable or unwelcome on campus, particularly from the slogans and rhetoric used during the protests. However, the punishments being meted out for protest on campus today at some of the most prestigious public and private "ivory towers" in the United States are largely targeted at one side of the political debate. At both a legal and an institutional level, a clear pattern has emerged of a securitized response to complaints against pro-Palestinian activists, with only condemnations directed at counter-protestors even when those protestors have been engaged in serious acts of violence. In the case of a pro-Palestinian protest encampment at the University of California, Los Angeles, during which off-campus actors showed up at night armed with chemical agents and sticks, police took three hours to arrive and then stood by to watch as students were violently assaulted before eventually intervening.[10]

Since October 7 and Israel's subsequent war in Gaza that has killed tens of thousands of Palestinians – including some due to a deliberate Israeli policy to induce famine in the Strip[11] – thousands of students from 970 academic institutions across the United States[12] have been engaged in protests calling for an end to the siege and war in Gaza and to the continued violation of Palestinian rights. Yet as many Americans question US policy, there's been a peculiar *omertà* in the halls of Congress. Consider that at the time of writing no congressional hearings have been held to reassess US policy amid credible reports of mass atrocities committed in Gaza[13] during the seven months of Israel's bombardment of the enclave, even as the destruction has far surpassed the worst bombings of World War II. Yet Congress has censured[14] the lone Palestinian-American legislator in its body for her speech against the war,[15] even as her other colleagues called for the use of nuclear weapons in Gaza or killing the entirety of its population unimpeded.[16] Lawmakers have expressed more concern about the nature of campus protests in support of Palestinian rights than over the indiscriminate bombing of civilians in Gaza. Amid widespread allegations of rising incidents of antisemitic,[17] anti-Palestinian[18]/anti-Arab, and Islamophobic speech and attacks,[19] three university presidents summoned before Congress at a hearing in December 2023 were primarily questioned about their university's response to incitement against Jewish students. The hate crimes against Palestinians on and off campus in the weeks before the hearing weren't seen as worthy of similar examination. Three Palestinian college students had been shot,[20] resulting in the permanent paralysis of one of them, and two Palestinian Chicagoans were stabbed, a child fatally so.[21]

For more than four hours, the presidents faced a barrage of questions about whether they believed Israel had a right to exist, and what they thought about words like "intifada" (Arabic for "shaking off" or "uprising") and phrases such as "from the river to the sea" (part of a protest chant that ends with "Palestine will be free"),[22] before the questions deviated into campus policy on diversity, equity, and inclusion,[23] a subject conservatives usually deride as part of "woke" culture.[24] Within weeks, two of the presidents would be forced to resign from their positions,[25] one following immense pressure from "deep-pocket donors" and "bipartisan political pressure"[26] and the other facing allegations of plagiarism resulting from a coordinated campaign to force her ousting.[27]

More than six months on from the start of Israel's war in Gaza, 99% of the pro-Palestinian, anti-war protests on college campuses have remained peaceful according to a May 2024 report published by the Armed Conflict Location and Event Data Project.[28] Yet much of the media coverage of the protests seems to suggest a causal link between the very real rise of incidents of antisemitic harassment and the campus protest movement against the war in Gaza[29] when, in fact, Jewish groups such as Jewish Voice for Peace and IfNotNow have been a prominent part of many of the protests on and off campus and have been arrested alongside their comrades.[30] Alternatively, some have suggested that the protests have been orchestrated by outside agitators,[31] a storied canard used to discredit civil rights and social justice movements in the United States.

Among the demands of most of the protests on campus has been for universities to "disclose and divest."[32] Like their counterparts in the anti-apartheid campus protests of the 1980s, students today want to know whether their university's investment portfolio includes support for companies complicit in human rights abuses abroad and, if so, they want the university to divest. This demand for divestment has become more urgent after the International Court of Justice ruled in January 2024 that Israel must take immediate and effective measures to prevent a genocide from taking place in Gaza.[33] Some administrators and students have been able to reach an agreement that would allow for greater transparency concerning the university's holdings and a process for considering divestment.[34] However, most colleges and universities have resisted the call for divestment. Besides concerns about loss of donor support, administrators are concerned that the university might run afoul of state law.[35] Thirty-eight states[36] have laws that prohibit state contracts with companies (including non-profit institutions) that boycott Israel or its illegal settlements. Some states require contractors to certify in writing that they are not and will not boycott Israel or its settlements during the contract.[37] Universities also fear that divestment from Israel could put them at risk of violating federal antidiscrimination statutes, given that lobby groups have sought to redefine hate speech to include activism targeting Israel's regime over Palestinians.

While college administrators are risk-averse, their students are not. Many of those protesting may pay a heavy price for their activism. They are risking their physical safety, arrest, reputational smears, loss of their student status, deportation, and job opportunities. Unlike the Vietnam War demonstrations, but similar to those opposing apartheid in South Africa, most college students protesting Israel's war in Gaza have no direct interest – they will not be drafted to fight. And most are not personally impacted by the violence in Gaza. But most importantly, the students – though they number in the thousands – only constitute a small minority of Americans. Why have their actions become the subject of countless front pages – and why have matters concerning Palestine/Israel become so divisive? Why is advocating for Palestinians treated so differently from other human rights activism? What is going on?

PALESTINE VERSUS ISRAEL: THE CONTEST OVER CIVIC SPACE

Engaging in activism or public debate concerning Israel and the situation of Palestinians living under Israeli military occupation has become an incredibly fraught endeavor. This is true even outside of academic settings, whether one lives in Israel, in the occupied Palestinian territories, in a liberal democracy such as the United States, or under autocratic rule in the Arab Middle East. That American classrooms and college campuses – so often idealized as safe spaces for ideas to be debated – have become deeply contested terrain is no accident. Since the 1960s, it has been on college campuses that movements for social and political change have begun, gained momentum, and produced policy change.

Conventionally, the ivory tower prides itself on cultivating freedom of thought, facilitating debate and allowing people to voice their opinions without fear of reprisal. At Columbia University, another campus that one law professor asserts[38] has been overregulating pro-Palestinian speech, the university policy states that the campus "has a vital interest in fostering a climate in which nothing is immune from scrutiny" and that a "clash of opinions on campus" is welcome. Furthermore, it asserts that "the role of the University is not to shield individuals from positions" but to test them, "so that members of the University community can listen, challenge each other, and be challenged in return."[39] However, the vast majority of American academics confess that they self-censor when talking about Israeli–Palestinian issues – but mainly, more than 80% say, if it involves critique of Israel.[40] Only 11% feel the need to self-censor when the criticism is directed at Palestinians.⁴¹ It is not only academics who feel unable to express their views. Following Israel's bombardment and ground invasion of Gaza in 2023–2024, more than a third of Democratic and Independent voters say they are careful when discussing the Israeli–Palestinian conflict outside their home.⁴²

This reticence is especially problematic when the issues at stake are ones involving allegations of genocide implicating the United States. With only 15% of Democrats and 34% of Independents believing that Israel is defending its interests and its actions are justified,⁴³ and a majority of Americans questioning the war and supporting a permanent ceasefire,⁴⁴ more debate is needed, not less. This especially applies when President Biden can recognize that Israel is bombing Gaza indiscriminately,⁴⁵ while blocking UN Security Council action calling for a permanent ceasefire to end the violence.⁴⁶

Beyond classrooms and the traditional public square, a virtual battlefront has also opened up on social media platforms where a growing number of young people get their news and share their assessments of what is going on in the world.⁴⁷ Interest groups and sometimes government actors have put pressure on content moderators to create standards on their platforms, take positions on what constitutes incitement or hate speech, and regulate user posts accordingly. The efforts around content moderation have resulted in more frequent removal of posts and user deplatforming for content that is pro-Palestine or critical of Israel. The volume of views for posts with hashtags sympathetic to the plight of Palestinians combined with the yet-to-be substantiated inference that young Americans are being brainwashed through algorithmic manipulation⁴⁸ has reportedly mobilized members of Congress⁴⁹ and the Biden administration⁵⁰ to support a ban on TikTok, a social media platform popular among Gen Z. In the charged political environment that surrounds discussions about Palestine/Israel today, even reporting that excessive criticism of Israel on the platform is what galvanized congressional and White House support for the ban results in claims of antisemitic bias.⁵¹

It is peculiar for a foreign policy matter to hold such a prominent place in US public debates, alongside other hot-button topics like abortion rights, gun regulation, and the role of religion in public life. Foreign policy does not generally hit the radar screen of Americans outside of the Washington Beltway, unless it involves US boots on the ground and puts soldiers in harm's way. Most Americans do not rank foreign policy high on their list of kitchen-table concerns, even less so when it comes to Middle Eastern wars.[52] But the subject of Palestine/Israel is as much a domestic political concern as it is a foreign policy matter due to the myriad domestic interest groups and political constituencies with a stake in outcomes who can make or break elections. These include legacy Jewish organizations and pro-Israel lobbyists, Palestinian diaspora populations in key US states, the Evangelical wing of the Republican party, weapons manufacturers and defense contractors, and the various national Arab and Muslim American organizations and progressive groups that have made Palestinian human rights concerns a priority issue and a litmus test for whether America is living up to its highest ideals and principles. The domestic political engagement of these stakeholders has given Palestine/Israel an outsized influence in American politics and election cycles.

Even average Americans, who do not rank Palestine/Israel high on their list of concerns, have expressed a preference for an even-handed US approach between Israelis and Palestinians for many years now. Despite the proliferation of state bans against boycotts of Israel, a majority of Republicans and 82% of Democrats oppose legislation that would restrict activism aimed at compelling Israel's compliance with international law.[53] In a poll conducted some months after October 7 and the start of Israel's war on Gaza, almost 60% of Democrats and nearly 50% of Republicans said they support conditioning aid to Israel based on meeting human rights standards.[54] Over 60% of Americans would also condition aid if Israel refused to stop building illegal settlements in the West Bank[55] and a majority of Democrats said in a February 2024 poll, following the deaths of over 20,000 Palestinians in Gaza during Israel's military campaign, that they would be less likely to support a candidate for public office who sends aid to Israel.[56]

While most Americans still say they sympathize more with Israelis than Palestinians,[57] the majority favor a political solution that respects the equal dignity of both peoples.[58] They oppose making the apartheid situation Palestinians currently experience permanent.[59] The trendlines point in the direction of more consensus on issues concerning Palestine/Israel, not less. Young Americans across all major subgroups express support for a permanent ceasefire in Gaza at a five-to-one ratio and only 21% believe that Israel's response to the Hamas attack in October 2023 was justified.[60]

Despite the direction of travel of public opinion and the overwhelming American sentiments favoring a ceasefire in Gaza, in the months since October 7, the White House[61] and many lawmakers[62] have been largely indifferent.

In general, what role do you want the United States to play in mediating the Israeli-Palestinian conflict?

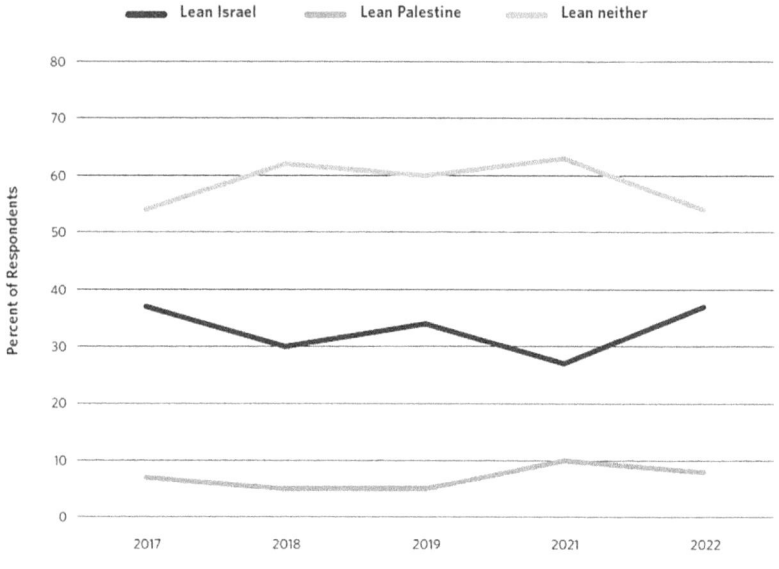

N = 2,138

Source: University of Maryland Critical Issues Poll, https://sadat.umd.edu/sites/sadat.umd.edu/files/american_attitudes_on_israel-palestine.pdf; https://criticalissues.umd.edu/sites/criticalissues.umd.edu/files/UMCIP%20Questionnaire%20Sep%20to%20Oct%202018.pdf; https://criticalissues.umd.edu/sites/criticalissues.umd.edu/files/UMCIP%20Middle%20East%20Questionnaire.pdf; https://criticalissues.umd.edu/sites/criticalissues.umd.edu/files/American%20Attitude%20towards%20Middle%20East%20Policy-%20June%202021.pdf; https://criticalissues.umd.edu/sites/criticalissues.umd.edu/files/UMCIP_11.3-5.2023_Israel-Gaza_Results.pdf

Even as elections were looming large, and at a time when the incumbent Democratic president (before his exit from the race) was polling 11% below his Republican challenger among a key constituency of 18- to 34-year-olds[63] and trailing in battleground states,[64] the administration's decision-making processes appear to be impervious to external pressures. What explains the firewall that seems to exist between public opinion and US foreign policy?

THE IMPACT OF COUNTERTERRORISM MEASURES AND EFFORTS TO REDEFINE ANTISEMITISM

US policy toward Palestine/Israel has long centered Israeli narratives about the nature and causes of conflict between Jews and Arabs. This Israel-centricity and the commitment of successive US presidents to "no daylight" between US policy and support for Israel holds even when American interests and values do not align with Israeli policy. This divergence was on full display during the Israel–Hamas conflict in 2023–2024. For the United States, the objectives were to return American and Israeli hostages, limit Palestinian civilian casualties, and prevent regional escalation. The Israeli prime minister Benjamin Netanyahu sought to prolong and expand the war, to delay accountability for the intelligence failures during his watch, and to escape conviction for corruption. Moreover, Netanyahu stands at the head of a governing coalition that includes the far right, who want the "voluntary immigration"[65] of Palestinians from Gaza. The ethnic cleansing of both Gaza and the West Bank is also favored by members of Netanyahu's own party, Likud.[66] Even though Israel's actions risk implicating the United States in what the International Court of Justice has ruled could amount to a genocide, American policymakers have thus far been reluctant to reassess the US–Israel special relationship.[67] The lack of willingness among most lawmakers to engage in robust debate about or schedule hearings concerning the human rights situation in the occupied Palestinian territories means Israel's security justification for keeping over two million Palestinians in Gaza for almost two decades under a strict siege and blockade, depriving them of the right to freely travel and trade, or have any semblance of a normal life, goes unquestioned. If this were not problematic enough, when lawmakers hear Palestinian expressions of desire for a liberatory future free from occupation and regularized violence, this has been interpreted as a threat to Israel's security and they are mobilized to pass resolutions and legislation that tend to undermine US stated policy that favors bilateral Israeli-Palestinian negotiations toward a two-state solution.

In fact, in responding to this perceived threat, Congress has imposed a regulatory regime over the course of many years to circumscribe and restrict Palestinian advocacy and agency. Though the impetus was to prevent individuals posing a security threat and their dangerous ideas from coming to American shores, the counterterrorism measures enacted went far beyond those aims. McCarthy-era ideological exclusion and deportation laws targeting communists and other "subversives" were an early tool used to prevent Palestinian political leaders and foreign students from advancing Palestinian self-determination in the United States.[68] Holding communist sympathies became the pretext for an initial 1987 deportation case against seven Palestinians and a Kenyan activist. FBI surveillance confirmed that the

"LA Eight," as the group came to be known, had committed no crime;[69] the basis for the deportation of members of the group related entirely to their pro-Palestine advocacy. And though the closure of Palestinian information offices and the de facto Palestine Liberation Organization (PLO) mission in the United States in the 1980s was claimed to be on the basis of concerns related to the US national interest,[70] Congress aimed to limit Palestinian advocacy to signal to the Reagan administration its displeasure with the opening of secret talks with the PLO.[71] When Congress decided to pass legislation to limit[72] and then finally end[73] the practice of travel bans based on mere association (including a specific ban on Nazi party members) and viewpoint discrimination in immigration laws, a special exception was left for members and spokespersons of the PLO.[74] In fact, Congress created an irrebuttable presumption by law that speech on behalf of or membership in the PLO – an umbrella organization representing virtually all Palestinian political factions, labor unions, syndicates, women's and student organizations, notable figures, and thought leaders – was the same as engaging in terrorism.[75]

Laws restricting Palestinian rights advocates from American shores was not enough. In 1987, Congress found that the PLO and all its affiliates were terrorist organizations,[76] a determination that has shown great persistence even as Palestinian political violence waned and Israel recognized the PLO as its interlocutor in peace talks and signed a series of agreements with the organization, and despite the fact that the United States regularly hosted PLO officials at the White House. Rather than repeal the antiquated law, the US granted time-limited waivers to its application so that Palestinian officials could enter the United States for meetings and open an office – but only so long as Palestinians were participating in peace talks with Israel. When in 2017 the PLO refused to engage on a new US peace plan after the United States recognized Jerusalem as the capital of Israel, the United States pulled its waiver from the PLO and all official PLO presence in the United States was forced to end.[77] Because of another law that would make the PLO or the Palestinian Authority (PA) liable for previously dismissed terrorism-related claims if Palestinian officials are present in the United States or open an American office outside of the Palestine Mission to the UN in New York, Palestinian officials only enter the United States today to attend official UN meetings or at the specific invitation of the State Department or members of Congress for the limited purposes allowed by law. Thus, when the Palestinian foreign minister was invited to the United States in 2023 for meetings with

US officials, he was forced to remain silent during a public event hosted for Arab diplomats to discuss the Israel–Hamas war.[78] If he spoke about the situation in Gaza, he would have triggered the jurisdictional predicate that would have made the PLO and PA liable for $655 million in civil damages.

Today, it is Palestinian civil society that is effectively facing a gag order. Foreign persons – and sometimes dual US citizens – may be subjected to travel bans and be prevented from entering the United States if they are associated with organizations Israel has designated as terrorists. Because Israel deems support for campaigns to boycott, divest from, and sanction Israel a national security threat, Americans may also face travel bans and be denied entry to Israel and the occupied territories for matters of personal conscience. Members of Congress critical of Israel have even faced bans on this basis.[79] Because of Israel's hermetic control over the occupied territories, these entry restrictions impact academic and cultural exchange with Palestinians and prevent local NGOs from benefitting from the expertise of foreign experts where those persons are deemed problematic by Israeli authorities.

For Palestinians smeared by Israel as a security threat or designated as terrorists, they and their civil society organizations may be treated as untouchables by current or prospective funders, financial institutions, contractors, and international NGOs due to the risk posed by material support for terrorism laws in the United States. Israeli designations of Palestinian NGOs have also resulted in US government officials limiting engagement with them or their staff[80] even while the State Department asserts that it has not changed its assessment of the organizations and has not seen evidence that would cause them to be listed as terrorist organizations under US law.

An Israeli terror designation or a mere accusation may have a devastating impact on Palestinian civil society organizations and on those in the United States who want to support their work. In the case of six prominent Palestinian community-based organizations and human rights groups, the impact of their designation resulted in attacks on their facilities, arrest of their staff, confiscation of computers and client files, suspension of their donor funding, and uncertainty about whether local banks would close their accounts to limit their own legal liability.[81] Some have had to move part of their operations abroad.

American NGOs and civil society actors must also be careful about their engagement with entities abroad. Beyond the criminal liability they might face in the United States if they are alleged to have links to terrorism, US organizations may face civil suit under material support for terrorism laws. The mere filing of such a suit against the American charity UNRWA USA National Committee[82] forced the organization to suspend its fundraising activities in support of the eponymous UN agency that was its sole beneficiary.[83] The UN Relief and Works Agency for Palestine Refugees (UNRWA) has long been the target of an organized campaign[84] to shut down its operations by those who believe terminating the standing UN body responsible for sustaining refugees as a recognizable community would also end the rights and claims of refugees to return to and seek reparations from Israel. Following the Israeli government's lodging of unsubstantiated terrorism allegations against the UN agency after the start of the Israel–Hamas war,[85] the Biden administration suspended its voluntary contributions and Congress passed legislation prohibiting appropriations to UNRWA until March 2025.[86] The suspension of funding to UNRWA came amid Israel's man-made famine in Gaza[87] and after a World Court ruling requiring Israel to allow immediate and effective aid to enter the area, with UNRWA the only humanitarian body with capacity to deliver food across the besieged enclave. The effort to discredit and defund UNRWA will have a profound impact not only on the over two million Palestinians facing starvation in Gaza, but also on the rest of the 5.8 million registered Palestinian refugees UNRWA serves throughout the West Bank, Jordan, Lebanon, and Syria.

And if a new bill advancing in Congress passes, non-profit organizations in the United States may be stripped of their tax-exempt status with little due process under the claim that their advocacy supports terrorism.[88] The bill has wide-ranging consequences beyond Palestine/Israel. All it will take is a determination by the secretary of the Treasury that an NGO is furthering the agenda of a proscribed organization and that NGO will lose its charitable status, crippling its fundraising capacity.[89] The potential for misuse of this power cannot be overstated.

ANTISEMITISM VERSUS UNCOMFORTABLE SPEECH AND THE SILENCING OF CRITICISM OF ISRAEL

Along with expansive application of counterterrorism measures, overly broad and vague definitions of antisemitism are being deployed to silence critique of Israeli policy. Expressions of Palestinian identity[90] and the teaching of Palestinian history and lived experience[91] have also been attacked as proxies for anti-Jewish animus. A still-in-effect Trump administration executive order empowers federal agencies including the Department of Education to rely on[92] a definition of antisemitism developed by the International Holocaust Remembrance Alliance[93] (IHRA) that conflates particular criticism of Israel with antisemitism. Six examples contained in the IHRA definition concern or relate to Israel and some are likely to chill otherwise protected political speech. The executive order instructs the Department of Education to consider the examples as prohibited ethnic, racial or national origin discrimination. This is causing some confusion for colleges and universities receiving federal funding[94] where compliance with federal law is at odds with institutional commitments to academic freedom. The Biden administration's National Strategy to Counter Antisemitism released in 2023 only added to the confusion, choosing not to align with any one definition of antisemitism – at least not for the purpose of setting domestic policy.[95] Rather, federal, state, and local agencies, along with civil society organizations, are instructed to make their own determinations based on one of three recognized definitions of antisemitism. In the very same policy document, however, the White House relies on a questionable source[96] for documentation and data collection on antisemitism, an NGO that actively advocates for IHRA's use and attempts to normalize the notion that opposition to Zionism, a political ideology, is the same as anti-Jewish hate. If a new bill, the Antisemitism Awareness Act,[97] which passed in the House in May 2024 and is now being considered in the Senate, becomes law, this confusion will be resolved: colleges and universities will be in violation of federal law if they do not punish certain campus speech critical of Israel if it falls within IHRA's examples. Two of IHRA's examples of antisemitism in particular – describing Israel as a "racist endeavor" or applying "double standards" to Israel – are so open to interpretation that they could be used to shut down a substantial portion of criticism of Israel. College administrators will be forced to police faculty and staff, undermining their institutional mandate for academic freedom and repressing the free expression of ideas.

Beyond college campuses, much of the debate around what constitutes antisemitism today involves the digital space. Social media has been an important feature of the Palestine/Israel public opinion war since the 2008–2009 Israeli bombardment of Gaza known as Operation Cast Lead.[98] Palestinian civil society has taken to social media to document the violence they experience during heightened tensions. This has spurred a corresponding Israeli information architecture involving public-private networks including civil society groups and online "bloggers and backers" to counter images Palestinian users share of their wounded and killed during Israel's various military campaigns.[99] According to Alessandro Accorsi, "for some time the Israeli efforts weren't quite as successful at influencing global public opinion as the organic and dynamic, albeit less organized, pro-Palestinian campaigns."[100] But it has not been for lack of trying. Israel invests millions on a strategy to counter pro-Palestinian speech and activism,[101] even measuring the amount of airtime Israeli narratives get on news channels during high-intensity violence with Gaza in comparison to Palestinian narratives.[102] During the course of the latest Israeli campaign against Gaza, social media researchers have found an Israeli influence operation being conducted over multiple platforms using hundreds of fake accounts to target young English-speaking audiences in Western countries.[103] The tactics of the campaign included amplifying Israel government claims about the Israel–Hamas violence, including those about UNRWA staff connections to Hamas and to the October 7 attacks. Israeli authorities also actively engage with social media content moderators. According to an independent study commissioned by Meta following the 2021 Israel–Hamas war,[104] the company denied Palestinian users their freedom of expression by removing their content and over-moderating Arabic-speaking users when compared to Hebrew-speaking users.[105]

Another battlefront has already been open at the state level for years. Dozens of state legislatures or governors across the US have taken measures to curb Palestinian advocacy within their borders.[106] Some penalize those supporting boycotts of Israel, requiring those wanting to contract with the state to certify that they have never or will not engage in such activity. Others involve use of unreasonably vague or broad definitions of antisemitism under state civil rights laws or criminal statutes on hate crime. While such efforts appear to violate existing US Supreme Court precedent, at least one federal appeals court has upheld a state law requiring certification from state contractors that they will not engage in boycotts of Israel.[107] The potential for further restrictions on dissent abound. Some states have begun passing legislation that penalizes organizers of mass protests if any criminal act occurs during the mobilization,[108] including such violations as obstruction of traffic, normal fare during most protests.

The US Supreme Court has recently refused to hear a challenge to such laws, keeping them in place in three states. With so much pro-Palestinian advocacy today taking the form of mass protests – taking over bridges,[109] freeways,[110] train stations, and public spaces – the effort to impute liability to organizers could shut down yet another well-established tool used by civil and human rights advocates when policymakers have refused to respond to their concerns.

On the international level, the Biden administration has taken an unambiguous position on what constitutes anti-Jewish hate: delegitimization of Israel, or calling into question Israel's privileging of Jewish identity over other identities, is antisemitism.[111] One lawmaker is now seeking for the first time to prohibit the appropriation of funds to international organizations that engage in conduct that is antisemitic as defined by IHRA and has added to that definition that any critique of Zionism as racist or that states that Zionism or Israel is guilty of apartheid is also anti-Jewish hate speech. If this measure becomes law, the United States will be barred from funding the UN or any other international organization if they criticize Israeli policies or the ideological basis for its policies.

SHRINKING PALESTINIAN CIVIC SPACE, RISING ILLIBERALISM IN ISRAEL, AND ARAB AUTHORITARIANISM

While it is often said that a vibrant civil society is essential for democracies to breathe, in repressed societies or places under foreign military occupation, restrictions imposed on civil society are a defining feature. During the many decades of Israeli occupation and before the Oslo peace process was launched in 1993, Palestinian civil society – including private entities, civic organizations, faith-based charities, unions, and syndicates – had some latitude to function, but only as a social safety net in place of public institutions. This was all under the watchful gaze and tight grip of the Israeli military administration which criminalized political activity and protest and designated the PLO and all Palestinian political factions as terrorist organizations. After the PA was established in an agreement signed between Israel and the PLO in 1994, Palestinian civil society had to contend with a new layer of regulation and oversight. What is the state of civil society and civic freedoms in the occupied Palestinian territories today? In one word, "repressed," according to CIVICUS.[112] Most Palestinians are likely to call that a gross understatement.

Alongside the failure of the Oslo peace process, and as successive Israeli governments have lurched further and further to the right of the political spectrum to incorporate the racist and annexationist political agenda of parties like Jewish Power and Religious Zionism, efforts have accelerated to consolidate Israel's settlement enterprise and entrench Jewish control over the occupied Palestinian territories. To prevent Palestinian protest and resistance to the changes taking place on the ground, Israel has imposed ever more repressive measures on Palestinian civil society and has allowed settler violence to run rampant. In addition to treating virtually all Palestinian political activity as terrorism, the Israeli government and its military administration have applied the designation to community-based organizations, humanitarian groups, and human rights defenders. Civil society actors also face smear campaigns and malicious litigation for unsubstantiated allegations of supporting terrorism that can result in a loss of donor funding, closure of bank accounts and/or loss of access to financial services, and other secondary effects which cripple operations and end the important work that these organizations do.[113] And as the Fatah-ruled PA has attempted to maintain its relevance as Israel's peace partner – despite the enduring occupation and the intractable political schism existing between Fatah and Hamas which has controlled Gaza for almost two decades – measures have proliferated to restrict criticism of and protest against the PA as well.[114]

In the Arab Middle East, civic protest and activism related to events in Palestine/Israel are either instrumentalized for the regime's agenda or they are repressed altogether for fear they might spill over into an Arab Spring 2.0. Efforts towards Arab–Israeli normalization and the transfer of invasive surveillance systems between Israel and Arab states are causing Arab constituencies in the Middle East to draw linkages between their lack of democratic freedoms and warming relations with Israel. With space for dissent becoming more and more circumscribed as Arab governments increase ties with Israel, the relationships between Arab populations and their governments are likely to continue to face strain.

THE NEW FACE OF REPRESSION, ITS LONG ARM, AND THE FUTURE OF CIVIC FREEDOMS

Many of the tactics used to quash debate are no longer the domain of government authorities alone. In 2015, Israel established the Ministry of Strategic Affairs to coordinate with civil society actors and interest groups abroad not only to influence public opinion, but also to take action to restrict dissent, impacting the civil rights of Americans.[115] Much of this activity is done in the open, involving strategic litigation, pressure and smear campaigns, and advocacy in support of legislation to delegitimize certain speech and protest. Yet the State Department does not recognize such activity as constituting transnational repression,[116] deeming the label inapplicable to its close ally in the region. The State Department is not alone in this determination. Other influential authorities on the subject have excluded Israel from scrutiny. For example, Freedom House's report, "Addressing transnational repression on campuses in the United States,"[117] omits examination of the links between those doxing and harassing students for their pro-Palestine speech and Israeli intelligence, though such activity targeting students has been an issue of concern for years now.[118] And despite the fact that half the population under Israeli control have been denied political and civil rights for fifty-seven years and a growing consensus has emerged among legal experts and human rights organizations that Israel's regime over Palestinians is one of apartheid,[119] the Freedom Report's rating of people's access to political freedoms and civil liberties in 210 countries and territories indicates Israel is "free."[120]

That a liberal democracy such as the United States might restrict certain political speech and activism of Americans on a matter of international peace and security for the sake of its special relationship with a foreign government foreshadows a troubling future. Might the restrictions imposed on dissent concerning Palestine/Israel become a blueprint for shutting down debate on other issues of domestic or global concern? Are we already headed down a slippery slope where both public and private regulators of civic spaces are privileging some speech over others? What does it mean for our First Amendment freedoms – to protest, to organize, to boycott, to dissent – if public and private actors working in parallel or in coordination with foreign governments can close off mechanisms for non-violent social and political change? What becomes of informed foreign policy and the US objective of securing a just and durable peace between Palestinians and Israelis – or on any other foreign policy challenge – as the marketplace of ideas becomes more and more heavily policed? The United States is the single most influential actor on the international stage. Measures adopted in Washington, or even at the state level, to limit dissent are sure to be felt beyond American shores. The contributors to this book put the particular case of Palestine/Israel under the microscope as a way to illustrate the problem and to begin a conversation to address it.

PART ONE

CIVIL SOCIETY IN PALESTINE AND ISRAEL

1

Palestinian Civil Society in the Shadow of a One-State Reality: Managing the Terms of Subjugation after the Oslo Accords ... Resentfully and Ineffectively

Nathan J. Brown

Palestine has a civil society but not a state. Or rather, the state that governs Palestine, however geographically defined, is Israel. The state of Palestine, while widely recognized internationally, exercises nothing like sovereignty on the ground. Yet a host of NGOs, private voluntary associations, professional associations, unions, youth clubs, community centers, and interest groups – what people who speak of "civil society" are referring to – exist. Some are led by those who regard themselves quite self-consciously – or are regarded by others – as part of "civil society"; others do what they do without concern about whether they merit the label.

The constraints on Palestinian civil society have always been formidable but they have varied. And for a while building civil society was an alternative to (or a substitute for) a Palestinian state. In the 1990s, during the Oslo peace process, the prospect of a Palestinian state and international support for some aspects of Palestinian institution building led to a great increase in groups that presented themselves as "civil society." And for some prominent organizations – especially those focused on human rights – that led to their positioning themselves as a voice of critical opposition to both the Israeli occupation and the Palestinian national leadership. The end of the Oslo process, the entrenchment of Israeli control over all of Mandatory Palestine, and the resurgence of conflict have combined to form an environment that is hostile to Palestinian civil society in the West Bank and Gaza in all its forms.[1]

WHAT IS PALESTINIAN CIVIL SOCIETY?

The term "civil society," meaning ways in which people organize outside of official structures, was generally restricted to scholarly and philosophical circles until the waning days of communism in Central and Eastern Europe, when it gained a more public and confrontational potency: when citizens of those societies organized themselves outside of official circles, they spoke and eventually mobilized in a manner that challenged existing regimes, leading to their rapid collapse as Soviet support shriveled. Global efforts to create liberal and democratic societies came to be built in part on support for "civil society," with that concept applied most frequently (if sometimes unconsciously) to professionalized organizations based around a specific issue (human rights, public health, education, gender equality) through organization and programming rather than primarily through a political process of party-building and elections (links between "civil society" and "political society" might occur but they were not the centerpiece of such efforts).

In the Palestinian case, the term "civil society" has come to have several different meanings, most of which are positive – though occasionally the term can be used in a barbed fashion suggesting that it consists of elitist organizations. That range of meanings – including the negative ones – steers our attention in a number of directions: at professionalized human rights organizations, semi-official bodies for licensing dentists, and local youth clubs. All these kinds of civil society organizations have navigated a difficult and shifting political reality: division, occupation, and failed attempts at state building. And now they are coping with a reality that few can regard as temporary or ad hoc but instead as the deepening reality of a single state that, through a myriad of structures, places sharp constraints on organizational activity. But the established components of Palestinian society, especially in the West Bank and Gaza, have largely soldiered on over the past half-century right up to the present.

Over the course of the twentieth century, Palestinians slowly built the components of a national movement, one that was designed to support the creation of a state of Palestine that would take its place in the international arena – and to operate in its absence until it emerged. Unions, parties, schools, newspapers, universities, and movements arose, often operating under the watchful and restrictive eye of whatever state or authority governed the territory where they were based. Some were closely or loosely affiliated with what Palestinians came to call "the factions" – organized movements designed to lead the way toward liberation and statehood. In the last third of the twentieth century, many (but not all) of these organizations tended to gravitate toward the Palestine Liberation Organization (PLO) as the "sole, legitimate representative of the Palestinian people" – and perhaps the seed of a Palestinian state.

But the reality of Palestinian life involved deep divisions as well. Palestinian citizens of Israel, those in the West Bank, Gazans, and those in the diaspora all tended to have separate organizations despite efforts by the PLO and others to knit them together. After 1967, all Palestinians between the Mediterranean Sea and the Jordan River came under Israeli control. After two decades, the Palestinian national leadership, based then in the diaspora, came to accept the idea of partition according to which a state of Palestine would emerge in the West Bank and Gaza alongside Israel. That led the leadership to sign the Oslo Accords, relocate from the diaspora and return to historic Palestine, and begin building a Palestinian National Authority (PA) as the kernel of a Palestinian state.

The state-building project started steadily decaying in the first decade of the twenty-first century and has now completely collapsed, leaving behind a shriveled PLO, a PA that administers and polices but serves no long-term purpose, and a splintered national movement with a major faction (Hamas) standing outside the leadership structure. Today, there is no Palestinian state on the horizon, and it is very difficult to find anyone other than hapless diplomats who pretend otherwise (and even many of them are giving up). But what of Palestinian society? While the state-building project has failed and the structures of the national movement are either desiccated or divided, how do Palestinians work collectively? Palestinians have not disappeared; their national identity has not been erased; and local fields of action persist. The increasingly hostile environment is shared by all of Palestinian civil society, but its component parts still operate quite differently. How do they organize and what do they do – and what does this portend for the future?

SELF-CONSCIOUS CIVIL SOCIETY

The most visible Palestinian organizations internationally are those that present themselves explicitly as "civil society." And indeed, Palestine has a rich and diverse set of well-established NGOs, some of them decades old, with formal structures and bylaws, professional and highly trained staff, domestic reach, and global audiences. They focus on human rights, education, and medical care, advocating for and providing services to constituencies who are often not organized. While they all were built under difficult circumstances and in the absence of a Palestinian state, the current entrenchment of the one-state reality is hemming them in on all sides, with global backers, local officials, and Palestinian constituencies all making it more difficult for them to operate.

These NGOs arose at a time in which many Palestinians living in the West Bank and Gaza – especially a younger generation of educated professionals – consciously and deliberately aimed to build a society that was able to assist and guide Palestinians at a time when the external leadership was weak and even friendly Arab countries were more likely to support Palestinians financially than through pursuing any effective diplomatic or military path. Formal political links with Jordan were attenuating and the PLO's longstanding concern that strong organizations in the West Bank and Gaza might eventually produce an alternative national leadership began to ebb, albeit partially and slowly. New spaces – universities and newspapers – operated under heavy Israeli oversight but still provided friendlier turf for organizing and discussing than had existed in the past. The First Intifada was based on a strong collective spirit and increased the international audience for reports on human rights violations and Israeli settlement activity.

The Oslo process greatly changed the environment for these organizations. First, it created the PA, a new body to administer the affairs of Palestinians in the West Bank and Gaza. And while US and Israeli officials studiously refused to speak at that time of a "two-state solution" or of the PA as the foundation of an independent Palestinian state, the PA leadership – and the PLO leadership from which it drew – had no such qualms. A group of activists who had self-consciously positioned themselves outside of the structures of political authority now had to figure out how to position themselves vis-à-vis this new state in the making.

Second, the "peace process" – which in the 1990s operated, however fitfully, as more than a slogan – occasioned a burst of international generosity toward Palestinian institutions, both those that formed part of the PA and those that were parts of what now were labeled both inside and outside of Palestine as "civil society."

Palestinian civil society, now conceived and supported explicitly as "civil society," tended to have three characteristics during this period. First, it was led by professional staff (and professionalized in other ways as well, with formal governance structures, annual reports, mission statements, and all the trappings of institutionalized organizations). Second, it was oppositional in nature – critical of the occupation, of course, but also willing to issue statements and reports critical of the PA, as it was being built, for corruption, authoritarianism, and undemocratic behavior. And third, Palestinian civil society was led by organizations with boards, funders, and structures of financial and administrative oversight – but no members. As opposed to a trade union, for instance, the leadership of a human rights or educational organization in what came to be called the "NGO sector" may have represented the interests of humans or students but was not selected by them or answerable directly to them.

These characteristics led to some pushback – among Israeli and Palestinian officials to be sure, but sometimes by a wide variety of Palestinians (or by politicians seeking to discredit them) who could suggest that "civil society" consisted of a set of overly negative, self-appointed, and elitist individuals. And the grumbling was reciprocated by many civil society leaders. There were also fears that the resulting "peace process" would lead not to a Palestinian state but a series of "Bantustans" dividing Palestinians. Many noted that the Palestinian diaspora had been marginalized and feared they would be forgotten by leaders now based only in the West Bank and Gaza. Authoritarian behavior by PA officials added to the discontent and led to a widening gap between the would-be state and those understood to be civil society leaders.

It was not just reverse snobbery that created concerns about Palestinian civil society. Even some critical intellectuals in Palestine and the diaspora saw a "civil society" that was not well connected to the society from which it was supposed to spring and that effectively supported a peace process that was not leading to Palestinian self-determination. The resulting political environment became difficult to navigate. The generous international funders for Palestinian civil society came under political pressure and sometimes legal restrictions when some Palestinian NGO leaders showed up at the World Conference against Racism in Durban, South Africa in 2001 to criticize Israeli policy; when Western legal moves against terrorism became increasingly mechanized into controls over banking; and when the bitterness of the Second Intifada led some groups (especially in Israel and the United States) to police Palestinian rhetoric.

Yet the activity of such groups continued and most funders (especially European ones) showed some staying power. The more established Palestinian NGOs continued to operate even as the Israeli occupation became more intrusive, the islands of Palestinian autonomy retreated, the PA became increasingly authoritarian, and international donors showed increasing squeamishness. Yet in the past few years the ability of NGOs to maneuver in this environment has decayed and the assortment of forces arrayed against them has grown more powerful.

First, Israel, by alleging terrorism, has launched crackdowns on some of Palestine's most prominent NGOs (such as Al-Haq, one of the oldest and most reputable human rights organizations). Its evidence of terrorism has persuaded no other governments. Many Palestinian NGOs were initiated by individuals with ties to particular political factions; some factions – such as the Popular Front for the Liberation of Palestine – have been designated by some Western governments as "terrorist organizations," and most evidence produced publicly relied on the partisan affiliation of these particular individuals, sometimes dating back decades. It is difficult to escape the impression that it is the credibility of these NGOs and the documentation that they circulate internationally (and even within Israel) that is the real concern of an Israeli leadership that has identified the Boycott, Divestment, and Sanctions movement as a threat (one initially heavily boosted by a coalition of leading Palestinian NGOs). But as implausible as the terrorism charges are, Israeli authorities have acted on them, preventing travel by NGO leaders and raiding offices. And the environment after Hamas's October 7 massacre of Israeli civilians made some previously bold European funders begin to lose their nerve.

Second, the PA itself has suppressed civil society in a less selective manner with far wider impact, using a variety of legal and extralegal tools. With regard to the former, a restrictive NGO law, modeled on that promulgated by other authoritarian states in the region, places limits on international funding and requires them to report to official actors. Those NGOs that do not comply find their accounts frozen. A restrictive social media law hangs over vocal critics of the leadership. While such legal obstacles have proven onerous for some, probably more problematic is the assortment of extralegal tools that have been deployed. Independent NGOs have felt pressure to appoint individuals loyal to Fatah, the ruling party in the PA, to their boards or senior positions in order to be allowed to operate and avoid having security services visit their offices.

It is not only increasing obstructions but also decreasing access that has affected the effectiveness of large NGOs. Those that have focused on pursuing legislative change have no clear lobbying path. Certainly the Israeli state and occupation authorities do not show themselves amenable to persuasion on how to modify the legal framework of the occupation or patterns of enforcement. Palestinian officials are a less hopeless case, but the suspension of the parliament since 2007 has robbed NGOs of a public forum and a set of elected legislators responsive to popular concerns. There is an ad hoc legislative process that goes through the cabinet to the president, who issues decrees with the force of law, but that leaves organizations campaigning for change – say, on domestic violence – trying to persuade a particular minister, arming him or her with arguments to persuade unaccountable officials and a president who does not face election.

Large, professionalized NGOs still do operate with some level of protection because of their prominence and international reputations. But that protection is ebbing with growing donor disinterest (and even despair), a continued reputation for elitism, and an Israeli leadership aiming to undercut their credibility if they criticize the occupation. The space for their work is shrinking slowly and thus edging them out of the limelight. This marginalization appears especially stark when placed in a long-term perspective, comparing today's situation with the role of such NGOs in the past and projecting into an uncertain and unpromising future. Almost all members of the Palestinian NGO Network (PNGO) fall into this category of professionalized and prominent organizations, dealing with constrictions and donor nervousness.

SEMI-OFFICIAL CIVIL SOCIETY: NOTHING TO DO WITH ISRAEL AND EVERYTHING TO DO WITH ISRAEL

What is happening for the formal NGO sector is also happening for a group of formal organizations that are not, strictly speaking, non-governmental

– unions, professional syndicates, and other associations licensed by political authorities to organize their sector of society and granted some autonomy to do so. And over the past decade, they have been the most active and vibrant; in the 2022/2023 school year, many Palestinians were highly focused on a sustained teachers' strike that almost escaped international attention. For reasons that ostensibly have to do with the PA's fiscal crisis and growing authoritarianism – but fundamentally stemming from the entrenchment of the one-state reality – they are still finding the space for autonomous action shrinking.

Semi-official organizations have diverse origins – some were affiliated with the PLO; others date back to Jordanian, Egyptian, or even Mandatory rule; and some are newer. Those that are recognized and granted legal status by the PA are generally referred to as syndicates (*niqabat*); those that are associated with the PLO are generally known as unions. And there are some other vital organizations as well that are similarly semi-official, most notably alms (*zakat*) committees, organized on a local basis and overseen by the Palestinian Ministry of Religious Affairs, but generally relying on reputable (and pious) local volunteer staff and private donations. Similarly, student associations at each university are not self-constituting but overseen by universities that are in turn overseen by the Ministry of Higher Education.

In the 1990s state-building period, most of these bodies, especially those involving the professions, experienced internal tensions. With the prospective emergence of a Palestinian state, some members sought to focus on professional concerns (training, licensing), member needs (pay, working conditions), or internal governance (elections). For others, the shift from focus on the Palestinian national movement to professional demands was premature. A second internal division was political: many unions and associations had partisan leaders, with Fatah stalwarts heading them. Dissidents within each body – those unwilling to bow to factional leadership – often placed professional demands at the forefront but were sometimes suspected of acting on the basis of their own factional loyalties. A third problem involved the operation of multiple bodies (in Gaza, in the West Bank, connected with Jordan, and with strong links to the diaspora) in the same field, contrary to the idea of a single, officially recognized body.

When the peace process collapsed and the Second Intifada erupted in 2000, the dynamic changed completely; it has never recovered. The idea of refocusing professional syndicates largely on professional matters seemed inopportune at best; struggle among the factions became more pronounced (especially after the West Bank/Gaza split of 2007) and even struggle within factions intensified. Because recognized unions and syndicates are represented in the Palestinian National Council – a barely functioning and rarely convened body, but still one that is on paper the ultimate source of authority for all Palestinian institutions – the national leadership seemed inclined to keep syndicates under the control of loyalists.

Some semi-official bodies have suffered even more. *Zakat* committees, organized in each locality and recognized under the relevant laws, generally consist of individuals with strong reputations for probity and piety; they receive alms donations and distribute them to those they determine are needy (and in recent years have gone beyond distribution to development projects). While thus licensed and regulated by an official body (with oversight in the West Bank handed over from the Jordanian Ministry of Religious Affairs to the Palestinian one since Oslo), they have been autonomous. After the West Bank/Gaza split of 2007, and with accusations from Israel (given credence by United States prosecutors) that West Bank *zakat* committees were connected to Hamas, Palestinian authorities in Ramallah have placed *zakat* committees in the West Bank under much stricter political scrutiny, appointing politically loyal figures – and reining in their autonomy.

But there are two exceptions to these trends, albeit only partial and episodic in nature. First, each Palestinian university has a student council elected by the student body. Elections focus on student concerns to be sure, but they are also sites for Palestinian political factions to organize slates – leaving PA and university officials nervous about them and often finding ways to obstruct them. Even Hamas has sometimes been able to field credible candidates, presenting themselves as concerned with students, earnest, and not coopted by national leaders seen as corrupt and oppressive and university leaders insufficiently responsive to student concerns. And that means they are seen as surrogates for national electioneering. It is not yet clear what the Israeli determination to destroy Hamas as an organization will mean in the West Bank.

Second, the upsurge in activism by teachers has been quite formidable and difficult to contain on the occasions it has broken out – with the most serious wave coming in 2023 (with the issues raised then still unresolved as of the time of this writing). The teachers' union is attached to the PLO (and therefore not a PA-recognized syndicate) with a leadership that is largely (but not exclusively) Fatah-dominated. Dating back almost a quarter-century, wildcat strikes and impromptu efforts at independent unions have recurred, generally over issues of pay but also advancing complaints that the PLO-affiliated union represents the national leadership more than it represents teachers.

In the late 1990s and early 2000s, a network of "coordinating committees" arose, sometimes organizing short-term strikes. At times, leaders of these movements have been arrested or subject to disciplinary action. In 2023, the PA's fiscal crisis and failure to pay full salaries led to a group of syndicates and unions striking (including lawyers and doctors), but the formal leaders of each of these bodies saw the action as a short-term protest. Teachers engaged in a more protracted strike, led not by their union but by a "movement" (*hirak*) with an anonymous leadership, reputed to be organized in part by those involved in the "coordinating committees" of earlier decades.

The 2023 strike brought much of the public education system to a halt, affecting the majority of Palestinian families throughout the West Bank. In conversations with Palestinians (including some students) in the summer that year, I found sympathy for teachers much more marked than sympathy for the cash-strapped PA, even though the strike threatened to disrupt an educational process just beginning to recover from Covid-era shutdowns. The strike did have some critics, to be sure, mostly those who saw it as motivated by factional leaders (from both the leftist and Islamist camps) seeking to embarrass the national leadership and advancing unrealistic demands during the PA's dire fiscal crisis.

That fiscal crisis – made existential in 2024 with draconian Israeli measures designed to choke off the transfer of tax revenues from Israeli to PA bodies as stipulated by the Oslo Accords – has led to an even more precarious situation for such organizations. Semi-official bodies are harnessed to a decaying and sidelined national movement as the Israel–Hamas conflict erupts, with no ability or interest to create alternative social or political visions.

GRASSROOTS SOCIETY AND YOUTH

Palestinian civil society is richer the closer one looks to the ground: what looks from the outside or the top as a set of professionalized NGOs can appear at the grassroots level as a web of youth clubs, volunteer organizations, charities, and women's associations. The factions undertook strong efforts in the 1980s to build such organizations, some of which are thus seen as loosely (or sometimes tightly if informally) affiliated with them. The First Intifada was built in part on such organizations and the efforts to build local coalitions across factions. The Second Intifada saw a similar wave, though Palestinians who were not part of armed groups remember that period as characterized by "militarization" that marginalized many activists dedicated to "popular" unarmed resistance – demonstrations, strikes, and other efforts to mobilize on a local level.

Grassroots society is still very much alive – but it may be losing its ability to organize a youthful generation less inclined toward coordinated action. Recently, their response to the one-state reality is taking different, and very worrying, forms.

Some of these grassroots organizations are linked to factions (in the West Bank, Fatah in particular has an extensive presence; Hamas did before the split but many of the Islamist-oriented or even religious grassroots organizations have been placed under watchful eyes). Such factional links are often informal through a prominent local factional leader, often giving an organization a strongly partisan reputation despite a lack of formal ties. Many youth clubs in camps on the West Bank, for instance, are all but formally affiliated with Fatah and follow a local leader.

In past organizing waves, networks have drawn some of these organizations together either by imitation or quite formally. The 1930s saw women's organizations spring up in many cities. The period before and during the First Intifada saw local volunteer efforts by groups (students, medical personnel, and others), often initiated by factional leaders and sometimes evolving into professionalized national organizations (for example, the Union of Palestinian Medical Relief Committees, initiated by volunteer medical professionals from the left in 1979, has evolved into the Palestinian Medical Relief Society, a major NGO).

Such organizations still exist and can be an important meeting space; in the past their connections with the factions have sometimes linked them to political activity or cemented political loyalties. While largely reliant on volunteer efforts, international assistance has helped formalize some organizations, either through direct financing through specific projects or working with major NGOs that partner with smaller, less professionalized local bodies.

Given the informal and local nature of many organizations, general statements are hard to make and even harder to document. But seasoned researchers tend to agree on a set of observations. First, in recent years, the extent of alienation and despair about the Palestinian national project cannot be overstated; such trends are particularly marked among youth who have grown up in a steadily more constrictive one-state reality, with a "leadership" that cannot lead, and factions who offer no strategic vision or even an attractive set of tactics for positive movement.

Second, while the factions do not seem attractive, they still seem inevitable as there are no alternatives arising, and most young people seem to gravitate toward a faction. Their allegiances are sometimes inherited from a past generation, and they align with some general tendencies (more religious people are more likely to gravitate to Hamas and those uninterested in religion still incline to the leftist factions). But ideologies and allegiances seem to be far shallower than they were in earlier generations.

Third, Palestinian politics is less personalized than it has been in the past. Fatah is divided up into rival camps often more on the basis of personality than principle. Other factions – and Hamas in particular – seem to function better as organizations, though of course rivalries still exist. But most national heroes discussed by Palestinians are no longer alive. And that is particularly true among the young. When asked about Marwan Barghouti, a prominent Fatah leader imprisoned in Israel, one young Palestinian answered me, "Is that the guy who is in jail?" As one knowledgeable Palestinian academic told me, "This generation has no heroes." This is an environment in which it is difficult for an individual or faction to lead, even if they had any idea where to go.

Fourth, with the decay in Palestinian governance structures, individuals with problems are far more likely to go to senior security officials or rely on tribes and informal structures. Organized bodies in civil society are weak and the elected parliament no longer exists (only local officials are elected). Some reach out directly to the "civil administration" – the Israeli body that directly or indirectly oversees much of their lives, especially if they wish to travel. And it has thus become something of a staple of Palestinian political discussions to observe that Israel is finally succeeding in building "village leagues" – an initiative of the early 1980s when Israeli authorities sponsored a series of local strongmen in an attempt to administer Palestinian society through a system that appeared to those living under it to be tantamount to governing through coopted warlords.

But most notably, this younger generation is radical – and, as one person knowledgeable about public opinion polling suggests, more radical the younger one is. The radicalism is not in the ideological realm but in the distrust of any institutions and authority and willingness to countenance any form of resistance. The upsurge of violence seems therefore more about self-expression than either collective or strategic action.

IMPLICATIONS: TUMBLING FROM A MURKY PAST INTO A DARKER FUTURE?

The trajectory for Palestinian civil society has never been straightforward; each new threat has also opened new opportunities. But in the years since the collapse of the Oslo process, almost all trends at work have been pernicious if gradual in their effects. Internationally, there have been growing restrictions placed by donors (both formally, often through anti-terrorism regulations; and informally, through nervousness about activities that are subject to criticism in the donor society). Israeli authorities have closed down organizations on occasion: first those accused of links with Hamas; in 2023, the net was cast far more broadly. The 2023–2024 war against Hamas in Gaza is likely to have severe if still undetermined repercussions in the West Bank.

For their part, PA leaders have tightened the law and developed other tools of pressure. And civil society is as factionalized as all other aspects of Palestinian political life. For all the mounting political obstacles, the social obstacles are also daunting: official and popular suspicions of large NGOs; youth disengagement; and a mounting cross-generational sense of the futility of concerted action. Palestinian civil society offers at best a way of coping with the worst effects of the one-state reality, and it does not generally do so in a promising manner.

Almost all affected actors will likely feel the harmful effects of this decay: international actors who have sought a just and peaceful outcome to – or less ambitiously, a just and peaceful way to manage – persistent conflicts over land, control, and occupation; Palestinian actors of all political stripes;

and most Israeli actors. But there is an exception. The vision articulated intermittently on the Israeli right – going back to the 1970s and up to recent statements by Prime Minister Netanyahu – of Israeli sovereignty over most or all of the territory without rights of citizenship or voting for most Palestinians – is beginning to be recognized even within much of Israeli political debate as a form of apartheid. The afflictions of Palestinian civil society might seem to serve that vision.

But it is hardly clear that the set of arrangements increasingly decried by critics as fulfilling the legal definition of "apartheid" is likely to be peaceful or stable over the long term. The first two intifadas were preceded by the strengthening of informal networks and even formal ones at the grassroots level. These networks were often led by factions or involved cross-factional alliances. That does not seem to be taking place now. What appeared in 2022 and 2023 from afar to be a wave of impulsive but isolated actions looks the same way up close, unaffiliated with any factions. The impotence of the Palestinian national leadership in the Israel–Hamas war hardly strengthened the credibility of the factions. The waves of youth violence and opportunistic attacks that have grown in recent years seem more expressive than strategic or even tactical in nature.

Unlike the Oslo period, there is no clearly identifiable diplomatic or political process that various actors can sign up to support. And the response of most external actors to worrying trends has been vague rhetorical warnings about the future, coupled, when needed, by short-term crisis management. It may be time for a more sustained approach that is less about a final status agreement between Israel and the Palestinian national movement and more about strengthening protection for basic human rights for all concerned.

2

The Oslo Framework and Palestinian Authoritarianism

Dana El Kurd

INTRODUCTION

In the aftermath of the October 7, 2023 attack, in which Hamas-led Palestinian militants attacked Israeli communities across the Gaza border and Israel began its assault on the Gaza Strip, there has been renewed discussion and urgency around the topic of Palestinian leadership. Analysts and policymakers wondered who could step in to govern Gaza if Israeli forces allowed anyone other than the military to do so. Moreover, analysts lamented the seeming lack of leadership that existed in the Palestinian political landscape, given the low level of popularity and legitimacy of both the Palestinian Authority (PA) in the West Bank, and Hamas in the Gaza Strip.

What this discussion often overlooked, however, was the root cause of this vacuum in political leadership, and why alternatives seemingly could not be found. The reality is that, since the Oslo Accords, the Palestinian public has been subjected not only to occupation and repression from the Israeli government, but also authoritarian conditions imposed by their own leadership. Furthermore, this state of affairs is not accidental, but rather actively supported by the international community – with the US at its helm. These authoritarian conditions have repressed the Palestinian public, and hollowed out formal institutional political bodies, such as the PA and the Palestine Liberation Organization (PLO). Thus, it is not a shortage of potential leadership, talent, or expertise of Palestinian political actors that is the problem. The crux of the issue is that internationally backed authoritarian actors and structures have stymied potential alternatives to the status quo.

This chapter outlines the development of Palestinian authoritarianism in the occupied territories; in particular, the relationship of Palestinian authoritarianism to the Oslo Accords, the ongoing Israeli occupation, and American and broader international intervention. First, the chapter will demonstrate the ways in which the PA has been empowered to engage in cooptation and repression to dodge accountability to the Palestinian public, and to remain in power to fulfill its role vis-à-vis the peace process. This dynamic has hollowed out alternatives to the PA's rule, and worsened conditions for Palestinians in the occupied territories. The role of Hamas as a governing body in the Gaza Strip will also be addressed. Despite the different model of governance, Hamas's function can also only be understood through the state-building paradigms imposed by the Oslo Accords. Second, the chapter will highlight sources of opposition to the authoritarian status quo, including a variety of grassroots alternatives.

THE CREATION OF THE PALESTINIAN AUTHORITY

The PA is an agent of the PLO, created under the Oslo Accords, which are a series of agreements concluded between Israel and the PLO. The PA was conceived as an interim body that would have degrees of autonomy in parts of the occupied Palestinian territories from which Israeli troops would be redeployed over time. In the aftermath of the 1987 Palestinian uprising, commonly known as the First Intifada, the Oslo Accords have been heavily criticized as compromising the rights and claims of Palestinian refugees and exiles in favor of limited rule in parts of the occupied territories and without guarantees of an end to Israeli control.

To conclude the agreement, the PLO, headed by chairman Yasser Arafat, bypassed local Palestinian leadership in the occupied territories who were engaged in bilateral peace talks with Israeli counterparts in the negotiations track established by the Madrid Conference, convened by the United States and the Soviet Union in 1991. The agreement was heavily criticized by the local leadership because of the risk that the PA would be coopted by the Israeli occupying power.[1] The PLO's leadership, on the other hand, largely functioning in the diaspora, argued that the deal would be a stepping-stone in achieving Palestinian sovereignty within five years and that the international community, particularly the United States, would help mitigate the risks. For the PLO's leadership, returning to some part of the Palestinian homeland was seen as critically important after decades of operating abroad, where the PLO's welcome was never guaranteed.[2]

Israeli leaders, however, did not hide their intentions or their interpretation of the deal. According to the then Israeli prime minister, Yitzhak Rabin, when he addressed the Knesset shortly after signing the Oslo Agreement, Palestinians would only ever get something "less than a state."[3] Regardless, the PLO leadership returned to the occupied territories to take control of certain service provisions and begin the process of building a functioning state under occupation.

Following a series of Israeli redeployments, the PA was given civil authority and internal security control over 18% of the West Bank (Area A) and shared internal security control in another 20% (Area B). Israel retained full authority over the remaining 62% of the West Bank (Area C) where illegal Israeli settlements are located, as well as East Jerusalem, which would be the subject of permanent status negotiations.[4]

STAGES OF DEVELOPMENT

In the first stage of the PA's development – 1994 to 1999 – the PA had to contend with some degree of societal pressure. Opposition parties outside the PLO umbrella, including Hamas, had to be tolerated, and given space to operate. Nevertheless, the creation of the PA immediately changed two major dynamics in the Palestinian political landscape.

First, the state-building process and the associated channeling of donor funding to the PA undermined the status of the PLO. The PLO as a national liberation movement that spoke for, and incorporated, Palestinian aspirations across the diaspora – however imperfectly – became a zombie organization, effectively subordinate to the PA.[5] Second, the PA coopted local civil society leaders inside the occupied territories as well as hollowing out grassroots organizations that Palestinians under occupation had come to largely rely on before 1994.[6] Those organizations were responsible for the ability of Palestinians not only to resist the occupation, but to mobilize at the levels seen during the First Intifada. But with international backing, the PA replaced civil society organizations as the focal point. International donors pushed Palestinian civil society organizations to "professionalize," and become more formalized NGOs. This process of "NGOization" greatly reduced the efficacy of Palestinian civil society in addressing the needs of the communities they served. It also ignored the political context within which they worked and put pressure on them to limit the scope of their activities.[7]

Then, Camp David failed to secure a final deal in 2000 and the Palestinians launched the Second Intifada. This was the second stage of the PA's development: an era of great instability and collapse of order (*infilaat amni*).[8] The fragmented nature of Palestinian politics during this time meant that the Second Intifada was less coordinated, and thus more reliant on armed resistance and political violence.[9] It was also during this time that not only did a militant wing emerge out of Fatah (the Al-Aqsa Martyrs' Brigades) but the political Islamist groups engaged much more frequently in tactics such as suicide bombing.[10] According to B'Tselem, 5,512 Palestinians were killed during this time, with 605 killed by other Palestinians. The armed militias also inflicted costs on the Israeli side that had not been seen before, with 492 Israeli civilians and 89 Israeli security personnel killed.[11]

The Palestinian people incurred costs during the Second Intifada that did little to achieve a two-state reality afterwards. Instead, the international community and the Israeli state took steps to avoid the possibility of such an uprising being repeated. This included empowering a PA under the leadership of Mahmoud Abbas, sidelining President Yasser Arafat until his death. Thus began the third stage of the PA's development, in which the PA consolidated its control over society more fully and funding of their security apparatus rose to new levels. The US Security Coordinator in Jerusalem, an American-led multilateral mechanism established after the end of the Second Intifada, expanded and retrained the PA security apparatus, ensuring that the PA would absorb their primary mandate: subduing opposition from within, and coordinating security with the Israeli state.[12] United States funding and involvement in Palestinian security matters helped to remind PA decision makers of the costs of another popular uprising.

This objective became even more important to the international community in the aftermath of the 2006 parliamentary elections, in which Hamas won a plurality in the Palestinian legislature. The PA's leadership as well as its international backers fully committed to the idea that the PA would continue as it was, even at odds with the people it claimed to represent. As a result, a great deal of Western pressure and funding went into disregarding the election results and preventing Hamas from entering a coalition government. This culminated in the split in governance between the Fatah-ruled PA in the West Bank and the Hamas authority in the Gaza Strip that persists to this day.

A CONSOLIDATED PALESTINIAN AUTHORITY

After the 2006 elections, the feedback loop between the PA leadership and Palestinian civil society was severely disrupted. Since then, other mechanisms by which Palestinian society could channel their concerns or aspirations were also narrowed significantly, if not made completely irrelevant. This included not only the cooptation of certain grassroots organizations, and the repression of others, but also the dismantling of the Palestinian Legislative Council, a unicameral elected legislature.[13] Furthermore, the PA was able to pursue such a tactic without fear of societal discontent or significant challenge due to international, American, and Israeli support. The consolidated PA cemented authoritarian control over Palestinian society through both cooptation and repression strategies.

First, to coopt civil society actors who might operate in opposition, the PA offered jobs. The PA is a major employer in the occupied Palestinian territories.[14] Jobs made potential critics beholden to the PA and invested in its continuation. Many Palestinians were thus limited in their ability to criticize or imagine alternatives. Research has also shown that this impacted the preferences of PA-employed Palestinians, creating a divergence in public opinion between those in society who were dependent on the PA in some fashion, and those who were not.[15]

Following the Second Intifada, as the Israeli government began building the thirty-foot-tall separation wall and expanding illegal settlements inside the West Bank, community-based organizations (CBOs) emerged, especially in villages that were directly affected by the wall. The separation wall often cut farmers off from their lands and seized large segments of the territories intended, theoretically, for a Palestinian state. These organizations challenged the Israeli state restrictions on movement and access and were successful, to a limited degree, in that they captured international attention, united village members from across the political spectrum, and also challenged the PA – and its inaction – directly.[16] Second, to deal with CBOs, particularly in Palestinian communities in Areas B and C, the PA utilized the committee (*hay'a*) system.[17] This strategy entailed creating committees that answered to the president's office on a particular issue area of CBO concern. The issue areas included settlement expansion, land expropriation, and access to water and agricultural land.

The *hay'a* system targeted members of these CBOs, offering opportunities to "coordinate" with PA authorities, and sometimes even employment. Many individuals involved in grassroots organizing in their locales were essentially rerouted to work for the PA, spending less time in their actual village organizations and more time as government bureaucrats in Ramallah. This dissipated the impact of the CBOs. In just a few years, international visitors at the village protests outnumbered actual villagers. The grassroots were thus unable to challenge settlement activity, land appropriation, or PA inaction, effectively or significantly.

Finally, the PA was able to coopt the Palestinian upper and middle class through development projects and economic reform activities led by the International Monetary Fund economist-turned-Palestinian prime minister Salam Fayyad. Under Fayyad's leadership from 2007 to 2013, development projects and investment opportunities were offered to Palestinian businessmen, and debt and consumption were encouraged. For example, they developed the new city of Rawabi outside Ramallah. Although a private project, it featured prominently in the PA's outreach and discourse, and was often described as a "national project" and as a form of state-building.[18] Promises of a planned city, as an opportunity for investment as well as an upgraded housing area, garnered a great deal of attention from the international community and from upper-class Palestinians. This helped to coopt Palestinians of a particular income level (or those who aspired to it), even as Palestinians in surrounding villages had their land bought up at low value and articulated openly that they were concerned about being subsumed by the project. Finally, in the context of the occupation, Rawabi could not guarantee safety and security for its inhabitants, but those who aspired to live in such a planned city set aside these concerns.[19]

Rawabi as an investment project is one example of how Fayyad's tenure became synonymous with the idea of liberation through economic development. However, this mode of governance was heavily criticized by Palestinian scholars and activists not only for coopting segments of the

Palestinian public, but also for sidelining political questions in exchange for small, and largely unsustainable, improvements in living conditions that only impacted a sliver of Palestinian society.[20]

Secondly, the PA also relied heavily on repression strategies to control Palestinian society. This manifested in both overt and covert repression. Covert repression entailed limiting the space for criticism, for instance by passing "electronic crime" laws to target activists working to mobilize people in online spaces. The law included penalties and punishments for those who criticized the PA and was soon used – in the aftermath of its executive decree – to target journalists and human rights advocates.[21]

Surveillance and security coordination with the Israeli state also became more heavy-handed. Indeed, Palestinian analysts refer to a "revolving door policy," "whereby Palestinian activists, resistance fighters, and members of the opposition are imprisoned by either Israeli or Palestinian authorities and then indirectly handed over to the other once released."[22] Because the handover is done covertly, the PA is able to maintain plausible deniability. Overt police repression includes public arrests, use of torture, and crackdowns on protest.[23] These tactics are often used to send a signal to the Palestinian public that the PA security apparatus can operate with impunity.

As the PA consolidated its control through both cooptation and repression strategies, the Israeli occupation increased measures to fragment and repress Palestinians. Following the Second Intifada in particular, Palestinian freedom of movement within the West Bank was being increasingly restricted. Israeli checkpoints proliferated throughout the West Bank, as did illegal Israeli settlements. In 2023, the UN Office for the Coordination of Humanitarian Affairs reported 565 "movement obstacles" in the West Bank and East Jerusalem, including 49 permanent checkpoints.[24] Expanding settlements also meant greater Israeli repression of the Palestinian population, even in areas under direct PA security control. By 2023, there were 279 Israeli settlements in the occupied territories, and over 700,000 settlers.[25] Thus, activists had to contend with both the PA and the Israeli occupation as they challenged the status quo. The physical fragmentation imposed on Palestinians, not only between Gaza and the West Bank but also between communities in the West Bank and Jerusalem, made coordinating collective action and shared objectives more difficult. The increasingly authoritarian and unaccountable PA, and the increasingly repressive occupation working in tandem, greatly reduced the potential for Palestinian mobilization.

IMPACT ON LEADERSHIP AND ON SOCIETY

The demobilization of Palestinian civil society impacted decision making within the PA. Without an effective feedback loop between the PA and civil society, the PA's decisions were unopposed and therefore unaccountable. PA decision makers rationalized the situation by claiming either that Palestinians were not ready for accountable governance, or that the PA was doing what needed to be done to avoid Israeli and international backlash – as had happened following the 2006 elections when the international community boycotted the Hamas-led PA government. In particular, they cited American intervention in Palestinian politics and the sanctions it imposed for why the PA maintained its security cooperation with the Israeli occupation.[26]

This authoritarian mode of governance has had a toll on internal politics within Fatah as well. Fatah, led by the Palestinian president Mahmoud Abbas, is the ruling party within both the PA and the largely defunct PLO. Fatah has itself become less dynamic, responsive, and accountable to its own party members. Fatah general congress meetings in 2009 and 2016 are evidence of this, as the convenings were largely seen as opportunities to consolidate Abbas's control over the party.[27] With Israel's support, which allowed only pro-Abbas members, party leadership was able to effectively sideline the role of young cadres. Party leadership also refused to articulate a new political program, instead insisting that Fatah (and by extension the PA) maintain its pursuit of negotiations with Israel despite Israel's refusal to commit to the Oslo Accords framework.[28] Not only have Fatah members expressed frustration at the party's "internal disarray and leadership crisis," but scholars argue that internal party politics have become "irrelevant" to the national liberation movement.[29]

Palestinian civil society in the West Bank has been heavily impacted by these authoritarian dynamics as well. Besides being geographically and politically fragmented and demobilized because of both PA and Israeli repression, civil society became polarized between those who had a dependent relationship with the PA, and those who eschewed the PA altogether as Israel's security guarantor. Still others saw an opportunity to change the status quo through elections. The PA in 2021, attempting to prove their relevance to their international backers, floated the idea of elections and began preparations.[30] Some civil society actors reacted positively, leading efforts to mobilize Palestinian youth and serious challengers to more established candidates. Many saw the renewal of the PA as an opportunity to express dissatisfaction with the current leadership and to hold it to account for its failings. However, the elections were canceled.[31] Thus, PA politics often diverted attention from the national liberation project and stunted the development of alternative parties.

HAMAS, 2007 TO 2023

In Gaza, Hamas became the governing body following the 2006 elections and the 2007 rupture with Fatah. This meant the West Bank and Gaza were now effectively governed as separate territories, which benefited the Israeli government, as a fragmented Palestinian body politic provided a convenient excuse for Israel to avoid engaging in peace talks.[32] Although Israel had already enacted restrictions on Gaza after its so-called "disengagement" from the Strip in 2005, it imposed a new and more severe form of blockade over the territory after Hamas took control. Palestinians in Gaza have lived under blockade since, without any change in political leadership or opportunity for elections.

Hamas has been engaged in a difficult balancing act since its takeover. Even prior to 2006, it was divided into militant, political, and social services/charitable wings. Its 1988 charter and parts of its 2017 "political document" emphasize Hamas's objective in armed resistance against the Israeli state.[33] At the same time, Hamas's attempted engagement with elections, their role as a Palestinian political representative abroad, and the same 2017 political document suggested the simultaneous pursuit of governance objectives, as well as an interest in engaging in the political process.[34] This led some scholars to describe Hamas as both "anticolonial" in their continued armed resistance and internal reasoning, as well as "postcolonial" in their operation of a "state-like governance."[35] During this time, Hamas offset its governance failures with diplomatic engagement and foreign aid.[36] Importantly, Iran and its proxies around the region provided Hamas with key support, and sustained their ability to survive despite marginalization and containment.[37]

The Palestinian people's experience of Hamas governance in Gaza, nevertheless, is authoritarian.[38] As scholar Somdeep Sen writes: "In many ways the Hamas-ruled Palestinian Authority replicated the postcolonial state in having to struggle continually to emphasize its own existence to a citizenry for whom the state is either illegitimate or illegible."[39] Polling of Palestinians in Gaza before the October 7 Hamas attack showed that while Hamas polled better than Fatah in the estimation of respondents, the legitimacy and popularity of the group was still quite low. For example, only 27% of respondents believed Hamas was the most "deserving" to lead the Palestinian people, 72% of respondents complained of corruption in Hamas-led institutions, and, tellingly, 59% of respondents believed that criticism of the Hamas government was not possible.[40] Additionally, in July 2023, there were large-scale protests against the Hamas government and its failures in governance and service provision, which Hamas security forces quickly dispersed.[41] Evidence has accumulated over time, in both scholarly sources and human rights advocacy reports, that Hamas often took advantage of the fog of war to neutralize its opponents, and imposed both political and social restrictions on Palestinian civil society in Gaza.[42] For that reason, though Hamas governance is cloaked in political Islamism and the doctrine of resistance to the occupation, Palestinians in Gaza face authoritarian conditions similar to those of their counterparts in the West Bank and little opportunity for recourse vis-à-vis governing authorities.

Hamas's trajectory, despite their role as armed resistance, can only be understood in the context of the state-building paradigm responsible for the creation of the PA as well. Although Hamas receives funding and support from very different sources than the PA (Iran for militant activity, donor funding from countries like Qatar), the fact that a group like Hamas is engaging in governance at all is a testament to the futility of the state-building paradigm imposed on Palestinian political actors through the Oslo process.

ALTERNATIVE STRUCTURES

As a result of the dynamics described in this chapter, and the status quo of split governance, formal and institutionalized politics have been effectively hollowed out. The PA is described as nothing more than a subcontractor of occupation, and the Hamas authority in Gaza has proven to be largely uninterested in accountability or representative governance.

Attempts to articulate an alternative to the status quo have emerged from civil society. Both the West Bank and Gaza have witnessed protests in recent years that have attempted to challenge the quasi-state authorities. In Gaza, civil society activists conceived of and organized the Great March of Return beginning in March 2018. This Great March was a large protest and encampment movement at the de facto border between Gaza and Israel. Although initially civil society-led, Hamas supported participation in the initiative. The objective of activists, most of whom had never known anything but life under blockade and who were descendants of Palestinians displaced in the Nakba ("catastrophe") of 1948, was to end the Israeli blockade and reassert the right of return for Palestinian refugees. Undoubtedly, the intended audience was also international, demonstrating the grievances and demands of the Palestinians in Gaza in a way that could not be immediately dismissed.

Despite lasting for over a year, the Great March of Return could not achieve a long-term alternative to the formal structures governing Palestinian lives. The Israeli response to the March was predictably violent, although the protest movement was largely non-violent. As Amnesty International noted in a report, "the Israeli army reinforced its forces – deploying tanks, military vehicles and soldiers, including snipers, along the Gaza/Israel fence – and gave orders to shoot anyone within several hundred metres of the fence." Furthermore, the report states that "eyewitness testimonies gathered by Amnesty International, Palestinian and Israeli human rights groups show that Israeli soldiers shot unarmed protesters, bystanders, journalists and medical staff approximately 150–400m from the fence, where they did not pose any threat."[43] The death and injury toll was high, with over 200 killed and over 9,000 injured. It also left a generation of Palestinians in Gaza disabled as a result of sniper fire to their limbs, often requiring amputation.

In 2021, another alternative to the status quo emerged in the form of the Unity Intifada. This was a large-scale protest movement across Jerusalem and the West Bank, as well as among Palestinian citizens of Israel for the first time since the second uprising. The Unity Intifada began as a result of organized efforts in Jerusalem, in the face of Israeli attacks and restrictions on worshippers during the month of Ramadan as well as expulsion of Palestinians from East Jerusalem neighborhoods. Organizers in Jerusalem linked with organizers within Palestinian communities in Israel to assert the shared objectives of Palestinians no matter where they happened to live, and to challenge imposed fragmentation and Israeli, as well as PA, control. The Unity Intifada also sparked organizing at a larger scale across the Palestinian diaspora, and both the language/framing and objectives across different Palestinian communities began to converge.

The medium- to long-term outcomes of this episode were the increasingly shared frames for the conflict from Palestinians both within their historic homeland and in the diaspora, as well as linkages between Palestinians in different communities. Institutionalized politics became ever more irrelevant and illegitimate, especially in the aftermath of the PA crackdown on protestors and the use of gender-based violence. Nevertheless, the Unity Intifada, like the Great March, did not translate into the creation of more permanent organizing structures for civil society, and there was no emergence of a new Palestinian leadership. As the Israeli state repressed Palestinian activism following the Unity Intifada, the efforts of activists and organizers on the ground turned to defending community members from legal persecution. Civil society organizations and advocacy organizations in the diaspora became a focal point in the pro-Palestine advocacy ecosystem. This created in some cases, or strengthened, an infrastructure for pro-Palestine advocacy in the face of Israeli aggression, which activists in the occupied territories would face in the future, but did not create an alternative to the status quo. Little effort was channeled into revitalizing Palestinian national bodies such as the PLO, or political parties, such as Fatah, or addressing gaps and shortcomings within internal dynamics.

Other alternative structures that have emerged to challenge the PA–Hamas status quo are militias that have arisen in the West Bank. These militias are essentially non-partisan, encompassing individuals from a variety of political backgrounds, spanning the political spectrum from Islamist to leftist. Members are also quite young, having grown up with the political dynamics that followed the Second Intifada. The militias, unlike Hamas, are not interested in taking part in the political process or engaging in governance. Indeed they do not claim a political platform beyond armed resistance tactics against the Israeli state.

These militias were able to challenge Israeli authorities to a limited degree. Moreover, they achieved a great deal of popularity in their local communities and across the occupied territories. The PA, often tasked with dealing with "security concerns" vis-à-vis the Israeli state, was to a large extent constrained in their ability to curtail the militias, specifically because going after these groups would have incited a huge backlash from the Palestinian public. The Israeli army responded to the rise of the militias by engaging in large-scale incursions, in places like the Old City of Nablus and the Jenin refugee camp, to assassinate members of these groups and deter other militancy. Thus, given the high level of surveillance, and the heavy use of force on the part of the Israeli military, these militias faced high costs.

CONCLUSION

The dynamics of Palestinian authoritarianism that have emerged in the occupied territories stem from the undemocratic practices of both major parties – Fatah and Hamas – as well as the state-building project launched by the Oslo Accords and international support. Palestinian political leadership in both territories has been sustained by outside intervention. This has disrupted the feedback loop between political leaders and Palestinian society and has made political leadership less accountable to public pressure.

Furthermore, this lack of political accountability has meant that neither the PA nor Hamas has attempted to seek sustainable resolutions to Palestinian national claims, instead settling into certain equilibriums. For the PA, its equilibrium is to act as a subcontractor to the occupation for the sake of maintaining its authority, and persisting in its role internationally as the representative of the Palestinian people. For Hamas, until the October 7 attack and its aftermath, its equilibrium has been to act as armed resistance to the occupation, in what experts refer to as a "violent equilibrium," while maintaining its grip on the Gaza Strip as the sole actor in charge of governance. Both the PA and Hamas attempt to maintain the illusion of functioning quasi-states, despite their undemocratic practices and the backdrop of continued occupation.[44] This dynamic has not only subverted accountability, but hollowed out alternatives, thus effectively fragmenting Palestinians and reducing the efficacy of public pressure.

3

Between a Rock and a Hard Place: The Impact of Israel's Occupation and Palestinian Authoritarianism on Community Organizing and NGOs

Zaha Hassan and Layla Gantus

The ability of civil society to work for social and political change within Palestinian civic spaces is critical to the twin goals of achieving Palestinian representative governance and advancing pathways for a just and durable political solution between Palestinians and Israelis. In moments of high-intensity violence and communal trauma, such as have been seen since October 7, the vital role played by civil society in supporting relief efforts and responding where governing authorities have failed the people is appreciable. But civil society is much more than this. It is essential to building and preserving the bedrock for a future free society where the right to organize into collectives, to peaceful assembly, to protest, to publish, and to express oneself without fear of persecution is respected. The attacks on Palestinian community-based organizations, journalists, human rights defenders, doctors, educators, and humanitarians documented in Gaza and the West Bank (including East Jerusalem) will severely complicate the postwar recovery efforts and the ability of Palestinians to stay on their land. It will also make sustaining the Palestinian national movement inside Palestine more difficult than ever. But Palestinian civil society has never had the luxury of operating when the guns are completely silent. And in the immediate future, it must operate in an active war zone.

The private actors and organizations that have grown over the decades and are part of the fabric of Palestinian civil society today remain both vibrant and vital though they struggle to maintain their operations. When the escalation of 2023–2024 abates, Palestinians will continue to depend on them along with international NGOs to help support the community's recovery, rehabilitation, and reconstruction. Palestinian governing authorities will undoubtedly be severely challenged. Their popular legitimacy will continue to suffer, and they will be hamstrung by ongoing fiscal constraints, opposition from an extreme right-wing Israeli political landscape, and a violent settler movement eager to consolidate control over the entire area between the Mediterranean Sea and the Jordan River.

In some ways, this moment is akin to the period before the Oslo peace process when all Palestinian political factions and national bodies were outlawed (they still are) and Israeli authorities actively enforced their exclusion from historic Palestine with an iron fist. At that time Palestinian civil society filled the void. The question is: will they be able to do so again under the much more difficult conditions of the moment? It is too soon to know the answer. For now, this chapter considers the nature of the restrictions Palestinian civil society actors face in the occupied territories and how the closing of Palestinian civic space has impacted their ability and that of international NGOs to fulfill their critically important mission.

ISRAEL'S REPRESSION OF NGOS AND COMMUNITY-BASED GROUPS

Ask most Palestinians what they believe the national movement's "superpower" is and they are likely to point to Palestinian civil society – the network of private actors, community organizations, and NGOs that provide human rights defense and documentation, social services to vulnerable communities, and humanitarian relief during myriad episodes of violence and crises. In particular, the support these collectives provide for sustaining Palestinian resilience – referred to as steadfastness or "*sumud*" – has been critical to the preservation of Palestinian national identity. The Palestinian Authority (PA) can come and go, the capacity of the Palestine Liberation Organization (PLO) can wax and wane, but most recognize that the national movement would be lost without its civil society organizations. They are what the Palestinian people draw upon to assert and insist upon the legitimacy of their national aspirations. And it is precisely this that makes them a target for public and private actors that oppose any notion of Palestinian sovereignty and aim to thwart the exercise of Palestinian self-determination anywhere in historic Palestine.

It has never been easy for civil society organizations operating in the Israeli occupied territories. Since 1967, Israel has banned more than 400 local and international organizations from operating there.[1] However, for many years now, particularly since Benjamin Netanyahu returned to the political scene in 2009 as prime minister, Palestinian civil society organizations have been experiencing a rise in repression. In particular, those organizations operating in the parts of the West Bank slated for construction of settler housing units have found themselves in the crosshairs of both the Israeli occupying power and private actors, including settler gangs, bent on preventing any Palestinian presence there.

Things came to a head in 2021. In March, the Office of the Prosecutor of the International Criminal Court (ICC) announced the opening of an investigation into the situation in Palestine[2] in what Netanyahu described as an "attack" against Israel.[3] Among the complaints submitted against Israel concerned Israel's settlement enterprise, the treatment of prisoners and detainees including children, and alleged Israeli war crimes during the 2014 bombardment of Gaza. Seven months later, in October, the Israeli minister of defense Benny Gantz designated as terrorists[4] six community-based organizations and human rights defenders,[5] including three that had provided information to the ICC prosecutor about alleged war crimes and crimes against humanity by Israeli officials.[6]

The counterterrorism legislation relied upon by the Israeli minister of defense defines terrorism in a broad and vague manner,[7] allowing authorities to effectively outlaw the oldest and most prominent Palestinian organizations operating in the occupied West Bank, including those providing legal aid to administrative detainees (Addameer Prisoner Support and Human Rights Association), documenting war crimes and violations of international humanitarian law (Al-Haq), providing research on Palestinian rights violations and community support to vulnerable populations (Bisan Center for Research and Development), and representing the rights of children detainees (Defense for Children International (DCI)-Palestine), women (Union of Palestinian Women's Committees), and farmers (Union of Agricultural Work Committees). The application of Israeli criminal law into occupied territory against

Palestinian organizations, and in an area that is supposed to be under exclusive PA jurisdiction, was unprecedented.

Israel claimed its action was necessary because the organizations were part of and provided financial support to the Popular Front for the Liberation of Palestine,[8] a political faction with an armed wing outlawed by Israeli military order. In fact, Israel has outlawed all Palestinian political factions including Fatah, the ruling party of both the PLO and the PA. UN experts strongly condemned the designations, noting that no credible evidence had been presented.[9] The executive directors of the designated civil society organizations believe that the terrorism designations were meant to preempt a public announcement they were scheduled to make.[10] Some of the staff were being subjected to "threats and other apparent acts of intimidation and interference"[11] for their work in gathering evidence of alleged Israeli war crimes, according to the ICC prosecutor. Staff of three of the organizations had discovered the presence of Israeli spyware on their phones.[12] Days before their planned public announcement, Israeli authorities informed a member of the legal staff at one of the organizations whose phone was among those infected with Israeli spyware that his Jerusalem residency permit was being revoked for "breach of allegiance to the state of Israel"[13] and the six organizations were then designated as terrorist organizations.[14] One of the organizations may have been designated to preempt a US State Department investigation. According to a former official at the Department responsible for reviewing human rights complaints against Israel, after the Department raised a credible case of sexual violence involving a child detainee represented by DCI-Palestine, Israel designated the organization as terrorist in nature and raided its offices.[15]

Nine months later, in August 2022, Israeli occupation forces raided the offices of the six organizations along with the Union of Health Work Committees, a community-based organization Israel designated in January 2020[16] that provides healthcare services to Palestinians in parts of the West Bank that Israel has earmarked for Jewish settlement. The Israeli army destroyed equipment and door locks, ransacked offices and cabinets, and took client files, computers, and documents.[17] The doors of the organizations were also sealed shut and notice left on them that the organizations were to cease their operations.[18] According to the EU High Representative for Foreign Affairs and Security Policy Josep Borrell,[19] and nine EU member states[20] which provide funding to some of the organizations, they were not provided with evidence to justify the designations which were executed without due process or transparency.[21]

Israel's actions against civil society organizations in 2022 has more alarming implications than first apparent. Like the extension of Israeli criminal law against Palestinian entities operating in the occupied territories, and the raid on the organizations' offices located in the heart of Ramallah, the part of the West Bank in which the PA is supposed to have exclusive security and administrative control, Israel's repression indicates they intend to treat the West Bank as part of Israel, that is, to permanently annex it and treat it as part of Israel's sovereign territory.

The designated civil society organizations have faced difficulty in continuing their critical work since the designations and closure orders. Though some have defied the order, unsealed their offices, and returned to work, they are relying on their international donors – the EU and influential European countries with working relationships with Israel – to discourage Israeli authorities from enforcing the order against them. Other organizations that do not receive foreign funding are more at risk and face serious challenges to fulfilling their mandate. Some of those challenges include suspension or loss of donor funding due to the reputational smear associated with the designation; travel bans; staff arrests and indefinite detention; loss of staff due to interrogations, harassment, and intimidation from Israeli authorities; and the persistent threat of de-risking from banks, and loss of access to financial services and payment platforms.

Even if Israeli authorities lift the designation and allow the Palestinian NGOs to operate again in the occupied territories, the stigma of having been once designated a terrorist organization will have lasting effects.[22] And when influential state actors such as the United States fail to condemn Israeli repression directed against the most prominent members of Palestinian civil society,[23] it tends to give credence to even noncredible and unsubstantiated allegations. All it takes is one Google search for a prospective donor to determine that it is too risky or troublesome to engage with a particular NGO.

TOOLS OF THE TRADE: REPRESSION INSIDE THE OCCUPIED PALESTINIAN TERRITORIES

Movement restrictions and surveillance

By far, the most pervasive restrictions on Palestinian civil society organizations involve the inability of their staff to move freely between Gaza, the

West Bank, and East Jerusalem, and within the West Bank, from town to town and village to village. Palestinians require permits to access areas where they do not reside. Staff based in Ramallah have to seek Israeli permits to travel to East Jerusalem for meetings or events which are not readily granted.[24] Most staff will not be permitted to travel to or leave Gaza without clearing strict Israeli security checks that appear to be randomly applied: one application for a staffer may be cleared for a visit one month, while the next month it may be denied.

A majority of Palestinian civil society organizations need some type of permission for their staff.[25] Permits may be canceled at any time[26] with little to no transparency of the processes involved.[27] Sometimes staff will not get their approval for travel until after the reason for their travel – a training session, event, or appointment – has passed.[28] Some organizations find that it is not worth applying for permits for Palestinian staff, or visas for staff and volunteers holding foreign passports, because of the difficulty in meeting the vague and complex requirements.[29] Organizations often have to duplicate staff positions and/or maintain facilities in multiple parts of the occupied territories in order to avoid applying for permits, raising the costs of their operations, and straining their capacity.[30]

Israel also restricts where civil society organizations can build and operate in the parts of the West Bank reserved for Jewish settlement, known as Area C. The Israeli occupation forces have not only confiscated construction materials, but they also demolish any infrastructure including any funded by donor governments.[31] This discourages building infrastructure for essential services in locations where vulnerable communities not served by the PA need them most. Because of harassment targeting construction workers, getting certain projects completed in Area C is difficult or requires additional resources to cover the increased costs.

Palestinian civil society organizations also report being surveilled by both Israeli authorities and settlers living in illegal settlements in the West Bank[32] using drones, hacking technologies, and spyware.[33] Israeli authorities have the capability to access an organization's email communications and phone data including personal information about the directors, board members, and staff.[34] The surveillance is so pervasive it compelled veterans of an elite Israeli intelligence corps known as Unit 8200 to publish an open letter refusing "to continue serving as tools in deepening the military control over the Occupied Territories."[35] Israeli spyware has even been found on the smartphone of an American executive director of a Palestinian civil society organization.[36]

All NGOs operating in Gaza may also be subjected to monitoring from the de facto authority inside the enclave. Hamas is especially concerned with international workers whom it suspects are acting as spies or whom they believe may present a security threat.[37] Hamas has attempted to control NGO beneficiary lists by screening NGOs and intervening in needs assessments.[38] NGOs may be visited by authorities, subjected to spot-checks of documents, and have their equipment and work files confiscated.[39] Palestinian and international NGOs and their staff also report delays in getting projects approved, restrictions on access to certain locations, and harassment from authorities.[40]

NGOs operating in areas under the PA's administrative jurisdiction face similar difficulties. Palestinian security officers are known to harass organizers or student leaders and anyone seen as a threat to their authority.[41] For example, in June 2023, after an Islamist party member was elected as the head of the student council at Birzeit University in the Ramallah Governorate, he was dragged from his house, beaten, and imprisoned.[42] And when Palestinians in the West Bank organized protests to show solidarity with Palestinians in Gaza during Israel's bombardment of the enclave following the October 2023 Hamas attack and to protest the PA president's failure to respond, protestors were met with force and were violently dispersed with the use of stun guns and tear gas.[43]

Smears, harassment, and arrests
Smear campaigns, harassment, and arrests are common tactics used by Israeli authorities to undermine the effectiveness and mandate of Palestinian civil society organizations operating in the occupied territories. Whether a civil society organization is formally designated a terrorist organization or not, the mere accusation of support for terrorism can cripple it. The smear campaigns following the designation of the six organizations discussed earlier have not abated even though donor countries, the EU, and UN special mandate holders and experts have condemned the designations. One executive director of a designated organization reports still being subjected to an Israeli travel ban even though he has dual US-Palestinian

nationality.[44] Organizations operating in Gaza face special screening from foreign donors. Banks treat accounts held in Gaza as presumptively suspect simply because they belong to a Palestinian organization inside the besieged enclave.[45]

A smear campaign against a civil society organization can start with one malicious blog or social media post authored by individuals connected to foreign actors, think tanks, or pro-settler groups.[46] The material is referenced and reshared repeatedly over the internet or social media to increase its visibility and prominence with search engines. Or the smear could be the product of a whisper campaign passed during meetings between Israeli officials and European ministers from countries providing funding to Palestinian civil society.[47] The spreading of false and misleading information about a Palestinian civil society organization raises questions and concerns from the organization's donors to which the targeted NGO must respond. This diverts the organization's attention away from its human rights or social welfare work.[48] Administrative staff must take time to draft responses, hire outside legal counsel, and review the claims being made about their programs or outputs. The organization becomes consumed by responding to false allegations.[49]

Even UN agencies are not impervious to smear campaigns. Consider the case of the UN Relief and Works Agency for Palestine Refugees (UNRWA). UNRWA was set up after the 1948 Nakba, when 750,000 Palestinians were forcibly displaced from their homes, in order to provide the refugees with humanitarian assistance, healthcare, and education until a political solution could be reached for their plight.[50] Since more than 75% of Gaza's 2.3 million population are 1948 refugees or their descendants, UNRWA functions similarly to a municipality given the critical services it provides to the majority of the population.[51] Almost all UNRWA's staff are also Palestinian refugees[52] which makes UNRWA an important employer in Gaza. Thus, UNRWA in Gaza and throughout the Middle East has become tied to Palestinian national identity and associated with the unresolved refugee issue, making it a target of those who wish to undermine the right of Palestinians to return to their original homes in what became the state of Israel.

According to Israel's ambassador to the UN, UNRWA's "end goal is to use these so-called refugees and their libelous right of return – a right that doesn't exist – to flood Israel and destroy the Jewish State."[53] The ambassador's statement, made at the UN, came after Israel accused twelve staff of taking part in the October 7 Hamas attack without providing evidence.[54] However, an effort has been underway for decades to defund and dismantle UNRWA by impugning its work.[55] As a result of the Israelis' accusations, which came on the heels of the International Court of Justice finding that a plausible genocide is taking place in Gaza,[56] a cascade of countries suspended funding, including the United States, its largest donor[57] – on the cusp of a man-made famine in Gaza.[58] Months later, Israel has yet to produce evidence against the staff.[59] The damage has been done, however. Congress passed a bill prohibiting US funding for UNRWA until March 2025[60] and it is unclear whether US funding will resume in the future.

Smearing one NGO can impact the entire sector. According to the executive directors of some of the most prominent Palestinian NGOs, donors become skittish and demand onerous vetting of staff or board members or require censorship of the organization's programmatic outputs. Even the most established Palestinian NGOs report being unable to accept grants due to the impossibility of guaranteeing to funders that no staff or board member has ever been a member of a proscribed organization or has had associations with those that have been members of such organizations.[61] One prominent organization reports losing a grant from a potential investor because the organization's board member had once been held in administrative detention, a situation that many Palestinian men face because of the high incidence of detention without charge.[62] An executive director of an arts and cultural organization said it had to decline foreign funding altogether because doing so would mean that it would have to censor its artists and programming.[63] Some funders have adopted the International Holocaust Remembrance Alliance (IHRA) definition of antisemitism that can be applied to condemn particular criticisms of Israel. Artists in the occupied territories, like many artists, often create work informed by their social and political context. Yet to be critical of an occupying power that controls where they can work, live, and travel risks falling afoul of the policies of their funders, who rely on a definition of antisemitism that is open to misuse. The mere expression of Palestinian identity and history provoked a campaign against one NGO with the aim of pressuring a European donor into cutting its relationship with the organization.[64]

The Palestinian staff of NGOs also face regular harassment from Israeli state authorities, organized settler groups, and those Israeli and foreign NGOs hostile to a two-state solution that would involve the relinquishing of Israeli authority over the West Bank. About a quarter of the Palestinian civil society organizations surveyed by the International Civil Society Centre (ICSC) in 2021 have reported harassment[65] including physical threats and destruction of offices and equipment.[66] This is consistent with the conduct of Israeli authorities during the 2022 raid of the six Palestinian civil society organizations in PA-administered Ramallah. In Area C, where Israel has total administrative and security control, settlers and settler groups have initiated raids with support from Israeli occupation forces[67] in order to advance a particular planning agenda. The northern West Bank village of Huwara, for example, has been a long-time target of settler violence with the aim of clearing the area to allow for the construction of a highway to connect smaller settlements with a larger one in the area.[68]

Figure 1: Segregated road being constructed for Israeli settlers near a Huwara apartment building subjected to a settler pogrom on February 26, 2023. Photo Credit: Zaha Hassan

Figure 2: Huwara home and cars firebombed by Israeli settlers on February 26, 2023. Photo Credit: Zaha Hassan

In February 2023, Israeli settlers protected by the Israeli Defense Forces conducted what even the Israeli military commander for the West Bank, Yehuda Fuchs,[69] described as a pogrom in the village and the area around it. Settlers attacked Palestinians, firebombed homes with families trapped inside, and destroyed cars and property.[70] According to interviews conducted with the Huwara Village Council, the attack continued from 6:30 P.M. to 2:30 A.M. while Israeli forces prevented Palestinian civil defense from entering the area to put out fires.[71]

Physical harassment from Israeli occupation forces or settlers against Palestinian staff of civil society organizations often escalates into their arrest and detention. About 15% of organizations surveyed by ICSC have reported that their staff or volunteers have been arrested or detained by the Israeli authorities.[72] Some prominent staff and directors of organizations have been repeatedly detained.[73] Malicious prosecution of popular human rights defenders is common. Issa Amro, founder of Youth Against Settlements, was put on trial for his non-violent activism against Israel's

Figure 3: Members of the Huwara town council and eyewitnesses meet with human rights workers following the February 2023 attack. Photo credit: Zaha Hassan

illegal settlements inside the city of Hebron.[74] Moreover, Khaled Quzmar, director of DCI-Palestine, reports that once the Israeli authorities had him in custody, they told him they knew the names of his sons and where they worked and lived, implying some harm might come to them.[75]

The PA has also engaged in smear campaigns to silence its critics. One of the targeted NGOs linked to former Palestinian prime minister Salam Fayyad had its assets confiscated.[76] On occasion, the PA has detained the staff of civil society organizations immediately after they have been released from Israeli custody. Alternatively, Israel may detain the Palestinian staff after their release from PA custody,[77] leading to accusations among the Palestinian public that the PA is collaborating with the occupying power to harass and intimidate Palestinian activists.[78] Many human rights defenders feel that the PA does not support them especially against harassment from Israel.[79]

Restrictions on activities, reporting requirements, and onerous taxation

Israel's detention and intimidation of the Palestinian staff of NGOs obstructs them in fulfilling their missions. Social service providers, humanitarian workers, and human rights defenders who fill the gaps in the provision of essential services, given the lack of capacity of the PA in the West Bank and Hamas in Gaza, in particular, find themselves unable to do their jobs.[80] For example, due to the harassment, intimidation, and detention of staff of Palestinian healthcare organizations inside Area C, these organizations have been unable to provide services to 30,000 Palestinians who live without access to healthcare there.[81] In occupied East Jerusalem, 40% of healthcare services provided in schools are delivered by Palestinian NGOs that face severe challenges to their operations from Israeli authorities who aim to expand Jewish settlement in the city by forcing Palestinian families out.[82]

In Gaza, the situation of NGOs providing healthcare looks different. Foreign funding to support the work of these providers is impacted by the fact that the United States, the EU, and Israel have designated Hamas a terrorist organization.[83] Donors are therefore concerned about sending funds to Gaza where Hamas is the taxing authority because they may face charges of material support for terrorism. Providers in Gaza also suffer from smear campaigns and arrest of their staff, which can precipitate a loss of funding, bank account closures, or other de-risking measures. One healthcare center whose senior staff faced harassment including arrest was finally forced to close operations in 2022.[84] Many donors are also loath to make capital investments in Gaza because of the regular Israeli military bombardments conducted in the Strip.[85]

One healthcare provider in the occupied territories reports losing up to two-thirds of its operating budget over an eight-year period as a result of the increasing restrictions on its activities.[86] Others report that smear campaigns have resulted in the loss of up to 50% of their contracts. Even when they can maintain a contract with a funder, the paperwork and oversight become so onerous that more of their budget gets diverted to reporting and compliance. Planning from year to year is also challenging for providers operating in Gaza because of delays in processing bank transfers to the enclave. Funds may be delayed for several months or even sometimes a year.[87]

As for the situation of civil society organizations under the PA's jurisdiction, in recent years, restrictions have been increasing on their funding flows, activities, advocacy efforts, and free expression. All NGOs and associations must have their funding pass through the Ministry of the Interior before being transferred to their bank accounts[88] and they must report on the source of the funding.[89] If the Ministry of the Interior determines after scrutinizing an organization's activities that it does not comport with the mission of the organization or if they believe the funds have not been spent properly, they may take action against the organization.[90] Staff of NGOs also report being targeted by PA security forces if they criticize certain PA officials, particularly on Facebook.[91] In addition to these measures against Palestinian NGOs, the PA is pressuring international NGOs to pay income taxes to the PA in Ramallah for Gaza-based staff and have threatened to shut down their West Bank-based bank accounts if the taxes are not paid to the PA.[92] Meanwhile, international NGOs are unable to pay taxes to the Hamas authorities in Gaza due to the legal risk they face associated with anti-terrorism laws. Without agreement between the respective authorities in the West Bank and Gaza, the operations of international NGOs remain threatened.[93]

THE OUTLOOK FOR PALESTINIAN CIVIL SOCIETY

Palestinian civil society organizations have long operated under repressive circumstances meted out by different governing authorities, though the Israeli military administration represents an existential challenge to the continuation of the operations of such actors. As Israel's military campaign in Gaza continues, and as settlers eye an opportunity to establish permanent Israeli sovereignty over the West Bank, the outlook for Palestinian civil society is arguably in its darkest hour. Palestinian civil society organizations are likely to continue to be targeted with smear campaigns, almost insurmountable donor vetting requirements, intimidation and harassment from occupation forces and settlers, and loss of funding which is ultimately the point of these tactics. What might change the status quo and allow for Palestinian civil society to hold space and continue the important role they play? It will require a sustained donor commitment to not be cowed by those leading the campaigns to hinder the work of Palestinian civil society organizations.

The representatives of the Palestinian civil society organizations interviewed for this chapter are under no illusions. They recognize the challenges they face and are attempting to find ways to adapt as they plan for an uncertain future. Many have made the decision to stop accepting donor funding that comes with strict vetting requirements. Others are refusing to continue relationships with donors who have not called for a permanent ceasefire in Gaza or who have condemned Hamas's attack on Israel while remaining silent during the many months of Israel's indiscriminate bombardment and destruction of Gaza which the International Court of Justice ruled constitutes a plausible case of genocide. Conversations are also taking place today among Palestinian civil society actors about how Palestinians can engage in self-help and build community-based solutions rather than attempt to abide by a donor-focused agenda and aid conditionality. And with the banking restrictions imposed on Palestinians, some are looking into traditional financing and fundraising mechanisms that avoid reliance on the international banking system. Though it is too early to say what will come of these efforts, what is certain is that the Palestinian national movement will be unsustainable without the foundational civil society organizations that have built the movement and helped to keep Palestinians on the land for more than five decades.

4

The Rise, Weakening, and Resurgence of Civil Society in Israel

Dahlia Scheindlin

INTRODUCTION

Illiberal nationalist-populist political forces began to take over Israeli politics in the 2010s, alongside a wave of similar trends in both democratic and less democratic countries around the world.[1] The long-running nationalist right-wing dynamics in Israel had deepened over the decades, largely in response to the Israel–Palestine conflict. But in the late 2000s, political competition in Israel among the increasingly powerful right-wing parties led to an outbidding of ultra-nationalist themes, echoing trends in West European countries like the Netherlands, France, and Belgium earlier in that decade.[2] The strategies of illiberal leaders increasingly converged: among them, the attempt to restrict civil society and the independent, non-governmental sphere – to suppress critical movements and political opposition.[3]

Governments that sought autocratic powers, such as those in Hungary, India, Russia, Turkey, Serbia, and others, trained their policy and legislative assaults on the media, NGOs, universities, and oppositional civic movements. In Israel too, the government formed by Benjamin Netanyahu in 2009 soon began advancing similar policies in an incremental but methodical way.

Netanyahu's long rule aimed to turn political and national minorities in Israel into an internal enemy, intimidate and suppress critical political speech and activism, and weaken the institutions that protect independent civil activity, including the media and the judiciary. The government was aided by non-governmental actors – right-wing allies committed to its illiberal methods and nationalist agenda. At different points, activists critical of government policy faced alarming threats, and the left-wing community worried that the government would seriously undermine its foundations for political action, from legitimacy, to funding, to legal limits on the specific political or policy positions they could take.

However, the full picture is both more complex, and possibly more encouraging. A brief history of civil society in Israel shows an impressive evolution from the early decades, leading to a robust, diverse, activist, and oppositional civil society coming into its own between the 1980s and the 2000s.[4] During the 2010s this community was weakened but not deterred; by the next decade, Israel experienced a series of political crises, but civil society rallied. As the government became more extremist, civil society groups forged new partnerships and mobilized into a mass and unprecedented movement. In the immediate wake of October 7, in the weeks when the state seemed to recede entirely into its failures, citizens filled the void, providing direct services and taking prominent policy positions, even during wartime.

This article reviews the historic evolution of civil society in Israel, and the controversies civil society has generated; the backlash against left-wing civil opposition in the modern populist era; and the resurgent capacity of civil society demonstrated in 2023.

THE EVOLUTION OF CIVIL SOCIETY IN ISRAEL

The early years: all for the state

When Israel became independent in 1948, certain pre-state Zionist institutions continued to act as quasi-state bodies, continuing their missions of managing land bought or appropriated prior to statehood, as well as land acquired through dispossession of Palestinians following independence, settling Jewish immigrants, representing women's needs, and other social concerns. These included the Jewish Agency, the labor federation called the Histadrut, the Jewish National Fund, Na'amat (a women's organization), and others.[5]

In a similar vein, the Hebrew-language Israeli media in the early decades was almost uniformly committed to the national cause; as in many countries, most newspapers were arms of political parties.[6] Opposition newspapers, such as Communist party newspapers (in Hebrew and in Arabic), and the independent critical investigative publication *Ha'Olam HaZeh*, faced pressure from the authorities at certain points in the 1950s and 1960s.[7]

Shortly after the start of statehood, Israel placed Palestinians within its borders under a military regime based on British Mandate-era colonial emergency regulations, which remained in place until 1968 (implemented through military force until 1966). Under these regulations, the government intervened directly to limit press freedom, while suppressing independent civil society and political organization.[8]

When Israel saw its first transition of power in 1977, the new Likud-led government drove ambitious plans in particular to cut back on state centralization. In particular, the Likud government sought to erode the power of the country's central labor union, the Histadrut.[9] Although these plans were only partially implemented, this era nevertheless saw the reduction of the welfare state and social services, just as Israel entered a severe economic crisis in the early 1980s.[10] These forces prompted third sector organizations – neither government nor for-profit private sector groups – to augment social welfare, charity, and social service needs.

Civil society: more independent, more assertive, more organizations

The liberalizing ideology therefore coincided with policies designed to reduce the public's dependency on the state and its social welfare institutions, prompting the growth and increasing independence of civil society.[11]

When the military government that ruled Palestinian citizens ended in 1966, this community too enjoyed significantly more freedom to develop its own civic activities, including student groups and activist political movements.[12] Palestinian citizens were never as free as their Jewish counterparts; for example, the state cracked down on or suppressed certain activities, such as the Land Day protests of 1976 or the Congress of Arab organizations in Nazareth that was banned in 1980; further, by 1985, a new electoral law restricted parties that undermined the Jewish and democratic nature of the state, or incited racism.[13] Nevertheless, Arab citizens had more political and civil mobilizing opportunities than under the military government.

In 1990, Israel passed a law to establish a second broadcast authority for private television, which would break the state's monopoly on broadcast news. After delays, the new authority began broadcasting in 1993. Moreover, by mid-1994 the majority of Israelis could receive cable television, significantly diversifying the information environment.[14]

In the 1970s and 1980s, non-governmental groups emerged or expanded to deal with social welfare needs. But also at this time, social change groups became more prominent. Citizens formed organizations to advance gender equality and women's rights, environmental issues, or opposition to the Israeli occupation of Palestinian areas and Lebanon, or to advocate for individual rights and civil liberties rights.[15] These included the Association for Civil Rights in Israel, Peace Now, the Israel Women's Network, Yesh Gvul, and Women in Black. Collectively, these groups would be known in Israel as the "left." Over time, civil society groups advanced liberal social causes alongside peace and anti-occupation activities, effectively binding these two elements into the broad Israeli understanding of "left-wing."

But civil society activism was not limited to liberal or left-leaning causes; such activism included nationalist right-wing activism.[16] From the mid-1970s, non-governmental movements such as Gush Emunim advocated for settlement expansion, and the Ir David Foundation and Ateret Cohanim, established in the 1980s, were devoted to appropriating properties in the Old City of Jerusalem, which Israel captured and occupied in 1967, for Jewish settlement.

The 1980s to the 2000s also saw the expansion of movements advocating democracy and government accountability, civil rights, and the adoption of a constitution, including the Public Committee for a Constitution for Israel, the Movement for Quality Government in Israel, the Movement for Freedom of Information in Israel, and the Israel Democracy Institute, as well as environmental groups and advocates for the separation of religion and state, among others.[17]

Two further observations are important: first, many of the educated social, cultural, academic, and political elites leading the critical civil society challenges may have been responding to the decline of political power given the heavy overlap between these social institutions and the Labor party, which had governed for decades before its decline. Now the Labor party was out of power, other than short-lived revivals, these well-placed elites began to embrace civil liberties and individual rights through civil society activities, which the Labor party had historically discouraged, blocking the institution of a bill of rights for its first three decades in power. By the 2010s, the far right would accuse the collective "left" of advancing its interests through civil society and the courts themselves, as an embittered elite unable to win elections.

Second, a prominent segment of civil society activism from the 1970s onward centered on peace with the Palestinians, opposing settlements and ongoing occupation. Peace Now opposed occupation from the late 1970s, while B'Tselem became the first anti-occupation human rights group, from 1989, in the wake of the first Palestinian uprising (Intifada) and Israel's crackdown. The Public Committee Against Torture in Israel was established in 1990 mostly to oppose the treatment of Palestinian detainees by Israeli security services. HaMoked was founded in 1988 to handle human rights violations of individual Palestinians, and other groups. As settlements and occupation spread, peace talks failed, and the Second Intifada raged in the early 2000s, still more organizations emerged to confront the diverse aspects of occupation. Yesh Din was founded in 2005 to provide individual legal representation and oppose occupation policies through legal channels, while Gisha focused on Palestinian freedom of movement. In other words, ongoing violation of human and civil rights spurred civil society-led opposition to become more assertive, vocal, and creative over time.

In sum, from roughly the 1980s, civil society became more robust, professionalized, independent, and politically diverse. Citizen-driven movements achieved some liberal aims, such as advancing gender equality and equal pay legislation, as well as anti-discrimination and freedom of information laws. Civil society became one of Israel's stronger pillars of democracy, despite the country's deeply mixed democratic record.

THE YEARS OF BACKLASH

The roots of the backlash
The Oslo Accords of the 1990s institutionalized the idea that peace needed to be built from the grassroots, following the top-down political agreements. The 1995 Interim Agreement outlined detailed areas of civic cooperation, dialogue, and grassroots "people to people" peace activities, which proliferated in the 1990s.[18]

But by the 2000s, much of the cooperative work unraveled, due to violence, movement restrictions on Palestinians, and mutual collapse of trust. Israelis who opposed occupation gravitated toward activism to protect Palestinian human rights. When a war broke out between Israel and Hamas in Gaza in late 2008 many of the existing, already demoralized peace and human rights groups no longer believed that they could change the attitudes of Israeli society.[19]

Some of these groups increasingly appealed to the international community, emphasizing international law and universal justice, on the one hand, while appealing to domestic Israeli courts for human rights claims to challenge state policies, on the other.[20] Human rights defenders pursued such claims at Israel's Supreme Court, which functions as the high court of justice for claims against the state and as the highest court of appeals.

In addition, during the years of the Intifada, Palestinian civil society in Israel became increasingly active in advancing equal citizenship. At the start of the Second Intifada, Israeli police forces killed thirteen Palestinian citizens of Israel demonstrating in solidarity with Palestinians. The landmark collective trauma was part of what motivated Palestinian civil society in Israel, alongside renewed efforts in Jewish civil society to draft a comprehensive constitution. Arab leaders felt the efforts led by Jewish civil society leaders and academics neglected the rights of Palestinian citizens. Palestinian civil society produced a number of "vision documents" mapping out their proposals for citizen equality, some of which involved ending Jewish privileges or the exclusivist Jewish identity of the state. Certain right-wing Jewish leaders viewed these as an egregious threat to the identity of the state.[21] All of these activities contributed to a backlash.

In 2009, Benjamin Netanyahu returned to power in Israel. Over the course of the 2000s, a new type of global populism was arising in Western Europe. Far-right politicians began to embrace a nativist and anti-immigrant agenda.[22] Their anti-elite messages pitted the people – in exclusivist, nationalist terms – against the liberal-minded, universalist political elite. These messages exploited widening socio-economic gaps generated by globalization.

From roughly 2009, Netanyahu and other right-wing political forces avidly embraced the new currents. His governing coalitions began to target left-wing activism – that is, human rights advocacy, anti-occupation activism, and broader liberal causes – accusing them all of acting to subvert the Jewish state and override the nationalist-oriented will of the people. Right-wing populist forces accused the Palestinian Arabs in Israel of undermining the Jewish identity of the state, leveraging endemic public fears due to the ongoing violent ethno-national military conflict.

After the war with Hamas in late 2008–2009, the UN appointed an investigating commission to examine accusations of war crimes from both sides; the Israeli government refused to cooperate, but certain Israeli human rights organizations helped provide information to the commission.[23]

Israeli society was furious: the Goldstone Commission report, as it became known, ignited the first wave of both right-wing civil society and government-driven attacks on non-governmental groups.

Assault on civil society

During the term of the 18th Knesset (2009–2013), a series of bills and Knesset hearings launched the first vitriolic attacks on human rights groups who opposed occupation. Right-wing media amplified rhetorical attacks on the "left" at large.[24] The government advanced policies and bills to target their funding, including mechanisms tailored to apply to anti-occupation/human rights groups. In 2016, the first bill passed into law, designed to brand anti-occupation NGOs as foreign agents under the guise of "funding transparency." The punitive tax bill for NGOs stalled, but returned in 2023 as a bill targeting "public advocacy" groups with tax rates of 65% – making continuing their operations untenable (it has not advanced as of this writing).[25]

Additional legislation sought to intimidate civic political opposition or expression. In 2011, Israel passed the anti-boycott law, making anyone who called for observing an academic, cultural, or economic boycott of Israel (a common tactic in the international Palestine solidarity movement) liable to pay civil damages. Another law stripped public funding from institutions that observe the Palestinian Nakba on Israel's Independence Day. A 2017 law targeted NGOs advancing voter turnout activity among center-left constituencies.[26] In practice these laws created only minor obstacles to expressing such positions, with ample workarounds available. But the laws generated a chilling effect among the political opposition, while legitimizing an anti-liberal policy and legislative agenda.

In the early 2010s, the government, alongside influential right-wing figures, began a campaign against the Israeli Supreme Court and the judiciary. The initial efforts mainly sought to erode the institution most likely to limit the illiberal legislation designed to threaten and intimidate political opposition in civil society.²⁷ The judicial criticism would eventually escalate into a full-out assault that rocked the country in 2023.

Netanyahu and his governments also railed against the media, advancing pressure especially on outlets deemed to be critical. Netanyahu's governments heaped financial burdens on a private television station perceived as critical, while eroding the viability of the public broadcaster.²⁸

The populist right also established its own civil society groups: independent but close to the government, and heavily funded by foreign, usually anonymous, donors.

Im Tirtzu, founded in 2006, was an aggressive McCarthyite group persecuting those it deemed insufficiently devoted to Zionism, particularly in higher education.²⁹ Together with Im Tirtzu's more extreme affiliates, such as the Institute for Zionist Strategies, these groups established networks of imposters and informers, working like a quasi-state intelligence service, infiltrating the organizations they hoped to undermine.

The Kohelet Policy Forum was founded in 2012, devoted to an illiberal nationalist agenda, putatively in the name of "conservative" ideologies. Kohelet was no opposition group; it worked closely with populist right-wing politicians, feeding policy, messages, and legal and political analysis in support of the shared agenda.

These organizations contained an inherent contradiction: Kohelet too was funded by anonymous foreign donors. Kohelet exploited the freedom of civil society in order to advance policies to suppress civil society activity of groups whose agenda Kohelet and its political camp opposed. As a result, such policies were always intricately tailored to apply to left-wing causes, leaving their own activities untouched.

The political, top-down campaigns against the left, Palestinian Arab communities, human rights causes, and liberal issues intensified severely during the 2010s. Civil society fought these policies or laws through the High Court of Justice. In response, far-right politicians trained their crosshairs on the courts, concentrating their efforts to undermine the Israeli judiciary. Kohelet worked closely with policymakers on the agenda of weakening judicial oversight (or extending executive control), particularly from 2015 onward, when the minister of justice adopted its agenda and other lawmakers shared their aims.³⁰ When Netanyahu was indicted in late 2019, he too seized the reins on rhetorical, political, and legislative attacks on Israel's judicial branch.

The left wing, and increasingly Israel's centrist-liberal camp, argued that the leadership was destroying democracy. The right wing hit back that the left had never accepted its loss of political power and sought to impose despised liberal universalist values on the true nation (Jewish Israelis), through a cabal of elites. This argument came close to a "deep state"-type conspiracy and drove ever more extreme campaigns against the judiciary. Civic space was increasingly threatened – on one side of the political map.

Yet by the late 2010s, Israel had developed a seasoned and savvy cadre of oppositional left-wing civic activists. The decades-old anti-occupation struggle meant that the organizations evolved and grew over time, attracting energetic leadership and creating global networks of peers to exchange lessons and best practices.[31]

The government-led campaigns against NGOs sapped energy, human resources, and funds; but they also sparked defiance. The political attacks mostly failed to restrain or suppress such activism. In fact, the attacks on liberal causes had a boomerang effect, galvanizing liberal Jewish diaspora networks, and often spurring donations. Progressive Jewish communities in the US could lobby public officials and media in the US to raise awareness, and younger diaspora Jewish communities increasingly opposed occupation, supporting these embattled NGOs in expressing their views. Further, the more extreme the behavior of Israel's government toward political opponents, the more its actions alarmed even stalwart pro-Israel allies in the US. Eventually even conservative supporters of Israel would become concerned about these, primarily when the government appeared to threaten free speech, or the civil rights of mainstream Jewish communities.[32]

2023: CIVIL SOCIETY FIGHTS BACK

From 2019, Israel experienced severe political instability, multiple non-decisive elections, temporary or interim governing coalitions, and short legislative sessions. The Covid-19 pandemic exacerbated fears of government overreach, in the form of restrictions on personal freedom. After Netanyahu's trial opened in 2020, more parties refused to join a coalition under his leadership, leaving him dependent on ultra-right-wing parties for his coalitions. In May 2021, Israeli efforts to evict Palestinian residents of an East Jerusalem neighborhood and restrict Palestinian movement to the Al-Aqsa compound sparked demonstrations by both Palestinians under occupation, and citizens of Israel. These led to a new escalation between Israel and Hamas and a nearly unprecedented bout of inter-ethnic conflict between Arab and Jewish citizens within Israel proper. The physical clashes among citizens both reflected and fed into the fear and fury around the broader Israel–Palestine conflict.

Netanyahu briefly lost power but was voted back into office in late 2022. He was still on trial and still limited to the most fanatical, messianic, theocratic, and ultra-nationalist politicians, undemocratic to their core, as his only political allies. But by now, his Likud party fully shared the populist and illiberal agenda, even if they were motivated more by a secular nationalist agenda that included territorial maximalism and annexation. The same populist nationalism fueled Likud's enthusiastic attempts to consolidate control, destroy constraints on government power, legitimize corrupt leaders, and keep its messianic coalition partners on its side.

Government against the people, and the people's protest

In January 2023, a Likud minister of justice declared a sweeping plan to eviscerate the Israeli judiciary; the proposals included laws allowing the Knesset to override a Supreme Court ruling, turning ministerial legal advisors' roles into political positions, and exerting more executive control over judicial appointments, aiming to re-engineer the Supreme Court. These and other reforms were designed to minimize judicial oversight of the state. By then Kohelet's ideas had been completely absorbed into Israel's far-right parties, from Likud to the erstwhile Jewish Home which held the justice ministry from 2015 to 2019, and were reflected in the judicial overhaul program of the Religious Zionism party, which it released shortly before the 2023 elections.[33]

But now, Israeli citizens snapped. Mounting concerns over Netanyahu's autocratic behavior burst into the streets within days, and even some erstwhile Likud voters were swept up by fear of the new government's attacks on a whole branch of government.

The judicial assault of 2023 galvanized civil society in a way Israel had never experienced. Israelis had held mass citizen-led demonstrations against the government in its past, but the size and endurance of the 2023 democracy movement were unprecedented; protests raged at least weekly for thirty-nine straight weeks (October 7 would have been the fortieth), involving hundreds of thousands of people *each week.* Citizens organized huge financial and mobilization efforts, as the private sector and even unions joined civil society. The movement was therefore able to call strikes with severe material consequences. In contrast to the country's social-economic protest for about six weeks in 2011, the 2023 democracy protests held disparate political groups together for far longer.

Further, the situation appeared to prompt deeper questions across political divides – feeding a re-imagining of political camps based on values related to constitutional principles, limitations on state power, good governance, democracy, and equality.

However, the movement frayed when it touched the most sensitive national identity issues that competed with those core themes: Jewish identity versus equality, as well as freedom and rights in the face of ongoing occupation.

Meanwhile, Palestinian citizens felt excluded by the heavily Jewish-oriented patriotic themes of the protest, which adopted the Israeli flag as its main symbol, and rejected Palestinian symbolism. Jewish protestors or security forces sometimes forcibly removed Palestinian flags from the crowd, prompting left-wing Jews and some Arab participants to display them more prominently. The organizers insisted that Arab speakers avoid raising the occupation or the Israeli–Palestinian conflict and focus instead on domestic issues.[34] And while Jewish Israelis fought to save democracy, many Arab citizens felt there was little democracy to be saved, and stayed away from the mainstream protests. However, surveys showed that a large majority of Palestinian citizens opposed the judicial assault and firmly supported the protest movement, even if they were unenthusiastic about participating themselves.[35]

These and other internal debates drove the sense of vibrancy and urgency among the civic movement. Some expected that after the phase of intense street-level activism, the movement might become an opening for a deeper reckoning on those issues, over time.

For its part, the new government appeared unprepared for the overwhelming civic rejection, but sought mainly to slow rather than stop the legislative blitz. First, the government divided the package into individual bills, to be advanced incrementally. The coalition and cabinet members hammered away at the message that electoral victory legitimized their assault on the judicial branch.

The openly anti-democratic government also frantically accelerated its attempts to smother civic space. This included the revived bill proposing to tax left-wing NGOs at a 65% tax rate on foreign donations, mentioned earlier.[36] The communications minister stated that he wished to shutter the public broadcast station, and that the entire media was too left-wing.[37] He later drafted media reforms that would further undermine the independence of the public broadcaster (a government-funded corporation). The reforms would have simultaneously boosted the visibility and viability of a sub-standard, loyalist, conspiracy-peddling television station.[38]

The government sought to extend political control over independent, publicly funded institutions. Netanyahu attempted to install a political lackey as head of the Central Bureau of Statistics; while the government tried to politicize the management of the National Library of Israel.[39] Each was met by vigorous reporting in the news media, and further inflamed the civic backlash. The public outcry led the government to back down from both appointments, at least as of this writing.

Under tremendous public pressure over the course of 2023, the government whittled down its judicial reforms to two signature pieces of legislation. One passed in July, limiting the legal grounds the Supreme Court could use for review of executive decisions, prompting fresh peaks of public protest. These included tent cities, blocking highways, and other disruptions. To implement these efforts, activists mobilized extraordinary civic funding efforts. Both existing and ad hoc groups made mass appeals for small donations, while large private donors directed resources to bankroll the efforts. The messy organizational sprawl of January 2023 gelled into a protest headquarters, with more than 150 different organizations coordinating protests across the country.[40]

No one could have predicted how fortuitous this mass civic organizational effort would become in the final quarter of the year.

October 7: civil society replaces the absent state
The 37th government of Israel not only failed to destroy Israel's tenuous constitutional order; on October 7, 2023, it turned out that Netanyahu and his government had violated the minimum contractual obligation between a state and its citizens: that of security. Hamas's unprecedented mass attack on Israeli sovereign territory against civilians, who were exposed and

vulnerable since many of the Israel Defense Forces had been diverted to support West Bank settlements over the Jewish holiday – as settler violence increased throughout 2023 – laid the security failures bare. Intelligence services botched their most important mission. The army was absent for the critical hours.

The following days and weeks exposed further evidence of a government in shambles. The state launched immediate military action, but it had gutted its own preparedness by slashing social and public services over the years and traducing the country's own civil service as a "dictatorship of the bureaucracy": "The government mismanaged ministries such as internal security so badly that the top professional staff had fled."[41]

During the crisis on October 7 and the chaos and displacement that followed, citizens were abandoned. Over 300,000 soldiers lacked basic necessities as they were called up by emergency orders. Civilians fled from the southern areas under relentless rocket fire, and soon from the north too – with no government plan to assist them.

Civil society filled the void. On the day of the attack itself, the government was caught unprepared to act efficiently in the crisis and failed to provide information; it was the Israeli media that rushed in to collect, vet, and convey information in real time, while state institutions floundered.

In the immediate aftermath, one of the most prominent groups from the democracy protests, Brothers in Arms, transformed itself almost instantly into a national network for the home front, especially to support evacuees. The group set up headquarters around the country, including collection points for donations that poured in from citizens – food, toiletries, clothing – to distribute them to army bases, and to evacuees.

The private sector rallied to back these citizen-led efforts. Restaurants shut down to the public while frantically cooking and packing meals that were sent around the country, and hotels opened their doors to tens of thousands of people.

Social workers and psychologists volunteered time and professional attention for the traumatized victims; so much that local welfare administrators could barely coordinate the flood of volunteer efforts. The public mental health system had been starved of funding over the years and was unable to cope with the demand.[42]

On January 1, 2024, one author wrote that on October 7 and in its aftermath, "Authorities collapsed; the government ministries were absent.

Many of them are struggling to supply their needs even now."[43] The author, Roni Douek, was a longtime entrepreneur and civil society activist, among the founders of civil society infrastructure organizations; his groups initiated a massive effort in the days after the disaster, "rallying foundations, companies, private donations, for an investment of 40 million shekels in mental health efforts for children from the south, now living in hotels near the Dead Sea and Eilat."[44]

As months of war dragged on and Hamas continued to hold Israeli hostages, the hostages' families became desperate. They, too, mobilized, setting up tent camps in a public square in Tel Aviv, mounting creative and chilling visual displays in the same square that had once displayed the pro-democracy messages. T-shirts, dog-tags, yellow ribbons, and posters of the hostages replaced democracy slogans and became ubiquitous. The government, it appeared, had not initially prioritized hostage release, but following mounting public pressure it acceded to a temporary ceasefire with Hamas in exchange for the release of about half the hostages.[45]

But with no further deal forthcoming, as of this writing in early 2024, civic participation has swelled, and demonstrations are growing once again on Saturday nights, reaching 10,000 or more. Most of the protestors are demanding hostage releases, but growing numbers are angrily demanding the ouster of the government. A smattering of Israeli protesters even demands a permanent ceasefire, and an end to the occupation.

The state's last sigh

The post-October 7 reality is not a unidirectional story of civil society revival. Alongside full-blown war, the government rapidly implemented legal and political changes that most countries experience in wartime. Unlike Ukraine after the Russian invasion in February 2022, Israel did not declare martial law on its citizens; but the government did declare a state of emergency (a misleading concept, since Israel has technically been in a permanent state of emergency since its founding in 1948).

Broadly, the government justified constraints on civil society using several main arguments: first, to avoid a resurgence of violence among Palestinian Arab Muslim and Christian, and Jewish citizens of Israel, as in May 2021; second, to clamp down on public protest, dissent, or unrest that might generate security threats and require police resources, draining the capacity of security agencies for war-related efforts; and third, to mobilize civilians capable of augmenting the security forces, given that Hamas infiltrators had hidden in Israel and posed an active threat weeks later, alongside the threat of chain-reaction or copycat attacks. (Some of the local trained civilian security squads in southern communities had helped to fend off infiltrators on October 7.)

Predictably, in the service of these aims, the government took sweeping action that immediately raised alarms about violations of democratic practice. These policies, both formal and informal, included the following.

First, the police chief – seemingly influenced by the extremist minister of national security – announced early in the war that there could be no anti-war demonstrations. The police later clarified that they would review each permit application individually; but only following court challenges. In practice, the police denied permits in Arab towns,[46] and broke up demonstrations therein, while eventually allowing anti-war demonstrations in the wider Tel Aviv area.

Second, there were widespread arrests of Arab citizens, estimated at several hundred, for highly ambiguous statements on social media deemed supportive of the enemy – including expressions of solidarity with civilians in Gaza or advocating Palestinian liberation, including in posts written prior to the war. At least one Jewish citizen was arrested for a controversial social media post noting that Jewish forces had also committed atrocities during the 1948 war. Numerous other citizens have been harassed at work, fired, called for pre-termination hearings, or doxed – mostly Arabs, but also Jewish citizens.[47]

Third, the government passed emergency regulations that prevent foreign media channels from broadcasting in Israel, if deemed anti-Israel, or too sympathetic to Palestinian perspectives – or a national security threat, in the government's words. The effort was targeted and shut down Al Jazeera from broadcasting on Israeli television.[48]

CONCLUSION

Israel's worst-ever crisis was precipitated in part by long- and short-term policies undermining democracy. These included the ongoing occupation and the deadly "conflict management" approach which held that Palestinians could be suppressed in perpetuity without retribution. Over years, the ongoing authoritarian military regime ate away at democratic values and institutions, which in turn emboldened political forces determined to wreck what remained of democratic values, in order to complete the occupation's aims.

This very same assault on democracy, in its most extreme manifestation in 2023, might yet spur a resurgence of civil society in the face of efforts to smother precisely this arena. Some Israelis have speculated about a new crop of political leaders emerging from the democracy protests, or from the movement advocating hostage release.[49] Despite full-throated support for the war, polling in Israel over half a year later displayed abysmal levels of trust in the government and the prime minister, and Israelis commonly believe that the assault on the judiciary weakened the country so significantly that it contributed to Hamas's decision to attack.

The future is deeply unpredictable; but at the start of 2024, it seems unlikely that Israel's most discredited leadership will be able to subdue civil society, constrain civil space, and undermine the independent thinking, activism, and debate that its actions have sparked. This cannot be mistaken for a prediction that Israel will embrace dovish or conciliatory attitudes regarding the Israel–Palestine conflict. The war also unleashed Israeli state crackdowns on Palestinian citizens, while generating contradictory dynamics such as an acknowledgement that Arab leadership and the public mostly disavowed Hamas's actions, and that they too were its victims. At the time of writing, it is too soon to gauge the impact on citizen equality, but among Palestinians, neither the fear Israeli authorities have generated, nor the sense of a shared commitment to keeping the peace among citizens, will be forgotten. But for all Israeli citizens, civil society has a considerable opportunity for far greater influence. Those who do embrace peace and an end to occupation may well have far more freedom to act.

5

Neo-Kahanism: The Growing Influence of a Violent, Jewish Supremacist Ideology

Jessica Buxbaum and Katherine Wilkens

INTRODUCTION

> For Israel there is only one answer: removal of the Arabs from Israel, before the land turns into an ongoing nightmare of mutual communal horror.[1]

You might think these words were uttered after October 7, 2023, when Israeli politicians practically lined up to denounce Palestinian Arabs. But they were written in 1980 by Rabbi Meir Kahane, an American-born extremist. He did not beat around the bush: he called his book *They Must Go*.

While Kahane was shunned for his inflammatory, ultra-fascist rhetoric by most of the political elites of his time, today his views are embraced by growing numbers in the Israeli mainstream.[2] The rise of Kahane's ideological successors, Itamar Ben Gvir, the current Israeli national security minister and leader of Israeli political party Otzma Yehudit (Jewish Power), and his far-right partner, Bezalel Smotrich, current Israeli finance minister and leader of the political party Religious Zionist, to top cabinet positions in December 2022 is one of the most visible demonstrations of the sharply rightward progression of Israeli politics long before October 7, 2023. Kahane could only sit one Knesset term before he was disqualified from running due to his "incitement to racism." The party Kahane founded, Kach, was designated as a terrorist organization by both Israel and the US in the 1990s.[3] Now his ideological heirs can sit comfortably in senior governmental posts.

This chapter examines the context in which this militant religious Zionist movement was nurtured, and expanded over the last half-century.

BEGINNINGS

Meir Kahane, born Martin David Kahane in Brooklyn, New York in 1932, was part of the radical Revisionist youth group, Betar. Revisionism emerged in 1925 as a militant counterpart to the mainstream Zionist movement. Its founder, Ze'ev Jabotinsky, considered Labor Zionists too passive in their quest to establish a Jewish state in Palestine. Revisionists sought a Jewish majority in "Eretz Israel" (the land of Israel), an ambiguously defined geographic area generally encompassing pre-June 1967 Israel, the occupied Gaza Strip and West Bank including East Jerusalem – as well as Jordan.

The Revisionist movement had little patience for diplomacy; it supported armed struggle to address the problems facing the Jewish diaspora, and engaged in guerrilla-style warfare against the British[4] and attacks against Palestinian Arab villages through its paramilitary wing, Irgun. Jabotinsky was the first Zionist leader to preach no compromise with the Palestinian Arabs and no partition of Mandatory Palestine.[5]

As an ordained rabbi at the Orthodox Mir Yeshiva in New York presiding over a congregation, Kahane did not come to public attention until 1968, when he established the Jewish Defense League (JDL),[6] an organization that over the years became synonymous with a violent form of anti-Arab Jewish nationalism.[7] The JDL initially emerged in New York City amid the heightened racial tensions of the time between the predominantly Jewish teachers' union in the city, and Black residents who were seeking greater control over their neighborhood schools.

The group's logo, a clenched fist over a Star of David, expressed Kahane's militant form of Jewish nationalism.[8] It made headlines in 1971, when JDL members fought with Black students at Brooklyn College, and the JDL's use of vigilante patrols contributed to intensifying ethnic polarization in New York City. The JDL later escalated to terrorism, including bombings and shootings.[9] Three years after founding the JDL, Kahane was convicted of violating the Federal Firearms Act for manufacturing explosives[10] which led to his decision to emigrate to Israel where he established the political party Kach ("Thus" or "This is the Way").

When Kahane moved to Israel in 1971, he brought his hallmark racialized discourse with him, injecting it into the Israeli political conversation on Israel–Palestine. At the time, most of Israeli society rejected Kahane's ideas,[11] favoring a nationalist understanding of the conflict.

However, at the time, there was a growing focus on Jewish settlement. Four years previously, Israel had occupied East Jerusalem, the West Bank, Gaza, the Sinai Peninsula, and most of the Golan Heights in the Six-Day War against neighboring Arab states. The state's swift victory was considered a miracle, sowing the seeds for messianism, and created a push to establish settlements in Israel's biblical patrimony in Judea and Samaria. Such ideas contributed to the landslide 1977 electoral victory of Menachem Begin and the right-wing Likud party which ran on a platform that "between the Sea and the Jordan there will only be Israeli sovereignty." Campaign fliers were also distributed with the tagline "An Arafat State Will Not Be Created! – The Likud Will Prevent It!"[12]

The election of Begin in 1977 changed the face and dynamics of Israeli democracy.[13] He was the first conservative prime minister from the Likud, a party with ideological roots in Ze'ev Jabotinsky's Revisionist Zionism. Israeli expropriation of Palestinian land and settlement construction in the West Bank and Gaza Strip accelerated and, along with it, repression of Palestinians intensified.[14] These conditions contributed to the outbreak of the First Intifada in December 1987, twenty years after Israel gained control of the West Bank.

KACH AND KAHANE CHAI: A VIOLENT LEGACY

During this period Kahane was working to build a political base in Israel. After three unsuccessful attempts to be seated in the Israeli Knesset, Kahane's Kach party was able to reach the required electoral threshold in 1984, winning one seat for Kahane himself. As a representative, Kahane immediately proposed a set of racist laws including ones supporting the enslavement and deportation of non-Jews, ethno-religious segregation, and a prohibition on intermarriage and mixing between Jews and non-Jews in public spaces. He also advocated for stripping non-Jews of their Israeli citizenship and political rights. At the time, mainstream Israeli politics sought to marginalize Kahane and diminish his influence: 118 Knesset members would leave the chamber every time Kahane spoke.[15] Even Likud members such as Miki Eitan spoke out against Kahane's proposals.

The change in Kahane's political fortunes took place alongside the rise of the ultranationalist, right-wing, Orthodox settler movement, Gush Emunim, whose violent tactics to take over Palestinian land in the West Bank aligned with Kahane's racist ideology.[16] This period also saw brazen attacks against Palestinians committed by other Kach affiliates including Makhteret, a Jewish underground terror unit that attempted to blow up Al-Aqsa Mosque in Jerusalem and kill several Palestinian mayors in the West Bank.[17]

In 1985, a year after Kach secured a spot in parliament, the Knesset passed a law banning political parties that incite racism during their campaigning – effectively barring Kach from participating in the 1988 election and limiting Kahane's Knesset career to one term.[18] Some analysts have suggested that the effort to ban Kach was less about a deep disgust for the racist ideology the party espoused and more about fears that Kahane's growing support (polls indicated Kach could gain thirteen seats in the 1988 election) could damage Israel's reputation on the world stage.

Following Kahane's assassination in 1990, the Kach party split into two groups – Kach and Kahane Chai (or "Kahane lives").[19] Kahane Chai, which was run by Kahane's son, Binyamin Ze'ev Kahane, operates under several alternative names today,[20] with members concentrated mainly in the Israeli settlements of Kiryat Arba (where far-right lawmaker Ben Gvir lives) and Kfar Tapuach located in the occupied West Bank.[21]

Despite the fracture of Kach, the ideological fervor of its Kahanist supporters continued along with its violent attacks against Palestinians. Most notably in 1994, Kach supporter and ex-JDL member Baruch Goldstein gunned down twenty-nine worshippers at the Ibrahimi Mosque in the West Bank city of Hebron during the Jewish holiday of Purim. Goldstein died in the attack but became a hero to Kach followers, including Ben Gvir, then a fourteen-year-old Kach youth coordinator, who, until 2020, prominently displayed a framed photo of Goldstein in his living room. The Hebron massacre resulted in both Kach and Kahane Chai being designated as terror organizations in Israel in 1994. The United States followed suit in 1997.[22]

Both groups continued to operate. However, the massacre and designations set Kahanists apart from other violent pro-settler movements for nearly three decades. Already associated with the coarse, racist rhetoric that had barred Meir Kahane from the Knesset after his term ended in 1988, Kahanists were considered less "acceptable" for public embrace than other extremists.

When Binyamin Ze'ev Kahane was assassinated in 2000, Rabbi Yitzchak Ginsburgh took over as the top religious leader of the Kahanist movement while also heading the Od Yosef Chai Yeshiva in the notoriously violent Israeli settlement of Yitzhar.[23] In 2005, Kahane Chai member Eden Natan-Zada abandoned his army post and shot four Palestinian citizens of Israel.[24] Four years later, Kahanist Bentzi Gopstein founded Lehava (a Hebrew acronym for "Preventing Assimilation in the Holy Land") a racist anti-Palestinian, anti-Christian organization committed to preventing intermarriage and relationships between Palestinians and Jews.[25] In 2024, the Biden administration designated and sanctioned Gopstein for "engaging in destabilizing violence affecting the West Bank." Ben Gvir, a close personal friend of Gopstein, has long served as Lehava's attorney. Lehava/Kach flags can be seen waving side by side during the annual Jerusalem "Flag Day" march, a state-sponsored parade celebrating Israel's 1967 occupation of East Jerusalem which has become synonymous with intimidation and violence against Palestinian residents of the Old City.

INFILTRATING THE ISRAELI MAINSTREAM

Though Kach was outlawed as a political party and designated a terrorist group in 1994, it didn't end there. In fact, it was quietly beginning to gain prominence behind the scenes in the mid-1990s as anti-Arab and anti-left sentiments were bolstered among settler groups and more Zionist sects within the ultra-Orthodox community who were motivated by concern for the religious significance of the land in the West Bank and opposed to the two-state vision outlined in the Oslo Accords. Some in the ultra-Orthodox community viewed territorial concessions and cooperation with "the Arabs," spearheaded by the left, as rewarding Palestinian militant activity in the First Intifada.

The Oslo Accords presented a ready-made political opportunity for Benjamin Netanyahu, then a young rising politician who had served as Israel's ambassador to the United Nations from 1984 to 1988 and was the newly elected Likud party chairperson in 1993. Netanyahu worked to tap into anti-Oslo sentiment and launched an aggressive campaign denouncing the agreement as incompatible with Israel's right to security and with the historic right of the Jewish people to the whole land of Israel.[26] His fiery speeches incited settler-vigilante youth like Ben Gvir and yeshiva student and far-right extremist Yigal Amir. Following an anti-Oslo speech by Netanyahu in 1995, a teenaged Ben Gvir ripped the hood ornament off then prime minister Yitzhak Rabin's car, bragging to the press: "Just as we got to his [Rabin's] car, we'll get to him too."[27] Weeks later, Rabin was assassinated by Yigal Amir, a twenty-five-year-old law student at Bar-Ilan University, from an Orthodox Yemenite Jewish family.

The May 1996 Israeli general election after Rabin's death was the first election contested under the new 1992 electoral law – and the first time in forty-five years that a prime minister was elected on a separate ballot from the remaining members of the Knesset. Under the new procedure, Netanyahu was able to win the election even as his Likud party gained two fewer seats in the Knesset than Shimon Peres's Labor party and bested Peres by less than 1% – about 2,900 votes. Overwhelmingly viewed as a referendum on the matter of peace with Palestinians, Netanyahu's slim win was largely credited to the ultra-Orthodox, who, described as the "soft right" by Israeli right-wing expert and author Ehud Sprinzak, had become vital players in Israeli politics by 1996.[28] The ultra-Orthodox and Likud were increasingly united by a shared antipathy for Arabs and the pro-peace left – sentiments also shared by large numbers of new Jewish immigrants from the former Soviet Union who began arriving in Israel under the Law of Return in 1989. By 1996, their numbers had reached over 600,000.[29]

The entry of the ultra-Orthodox into political activism for the first time was also due, in part, to the increased enrollment in yeshivas. Beginning in 1977, more young men were exempted from mandatory Israeli military service to study Jewish law. Yet some of these young, religious, and impressionable men were not prepared for rigorous study, and became targeted for recruitment by Kahanists[30] and their message of violence "in the name of God." Over time, anti-Palestinian violence, like that of groups like the Hilltop Youth and the Price Tag movement, settlers who carry out vengeful attacks in response to the army dismantling their outposts, became an alternative path for more of these yeshiva students.[31] Together these factors culminated in growing support among factions in the Orthodox community for Likud's message – advanced by Netanyahu – of expansionism, control, and security.

In subsequent years, Kahanism further crept into Likud through the Israeli political party Manhigut Yehudit (Jewish Leadership), which evolved out of a protest movement against the Oslo Accords, led by Zo Artzeinu (This is Our Land). Founded in 1996 by radical right-wing nationalists Moshe Feiglin and Shmuel Sackett, the party managed to enter Likud in 2000 and, in less than a decade, became its largest faction. This strategic alliance with Likud was aimed at coopting Likud and moving the Israeli political landscape closer to the Kahanist agenda. The Kahanist ideology espoused by Sackett and Feiglin permeated through Manhigut Yehudit, which strove to make Israel a more Jewish state and eliminate the idea of a Palestinian one. Feiglin believed religious nationalists could have more influence in politics through Likud than by voting for niche parties.[32] Thus, the two worked to register settlers as Likud members. While Manhigut Yehudit eventually separated from Likud, the Kahanist links to the party have not.

NEO-KAHANISTS IN GOVERNMENT

Otzma Yehudit, the far-right ultra-Orthodox party of Itamar Ben Gvir, is widely considered the ideological successor of Kach. The party was founded in 2012 by Kahanists Baruch Marzel, Michael Ben-Ari, and Lehava founder Gopstein. Its platform is replete with Jewish supremacist thought, most prominently calling to establish "a national authority for encouraging emigration" of Palestinians.[33] The party's leader, Kahanist Ben Gvir, has also called for the expulsion of Palestinians. "I am not against all Arabs," Ben Gvir said in 2022, "but those who want to do harm … those who throw stones, those who throw Molotov cocktails, will first be sent to prison – and then we will strip them of their citizenship!"[34]

Netanyahu was largely seen as putting Kahanism back into the Knesset when he struck a political deal with Otzma Yehudit and brought them into his government coalition. Political pundits' assessment of this as a desperate move by Netanyahu to form a coalition with the only party willing to join his government and help him avoid corruption charges overlooks the historical record. Netanyahu's alliance with Kahanists stems back decades – to when he was first elected prime minister in 1996. It was then that he appointed former Kahane student Tzachi Hanegbi and ex-Kach member Avigdor Lieberman to his government. And during his second prime ministerial term in 2019,

Netanyahu allowed the racist and anti-immigrant activist Sheffi Paz to sit in on his cabinet meetings. (Though Paz rejects the Kahanist label, she helped campaign for Otzma Yehudit.)

Kahanism and Netanyahu's Likud party are also historically linked. When Israel was founded, Revisionism transitioned from an ideological movement to a political party called Herut. The party went through several iterations before eventually morphing into Likud. The territorial maximalism of Revisionism is reflected in Likud's long-standing policy favoring annexation of the occupied Palestinian territories. In fact, Likud's original party platform[35] declared the entire area from the river to the sea as under Israeli sovereignty and rejected a Palestinian state.

Netanyahu has not only allied with Kahanists, he seems to genuinely share their perspective. In 1989, while serving as deputy foreign minister, Netanyahu gave a speech at Bar-Ilan University lambasting the government for its failure "to exploit politically favorable situations in order to carry out 'large-scale' expulsions at times when 'the [political] damage would have been relatively small ... I still believe that there are opportunities to expel many people,'" he said. Throughout the 1990s, Netanyahu participated in protests against the Oslo Accords and their champion, Rabin. He even led a funeral procession in which the coffin bore the engraving, "Rabin kills Zionism."[36]

Netanyahu – the master of spin – has also espoused Kahanist-like rhetoric throughout his premiership.[37] In an infamous effort to propel Jewish voters to the polls in 2015 he issued a warning that "Arab voters are heading to the polling stations in droves." In 2019, he stated that "Israel is not a state of all its citizens." In his view, "Arab citizens have 22 nation-states ... they do not need another one."[38]

As Israel's longest-serving prime minister, Netanyahu's anti-Arab and anti-Palestinian views have become increasingly normalized within the Israeli public consciousness. Over the years, Netanyahu's rhetoric has allowed Kahanism to flourish, while the domestic political landscape in Israel has been the perfect breeding ground for the racist ideology.

Political unrest and upticks in violence between Palestinians and Israelis have long been exploited by Kahanists to garner support for their movement. Most Jewish Israelis viewed the Oslo Accords as the last chance to resolve matters between them and Palestinians and reach a peace deal. With the breakdown of negotiations and the start of the Second Intifada in 2000, many Israelis moved to the right[39] and anti-Palestinian notions festered.

This mistrust of Palestinians was deepened by leftists' disillusionment with peace talks,[40] resulting in a sense of hopelessness over the prospect of coexistence. The left's pessimistic attitude was further bolstered by the growing demographic imbalance between secular leftists, decreasing in number, and the burgeoning religious population.[41] These changes in Israeli society gave space for religious nationalists to take control. Thus, the balance of power in Israeli politics shifted away from the Labor party that had long dominated, toward the right which had become heavily influenced by the ultra-Orthodox.

Kahanist ideas of Jewish supremacy became much more visibly ingrained in Israel with the passage of the Basic Law: Israel as the Nation-State of the Jewish People in 2018, the quasi-constitutional measure that states that Jews have an exclusive right of self-determination in the state of Israel.[42] In addition, the law declared Jerusalem Israel's undivided capital, Jewish settlement in the biblical land of Israel a national priority, and Hebrew the state's only official language. Arabic language was downgraded to having a "special status."

Where Palestinian citizens of Israel may live has also become more regulated. In 2023, the Knesset broadened the scope of the Admissions Committees Law, allowing more so-called "community towns" to be established. The towns are empowered to create authorities to screen applicants wishing to reside in the towns based on whether the applicants are socially compatible with the other members of the community.[43] Thus, the Admissions Committees Law broadened the scope of permissible discrimination against Palestinian citizens of Israel in the area of housing and home ownership. Yet housing discrimination did not originate with this bill. The state has long sought to limit where Palestinian may live. Decades of Israeli government land confiscations and discriminatory planning policies have confined many Palestinians to densely populated towns and villages with little room to expand.[44] For instance, the 1970 Legal and Administrative Matters Law (and before that the Absentees' Property Law)[45] only allows Jewish property lost during the 1948 Arab–Israeli War to be returned to Jews and their descendants. No such right is afforded to Palestinians who also fled or were expelled from their lands during the war.

Similar to the restrictions on where Palestinian citizens of Israel may reside, measures have been taken to circumscribe the residence of Palestinians inside the occupied territories, including in East Jerusalem. One example of how the Israeli government does this in the occupied territories is the case of the Palestinian community of Masafer Yatta. According to an unclassified meeting transcript from 1981, former prime minister Ariel Sharon instructed the Israeli military to create training zones in Masafer Yatta, a rural area in the southern West Bank near Hebron, as a mechanism to displace the Palestinian residents there.[46] The legality of this artifice was resolved in 2022, when Israel's Supreme Court sided with the Israeli army to pave the way for the mass expulsion of thousands of Palestinians.[47]

In the same year that the Israeli Supreme Court sanctioned the evictions of the community of Masafer Yatta, Ben Gvir's Otzma Yehudit and the anti-LGBTQ Noam party united with and were subsumed by Smotrich's Religious Zionism party to create a joint list. Religious Zionism is considered the ideological successor of the ultra-nationalist, religious settler movement, Gush Emunim. Religious Zionism then allied with Netanyahu's Likud party to create a governing coalition following November 2022. Analysts have described the alliance of these parties as Israel's most right-wing governing coalition ever. In order to take the premiership, Netanyahu was forced to strike agreements with each of the parties under the Religious Zionism umbrella, even carving out new roles for the party leaders. Netanyahu made the notoriously homophobic Avi Maoz a deputy minister overseeing the establishment of "Jewish identity" programs in a new Jewish National Identity Office as well as being in charge of external programming for public schools. Smotrich snagged the role of finance minister and a Defense Ministry position granting him near full control over settlement construction in the West Bank. Netanyahu appointed Ben Gvir as national security minister, a new role broadening the powers of the previous public security minister to head Israel's national police force and, additionally, the Israel Border Police in the West Bank, which was previously under the Defense Ministry's domain.

The Religious Zionism alliance's main 2022 platform objectives were settlement expansion, specifically legalizing more than 100 settlement outposts (extensions of Israeli settlements built without official government approval), and further limiting Palestinian building in the West Bank. As part of Netanyahu's government, this platform agenda has now become policy.

Before entering the current government, Smotrich outlined his solution to the so-called Palestinian–Israeli conflict in his 2017 Decisive Plan for Israel. In this document,[48] Smotrich rejected Palestinian statehood in favor of Jewish self-determination from the river to the sea. He called for squelching any Palestinian nationalist aspirations and for expelling Palestinians who remain committed to Palestinian statehood. To achieve these goals, Smotrich stated, a campaign of aggressive settlement expansion and construction must be implemented. With his Defense Ministry appointment, Smotrich has been able to make significant strides to actualize the Decisive Plan.

In 2023, Smotrich directed representatives from various government ministries to prepare for the settler population in the West Bank to double, to one million in two years.[49] By 2024 – under the cover of war – Smotrich appears on track to reach that goal. According to West Bank Population Stats,[50] a pro-settler website tracking the settler population in the West Bank, the population grew by nearly 3% from 2023 to 2024, bringing the number of settlers today to nearly 520,000. This number does not include the approximately 340,000 settlers in occupied East Jerusalem. The group predicts the settler population will rapidly accelerate in the coming years because of Hamas's attack on Israel, which pushed Israelis farther to the right.

The year 2023 saw the highest record of settlement advancement since monitoring began in 2017, according to statistics collected by the United Nations[51] and Israeli settlement watchdog group Peace Now.[52] More than 24,000 housing units were advanced or approved within Israeli-military-controlled Area C of the West Bank. Settlers established a record number of twenty-six new outposts while the Israeli government retroactively legalized fifteen. The year 2024 may surpass 2023's record-breaking rate as within just the first two months of the year, the government approved the construction of nearly 3,500 settler homes.

Meanwhile Ben Gvir has been busy establishing a 2,000-strong nationalist militia to be deployed during times of "Arab unrest," essentially aimed at repressing any Palestinian protest or resistance. Juxtaposed to this project, Ben Gvir loosened the gun licensing regulations in the wake of Hamas's attack, thereby arming at least 100,000 Israelis. He has also been working to increase the number of rapid response squads, volunteer defense forces operating in emergencies when police have not yet been deployed. Traditionally, these units work in rural areas, but squads are now forming in settler outposts deep within Jerusalem's Palestinian neighborhoods[53] – acting as yet another way to quickly arm settlers.

"KAHANE WAS RIGHT"

In September 2023, nine months after the formation of the coalition government, a protest in favor of the judicial overhaul that would strip the Supreme Court of its powers of legislative oversight included a number of participants donning stickers proclaiming "Kahane was Right," "Baruch Goldstein was Right," and "Yigal Amir was Right." For these protestors, weakening the judiciary in favor of the Knesset would allow them to pursue their pro-settlement agenda unchecked by liberal judges. The events of October 7 have further pushed Kahanist ideas into mainstream Israeli society. One month after Hamas's attack, Israel passed an amendment to the 2016 Counter-Terrorism Law criminalizing the consumption of terrorist materials with a maximum penalty of one year in prison.[54] The vague and broad language of the amendment means even reading the Hamas Charter for informational purposes can be considered a crime. This comes against the backdrop of increasing arrests of Palestinians for their social media posts in solidarity with Gaza.

Speaking out against the war has become dangerous for both Palestinians and Jewish Israelis. While initially banned, anti-war protests are now frequently met with police brutality in Israel. Campus culture has become even more suppressive; the Hebrew University in Jerusalem suspended Professor Nadera Shalhoub-Kevorkian for distributing a petition calling for a ceasefire in Gaza and saying Israel is committing genocide in the Strip.[55] A few months later, Shalhoub-Kevorkian was arrested for "incitement." While labeling Israel's assault as genocide is grounds for punishment, genocidal rhetoric is welcomed now – from the upper political echelons to the everyday Israeli. "We are fighting human animals, and we are acting accordingly," Israel's defense minister, the Likud party's Yoav Gallant said, days after Hamas's attack. "We will eliminate everything – they will regret it."[56]

Several Israeli lawmakers called outright for Israel to enact another Nakba in Gaza, referring to the mass expulsion and massacre of Palestinians in 1947–1948 before and during Israel's establishment. At the time of writing, Israeli soldiers are proudly sharing videos and photos online celebrating their participation in violent and inhumane acts, often posting pictures of themselves blowing up property not justified by military necessity, plundering civilians areas, vandalizing homes, dehumanizing detainees and more. Israelis are blocking aid to Gaza at major crossings despite the man-made famine. One of the groups leading this effort is Jewish Truth, an extremist right-wing movement advocating for the ethnic cleansing of Palestinians from the West Bank. Its spokesperson is the Kahanist Marzel.

Think tanks intertwined with the state are promoting the mass expulsion of Palestinians. Israeli security think tank Misgav (or the Institute for National Security and Zionist Strategy) published a paper written by its researcher Amir Weitmann in 2023, weeks after Israel launched its war on Gaza, entitled "A plan for resettlement and final rehabilitation in Egypt of the entire population of Gaza: economic aspects." Weitmann is an activist with Netanyahu's Likud party and reportedly a close associate of intelligence minister Gila Gamliel. The report suggests the mass transfer of civilians in Gaza as part of Israel's "day-after-the-war" strategy. The report states:

> Israel ... [to] transfer as many Gazans as possible to other countries; Any other alternative, including PA [Palestinian Authority] rule, is a strategic failure. Therefore, Gaza's population should be transferred to the Sinai Desert and the displaced absorbed in other countries.[57]

There are also calls for the Israeli government to reestablish Jewish settlements in the Strip. As the war continues, recolonizing Gaza is turning from a niche concept into a popular idea as surveys and conferences suggest growing support among Israelis.[58]

Jewish supremacy manifests on even the most mundane levels as well, such as when the main taxi-hailing app in Israel, Gett, offered a "Mehadrin" service, in which drivers must adhere to strict Jewish regulations, allowing users to request a taxi that is not driven on the Sabbath. Unlike observant Jews, most Palestinian Gett drivers work on the Sabbath. A 2020 lawsuit ended this service.[59]

In Israel, districts are often segregated by ethnicity. West Jerusalem is Jewish, East Jerusalem is Palestinian. Tel Aviv is Jewish, Jaffa is Palestinian. For Palestinian tenants, this means their housing options are severely limited as many Israeli landlords refuse to rent to non-Jews.

With Kahanism's central idea – complete expulsion of Palestinians – gaining greater momentum in Israeli society, the space for Palestinian–Jewish coexistence and justice is rapidly shrinking. This is seen in Israel's designation of six Palestinian human rights groups as terrorist entities, in its brutal quelling of criticism of the state's actions, and, more recently, in a Knesset hearing claiming pro-Palestinian activists documenting settler violence in the West Bank are harassing settlers and police.[60]

CONCLUSION

During his lifetime Meir Kahane represented a fringe movement. Today neo-Kahanism has fully entered the bloodstream of the Israeli body politic. Though this process has been in the works for some time, the October 7 Hamas attack and the official Israeli response have been a windfall for extremism. The new cycle of violence that was born in the rubble of Gaza, Kfar Aza, and Be'eri will likely fuel the actions of extremists for decades. We have already seen the impact in apparent widespread violations in Gaza of the laws of war, open Israeli military support of settler revenge attacks against innocent civilians in the West Bank, and further denial of the basic rights of Palestinian and Jewish citizens of Israel seeking to peacefully express their disagreement or dissent.

Kahane's vision helped to spread a more racist, messianic form of Zionism. The official merger of this maximalist ideology with the Israeli state in December 2022, when Itamar Ben Gvir and Bezalel Smotrich entered the Netanyahu coalition government, was a watershed moment – for the first time fully embracing and legitimizing the violent supremacist beliefs of neo-Kahanism. The future of Israel–Palestine is uncertain, but one thing seems clear: it will be influenced more than ever by the views of a man who proudly preached that "No trait is more justified than revenge in the right time and place."

PART TWO

MECHANISMS TO REPRESS SPEECH, ACTIVISM, AND AGENCY

6

US Counterterrorism Law and Policy: Its Role in Shutting Down Palestinian Activism and Agency

Nour Soubani and Diala Shamas

INTRODUCTION

On October 25, 2023, the Anti-Defamation League (ADL) and the Brandeis Center sent a joint letter to the presidents of 200 universities and colleges, calling on them to investigate chapters of the student organization Students for Justice in Palestine (SJP) on their campuses. The letter accused SJP of potential violations of the ban on material support to foreign terrorist organizations. It cited 18 USC 2339A and 2339B, otherwise known as the material support statutes.[1] It characterized SJP's activities – normal student activism like participation in a National Day of Resistance, organizing toolkits for campus actions, and various statements – as support for Hamas, a designated "Foreign Terrorist Organization" (FTO).[2] In May 2024, the lawsuits building on those initial calls followed.[3]

The ADL and Brandeis Center letter drew immediate rebuke from leading civil liberties and civil rights groups as a brazen attack on the First Amendment. But the groups' letter and the subsequent lawsuits are not extreme outliers. They drew on decades of work by pro-Israel groups to deploy US counterterrorism law to chill Palestinian and pro-Palestinian civic engagement and political expression. For decades, material support laws in particular have been wielded powerfully and often without basis in fact by opponents of the Palestinian rights movement against civil society actors including humanitarian workers, Palestinian rights organizations, and human rights activists in the United States and abroad. Indeed, the material support laws invoked by the ADL and the Brandeis Center have historically emerged out of efforts to police and control Palestinian political movements and advocacy.

Through both criminal prosecutions and private civil suits or threats of litigation, material support laws have served to shrink the civic space for Palestine. They have had a chilling effect on engagement with Palestine in the US due to the threat of protracted litigation or criminal investigation. They have also tied up civil society resources by diverting funds, energy, and labor to defending against disinformation campaigns and politically motivated litigation – often called "lawfare." The motivation behind the expansion and application of antiterrorism laws has been about far more than regulating violence and ensuring safety. In fact, policing Palestinian movements has been a central component at key turning points in the laws' trajectory. Yet the ubiquitous presence of these laws and their dramatic impact on Palestinian civic space is not matched by any coherent policy response. Critical engagement with these laws has tended to focus on their restrictive effect on humanitarian aid, or the religious and civil rights of Muslim communities in the US. These conversations have largely ignored that the policing of Palestinians has been among the laws' most potent uses (or abuses) and a core feature of their history and expansion. This chapter hopes to contribute to future legal and policy discussions regarding the politicized abuse of antiterrorism laws in the context of Palestine.

THE ANTI-PALESTINIAN ORIGINS OF US TERRORISM LAW AND THE BAN ON MATERIAL SUPPORT

In February 2024, the Center for Constitutional Rights and Palestine Legal published a briefing paper authored by Professor Darryl Li, tracing the history of core pillars of US counterterrorism law. The central contribution of the paper is that Palestine – and efforts to suppress certain forms of Palestinian political expression – has been a principal motivating factor behind the development and expansion of US antiterrorism architecture from its inception. Indeed, the paper notes, the first mention of "terrorism" in US federal law was in 1969 in reference to restrictions on humanitarian aid to UNRWA, the United Nations Relief and Works Agency for Palestine

Refugees. The paper locates Palestine in similar foundational moments in immigration law's terrorism crosshairs, in designation schemes and blacklists, and in criminal law with the bar to material support for terrorism. The briefing paper traces the involvement of pro-Israel advocacy groups at these key junctures where counterterrorism law was developed or expanded. Ultimately, it concludes, the post-9/11 "War on Terror" policies, and the counterterrorism architecture as we know it now, were built on a pre-existing foundation of hostility to the Palestinian liberation movement.[4]

In the 1970s, "the Palestinian" began to emerge as the paradigmatic or "essential" terrorist in the international imagination and in US policy circles.[5] After the attacks by the Black September Organization at the Munich Olympics in 1972, Israel worked to develop a logic of international terrorism that linked Israeli security concerns to American interests. The Jonathan Institute, an Israeli think tank with Benjamin Netanyahu at its helm, "would play a decisive role ... in internationalizing the idea that terrorism was not just an Israeli problem but rather one that plagued the Western democratic world."[6] This outlook, whereby Israel's security concerns were framed as a broader problem that threatened Western values, set a foundation for pro-Israel interest groups in the US like the American Israel Public Affairs Committee (AIPAC) and the ADL to advocate for anti-terrorism legislation that targeted Palestinian armed resistance groups.[7] This marked the beginning of a long-term strategy to intertwine American and Israeli security interests through a robust counterterrorism regime. Today, this regime includes designations, criminal bars on "material support for terrorism," immigration bars, and extensive financial and regulatory enforcement. As anthropologist Lisa Bhungalia writes, it was "shaped in subsequent decades by transnational circuits between the United States and Israel."[8]

The end of the Cold War and the subsequent US geopolitical focus on the Middle East was an important turning point for the American counterterrorism apparatus. After the fall of the Soviet Union, Israel, whose military funding from the US "began as a way to contain Soviet expansion into the Middle East,"[9] used the specter of "Islamic" terrorism to secure continued aid.[10] Since the 1970s, proponents of the idea that threats to Israel were also threats to the US argued that these threats emanated from the Muslim world (with financial support networks partly inside the US). After the Cold War, what had been a developing but inconsistent political use of the terrorism category in US policy toward the Middle East was further entrenched and consolidated.

In this context, American efforts to combat terrorism in the region became increasingly filtered through the lens of Israel's fight against the Palestinians. A shift in foreign policy toward Israel, combined with lobbying by interest groups, gave rise to the development of enforcement mechanisms that punished and disciplined the Palestinian liberation movement which was seen as a threat to Israeli – and by extension American – stability in the Middle East. These enforcement mechanisms would evolve into an intricate transnational counterterrorism regime, at the heart of which is the ban on material support for terrorism.

Specifically, the Oslo Accords constituted a pivotal moment in which these policy shifts crystallized. Not only did the US act as "Israel's lawyer" during negotiations with Palestinians, according to former State Department official Aaron David Miller,[11] but it also deployed its emerging counterterrorism apparatus to suppress opposition by Palestinian political factions. In 1995, Bill Clinton signed Executive Order 12947, blocking the assets in the United States "of terrorists who threaten to disrupt the Middle East Peace Process."[12] This was the first US government list that triggered concrete legal consequences.[13] The order listed twelve organizations, including Hamas, Palestinian Islamic Jihad, the Popular Front for the Liberation of Palestine, and other significant Palestinian political factions.[14] As Bhungalia argues, "[t]his marks the beginning of the shift to a 'list-based' approach to criminalizing support for terrorism ... [and] set into motion processes that ultimately culminated in the passage of the US material support ban."[15]

That same year, the Oklahoma City bombing, perpetrated by an extreme right-wing white nationalist,[16] would become the catalyst for enshrining in law the "financial war on terror" through the material support statute. In the wake of the attack, and building on Executive Order 12947, Congress passed the Antiterrorism and Effective Death Penalty Act (AEDPA) of 1996. The AEDPA gave the secretary of state the power to designate organizations as foreign terrorists[17] and prohibited the knowing or purposeful provision of "material support or resources" to them.[18] The AEDPA's ban on material support relied on two important assumptions: first, that the prohibition on material support to designated organizations was irrespective of any intent; and second, that "money is fungible," meaning that giving support to aid an organization's peaceful activities frees up resources that can be used for terrorist acts. These assumptions would become central to the ban's broad reach, and specifically how it was used against Palestinian civil society.

Not only was tangible support to a designated organization outlawed under the AEDPA, but any contact, relationship, or interaction with it were brought within the orbit of the Act's prohibitions. In effect, the AEDPA concretized the terrorist designations that Executive Order 12947 had put in place and broadened their reach. Its language encompassed not only designated organizations, but any affiliation with them, including engagement by civil society. This would lay the foundation for material support laws to be used to suppress civil society actors, particularly those operating in a context like Palestine, where the major political factions are also designated terrorist organizations under US law.

Though precipitated by the Oklahoma City bombing, pro-Israel lobby groups championed passage of the AEDPA. They capitalized on the moment to entrench a discourse in which associations are made between terrorism, Islam, and the Middle East.[19] The AEDPA was, "from the outset, a transnational legal architecture established to curb a perceived foreign, racialized threat."[20] The material support ban has become the main feature of the US counterterrorism apparatus and its War on Terror. As Bhungalia writes, "[a]s pressure has mounted surrounding more controversial tactics of US warfare, notably torture and indefinite detention, US prosecutors have invoked the material statute more than any other in pursuit of the US global war on terror. The ensuing financial war on terror has come to dominate, in all its banal details, the preemptive focus of the war on terror."[21] Although passed in response to a white supremacist attack, it laid the foundation for the post-9/11 expansive material support regime which has been heavily criticized for its disproportionate application to Arab and Muslim communities.[22]

POST-9/11 EXPANSION OF "MATERIAL SUPPORT TO TERRORISM" LAWS

In the post-9/11 era, the material support ban grew as a central feature of the counterterrorism legal architecture and has persisted as a key challenge facing Palestinian civic and political space. The Global War on Terror facilitated an expansion of material support laws from what Wadie Said calls "traditional" material support laws to heavily politicized weapons of the war with serious implications for First Amendment rights.[23] Weeks after 9/11, the USA Patriot Act amended the definition of material support to include "expert advice or assistance."[24] In 2004, the material support statute was again expanded by the Intelligence Reform and Terrorism Prevention Act to include "property, tangible or intangible, or service."[25] These legislative expansions were in line with the Bush administration's vow to "impede terrorist funding."[26] They had the effect of broadening the ban's reach to more easily include civil society activities tied to Palestine.

The courts have upheld expansive interpretations of the material support prohibition in the face of challenges to their constitutionality. The most significant of these challenges, *Holder v. Humanitarian Law Project*, was brought by groups in the United States engaged in providing money, training, and advocacy for the Tamil Tigers, a designated FTO in Sri Lanka. The Supreme Court ruled that the statute's prohibitions on "expert advice," "training," "service," and "personnel" were not vague and did not violate the First Amendment. Moreover, the court's opinion stated that engaging in these efforts, even if not on behalf of the FTO, but in service of the FTO's political (non-violent) goals more broadly, was still a violation of the statute.[27] The foundations established in *Holder* would allow the ban on material support to have an outsized effect on transnational humanitarian and political activities, especially as related to Palestine.[28] The following sections trace some of the ways in which this has played out for Palestinians.[29]

MATERIAL SUPPORT LAWS AND SHRINKING CIVIC SPACE

State repression through criminal prosecutions

Some of the most canonical prosecutions under material support laws have targeted prominent Palestinian figures and organizations. Notably, these were often people and institutions Israel had already tried to push the US to criminalize before 9/11, with limited success. In the context of the Global War on Terror, however, the heightened rhetoric on international terrorism, especially "Islamic" terrorism, and the emphasis on cutting off purported terrorist financing, created an opportunity to renew interest in their cases. Expanded surveillance and prosecutorial authorities, more aggressive policing, and reduced oversight facilitated and bolstered terrorism prosecutions. As the US-declared War on Terror coincided with the Second Intifada raging in the occupied territories and the rise in the popularity of the Islamist movement, Hamas, in the West Bank and Gaza, humanitarian aid to Palestinians and Muslims abroad, particularly if conducted by US-based Muslim charities, faced heavy scrutiny.

The case of Muhammad Salah, a prominent Palestinian American figure in Chicago well-known for his service to the community both locally and in Palestine, illustrates this evolution. In 1993, Salah was arrested by the Israeli military while he was crossing a checkpoint to enter Gaza to deliver humanitarian aid. Israel claimed he was "a US based senior Hamas military commander"[30] and imprisoned him for five years, during which he was subject to interrogations under torture, resulting in a forced confession.[31]

Salah's case, based as it was on a coerced confession, became an emblematic example of how Israel was able to enlist the US in the fight against what it characterized as a transnational terrorist network.[32] Two years after Salah's arrest, US policy toward Hamas – and Salah – would shift more decisively in Israel's favor with Executive Order 12947. As a result of the Order, which listed Hamas as a terrorist organization, Salah, still in Israeli prison, was listed as a Specially Designated Terrorist (SDT). Despite his designation as an SDT, a terrorist financing investigation conducted in 1997 by the United States upon Salah's release from Israeli prison did not result in charges being brought against him when he returned to the United States. In fact, the Clinton administration subsequently closed the case against him in 2000 for lack of evidence.

It was not until after the terror attacks on the United States in September 2001, motivated by the politics of the War on Terror and a desire to show the public it was cracking down on alleged terror financiers, that the Department of Justice reopened Salah's case. He was prosecuted under the material support law. The case against him reflected a deep Israeli entanglement in the US courtroom. The prosecution relied overwhelmingly on the confession that the Israeli secret police (known as Shin Bet) extracted from Salah under torture as well as classified Israeli intelligence documents, most of which were not made available to him.[33]

Salah was eventually acquitted, suggesting the classified material presented to the judge failed to establish that his activities were linked to terrorism. Though Salah's name has been cleared, he had to sue to remove his name from the Treasury's SDT list.[34] Salah's prosecution put humanitarian workers and civil society actors working with Palestinians and Palestinian organizations in the occupied territories on notice that they could be subject to lengthy litigation based on secret evidence of links to terrorism. Moreover, Salah's coerced confession became a key piece of evidence in related prosecutions against Palestinians and civil society actors.[35]

In 2001, at the urging of the Israeli government,[36] then Representative Chuck Schumer, and the Investigative Project on Terrorism headed by Steve Emerson,[37] the US government seized the assets of the Holy Land Foundation for Relief and Development (HLF), the largest Muslim charitable organization in the US at the time, whose primary focus was delivering aid to Palestine. *USA v. Holy Land Foundation* was the first terrorism prosecution targeting a group other than al-Qaeda after 9/11, and it was one of many Muslim charities prosecuted during the War on Terror.

But the US–Israeli campaign against the HLF began well before 9/11. The United States had been surveilling HLF since 1994 for its alleged ties to Hamas. In the same year, the ADL and the American Jewish Congress launched a campaign to pressure the Internal Revenue Service to revoke the HLF's tax-exempt status. On December 4, 2001, the US government declared HLF a "Domestic Terror Organization" and shut down its operations under Executive Order 13224.[38] The allegations against the HLF were based on its support for *zakat* (charity) committees in the West Bank and Gaza. The *zakat* committees collect religiously mandated charitable contributions from Muslims across the world and distribute them to Palestinians in need. Rather than argue that the *zakat* committees were a front for terrorist activity, the government used expert witness testimony to link the *zakat* committees to Hamas and argue that by providing essential goods and services to Palestinians, they ultimately served to bolster Hamas's reputation through their charitable work.[39]

By supporting the *zakat* committees financially, the government argued, HLF was indirectly providing legitimacy to Hamas, an act that fell under the definition of material support. This interpretation went beyond the realm of security considerations tied to acts of violence or militancy for the enforcement of the material support laws. Instead, the government relied on "political calculations, with the issue of dangerousness and violence shunted off to the side."[40] As a result and combined with the outcomes of *Holder*, material support liability became a clear vehicle for articulating US foreign policy priorities, heavily influenced by the special relationship with Israel.

These prominent, multi-year criminal prosecutions sent a clear, chilling message to broad segments of the Palestinian community. Moreover, with the shadow of terrorism cast over charitable giving to Palestinians, it did not take long for US-based civil society organizations advocating for Palestinian human rights to be swept up in criminal investigations for material support to terrorism. In 2010, for example, the FBI raided the homes of and subpoenaed twenty-three anti-war and pro-Palestinian activists in the Midwest who had travelled to Palestine in a cross-movement solidarity delegation. Citing material support to FTOs, including the Popular Front for the Liberation of Palestine (PFLP) and Hezbollah, the government confiscated dozens of boxes of material related to Palestine, including videos of family trips, personal papers, computer files, and children's schoolwork.[41]

The raids targeted leaders of prominent Palestinian civil society institutions in the United States, including Maureen Murphy, an editor of the online magazine the *Electronic Intifada*, and Hatem Abudayyeh, the director of the Chicago-based grassroots organization Arab American Action Network. While the 2010 raids did not lead to any charges, the investigation served as a phishing expedition that eventually led to criminal proceedings against Rasmea Odeh, a Palestinian leader with deep roots in Chicago who had been widely recognized for her community organizing work.[42] The government charged Odeh with lying to immigration authorities about a terrorism conviction in Israeli courts which Odeh claimed was obtained through torture but was not allowed to present evidence of this in court.[43] She was eventually deported after decades living in the United States.[44]

In more decentralized incidents, Palestinians across the United States have reported being visited by the FBI in their homes and questioned either based on their political activism or simply because they are Palestinian.[45] In the aftermath of the October 7 attacks, FBI outreach for such "voluntary questioning" has increased, as have reports of law enforcement monitoring mass protests at the local, state, and federal level.[46] Similarly on college campuses, students have reported being questioned by the FBI for social media posts in support of Palestinian rights and say that private actors have created online blacklists based on unsubstantiated claims of support for terrorism which are then shared with the FBI. One such blacklist, Canary Mission, targets students for their activism, impacting their reputations and ability to find employment after graduation. These blacklists have been heavily criticized for their use of intimidation tactics against students and blatant conflation of protected speech against Zionism with antisemitism and terrorism.[47]

Private policing and civil litigation

Even when criminal cases are dismissed or go nowhere for lack of evidence, Palestinian civil society leaders and institutions still face ongoing harassment. For example, after the US government temporarily dropped charges against Salah in 2000, a civil case was brought against him and seven US-based Muslim NGOs, including the HLF, in *Boim v. Quranic Literacy Institute et al.* Brought as a test case by a group of pro-Israel lawyers who called themselves "private attorneys general" and supported by the ADL,[48] *Boim* plaintiffs alleged that Hamas was responsible for the death of their Israeli-American son in Jerusalem. The successful material support case resulted in a $156-million-dollar damages award against the HLF. One of the plaintiffs' lawyers, Nathan Lewin, was a board member of the Zionist Organization of America and the legal representative for AIPAC. He later testified in front of the Senate Judiciary Committee that "one of the purposes of the *Boim* litigation [was] to deter financial contributions to the US-based Palestinian relief organizations, irrespective of their charitable purpose."[49] Indeed, *Boim* set the stage for a far more restrictive environment for organizations doing work in Palestine. The Seventh Circuit found the argument that "money is fungible" persuasive. Therefore, any money given to Hamas, even if earmarked for social services, fell within the scope of liability for section 2333 of the Anti-Terrorism Act (ATA).[50] The practical implication was that individuals and organizations engaged in humanitarian or non-violent political activities in Palestine would find themselves within the ATA's orbit.

In the two decades since 9/11, civil damage actions using the ATA and the material support law framework have increased. Private actors have brought or threatened to bring cases against Palestinian civil society actors and/or the entities it relies on to operate, including banks, donors, and social media companies. In 2016, the ATA was amended further to expand liability to include those who "aid and abet" persons who commit acts of terrorism.[51] The amendments to the ATA have opened the door for private actors to engage in what is referred to as "lawfare": the filing of civil material support for terrorism suits – or threats to do so – against

Palestinian organizations. Over the course of the last decade, this strategy has increasingly been taken up by a range of organizations with ties to the Israeli government or Israel-advocacy groups.[52]

There are three prominent examples of the use of civil suits against US-based civil society organizations. In 2017, the plaintiffs in *Boim* filed another ATA suit, this time against American Muslims for Palestine (AMP), alleging that AMP is actually an "alter ego" or cover for one of the organizations previously named in their original complaint, which never ceased operation but instead rebranded itself and resumed operations. In another case filed in 2019, Keren Kayemeth LeIsrael, or the Israeli Jewish National Fund, an entity holding quasi-state status in Israel, sued the US Campaign for Palestinian Rights, a DC-based umbrella organization made up of grassroots member groups from around the country, for material support for terrorism. Represented in their appeal by the same lawyers as in *Boim*, plaintiffs claimed that the solidarity organizations had ties to a Specially Designated Global Terrorist organization. The US Campaign, widely known for its efforts to expand the movement supporting boycotts, divestment, and sanctions against Israel, was forced to defend against the costly and time-consuming multi-year litigation which ended in the case's dismissal and a denial of review from the Supreme Court.[53] A similar action was filed in March 2024 against UNRWA USA, a US-based non-profit that fundraises for the eponymous UN agency that provides humanitarian relief and social services to Palestinian refugees. The Israeli plaintiffs argued that fundraising for the UN agency amounted to aiding and abetting terrorism following unsubstantiated allegations that some UN staff participated in or supported the Hamas attack on Israel.[54]

The majority of ATA lawsuits, however, are not brought against civil society organizations. Since Congress passed the ATA in 1992, US federal courts have seen a proliferation of cases against deep-pocket defendants, usually banks and social media platforms, as well as governments accused of being state sponsors of terrorism. Plaintiffs have also brought ATA cases against ISIS and militant groups in Somalia, Iraq, and Pakistan, though many of the cases involve dual Israeli nationals or Israelis residing in the West Bank. With treble damages permitted under the statute, law firms have developed lucrative ATA practices by pursuing increasingly expansive theories of direct or secondary liability under the Act. Appeals in these cases regularly draw amicus briefs from pro-Israel advocacy groups.

In *Twitter v. Taamneh*, a lawsuit against social media platforms brought by victims of ISIS, the ADL submitted an amicus brief advocating for an extension of liability to social media companies that allow designated terrorist groups to use their platforms to further their goals.[55] Although the case dealt with ISIS, it has important implications for public discourse on Palestine. Social media has become an important source for news and reporting on Palestine, giving voice to Palestinians in the occupied territories in a way that traditional corporate media outlets do not. This dynamic was especially salient during the 2023–2024 assault on Gaza, during which social media companies routinely shadow-banned posts and otherwise censored content about Palestine.[56] An expansion of secondary liability under the ATA would put pressure on social media companies to heavily scrutinize posts expressing support for Palestinian rights or criticism of Israel to avoid the risk of legal liability. Thus, more content on one side of the political divide would face censorship or more accounts posting such views would be de-platformed.

Though the Supreme Court in *Taamneh* rejected the plaintiffs' arguments, holding that the tech companies were not liable for ISIS content on their platforms under the ATA, the impact of the action stands. Risk-averse companies find themselves vulnerable to lawsuits under the ATA and act accordingly by censoring information and speech on Palestine.[57] The ATA litigation against private actors has had a profound impact on banking and financial services and other private businesses holding accounts for civil society organizations and activists. Because the provisions of the ATA have been interpreted expansively and the cases tend to be high profile with large pay-outs including treble damages, the potential targets for the litigation have become extremely risk-averse. Thus, banks will choose not to open accounts for civil society actors supporting Palestinian rights. Social media companies will de-platform or censor content that might put them in the crosshairs of allegations that they are giving support to those linked to terrorist organizations. For example, Palestinians living in Jerusalem or Gaza have their content removed as a result of social media platforms' overcorrection in the face of suits like *Taamneh*.[58]

Those seeking to silence organizing in support of Palestinian rights need not resort to actual litigation; they are able to shut down access to funding, financial services, or the virtual public square by mere allegation or threat of a lawsuit.[59] They do not need to make a showing that would meet a legal standard for liability to restrict Palestinian rights organizing and advocacy. This environment has a chilling effect on these sectors, with direct impacts on Palestinian speech. Private companies ultimately make their own risk assessments when choosing whether or not to extend their services to Palestinians and are alert to the litigious environment around Palestine. They lack the proper tools to assess the politically driven nature – or the credibility – of the allegations presented to them in threat letters that they routinely receive.[60]

These private actors tend to have a low appetite for risk and, faced with the threat of litigation, err on the side of risk avoidance. The prospect of lengthy and costly litigation and the stigma that even a baseless accusation of material support to terrorism can carry are not negligible considerations. This often results in the de-platforming of Palestinian voices deemed too risky. For instance, in 2020, the Lawfare Project, an Israeli non-profit, successfully pressured Zoom into canceling an event with Leila Khaled held by San Francisco State University, arguing that hosting the event would violate the prohibition on material support for terrorism because of Khaled's links to the PFLP, which is designated by the US. Freedom of Information Act records released by the State Department reveal that the Lawfare Project sought a statement from the US government saying that the technical services offered by Zoom for the event would constitute material support.[61]

The impacts of US material support laws are not limited to the United States. US laws and institutions have significant extraterritorial reach, making this domestic statute a powerful tool of transnational repression. Any company, bank, funder, or organization seeking to operate in the United States will need to take into consideration not only the expansive nature of the laws, but the likelihood of their weaponization by lawfare groups. For example, legal advocacy organizations like the Zionist Advocacy Center have filed complaints against mainstream, international humanitarian organizations like Oxfam, Norwegian People's Aid, and Doctors Without Borders, invoking material support for terrorism. Although as a legal matter those cases have ultimately never prevailed on the merits, they alter the risk environment and have a real impact on these organizations' work in the region.[62]

This environment also encourages further repression by Israel. When the Israeli military designated six Palestinian human rights organizations as "terrorists," it appeared to be largely driven by a longstanding desire to convince their US and European donors to defund these organizations.[63]

Israel had failed to convince the US and European states to criminalize the organizations directly, but its designations – no matter how baseless – would trigger major obstacles for the funding needed to continue their work.[64] Similarly in the case against UNRWA, terrorism allegations by Israel led to the cutting off of funding by major European donors, endangering UNRWA's critical work during the ongoing genocide.[65]

CONCLUSION

From its inception, the architecture put in place to combat terrorism has had a profound impact on the movement for freedom and justice in Palestine. As we have shown, expansive US material support laws and related legislation have functioned to constrain and criminalize advocacy in solidarity with the Palestinian struggle. Especially since 9/11, criminal prosecutions have targeted prominent US-based individuals and organizations involved in humanitarian activities in Palestine. This scrutiny of humanitarian aid to Palestine through material support laws has expanded well beyond humanitarian support or charitable giving. It has swept up human rights advocates, student organizations, protestors, and other civil society actors.

Developments in the legal regime have effectively deputized private actors hostile to the Palestinian national movement, encouraging them and their lawyers to target civil society organizations or those it relies on to operate, with civil suits. This "lawfare," when aimed at pro-Palestinian advocacy and humanitarian organizations providing support to Palestinians abroad, detracts and distracts them from their mission, forcing them to divert resources to defend against protracted litigation and misinformation campaigns. Coordinated efforts by pro-Israel advocacy groups have also targeted social media companies, banks, and other risk-averse, deep-pocket defendants with the threat of litigation for association with Palestinian groups. The abuse of material support laws by private actors has created a chilling environment for Palestinian rights advocacy.

The scope of terrorism legislation is ever-expanding: in spring 2024, amidst the filing of new lawsuits and escalating accusations by law enforcement against student protestors, a bill was introduced in Congress to give the Department of the Treasury the power to revoke the tax-exempt status of "terrorist supporting organizations."[66] Although the bill's sponsors clearly intend to target pro-Palestinian organizations, the text and therefore consequences could sweep much more broadly. This expansion of the Treasury's powers builds on existing counterterrorism laws, and should it pass, will undoubtedly impact Palestinian organizations and those doing work on behalf of the Palestinian cause. It will also create new opportunities for private actors to attack non-profit organizations. If passed, the bill is one more step in the broad legislative and regulatory counterterrorism framework that restricts Palestinian civil society through enforcement mechanisms attached to the terrorism label.

By highlighting the centrality of Palestine within this evolving body of law, this chapter has sought to add an important dimension to the discourse on material support laws and other counterterrorism legislation. Legal and policy interventions to remediate the more problematic impacts associated with material support laws have been stymied by the highly charged, politically fraught discourse around Palestine, Israel, and terrorism. Left unaddressed, however, these overbroad and expansive counterterrorism measures will continue to constrict spaces for discourse in the United States, chill dissent, and complicate the important work of civil society organizations at home and abroad.

7

Israeli Mechanisms to Restrict Civic Space: From Surveillance and Repression in the Occupied West Bank to Policing Israelis Writ Large

Yael Berda

Israel inherited their initial emergency laws, still used to restrict civic rights, from the British Mandate in Palestine. Following Israel's War of Independence and the mass displacement of Palestinians from the nascent state of Israel, known as the Nakba, Israel used a patchwork of decrees meant to restrict Palestinian mobility for the purpose of settlement and control. Those measures, deployed in the first two decades of the Israeli state, were mostly enacted against Palestinian citizens of Israel, who were under military rule until 1966, and were also the basis of Israel's military rule in the occupied Palestinian territories from 1967 onward. The measures were developed, maintained, and intensified to control Palestinians in the territories, who were governed under the laws of belligerent occupation.

Since 2000, the measures have been gradually redeployed inside Israel against Palestinian citizens. More recently, during the 2023 mass protests against government plans to limit the authority of the Israeli judiciary (known as the judicial overhaul, or the "regime coup"), some of these measures have been used against Jewish citizens as well, though with limited scope. Since the Hamas-led massacre of October 7, 2023, and Israel's ongoing retaliatory assault on Gaza, the deployment has intensified and accelerated, along with the deepening of illiberal trends within Israel, and tighter restrictions over Palestinians in the occupied territories.

After Israel and the Palestine Liberation Organization failed to reach a comprehensive peace after signing the Oslo Accords in the early 1990s, the territorial divisions, administrative institutions, and security apparatus established during the Oslo years were used to control the millions of Palestinians in Gaza and the West Bank, including East Jerusalem. A sophisticated set of surveillance, monitoring, and data collection measures, presented as necessary to combat terrorism, served as tools of broad civilian repression and control, designed to prevent "hostile populations" from free movement, political organizing, and association, and of course, any form of insurgency or rebellion.[1]

Legal and technological advancements intensified Israel's repression of Palestinians during periods of violent insurgency and periods of relative quiet. In the events that sparked the Second Intifada in 2000, some of the practices used regularly in the occupied Palestinian territories were redeployed inside Israel, first as racialized tools targeting Palestinian citizens protesting the treatment of their counterparts living under occupation, and then sporadically against the Jewish dissenters as well. The contemporary expansion of surveillance and repression is due to a trinity of processes, involving the revocability of Israeli citizenship, annexation of the occupied Palestinian territories, and the attack on the liberal order in Israel. This triad – effectively a regime change – is advanced by formal legal and administrative means.

This chapter outlines how Israeli measures to surveil and control Palestinians in the occupied territories have transferred back to Israel as two related processes, one colonial and the other authoritarian. It argues that these processes aim to blur the distinction between the political status of Palestinian citizens of Israel and that of Palestinian subjects living under military occupation, while simultaneously dismantling the remaining boundaries between the colonial regime in the occupied territories, and the semi-democratic regime in Israel. Measures to shrink the rights and civic space of Jewish and Palestinian citizens of Israel who function as dissidents are essential to facilitate these processes.[2]

COUNTERTERRORISM MEASURES AND THE EROSION OF BOUNDARIES BETWEEN THE STATUS OF PALESTINIANS IN ISRAEL AND IN THE OCCUPIED TERRITORIES

The crux of the debate on the nature of Israel's political regime has revolved around the citizenship status of Palestinians.[3] For some analysts, citizenship of Palestinians in Israel is the marker of the state as a liberal regime, providing individual rights, while denying collective rights to the Palestinian population in Israel.[4] Others assert that the status of Israel's Palestinians citizens is proof of Israel's colonial policies to assimilate a remainder population.[5] Nimer Sultany and Nadim Rouhana argue that policies to diminish the rights of Palestinians in Israel enacted after the Second Intifada served as the harbinger of rising Jewish hegemony, accelerating the general erosion of citizenship.[6]

The increase in authoritarian rule under Israeli prime minister Benjamin Netanyahu is intimately linked with the erosion of status of Palestinian citizens in Israel. Two pieces of legislation mark this contemporary shift: the Counter-Terrorism Law (2016)[7] and the Basic Law: Israel as the Nation-State of the Jewish People (2018) (the "Jewish Nation-State Law").[8] These laws signify the unification of the colonial regime in the territories conquered in 1967 (in which Palestinians are subjects of a military occupation) with the regime of separation inside Israel, first established in 1948 (in which Palestinians are citizens with a limited set of rights). The reason for this separation or difference, though much debated, is that rights and privileges of citizenship in Israel are partially associated with nationality,[9] which elsewhere might be perceived as discrimination.[10] Political scientists have called this unification of the two regimes the "one-state reality."[11] Moreover, political scientist Yoav Peled identifies a major process for blurring the distinction between the political status of Palestinian citizens of Israel and Palestinian subjects in the occupied territories through laws, administrative practices, and criminal law enforcement.[12] The blurring of boundaries between political statuses of Palestinians, and between the regimes under which these statuses exist, accelerated through a set of events that made use of emergency laws. These events marked the shift toward authoritarian modes of governance for Palestinian citizens of Israel.

The Counter-Terrorism Law formalized the Defence (Emergency) Regulations (1945),[13] transforming eighty years' worth of British colonial emergency decrees and regulations deployed mainly against Palestinians in Israel and in the occupied Palestinian territories, into formal Israeli legislation. The revocation of citizenship for disloyalty has a convoluted history in the past two decades. Alongside the enactment of the Counter-Terrorism Law, in 2008 Israel amended the Nationality Law of 1952, granting authority and discretion to the minister of interior to revoke the citizenship of disloyal citizens, including for "acts of terrorism," as defined under the new counterterrorism legislation, espionage, or acts considered a "breach of trust." The constitutionality of this amendment was reified by the Supreme Court in 2022.[14] A more recent development was the promulgation of the Law for Revocation of Citizenship or Residency of a Terrorist who Receives Compensation for Carrying out a Terrorist Act, passed in February 2023.[15]

The transition from emergency regulations to counterterrorism legislation broadened possibilities for the government to act against its political opponents, whether that opposition utilized violent or peaceful methods. The Counter-Terrorism Law had some built-in flexibility: it allowed for both the legitimization of the use of different types of laws against different populations within Israel and the occupied Palestinian territories; and it also expanded the space for the regime to apply such legislation to all citizens in the future, including Jewish Israelis perceived as posing a security risk or presenting political opposition.

Two years later, the quasi-constitutional Basic Law: Israel as the Nation-State of the Jewish People (2018) enshrined an ethno-national hierarchy between Jewish Israelis and other citizens, proclaiming the exclusivity of Jewish self-determination and settlement of the biblical land of Israel; that is, including the occupied West Bank. The coupling of the Counter-Terrorism Law with the Nation-State Law has generated the possibility for the administrative revocation of the citizenship of Palestinians.[16]

EMERGENCY REGULATIONS AND DECREES: GRADUAL EXPANSION OF AUTHORITARIAN MEASURES

In 2020, during the Israeli government's declaration of a "Covid-19 emergency," more than forty emergency regulations were issued, as many as had been issued since Israel's founding.[17] The sheer quantity of emergency regulations relates to Israel's peculiarity: legally it has been in a state of war since 1948. The government can hence make emergency decrees any time without authorization from the Knesset.

As part of its efforts to battle the spread of Covid-19, the Israeli government's additional emergency regulations allowed the Israel Security Agency (Shabak) to track citizens' mobile phone geolocations. Previously, Shabak, the military, and the police limited the practice for use on Palestinian residents of the occupied territories including Palestinians from East Jerusalem.[18] Israel became one of the few countries in the world to use its security branches to resolve a civil-medical crisis using security surveillance for epidemiological tracking.[19] This unprecedented mass surveillance, which included Jewish Israelis, attracted extensive media attention, sparking vigorous public debate about its ethics. Using emergency powers to authorize Shabak to trace the private phones of Israelis pierced the invisible boundary of legitimacy surrounding Israel's security and intelligence services which, despite their capabilities and access, had previously refrained from compromising the privacy rights of Jewish Israelis.[20] Despite the public uproar, the government argued that the violation of privacy was proportional to the threat and temporary in nature. However, civil society organizations nonetheless continued to raise the alarm about this breach of citizens' rights.[21] In turn, during the protests in 2020 and 2022, and then more recently against the judicial reform in 2023, public suspicions circulated regarding the use of surveillance against Jewish Israeli protesters by the security services and police.[22]

The transfer of invasive monitoring and surveillance practices from the occupied territories to inside Israel has begun to collapse the distinctions between the two Israeli regimes: the military administration over occupied Palestinian subjects, and the civilian government under which Israeli citizens, Jewish and Palestinian, had enjoyed certain civil rights.

In October 2022, the Israeli minister of defense's designation of six Palestinian civil society organizations as terrorist organizations further entrenched Israel's use of security measures to restrict political rights. A broad interpretation of Israeli Counter-Terrorism Law[23] allowed the disabling of highly regarded human rights and community-based organizations in the occupied territories because of their classification as terrorist entities. Some of the staff of these organizations were Israeli citizens or maintained close ties to Israelis. Israeli authorities perceived the six to be part of a network of Palestinian organizations that enjoyed a longstanding reputation of legitimacy and credibility among international stakeholders while operating under the vulnerabilities associated with military occupation. The wide definitions in the Counter-Terrorism Law, targeting "infrastructure" and "incitement," enabled the Ministry to classify the organizations' political and public relations activities as terrorist and a security threat and thus to shut down their offices.

The case of Salah Hammouri underscored how precarious the status of Palestinians in the occupied territories had become by 2022 under Israeli law. In December 2022, Hammouri, a lawyer and researcher working for one of the six designated organizations, was arrested and placed in administrative detention. Because occupied East Jerusalem was officially annexed by Israel in 1980, and Hammouri is a resident of the city, he is entitled to certain legal protections under Israeli law that are unavailable to other Palestinians living under occupation in the West Bank. Despite these protections, his Jerusalem residency status was revoked because of allegations that he was a member of the Popular Front for the Liberation of Palestine, a political faction with a militant wing designated as a terrorist entity by Israel and the United States decades ago. Israel eventually deported Hammouri based on an amendment to the Entry into Israel Law[24] which allows the minister of interior to revoke the permanent residency status of anyone found to be disloyal to the state.

Though Hammouri's deportation garnered significant public attention, during 2022 over eighty other Palestinians from East Jerusalem would have their residency revoked, the largest number in five years. This granted the Israeli administration the right to deport them if they did not voluntarily leave. While the Israeli policy of revoking Palestinian residency rights known as "silent transfer"[25] has been in place since 1995, Hammouri's case was exceptional in that the Ministry of Interior boasted about his deportation and its flouting of international law, which prohibits deportation of occupied people from the occupied territory.[26]

Israel has recently moved to make Israeli citizenship conditional. The 2023 amendments to the Counter-Terrorism Law legislate that Israelis convicted under that law who receive "compensation" for their criminal acts can be deprived of citizenship.[27] Ninety-four out of 120 Knesset members (including a majority of the Jewish members in the opposition) voted in favor of this legislation: the first time the Israeli government made citizenship revocable.

The annexation of the West Bank through organizational and administrative changes,[28] and legal measures aimed at depriving Palestinians of citizenship, occurred in parallel with Netanyahu's 2022–2023 authoritarian maneuver to crush the institutions of Israel's liberal order. The attack on the independence of the judiciary and its subordination to executive power was intended to fortify the regime's repressive legislative infrastructure: the crowning achievement of which was the deprivation of nationality law. The protest movement, though vibrant and effective, was indifferent to the connection between the judicial overhaul efforts and the revocation of Palestinian citizenship rights. The opposition parties supported the deprivation law in the parliament.[29]

In order to understand shrinking civic space in the Israeli context, and how repressive practices in the occupied territories diffused back into Israel, we need to look more closely at how citizenship became enmeshed in security legislation.

REDEFINING CITIZENSHIP: THE COUNTER-TERRORISM LAW AND THE JEWISH NATION-STATE LAW

The major shift in Israel's citizenship regime, significantly derogating the legal status of Palestinian citizens of Israel, occurred with the two laws: the Counter-Terrorism Law and the Jewish Nation-State Law. However, Israel's securitized legal treatment of its Palestinian citizens, blurring the distinction between them and Palestinian subjects in the occupied Palestinian territories, began in the 2000 Palestinian uprising, known as the Second Intifada. In October of that year, twelve unarmed Palestinian citizens of Israel and one resident of the occupied territories were shot dead by Israeli police while protesting Israel's killing of other Palestinians from the occupied territories. Since that critical juncture, Israeli conceptualizations of the rights and privileges of non-Jewish citizens in Israel changed and became contingent.

With Palestinian citizens perceived by the government as a potential "fifth column" during the Second Intifada, Israel amended the Citizenship Law (2003), which diminished their citizenship rights by limiting their ability to apply for family unification if their spouse originated from the occupied territories. The law was based on a presumption that Palestinians from the occupied territories posed a security threat. This effectively meant that some Israelis (mainly Palestinian citizens of Israel) had to choose between living in Israel without their family or moving to the occupied territories. Knowing that such a decision was imminent also had the impact of disincentivizing marriages between the two Palestinian communities. The more substantive changes to Palestinian citizenship in Israel, however, would be enacted more than a decade later with the Counter-Terrorism Law (2016).

The Counter-Terrorism Law was not originally conceived to directly influence the rights and privileges of citizenship; rather, it formalized the Defence Regulations of 1945 from the British colonial regime. As mentioned, until the enactment of the Counter-Terrorism Law, Israel had used the British emergency regulations as a tool to maintain two separate legal regimes between Palestinians and Jews within Israel. The regulations allowed Jewish citizens and external observers to believe the fiction that Israel was a fully liberal democratic state, only resorting to the colonial measures to address legitimate security concerns in the context of Israel's permanent state of war.

The Counter-Terrorism Law completed two processes that redefined the relations between security laws and citizenship. The first process was to make the emergency regulations part of Israeli counterterrorism laws, which allowed for formalization of otherwise discriminatory treatment in a graded fashion, based on political affiliation, kinship (belonging to specific families), and demographic traits (belonging to specific age groups or sectors), deployed against Palestinians in Israel and the occupied Palestinian territories. The second process was more general – to give formal legitimacy to the differential treatment between Jewish and Palestinian citizens in Israel, with respect to the revocation of citizenship and other rights, following allegations of a security violation. The two processes transformed the colonial logic of separating populations on racial and national grounds, and managing them according to an axis of suspicion, into an integral tenet of Israel's effort to "protect the homeland" in the entire territory.[30]

The institutionalization of the emergency regulations is the historical moment that entrenched Palestinian status as a security threat in Israeli law, and established the scope for how executive power might determine the terms under which citizenship may be offered or withdrawn.

HOW DOES EMERGENCY LAW SHAPE CITIZENSHIP? A BRIEF HISTORY

Israel inherited the British colonial system for classification, identification, and surveillance of the population of Palestine when it accepted the UN Partition Plan in 1947, and allowed only a small Palestinian minority to remain in Israel after the Nakba. It treated the Palestinians who stayed as a foreign population: hostile and dangerous. Palestinians, who were later offered citizenship by the state, were perceived as a population on the wrong side of the border. They were therefore treated as belonging to a different political entity, permanently suspect, and de facto enemies of the state.

The British colonial power left Israel with a significant inheritance in the form of the emergency regulations: an organizational logic for managing a perceived hostile population that could prevent them from mounting any political opposition. Labeling people, following conquest, as a hostile population and a security threat was a common bureaucratic colonial practice. It informed the usage and content of the expanding emergency powers.

The British, and later Israel, classified the Palestinian population, creating blacklists and categorizing political and security prisoners, among others. This classification and taxonomy turned the Defence Regulations into a bureaucratic toolkit to prevent opposition to the regime. Administrative detention and other movement restrictions were used mainly against those who were suspected of opposing the regime. Labels such as "security threat" or "political threat" were fluid and unstable categories that fed into each other. The colonial regime understood national liberation movements, or any type of political activity, as a security threat and classified it as illegitimate or violent activity.[31]

The institutionalization of British regulations in the Counter-Terrorism Law gave legal authority to this colonial definition of citizenship.[32] The Counter-Terrorism Law labels populations by defining their status or activity as support for terrorism because of kinship or geographical area of residence. Earlier versions of the law enabled the minister of defense to define areas as "terrorism infrastructure areas" which then created a presumption that persons operating in the area are linked to terrorist activity. This wide geographical definition blurred the distinction between one's belonging to a place, and the designation of one's actions as constituting a security threat.[33]

Through democratic procedures, proponents of the Counter-Terrorism Law turned the draconian, controversial colonial measures contained in the Defence Regulations into legitimate primary law, allowing the law to be deployed against all Israeli citizens, including Israeli Jews, shifting from a long consensus that the use of security laws against them was limited.

WIDENING THE DEFINITIONS OF TERRORISM AND PROSECUTION OF SPEECH AND PROTEST

Since the Hamas-led massacre and atrocities of October 7, the Israeli government has enacted over eleven new emergency regulations, widening the definition of support for terrorism, and unleashing a series of measures that were previously practiced only against Palestinians in the occupied territories, including in annexed East Jerusalem. Alongside the revocation of citizenship, these highlight the extensive nature of the attack on civil rights. This has been shown most acutely with regard to the ability of Israelis to protest or voice opposition to Israel's war on Gaza. Some of the regulations included allowing the Israeli military to access cameras on personal computers,[34] and enabled it to override habeas corpus petitions in terrorism-related cases by holding hearings on video, rather than bringing the defendants to appear in court. This was first an emergency regulation for three months, and then prolonged as a temporary war provision, allegedly enabling severe detainee rights violations and custodial deaths.[35] One regulation previously used exclusively in the occupied territories grants the Israeli minister of communication the authority to shut down foreign broadcasting bodies, leading to the shutting down of Al Jazeera's media network in Israel.[36] Another measure allowed the state to access a person's biometric information in order to find dead or missing persons, although this did have a justification in determining whether someone had been taken hostage. However, Israeli security officials had already been collecting this data on Palestinians in the occupied territories for many years. Other regulations extended the period for preventing those charged with security offences from meeting their lawyers to 180 days; and for those arrested for security offenses, from fifteen to forty-five days, with possible extensions beyond ninety days.[37] Prolonged detention of Palestinian workers from Gaza was also permitted under the new regulations.

An amendment to the Counter-Terrorism Law was also passed which broadened the definition of terrorism to include the "consumption of terrorist publications."[38] The prohibition includes publications expressing praise or encouragement for an act of terrorism or documenting it. While the initial framing of the law was the prevention of dissemination of Hamas footage of atrocities of October 7, the law grants authority to the minister of justice to designate media platforms as terrorist entities under the specific provision. The law allows for surveillance of people's social media use, while the prescribed penalty for the offense is up to one year in prison.

The prohibition on consumption of terrorist material extends the dense social media surveillance in the occupied territories to the citizens of Israel. The monitoring of social media posts occurs alongside surveillance through facial recognition programs such as Blue Wolf,[39] used in the occupied West Bank, and Red Wolf, used in occupied East Jerusalem.[40] Surveillance of social media takes place using an automated system that builds on the recent "Police Ordinance (Amendment No. 40), 5784-2024,"[41] which formalized over a decade of unauthorized tracking of vehicles and travel logs through photos taken of their license plates while on the road.[42] It is not entirely clear which technologies are used on which populations, but the practices targeting Palestinian citizens of Israel have been seamlessly transferred from the occupied territories. The major difference now is that formal legislation is being enacted, rather than relying on emergency regulations.

After October 7, the government severely restricted the activity of hundreds of Palestinian citizens of Israel, and some Jewish Israelis, and prevented them from exercising their rights to freedom of speech, assembly, and protest. According to Adalah (the Legal Center for Arab Minority Rights in Israel), the crackdown on freedom of speech for those expressing support for or solidarity with the people in Gaza has led to prosecutions, including arrest and detention, and strict censorship, both on social media and within social settings. This crackdown on dissent, which had already been standard practice in the occupied territories, is a result of a concerted effort by government agencies, security forces, and right-wing civil society organizations, as well as private firms and academic institutions. Over 100 students have faced disciplinary measures over social media posts that purportedly support terrorism, including suspension or expulsion from twenty-five different academic institutions. Most of the posts were expressing solidarity with or grief for the people of Gaza.[43]

Palestinian citizens of Israel have also faced work-related penalties including suspensions, demotions, and termination due to their social media posts.

The Israel Civil Service Commission has also requested that all government agencies track and report any statements employees make on social media that express "hostile views to the state of Israel."[44]

Over 250 citizens, the vast majority of whom are Palestinian citizens of Israel, have been arrested or detained for social media posts or participation in demonstrations, and charged with violations of various provisions of the Counter-Terrorism Law, including incitement or support for terrorism. Adalah reports that the State Attorney's Office approved criminal investigations against 103 individuals under article 24 of the Counter-Terrorism Law:[45] at least 95% of the individuals were Palestinian citizens of Israel. For context, during the entire period between 2018 and 2022 (five years), the State Attorney's Office approved only seventy-eight investigations of this kind. More than seventy indictments for violations of the Counter-Terrorism Law have been brought, with most of these including an extension of detention until the end of proceedings.[46] Most recently, a full professor at Hebrew University, Nadera Shalhoub-Kevorkian, was arrested, searched, and interrogated four times on charges of incitement and support for terrorism under the counterterrorism legislation, on the basis that she participated in a podcast.

THE THREAT OF CITIZENSHIP REVOCATION FOR POLITICAL ACTIVITY

The most significant development involving the use of the counterterrorism laws to shrink civic space and declare political opposition a security threat is the introduction of a bill to revoke citizenship and residency rights for speech-related offenses.[47]

Another two proposals for amendments to the Entry into Israel Law and the "Citizenship Law" would authorize the revocation of permanent residency, or citizenship, of an individual convicted of an offense related to identifying with a terrorist organization or incitement to terrorism.[48] Less than a year after the first formal law making citizenship revocable due to terrorism-related acts, the Ministry of Interior sent a clear message to Palestinian citizens of Israel and Palestinian residents of Jerusalem that their political membership, legal status, and rights are contingent on their refraining from dissent or opposition to the government. The bill and the amendments represent another far-reaching step in collapsing the distinctions between Palestinians in the occupied territories and Palestinian citizens of Israel.

The proposed amendments to the Counter-Terrorism Law are practically superfluous, given that revocation of citizenship is already possible by resorting to the courts under the Revocation Law passed in February 2023, for which ninety-four members of Knesset voted.[49] However, passing such a bill will provide the government with legitimacy to strip citizens of their political status based on speech acts. There is little reason to believe, at the time of writing, that there will be significant opposition to prevent the bill enabling revocation of citizenship for speech-related acts.

CONCLUSION

The shrinking civic space in Israel is inextricably related to the erosion of status for the Palestinian citizens of Israel. This chapter has argued that a trinity of processes, namely the revocability of Palestinian citizenship, annexation of the occupied Palestinian territories, and the authoritarian attack on Israel's liberal institutions, all create a major shift in the status of people and territory controlled by the Israeli government. It has identified how two laws, the Counter-Terrorism Law and the Nation-State Law, created this shift by allowing practices of control and repression, used in the occupied Palestinian territories, to migrate into Israel.

The attack on the liberal order, and simultaneously the annexation, is doing away with the institutions that maintained separation between the military regime in the occupied territories and the civil regime in Israel, creating a "one-state reality" across the entire territory. The status of Palestinian citizenship is being quickly eroded, due to the revocability of citizenship through the wide definitions in the Counter-Terrorism Law, and the massive crackdown on freedom of speech, assembly, and any expression of the collective identity of the Palestinian citizens of Israel. Moreover, as we have seen, the distinctions between the political and legal status of Palestinians in the occupied territories, and the status of Palestinians with Israeli citizenship, are also being diminished. These two laws, and the trinity of processes, have also affected the rights of Jewish Israelis, creating a visible link between colonial practices in the occupied Palestinian territories, and the authoritarian coup within Israel.

8

Made in Palestine: Repackaging Apartheid as "Smart" Cities

Matt Mahmoudi

INTRODUCTION

Since Israel imposed a near complete siege on Gaza in October 2023, it has reportedly been using artificial intelligence (AI) – and communication technologies more broadly – to further streamline its campaign of relentless killing, destruction, violence, and unfolding genocide in Gaza.[1] Between the Habsora ("Gospel") and Lavender systems,[2] which purport to remotely,[3] biometrically, and automatically identify military targets and calculate the number of civilian casualties that can be expected with a strike; facial recognition deployed to identify Israeli hostages and Hamas operatives;[4] novel forms of social media surveillance;[5] and complete telecommunications control,[6] Gaza has gone from being the world's largest open-air prison[7] to an open-air exposition for technologies of violence.

Occupied Palestine and its cities are being instrumentalized for the development of vast architectures of surveillance and control. Experimentation with and development of surveillance tools using Palestinian communities is not new: it goes back to the post-1948 period of Israeli military intelligence operations.[8] However, since the end of the twentieth century, Israeli efforts have been animated by the rapid development of biometric technologies and data-intensive computing capabilities. Some of these capabilities had already been recognized for their potential for social control elsewhere, such as in apartheid South Africa in the 1970s, where they played a significant role in the expansion of white power.[9]

Yet it is under Israel's deepening occupation and apartheid regime over the Palestinian territories in more recent years that Israeli technologies developed an "international brand" (particularly resonant against the backdrop of the War on Terror),[10] allowing Israel to become a vanguard for practices of racialized surveillance, warfare, policing, and control with impact far beyond the region.[11] The infrastructures of violence in the occupied Palestinian territories and their logics constitute the modus operandi for the proliferation of "smart" or "safe" city interventions elsewhere, under a veneer of greater convenience and safety, but to profoundly devastating effect. In this chapter, I outline some of the key algorithmic practices undergirding Israel's system of apartheid against Palestinians, and how these logics, in turn, are promulgated globally in other contexts as diverse as border enforcement and smart city initiatives.

PALESTINE AND THE AUTOMATION OF APARTHEID

On November 17, 2023, amid Israel's military assault on Gaza, reports began to surface of Palestinians being held en masse between two large structures on Salah al-Din Road, the main north–south thoroughfare in Gaza. Israeli authorities had announced the opening of an evacuation corridor to allow Palestinians fleeing bombardment of their homes and neighborhoods in the north to move to Israeli-designated safe zones in the south. Before the military would allow Palestinian families to pass, however, they were forced to have their faces scanned. With airstrikes and shelling ongoing – which have killed over 39,000 at the time of writing – the Israeli occupying army required Palestinians, already the world's most heavily surveilled community, to submit to the extraction of their biometric information as a condition of their being allowed to reach safety.

The technology, operated by an Israeli military intelligence unit, combines software from Corsight – a subsidiary of the Israeli autonomous AI company Cortica – and facial recognition capabilities built into Google Photos, to purportedly identify Israeli hostages and Hamas operatives.[12] Yet the criteria for detaining Palestinians attempting to reach Israeli-designated safe zones in Gaza were left broad, paving the way for ordinary civilians to be mistakenly identified as linked to Hamas. This has led to cases such as that of Palestinian poet Mosab Abu Toha, who attempted to flee to Egypt with his family but was detained after Israeli soldiers, using the technologies, mistakenly identified him, and then beat and interrogated him in a detention center.[13]

In the occupied Palestinian city of Hebron, where Palestinian access to certain city streets and neighborhoods is restricted in favor of Jewish Israeli settlers, the Israeli occupation forces utilize the Blue Wolf system, which they have dubbed "Facebook for Palestinians."[14] Blue Wolf is a mobile application used by the Israeli military to centralize and automate remote biometric identification of Palestinians in Hebron.[15] Operating almost like a game complete with a leaderboard, military units are offered incentives to register as many Palestinian faces in the system as possible, with rewards going to the unit with the most images captured.[16] The use of Blue Wolf also facilitates ongoing military intelligence mapping exercises often involving unannounced night raids on Palestinian homes in an effort to make "the presence of the military felt."[17] In one example linked to the use of Blue Wolf, staff from B'Tselem – the Israeli Information Center for Human Rights in the Occupied Territories – filmed a raid in September 2021 in which a Palestinian family, including several children, were lined up in the middle of the night outside their home, while their photos were taken by soldiers.[18] Blue Wolf is in effect an upgrade to the more analog surveillance registry known as Wolf Pack. This older system relied on soldiers calling an operations room to retrieve information on detained individuals.[19]

Red Wolf, the latest innovation in a series of AI surveillance experiments, helps allow the few hundred Israeli settlers illegally residing in the city of Hebron in the southern West Bank to move freely among a Palestinian population of 250,000.[20] At military checkpoints such as Checkpoint 56, located in the part of the city designated as H2 where the Israeli military has exclusive security and administrative control, Palestinian egress and ingress are subjected to algorithmic decision making, intensifying and compounding the already draconian closure regime imposed on the city. Soldiers use the facial recognition program to scan the faces of Palestinians without their knowledge and consent to add them to vast databases, usually mounted in locations that Palestinians are likely to traverse to access shops or medical services, or to go to school or work.

About ten cameras around the checkpoint monitor an individual as they enter a turnstile. When the revolving gates lock behind and in front of the person, their face is scanned and data about the person is sent to a computer viewed by a soldier sitting inside a security booth at the checkpoint. If the system recognizes the individual, the soldier receives a message regarding whether they have appropriate clearance to pass or whether they are flagged for detention and/or interrogation.[21] If a Palestinian is unknown to the system, the soldier will require them to produce their ID which is then linked to the biometric information captured at the checkpoint upon entry and it is uploaded to the system. This increases the number of Palestinians within the Red Wolf system, in addition to the Blue Wolf and Wolf Pack databases from which it already draws.[22]

Only Palestinians are required to use these checkpoints; only Palestinians are subjected to these facial recognition-enabled arbitrary movement restrictions; only Palestinians are listed in the controversial databases used to exercise this racialized form of social control. Under the automated apartheid of Israel, Israeli settlers are not required to use these checkpoints, nor are they contained within the restricted zones that Palestinians are forced to make do with.[23]

Red Wolf is just the latest in a slew of AI-based surveillance tools deployed on Palestinians in the West Bank. Technologies such as anomaly detection systems (audio-visual tools that detect "abnormal" patterns in areas of interest), gait recognition (surveillance systems that purport to recognize individuals based on their manner of walking), and predictive analytics (for example, tools that purport to predict the probability of a crime occurring, often based on socio-economic, racial, and historical data related to the particular residential area of an individual) have also allowed Israeli authorities to make life for Palestinians the stuff of the worst imaginable dystopian nightmares by creating an automated system of control and domination. The system is eminently visible on the streets of Hebron: cameras are mounted on the sides of buildings, lampposts, surveillance towers, and rooftops. The omnipresent video surveillance compounds the already extreme segregation existing in the city, making inescapable for Palestinians the limits of their movement within H2, depriving them of access to places that may only be meters from their homes.

Installation of a high-tech checkpoint on a once thriving street in a neighborhood of Hebron has "killed all forms of social life" in the city.[24] According to one witness testimony collected by Amnesty International, if the system doesn't recognize someone, the Israeli soldier manning the checkpoint can stop them and deprive them of entry to their own home.[25] The presence of these technologies exacerbates fears among residents, which creates a "chilling effect"[26] on assembly and speech; communities avoid public protest, gathering, or expressions of dissent due to the surveillance and potential persecution or punishment. As quoted in Amnesty's report, *Automated apartheid*, "those who [protest] know that, even if they don't get detained on the spot, their faces will be captured by the cameras, and they can be arrested later."[27]

Though military occupations are meant to be temporary in nature under international law, the installation, expansion, and connectedness of Israel's AI-powered surveillance technologies – in particular to arbitrarily restrict the freedom of movement – has reified the permanency of Israeli occupation of Hebron, paving the way for annexation. What Israeli authorities call a *smart city* initiative in Hebron[28] is the automation of apartheid to Palestinians.[29]

In occupied East Jerusalem, these systems have been expanding in tandem with settlement activity. The Mabat 2000 system – a networked system of CCTV – connects the Old City to an Israeli command-and-control center to always allow the East Jerusalem District of the Israeli police to surveil Palestinians. The system's cameras have been in place since the beginning of the millennium. Between 2017 and 2018, it was upgraded to allow for facial recognition.[30] Israeli authorities are now able to scale up and automate apartheid policies so that Jewish Israeli settlers may live in illegal settlements within Palestinian communities in occupied East Jerusalem, like Silwan, under the gaze of Israeli police. Since 2021, when Israeli authorities sought to displace Palestinian families from the East Jerusalem neighborhood of Sheikh Jarrah, more cameras have been mounted there. Following a street survey of an area encompassing 10 km^2, one or two cameras were found for every five meters walked.[31]

The relationship between surveillance and forcible transfer has also been made increasingly clear, as researchers and human rights organizations alike report on how illegal settlement activity begets surveillance, and how surveillance, in turn, begets illegal settlement activity.[32] Biblical excavation projects in Silwan, for example, such as the City of David project, have been widely connected with the destruction of Palestinian homes, illegal settlement, and an expansion in surveillance infrastructure.[33] As the excavation project has expanded, so has the number of CCTV cameras. Human rights organizations have also reported extensively on the measures taken by Israel to generate a coercive environment intended to force Palestinians out of areas of strategic interest; the rapid expansion of high-tech surveillance systems are part and parcel of the reproduction of this environment.[34]

RACIAL CAPITALISM AND TRANSFERS OF "SMART" VIOLENCE

While surveillance of Palestinians in the occupied territories is powered by supply chains that span hardware providers across the globe, Palestinian communities, captive behind walls and checkpoints, are effectively contained within sites used to test Israeli technologies for export abroad.[35] For example, hardware, like the CCTV cameras used in Hebron and East Jerusalem, are developed by a Dutch company, TKH Group, and Hikvision, a China-based company.[36] However, Israeli police and border authorities along with security personnel in illegal settlements use these products as part of a mosaic of other AI-driven surveillance systems and smart city projects.

Tech giants such as Amazon and Google are also very much at the core of the supply chain of technologies adapted for repressive purposes, their brand names normalizing the trade. Both companies are engaged in developing a military and policing cloud service project especially for Israel called Project Nimbus, valued at $1.2 billion.[37] In January 2024,[38] Palantir, another American company, also announced its Artificial Intelligence Platform for Defense, using large language models (LLMs) and AI for defense and military organizations.[39] This came after the company announced in November 2023 that it had been supplying new products to Israel since the October 7 Hamas attack and Israel's near total blockade over Gaza.[40] These developments are symptomatic of a larger pattern of investments – in the hundreds of millions of dollars – in the militarization and datafication of societies within Western liberal democracies,[41] in a move that can best be described as automating and normalizing xenophobia.

Border enforcement regimes across the globe have also sought out Israeli high-tech products, emboldened by their successful use in the occupied Palestinian territories. The mass surveillance regimes in the occupied Palestinian territories have in many ways become the gold standard, even in liberal democracies like the United States and the European Union. On the US southern border, for example, US Customs and Border Protection is using dozens of surveillance towers set up by the Israeli company Elbit Systems "to improve border security and force protection" with the help of "artificial intelligence and automation."[42]

The Israeli company Oosto, a controversial AI-driven surveillance manufacturer formerly known as AnyVision, is now offering law enforcement agencies cost-effective facial recognition technologies with real-time watch-listing capabilities (generating lists of people of interest, continuously and automatically monitored over time).[43] Since Microsoft sold its 40% stake in Oosto's predecessor following revelations that its technology was being used at checkpoints in the occupied West Bank,[44] the company shifted its focus to the United States, where it has increased its presence.

Celebratory narratives of Israel as a start-up nation not only herald Israeli AI and surveillance exports as cutting-edge and crucial in the global quest to reinforce policing – as part of what Jeff Halper refers to as the "global pacification project"[45] – they also obfuscate the very fact that Palestinian lives and livelihoods were the price paid for this level of "seamless" and "smart" policing.[46] This narrative, in turn, paves the way for governments and cities across the globe to participate in the trade of these technologies, bringing the experiences of those at borders, in camps, at checkpoints, and in other liminal contexts where civil rights are suspended around the world, closer to home.

This, I argue, is a contemporary technological manifestation of *racial* capitalism; an economic system, first described by Cedric Robinson, which is fundamentally concerned with exploiting racialized populations for power and profit.[47] This is carried out in two ways. First, certain racial, ethnic, national, and religious groups are identified through social constructions as a threat to the public, creating the rationale for investment in sophisticated technologies to keep them at bay. Second, a techno-security industrial complex keeps fears of the threat alive through product marketing plans, creating a supportive environment for divisive and xenophobic politics. Thus, technology companies provide government entities with data derived from their products to give credence to certain political claims and that justify associated governance decisions, and, in turn, government bodies provide the products of these technology companies with legitimacy.

SMART CITIES AS APARTHEID

Packaged as products to enhance security in an urban context, the technologies explored earlier are drawn from military, border, prison, and policing environments. They often include biometric and AI-driven technologies such as facial recognition, anomaly detection, autonomous weapons and crowd dispersal systems, and robotics. They also include the enabling infrastructure such as cloud computing and services, storage, datasets, and processing facilities; in short, the often hidden tools that connect, power, and operationalize many of the technologies discussed in this chapter.[48] Together, these products and their target environments have been referred to as the "border-surveillance industrial-complex,"[49] the web of economic relationships made possible by securitized narratives concerning certain oppressed and marginalized populations. The narrative is what makes technologies used against Palestinians in Gaza, Hebron, and East Jerusalem transferable to places hosting other oppressed or marginalized communities in places like London and New York City. Under the auspices of greater convenience and safety for citizens and communities, governments around the globe have invested in highly securitized smart cities[50] that inevitably diffuse the same logics of control.

Across the world, these systems are increasingly adopted as almost inevitable in the growth and development of cities. Regimes of control in carceral urban spaces include automated welfare assessment,[51] prison systems,[52] refugee camp administration,[53] border control,[54] and management of so-called ghettos. In all cases, they follow many of the same racialized logics of control used in the occupied Palestinian territories.

As I have advanced elsewhere, digital urban infrastructure, deployed under a veneer of greater efficiency and safety, entangles historically racialized and marginalized communities with exploitative practices of technology production, in what I conceptualize as the *digital periphery*.[55] It is in these communities' names (think of the many narratives that posit AI as the solution to the plight of the poor, the racially marginalized, the otherwise excluded), and often to their detriment (think of the many instances in which these very tools are used to surveil, track, detain, deport, and in other ways penalize these very communities), that these systems gain traction, fame, and profitability.

Over the last decade in particular, cities have become a battleground over the spatial landscape for technology, from the Internet of Things which connects everyday infrastructures to cloud-controlled processes, for example, smart transit entry/exit systems for subways, audio-visual sensors, ambient sound detection technology, and AI-driven surveillance and early-warning systems. "Digital twinning" of municipal functions and services has also resulted in increased atomization of city life, while blockchain technologies that involve creating digital identities and e-citizen services, purportedly to generate greater transparency and control among citizens, generate inescapably inscribed identities, characterized by state authorities and corporations.[56] The drive toward smart cities has given governments the ability to erect a mirage of technology-based order and efficiency while allowing the technology companies to become an essential part of the performance of governance and social control (oftentimes without being openly acknowledged as such).

Smart city technologies have and continue to be weaponized toward practices rooted in dated racially discriminatory pseudo-science. Take for example attempts at ascertaining the race, gender, and perceived emotional state of an individual remotely – not only do these tools impart significance to machine-legible biological difference rooted in race science, but they also assume universal emotional expressiveness. These long-debunked problematic practices exacerbate existing policing processes by which minority communities are targeted, surveilled, and persecuted. The experience of residents of Hangzhou, Sanmenxia, and Wenzhou in China with the use of the SenseTime system is instructive.[57] SenseTime, a company that by 2022 had raised over $512 million, has developed facial recognition software that is being used to identify and profile Uyghur ethnic minorities, against whom China continues to commit crimes against humanity.[58] Or take New York City, where a facial recognition tool, the Domain Awareness System (DAS),[59] promises city-dwellers more efficient policing. Due to the system being deployed in areas where individuals are at greater risk of being stopped and frisked, the subjects caught in the surveillance dragnet are disproportionately non-white.[60] Thus, in addition to the existing technical biases that facial recognition systems are known for (in particular against women of color),[61] the technology is biased at the point of deployment, reinforcing and automating the existing racially discriminatory logics of policing. And construction of smart cities may also result in displacement of vulnerable populations. For example, in order to commence building of the futuristic desert megacity of NEOM,[62] a $500 billion initiative[63] incorporating AI and advanced surveillance systems purportedly to automate city management,[64] Saudi Arabia is evicting the Howeitat tribe residing in the villages of Al Khuraiba, Sharma, and Gaya.

Smart cities are making the entanglement of digital urban infrastructures with corporate power more commonplace. In New York City, for instance, the Mayor's Office appointed representatives from the major technology companies including Meta (formerly Facebook), Google, IBM, Microsoft, and Verizon, to its NYC Advisory Board and several other elite city committees.[65] This collaboration between the city and Big Tech served to ensure NYC achieved its mission of becoming a "testbed for new technologies [transforming] the relationship between city government, community, and the tech industry."[66]

Cities are quickly becoming data pipelines, cultivated, expanded, and fed by the everyday lives of the most vulnerable. This global development is especially worrying given the situatedness of cities as marginal sanctuaries, historically providing the scale and numbers for certain marginalized communities to be sheltered by the anonymity associated with the sheer vastness of urban environments. It also has implications for the contemporary and future distribution of power within cities, between the privileged and those living at the margins.

Peter Marcuse qualifies a distinction between the urban concepts of the "ghetto," in which members of a marginalized grouping are concentrated for the purposes of their domination or exploitation, and the "outcast ghetto," in which communities in their entirety are contained and excluded as a whole.[67] Denoting a stratification in what can be seen as urban class dynamics, Aaron Shapiro explores the emergence of the "mobile outcast ghetto" in our increasingly smart cities, where the containment of members of underprivileged and historically marginalized communities no longer takes on a geographical form of exclusion per se, but a digitally mediated one. Thus, "smart" logistics will be able to control and mediate the type of work, services, and amenities the digital urban underprivileged are able to access.[68] According to Shapiro:

> The "bad part of town" will be full of algorithms that shuffle you straight from high school detention into the prison system. The rich part of town will get mirror glassed limos that breeze through the smart red lights to seamlessly deliver the aristocracy from curb into penthouse.[69]

With expanding digital infrastructure in urban environments, private companies and their technologies become a central component of the state, further centralizing the city's power including over when and where to construct and upgrade infrastructure, to surveil, to distribute resources, to displace communities, and so on.[70] This in turn inserts technology companies into the business of governance, while digitally fusing characteristics that determine privilege and marginality such as race[71] to communities and their urban futures.

Reflection on the digital configuration of racial marginalization in cities requires recalling the conditions of Palestinians, whose restrictive life conditions emanate not only from Israel's apartheid regime over them, but also from the ever-evolving presence of digital control and domination. The management of Palestinians under apartheid directs a digitally reinforced Western orientalism toward the Palestinian subject,[72] stemming – in Edward Said's words – from an "inaccuracy produced by too dogmatic a generality and too positivistic a localized focus."[73] The differential construction of Palestinians as threatening others situates them as inferior populations that must be managed, contained, neutralized, or studied and closely surveilled. Even in occupied East Jerusalem – often posited as a melting pot – Palestinians are digitally flagged, persecuted, detained, and/or denied movement by virtue of their relationality to acts of deviance or resistance.[74] As such, contemporary occupied Palestine exists as a prototype for the reality and implications of the so-called "mobile outcast ghetto."[75]

While these structural logics and inequities are often hidden under digitization efforts – even at times coopted as the problem justifying the deployment of the particular technology in question – their effects are no less present. Ultimately, digital urban infrastructures often work antithetically to their purported objectives, while reliant on emancipatory framings such as the myth of extending access (to what?), connectivity (on whose terms?), and welfare (at what cost?).

These developments hint at an emergent consensus between technology companies and local, state, and federal authorities to share in the governance of surveillance, social welfare, migration, and urban life writ large. Big Tech-spearheaded partnerships in the service of humanitarian causes and international organizations in particular have experimented with interventions ranging from digital blockchain-based identity systems to algorithmic resettlement schemes.[76] Meanwhile, allegations that Big Tech is complicit in repressing marginalized communities around the globe are met with the retort that the products perform public goods such as stopping human trafficking, finding disappeared children, or feeding the poor and displaced, while there is woeful silence on any data proving such acts of algorithmic altruism. Even allowing for the benefit of the doubt, if the technologies do facilitate some public good, the question remains whether that good outweighs the associated societal harms.

CONCLUSION

As military occupation and apartheid structures become entrenched over Palestinians, Israel has become a global vanguard for practices of racialized surveillance, warfare, policing, and control. By situating the automated apartheid in Palestine as an open-air technology exposition, I have attempted to weave together the development and deployment of the repressive technologies and their attendant global supply chains with the future of urban life in so-called smart cities around the world. The technologies discussed in this chapter have had a significant impact on how marginalized communities are repressed and governed. Big Tech has become implicated in the exacting conditions of segregation and apartheid as their technologies are incorporated into products and practices used to control Palestinians in the occupied territories. These systems are also used for the passive or active repression of marginalized communities in the United States and around the world. The problematic underpinnings of otherwise seemingly innocuous "smart" technologies – sold as being in service of community safety – subjects the most quotidian engagements of everyday life to aspects of the oppression foisted on Palestinians. To understand this relationship between power and profit is to understand the racialized capitalist logics that tie the emergence of smart cities in New York and London, to the smart violence in East Jerusalem, Hebron, and Gaza.

9

Digital Repression: How Palestinian Voices are Censored, Surveilled, and Threatened Online

Marwa Fatafta

Over a decade ago, the United Nations recognized the role of the internet and new technologies in enabling people's enjoyment and exercise of human rights.[1] From freedom of expression to the right to privacy, the UN has repeatedly asserted that in the digital era human rights apply online just as they do offline.[2] However, the promise of the internet as the "digital public square" sowed the seeds of its own demise.[3] The last decade has witnessed the rise of digital authoritarianism. State and non-state actors have weaponized the internet to police, censor, and spy on individuals and communities, manipulate public discussions, spread disinformation, interfere in elections, and assert control over civic space.[4] Big Tech – made up of the largest tech companies including Meta, Alphabet, Amazon, Apple, and Microsoft – entrenched surveillance capitalism by building technologies that profit from amassing the personal data of billions of people with little regard to human rights outside the realm of regulation.[5] The proliferation of commercial spyware by opaque and shady private companies has also facilitated transnational repression and human rights abuses on a massive scale.[6] The Palestinian civic space, both online and offline, is no anomaly in these global trends.

Digital platforms offered a space for the geographically and politically fragmented Palestinian populace to connect with each other and facilitate intra-Palestinian discussions about their current reality under the Israeli military occupation and possible future solutions for independence and liberation. A new generation of Palestinian activists and scholars have utilized online civic spaces to break through the retired framing of the "Israel–Palestine conflict" and the two-state solution and advance a new narrative that best captures their reality under a system of settler colonialism and apartheid.[7] Social media platforms have also enabled Palestinians to build and cement cross-border solidarity and allyship with other social justice struggles. The Sheikh Jarrah protests and the Unity Intifada in May 2021, in which Palestinians have successfully mobilized across historical Palestine in response to Israel's attempt to expel Palestinian families from their homes in the neighborhood of Sheikh Jarrah in East Jerusalem, offer a solid example of the advantages that can be achieved through such digital means.[8]

However, new technologies have ushered in an unprecedented level of repression and attacks on Palestinian civil society, human rights defenders, and journalists – expanding the Israeli digital occupation and population control to alarming dimensions. Palestinian and pro-Palestinian voices are at the mercy of non-transparent and discriminatory private tech giants. Fueled by the War on Terror and pressures from the Israeli authorities, social media companies have censored and penalized Palestinians under the pretext of eradicating extremism and incitement to violence on their platforms. Meanwhile, Israel has successfully created a digital surveillance laboratory in the occupied Palestinian territories, prototyping, deploying, and testing spyware and biometric surveillance technologies in order to automate its military occupation and facilitate a stricter control of the Palestinian population.[9] In the same vein, Palestinians have been subject to brutal policing over their online speech and activity.

Since these issues are intrinsic to understanding the current status quo of the Palestinian civic space, its challenges, and its threats, this chapter delves into the landscape of Palestinian digital rights and the impact of the escalating digital repression of Palestinian human rights defenders and civil society on the Palestinian people's quest for justice, freedom, and independence.

THE SYSTEMATIC CENSORSHIP OF PALESTINIAN VOICES

Palestinians have championed online activism. One of the earliest uses of social media platforms for political activism took place during the Gaza war of 2008–2009, followed by the Iranian Green Movement in June 2009 and later the Arab Spring revolutions in 2011. During that time, tech-savvy internet users in Palestine and across the Arab world coalesced on Facebook to share updates and mobilize global support for Palestinians in Gaza.[10] The words "Gaza" and "#gaza" were among the top ten trending topics on Twitter during the weeks of the war.[11] Protestors even took to the virtual gaming space "Second Life" to demonstrate against Israel's war on Gaza and the killing of civilians.[12]

Undoubtedly, the internet promised an alternative civic space for Palestinians, a space they have been deprived of under Israel's military occupation since 1967. In the words of internet philosopher John Perry Barlow – stated in his celebrated manifesto "A declaration of the independence of cyberspace," written in 1996 – the internet created "a world where anyone, anywhere may express his or her beliefs, no matter how singular, without fear of being coerced into silence or conformity," a world where the legal concepts of "property, expression, identity, movement, and context do not apply."[13] The internet provided Palestinians, who have long been fragmented and historically silenced by international mainstream media, with "a mediating space through which the Palestinian nation is globally 'imagined' and shaped."[14]

This freedom was short-lived, however. Soon enough, social media platforms turned into a space where Palestinians are monitored, doxed, censored, and threatened. In the aftermath of Israel's war on Gaza in 2014 and the ensuing lone-wolf attacks by Palestinians against Israelis in East Jerusalem and the West Bank, the Israeli authorities turned their eyes to social media with the accusation that these platforms are hubs for breeding terrorism and incitement to violence.[15] In late 2015, hundreds of Palestinians in the West Bank, Jerusalem, and Israel proper were arrested and prosecuted in connection with their social media posts.[16] Israeli security agencies deployed a predictive policing system – a disturbing AI-powered tool that allows authorities to "predict" crimes before they occur – to comb through Palestinians' social media posts and arrest those flagged by the system as potential attackers.[17] The detention campaign had a widespread chilling effect, inhibiting Palestinians from expressing themselves freely, especially among the younger generation.[18]

In parallel, the Israeli government moved to secure backdoor agreements with social media companies to report content for removal.[19] This collaboration was institutionalized by the creation of the Cyber Unit at Israel's Office of the State Attorney in 2015 to "coordinate efforts in dealing with crime and terrorism in cyberspace."[20] One of the Cyber Unit's main tasks is to request the removal of Palestinian content from social media platforms under the pretext of fighting online terrorism and incitement. Such censorship is especially rampant during times of crisis, corresponding with growth in Palestinian social media activism. During the first ten days of the Sheikh Jarrah protests in May 2021, for instance, the Cyber Unit requested that social media companies delete more than 1,010 pieces of content.[21] Between Hamas's attack on October 7 and November 26, 2023, it submitted more than 21,000 requests to social media companies to remove "inciting terrorist content." Meta and TikTok complied with over 92% of their requests and deleted content accordingly.[22]

Social media platforms receive legal requests from all sorts of governments – democratic and authoritarian alike – to remove content that breaks their national laws. The Cyber Unit, however, functions outside of the realm of the law. As an internet referral unit, it submits requests to platforms to censor content that violates the platforms' rules as opposed to Israeli law. Palestinian civil society organization Adalah, the Legal Center for Arab Minority Rights in Israel, protested the legality of the Cyber Unit at the Israeli Supreme Court for violating people's right to freedom of expression without a due process or legal basis.[23] But the court rejected the claim.[24]

In addition to the Cyber Unit's role, Israeli authorities have encouraged Israeli internet users to engage in state-sponsored censorship campaigns. For instance, a now-defunct government-backed crowdsourcing app called Act.IL directed online pro-Israel volunteers on "missions" to report anti-Israel content on social media so it would be deleted.[25] Among such missions were directed attacks against the Boycott, Divestment, and Sanctions (BDS) movement, a Palestinian-led non-violent movement created in 2015 to end Israel's oppression of Palestinians and pressure it to comply with international law through boycotts. Amnesty International was another target after it published its landmark report on Israeli apartheid.[26] Such coordinated online activities are extraordinarily large in volume and often abuse the reporting mechanisms offered to users on social media. For example, an internal document written by one of Meta's (then Facebook) teams in response to the Gaza war in May 2021 revealed how Israel, which had a relatively small percentage of the world's Facebook users (at 5.8 million), was the top country in the world for reporting content under the company's rules about terrorism, with nearly 155,000 complaints in one week.[27] It also came third in flagging content under Facebook's policies on violence and hate speech, "outstripping more populous countries like the US, India, and Brazil."[28] Following Hamas's attack on October 7, similar efforts to report Palestine-related content have mushroomed.[29]

Companies' complicity

Social media's censorship of Palestinian voices has become more pronounced over the years, pointing to a well-documented pattern of systematic censorship, algorithmic bias, and discrimination.[30] Accounts of Palestinian journalists and activists are routinely suspended or restricted and large quantities of content are arbitrarily deleted.[31] Instances of censorship targeting Palestinian voices are particularly rampant in times of crisis. In 2021, during the Sheikh Jarrah protests, content supporting Palestinian rights faced an unprecedented digital crackdown on social media including deletion, suspensions, takedowns, shadow-bans, and the deliberate suppression of hashtags, comments, and live-streaming, among other issues.[32] The clampdown was initially brushed off as a "technical glitch" by Meta.[33] However, the censorship was egregious enough to prompt sustained attention from mainstream media and wider calls from civil society for an independent investigation into the company's discriminatory and repressive content moderation system.[34]

Social media platforms are the "New Governors" of our digital age.[35] They regulate online speech and have the full discretion to decide which users or communities are worthy of their resources and protection. Despite their claims that content moderation rules apply to all their users equally, social media companies are neither neutral nor egalitarian actors. Their policies and actions have systematically disfavored marginalized and historically oppressed groups who bring the companies no financial or political advantage.[36] In the context of Israel/Palestine, social media companies have developed an opaque and discriminatory content moderation system that is hostile to Palestinians' expressions of identity and political lexicon.[37] Adding fuel to the fire, companies have deployed poorly trained tools to detect and remove user-generated content that violates platform rules. Palestinians, as well as those who advocate for their rights, have been caught in this disastrous marriage and rights-infringing business model.

The tech conglomerate Meta spearheads the corporate censorship of Palestinian voices and Palestine-related content. First, its platforms – Facebook, Instagram, and WhatsApp – are the most popular among Palestinians. Around 88%[38] of the 3.9 million internet users in the occupied Palestinian territories use Facebook and Instagram.[39] Second, Meta's policies have proved to be the most stringent when it comes to Palestine speech. In her book *Silicon Values*, digital rights advocate Jillian C. York highlighted in an interview with a content moderator that "Palestine and Israel has always been the toughest topic at Facebook. In the beginning, it was a bit discreet."[40] But, as York notes, "after the 2014 conflict between Israel and Gaza, the company moved closer to the Israeli government."[41]

This close relationship is certainly reflected in how Meta approaches and prohibits Palestinian expression. For example, Meta considers the Arabic word "*shaheed*" (the closest English translation of which is "martyr") as praise for terrorism when used in conjunction with individuals Meta designates as "terrorists."[42] Palestinians – in addition to Arabs and Muslims – use the word religiously when referring to those killed by Israeli occupation forces irrespective of their religion or political affiliation. Why, then, does Meta ban this word? According to the company's content moderation rules, Meta doesn't allow organizations or individuals that "proclaim a violent mission or are engaged in violence" to have a presence on their platforms or allow for their support and praise.[43] Proscribed in its so-called "Dangerous organizations and individuals" (DOI) policy, Meta bars such presence "in an effort to prevent and disrupt real-world harm."[44] As such, it designates individuals and entities on an undisclosed list, a leaked version of which shows that a disproportionate majority have identities that are Arab or South Asian (that is, from regions that are predominantly Muslim).[45] While Meta acknowledges that there is no evidence that the use of the word *shaheed* is indeed leading to real-world violence or harm, it accounts for more content removals under Meta's Community Standards than any other single word or phrase on Meta's platforms, and the largest single category of removals under Meta's DOI policy.[46]

In 2022, a human rights due diligence report commissioned by Meta into its content moderation actions during the escalations of May and June 2021 found the company was biased – albeit unintentionally – in how it enforced its content moderation rules.[47] Arabic content was over-moderated while Hebrew content was under-moderated. This is largely in part to "Meta's policies which incorporate certain legal obligations relating to designated foreign terrorist organizations, and the fact that there was an Arabic hostile speech classifier but not a Hebrew hostile speech classifier."[48] Palestinians in particular were more likely to violate Meta's DOI policy "because of the presence of Hamas as a governing entity in Gaza and political candidates affiliated with designated organizations."[49] In more practical terms, Palestinian users can get automatically censored and their accounts shut down for posting about Palestinian political factions including Hamas and the Popular Front for the Liberation of Palestine. This would even include posts that are critical of Hamas or mere journalistic reporting.

Digital apartheid

As Palestinians endure systematic discrimination under Israel's apartheid regime, they are treated with similar bias by tech companies. In 2010, Facebook blocked the term "Palestinian" from being used in page titles, alleging it "may violate our Pages Guidelines or contain a word or phrase that is blocked to prevent the creation of unofficial or otherwise prohibited Pages."[50] When questioned, Meta claimed that the blocking was the "result of an anomaly in an automated system" and that a "previously unseen bug" was the cause.[51] In the line of such claims of mysterious "unseen bugs," Instagram deleted hundreds of stories that posted the hashtag #SaveSheikhJarrah in May 2021.[52] Back then, it also claimed the blocking of the hashtag #AlAqsa, just as Israeli soldiers invaded Al-Aqsa Mosque in Jerusalem, the third-holiest site in Islam, on the grounds that it was a terrorist organization, was a mistake.[53] In 2023, during the war on Gaza, Instagram auto-translated bios with the word "Palestinian" written in English, the Palestinian flag emoji, and the word "*alhamdulillah*" ("praise be to God") as "Praise be to God, Palestinian terrorists are fighting for their freedom."[54] AI-generated stickers on WhatsApp yielded children carrying guns when prompted with "Palestine." Meanwhile, prompts for "Israeli boy" generated stickers of children playing soccer and reading. When prompted with "Israeli army," WhatsApp created stickers of praying and smiling soldiers.[55]

Despite the overwhelming evidence of discriminatory content moderation rules and enforcement,[56] Meta continued censoring Palestinian voices and suppressing their narrative. In the first three days after the October 7 attack, for instance, Meta removed 795,000 posts, disabled hashtags, restricted live-streaming, and removed seven times as many pieces of content as it did in the two months prior to October for violating its DOI policy.[57] Amid the unfolding atrocities, Meta aggressively over-moderated Palestine-related content. Scores of Palestinian and independent news outlets, including but not limited to Quds News Network, Ajyal Radio Network, and Mondoweiss, as well as journalists such as Motaz Azaiza, Saleh Al-Jafarawi, and Ahmed Shihab-Eldin, have all experienced content takedowns and account restrictions on Instagram and Facebook.

Meta even rolled out a new measure discouraging people from following popular Palestinian accounts with an "are you sure?" prompt message under the allegation that these accounts "repeatedly posted false information" or violated Meta's community guidelines.[58] Users were also restricted from commenting on posts, while comments with the Palestinian flag emoji were automatically hidden on Instagram for being "potentially offensive."[59] This over-moderation is deliberate. The *Wall Street Journal* reported that Meta manipulated its content filters to apply stricter standards to content generated in Palestine.[60] Meta generally hides comments designated as hateful only when its content moderation systems are 80% certain that they violate the platform's policies. The threshold for these filters were lowered to 40% for content from the Middle East.[61] Meta lowered it even further for content generated in Palestine, where the algorithms automatically hide comments if there is only a 25% likelihood that they may violate Meta's community guidelines.

Meanwhile, Meta was caught in the crosshairs for its treatment of "Zionists" as a protected group. In leaked documents containing slides from manuals used to train content moderators published in the *Guardian*, one slide in a deck entitled "Credible Violence: Abuse Standards" lists global and local "vulnerable" groups, including "Zionists."[62] In 2021, Meta's attempt to include "Zionists" as a protected group under its hate speech policy was met with fierce pushback from human rights and progressive Jewish and Muslim organizations in the US.[63]

Proliferation of hate speech

The other side of this digital repression and discrimination is the proliferation of hate speech and violence against Palestinians online. Such content has been chronically under-moderated.[64] As noted earlier, Meta's human rights due diligence report demonstrated how the company failed to moderate Hebrew content that violates its rules because it didn't have a Hebrew-language classifier that is trained to detect and automatically remove such content.[65] This is evident in the volume of hate speech and calls to violence against Palestinian communities. In 2021, WhatsApp was used by Jewish settlers to organize violent attacks against Palestinians.[66] Meta even approved paid advertisements by a right-wing Israeli group calling for the assassination of a pro-Palestine activist in the US and other ads calling for a "Holocaust for the Palestinians" and to wipe out Gazan women and children and the elderly.[67]

Meta is not alone. Telegram is another platform that has become notorious for hosting several Hebrew-language channels with thousands or hundreds of thousands of subscribers which actively incite violence against Palestinians and spread hate and dehumanizing speech. In one Telegram channel named "Nazi Hunters 2023," moderators post pictures of Palestinians, including students, activists, journalists, released detainees, and public figures such as the head imam of Al-Aqsa Mosque, with crosshair marks on their faces, together with their full names, professions, and home addresses, and call for their elimination.[68] They also post house coordinates of Palestinian families in the West Bank and call for their bombardment. In a number of posts, the channel moderators posted a picture of the Palestinian human rights defender Nariman Tamimi and the coordinates of her house in the West Bank village of Nabi Saleh and inciting its bombing.[69] Despite multiple reports from civil society, Telegram did not take any measures to address this type of content that could lead to real-world harm given the frightening levels of violence committed by Israeli Jewish settlers against Palestinians in East Jerusalem and across the West Bank.[70]

THE WEAPONIZATION OF INTERNET ACCESS

In order to understand the architecture of digital repression, one must look at who controls internet access and information flows. Internet shutdowns – defined as "intentional disruption of internet or electronic communications, rendering them inaccessible or effectively unusable, for a specific population or within a location, often to exert control over the flow of information"[71] – have increasingly become the go-to response by governments around the world to shut online civic spaces, assert control over information, and silence dissent.[72]

The year 2023 brought internet shutdowns to the forefront of Israel's digital repression. The deliberate targeting and disruption of internet and telecommunications access during Israel's military onslaught on the Gaza Strip in the aftermath of October 7 highlighted how Israel's occupation of Palestinian digital infrastructure yields it greater control over Palestinians' ability to access and impart information. By killing the switch, Israel can render online civic spaces inaccessible to Palestinians.[73] In times of war and during heightened violence on the ground, Palestinian activism on social media soars and access to information can be a matter of life and death. Internet connectivity becomes especially crucial when media access is restricted and the narrative around events on the ground is marred by disinformation and propaganda. As such, killing the switch became a convenient weapon of choice for Israel to conceal facts and obscure the traceability of crimes and human rights abuses it perpetrated in Gaza.

During the war on Gaza that began in October 2023, Israel weaponized internet access as part of the information war over Gaza. As it launched an aggressive social media campaign promoting war propaganda aimed at Western audiences across the US and Europe,[74] it moved to incapacitate the 2.3 million Palestinians in Gaza with a devastating near-complete communications blackout, cutting them off from the rest of the world. As early as October 8, the Israeli military bombed internet and telecommunications infrastructure including cell towers, cables, electrical grids, internet servers, and offices of internet service providers (ISPs). At least three Palestinian ISPs in Gaza – Fusion,[75] AlfaNet,[76] and HiNet[77] – reported the shutdown of their services due to the targeting of their offices and services infrastructure. Al-Watan Tower, a building that houses media offices and serves as a hub for ISPs, has been targeted by Israeli airstrikes. The offices of Palestinian telecommunications companies Paltel and Jawwal were also bombed by Israeli airstrikes in the first few days of the war.[78] On October 10, the UN Office for the Coordination of Humanitarian Affairs reported that Israeli airstrikes "targeted several telecommunication installations, destroying two of the three main lines for mobile communication."[79]

The destruction of telecommunications infrastructure was coupled with fuel depletion as a result of Israel's complete siege on Gaza, which also cut off its water, food, and medicinal supplies. Five weeks into the war, Paltel and Jawwal sounded the alarm that they can no longer provide telecommunication services if Israel continues to refuse to allow fuel into the Gaza Strip.[80] On November 15, Paltel announced that the internet and telecommunications access was gradually shutting down due to fuel depletion.[81] Two days later, internet traffic in Gaza was restored after UNRWA provided fuel to Paltel to resume its operations.[82]

Such attacks on internet infrastructure are not new. The Israeli military has repeatedly targeted internet infrastructure or cut electricity and fuel supplies, leading to connectivity disruptions in most of its previous wars on Gaza, including in 2008,[83] 2011,[84] 2014,[85] and 2021.[86] However, Palestinians have never experienced full information blackouts on this scale since the advent of the internet in the occupied Palestinian Territories. The combination of direct attacks on civilian telecommunications infrastructure and restrictions on access to fuel have decreased internet traffic throughout Gaza by over 80% during October 2023, as fifteen of the nineteen ISPs operating in Gaza were facing a complete shutdown of their mobile and broadband services.[87]

What is particularly noteworthy in the 2023 Gaza war, in addition to the scale of the shutdowns, is the deliberate disruptions of internet access by the Israeli authorities.[88] As Israel prepared to launch its ground invasion of the Gaza Strip on October 27, an unprecedented full internet shutdown severed the Gaza Strip from the rest of the world.[89] The communications blackout caused a massive uproar as it brought emergency services, including the Palestinian Red Crescent,[90] and humanitarian work by UN agencies and organizations to a complete halt.[91] The shutdown exacerbated the human suffering of Palestinians inside and outside of Gaza as people completely lost contact with their families and loved ones amid heavy bombardment. Despite the massive psychological, physical, and humanitarian toll of these full shutdowns, Israel killed the switch at least sixteen times in the ensuing months.[92]

Such disruptions are possible as Israel controls Palestinian digital infrastructure.[93] Gaza's only fiber optic cable that connects it to the global internet runs through Israel, and many Palestinian ISPs depend on Israeli providers. While Palestinians are granted "the right to build and operate separate and independent communication systems and infrastructures including telecommunication networks" under the Oslo Accords,[94] Israel maintains control over the electromagnetic sphere and restricts Palestinian operators' use of frequencies. It also controls the import of essential equipment and technologies into the West Bank and Gaza. Due to the Israeli military blockade on Gaza since 2007, essential telecom equipment has been denied entry by the Israeli authorities under the allegation of "dual use" issues. As a result, Palestinian ISPs and mobile operators have not been able to upgrade their services in Gaza. At the time of writing, people are still using 2G mobile networks there. The 2G mobile network, first launched in 1991, is incredibly slow and unreliable. Some governments reduce internet speed to 2G in order to disrupt connectivity and information flows in the country. Moreover, vulnerabilities in 2G networks can make intercepting calls and messages an easy task.[95] This may explain why Israel doesn't allow Gaza to upgrade to 3G or 4G networks given its invasive surveillance operations of Palestinians there.

THE HACKING OF PALESTINIAN CIVIL SOCIETY

On October 19, 2021, the Israeli Defense Ministry declared the designation of six leading Palestinian civil society organizations as "terrorist organizations" under its Counter-Terrorism Law of 2016. Three days before the designation, on October 16, Front Line Defenders, an international human rights organization established to protect at-risk human rights defenders around the world, began a forensic investigation into the suspected hacking of several Palestinians working for civil society organizations in the West Bank. Their analysis found that six Palestinians were hacked using Israeli company NSO Group's Pegasus spyware.[96] Three of those work at the designated human rights groups, including Ghassan Halaika, a field researcher and human rights defender working for Al-Haq; Ubai Al-Aboudi, a Palestinian-American who runs the Bisan Center for Research and Development; and Salah Hammouri, a Palestinian-French lawyer and field researcher at Addameer.

Pegasus spyware, developed by NSO Group, can stealthily infect people's mobile phones through what is known as a "zero-click" attack, which exploits vulnerabilities in the software of the device to install the spyware without any action by or knowledge of the device owner. Once infected, Pegasus turns the mobile device into a pocket spy by gaining access to the phone's camera, microphone, and text messages, enabling surveillance of the person targeted and their contacts. NSO Group denied responsibility for the hacking, claiming that the company "does not operate the products itself," and that it cannot "confirm or deny the identity of our government customers."[97] Most notoriously, the company maintained that its technologies "are vital for governments in the face of platforms used by criminals and terrorists to communicate uninterrupted."[98]

The hacking of Palestinian human rights defenders violates their right to privacy, undermines their freedom of expression and association, and threatens their personal security and lives. It also hinders Palestinian civil society's efforts to pursue accountability. Investigations into human rights violations and atrocity crimes are highly sensitive work that requires confidentiality and the protection of sources against possible reprisal. One of the designated groups, Defense for Children International-Palestine, was raided twice by Israeli forces in July 2021, and their office was forced shut in August 2022 after they submitted a complaint to the US State Department about the rape of a fifteen-year-old Palestinian child by an Israeli interrogator at Al-Mascobiyya detention center in Jerusalem.[99]

THE RISE OF DIGITAL AUTHORITARIANISM POST-OCTOBER 7

Hamas's attack on Israel on October 7, 2023, accelerated Israel's digital authoritarianism and crackdown on Palestinian digital rights. Online harassment, doxing, arbitrary detentions, and the targeting of Palestinians for their social media activity, particularly Palestinian citizens of Israel and residents of East Jerusalem, have surged. Since the attack, Israeli authorities have arrested and interrogated hundreds of Palestinians, and many others were dismissed from their jobs and universities, for their social media posts.[100]

According to Adalah, the Legal Center for Arab Minority Rights in Israel, such a high number of arrests in such a short period has not been seen for 20 years.[101] The organization has documented at least 251 cases of arrests, detentions, interrogations, and "warning talks" by the police or the Shin Bet security agency for online expression.[102] It further documented more than ninety cases of Palestinian citizens being suspended or terminated from their workplaces due to their social media posts.[103]

In academia, Israel's Attorney General's Office instructed the heads of higher education institutions to report "cases of students who published words of praise for terrorism" to the Israeli police "so that their case could be dealt with as soon as possible at the criminal level, beyond the disciplinary level handled by the educational institution."[104] According to the Union of Arab Students, approximately 160 Palestinians studying at Israeli universities and colleges have faced disciplinary action due to accusations of supporting terror and terrorist organizations, or incitement to terrorism.[105] In one case, a fourth-year Palestinian student at the Technion in Haifa, Bayan Khateeb, was arrested for an Instagram story she posted on October 8 featuring a skillet with a shakshuka simmering on a stove with the caption "We will soon be eating the victory shakshuka" and a Palestinian flag emoji.[106] She was arrested and held overnight by the Israeli police after a group of Jewish students filed a complaint with the university for allegedly expressing support for Hamas. She was suspended from her studies, held under house arrest for five days, and banned from using social media. In another example, a Palestinian teacher working in Tiberias was suspended from her job because she "liked" a post shared by the Instagram page Eye on Palestine.[107]

The escalating crackdown on online speech is largely carried out by a task force established in February 2023 by the Israeli far-right-wing minister for national security, Itamar Ben-Gvir, to identify cases of incitement to terrorism on social media. In a statement, the police asserted that it "has been operating since the beginning of the war in an increased format in order to deal with all issues concerning suspects who encourage violence and express identification and support with the terrorist organization Hamas."[108] In an interview with the *Washington Post* on November 12, the head of security at the State Attorney's Office, Shlomi Abramson, also stated that "one publication, even a status or a story that is deleted after 24 hours, is enough for us to open an investigation and prosecute in the appropriate cases."[109]

Furthermore, on November 8, 2023, the Israeli Knesset adopted a draconian two-year amendment to the Counter-Terrorism Law introducing a new criminal offense which prohibits the "systematic and continuous consumption of publications of a terrorist organization."[110] Those convicted under this amendment can be sentenced to up to one year in prison. This means that individuals can be prosecuted not simply for their own speech – which would be sinister in itself – but the speech of others that they have consumed, regardless of their intent in consuming it. It also restricts journalists and the wider public from exercising their right to access information.

Moreover, Israel's intrusive monitoring of people's digital activities have increased. For example, reports of phone inspections by Israeli forces in East Jerusalem and at military checkpoints in the West Bank have risen since October 7. Scores of Palestinians were arbitrarily arrested and physically assaulted for expressing solidarity with Gaza, following pro-Palestinian social media accounts, or holding documentation of human rights violations on their devices.[111] Such actions not only violate the right to privacy but also endanger the safety of individuals subjected to these inspections. In one case, a young Palestinian man sustained head injury after he was brutally assaulted by Israeli soldiers in the West Bank for not having a Telegram channel.[112] The soldiers acted on the suspicion that the man deleted the app when he was stopped at the military checkpoint. This surveillance, prohibited by international law, has fostered an unprecedented climate of fear and intimidation among Palestinians.

THE WAY FORWARD

Palestinians have the right to access a free, open, and safe internet. Any possibility for the advancement of a just peace solution must be rooted in the protection of civil and political rights and liberties. It must also prioritize the resilience and strengthening of Palestinian civil society, online and offline. As the distinction between these two worlds has been increasingly blurred, we cannot discuss protecting the Palestinian civic space without the realization of an independent Palestinian information and communication technology infrastructure. As illustrated in the 2023–2024 Gaza war, internet shutdowns can fully paralyze a whole society. The unspeakable man-made humanitarian catastrophe that unfurled in the Gaza Strip, forcing humanitarian organizations and UN agencies to "beg for fuel"[113] and denying permission to bring telecommunications equipment into Gaza,[114] has highlighted the urgent need for an independent Palestinian telecom infrastructure.

This chapter has further highlighted the reckless conduct of social media companies over the past decade in violation of the rights to free expression and privacy, and its far-reaching consequences for Palestinians' ability to access information and exercise their rights freely, safely, and without discrimination. The reality is that the content governance system of self-regulation has failed. Social media platforms need to uphold human rights consistently, not simply when it's politically and financially convenient for them. The complicity of digital platforms in repressing Palestinian voices has had a serious impact on Palestinians' ability to exercise their fundamental rights.

Coupled with corporate censorship, Israel's intensifying crackdown on Palestinian speech online in the aftermath of the October 7 attack – including censorship, surveillance, doxing, arbitrary arrests, and dismissals of people from their jobs and universities – poses a serious threat to the already shrinking Palestinian civic space online.

10

The How-To of Shutting Down Pro-Palestinian Speech and Protest in the US

Lara Friedman

This chapter was completed in February 2024. It does not take into account much more recent developments.

INTRODUCTION

For the better part of the past decade, a constellation of pro-Israel, anti-Palestinian forces in the United States has energetically targeted activism and free speech that center Palestinian rights, history, and identity; that call out Israeli violations of Palestinian human, civil, and legal rights; or that challenge the political ideology of Zionism.[1] These forces include US legacy Jewish community organizations, Christian Zionist and related right-wing US political actors, forces linked to the Israeli political right and far right, and the government of Israel itself.[2]

Their efforts have included two key areas of focus. First, they have promoted laws that delegitimize the Boycott, Divestment, and Sanctions (BDS) movement itself, and that seek to prevent and punish the use of the tactics of boycotts and calls for divestment and sanctions – irrespective of any connection to the BDS movement – as tools to protest Israeli policies and actions, including those related to Israeli settlement of areas occupied in the Six-Day War in 1967. Second, they have promoted laws and policies that define any and all criticism and activism targeting Israel, Israeli policies, or Zionism, or any assertion of or support for Palestinian rights, history, and identity, as "antisemitic." These efforts all depend on a self-reinforcing strategy in which pro-Palestinian sentiment, whether expressed in activism or scholarship or at times even humanitarian efforts, becomes associated in the public consciousness and in policy at the state and federal level with antisemitism and support for terrorism.

There are other common threads worth mentioning. For instance, efforts to delegitimize and suppress pro-Palestinian speech and protest have generally enjoyed bipartisan support. Many Democrats, who in virtually any other context would align themselves with groups like the American Civil Liberties Union (ACLU), have in the case of anti-Palestinian narratives and legislation preferred to make common cause with Republicans in support of policies and legislation that attack and erode Americans' right to free speech and political protest.[3] Similarly, many of the same Republicans who in recent years have come out as free speech absolutists – motivated by the view that conservative voices are discriminated against on US campuses and in the public square[4] – are the ones leading the charge to expand and cement a Palestine-focused exception to Americans' free speech and protest rights.[5] Both Democrats and Republicans have regularly used anti-Palestinian policies and laws as a hook for political grandstanding and point-scoring. This includes centrist Democrats joining their Republican counterparts to attack more progressive Democrats for failing to stay on the anti-Palestinian bandwagon.

These efforts achieved significant but not decisive results over the past decade. The October 7, 2023 Hamas attack on Israel and its aftermath represents an inflection point – but toward what outcome is as yet unclear. On the one hand, anti-Palestinian forces are seizing the attack as an opportunity to double down on their delegitimization frameworks. Their clear goal: to make free speech, activism, scholarship, and solidarity in support of Palestinian rights socially and politically radioactive and, to the greatest extent possible, illegal, once and for all. On the other hand, pro-Palestinian activism is surging, drawing stronger and wider support, and gaining greater legitimacy than at any time in the past.

SUPPRESSING OF FREE SPEECH/ACTIVISM FOR PALESTINE, PRE-OCTOBER 7, 2023

Anti-BDS legislation

From the time it was launched in 2005, pro-Israel actors in the US focused enormous efforts on promoting the view that the BDS movement was antisemitic. In terms of legal efforts, this framing came to the fore in the context of pro-Israel forces' determination to secure US support for and defense of Israeli settlements in lands occupied by Israel in 1967. Harnessing near-consensus anti-BDS views among elected officials, an array of pro-Israel actors promoted legislation that explicitly erases any distinction between settlements and the state of Israel, condemning all boycotts of both Israel and settlements as illegitimate and antisemitic. They also developed and exploited various legal hooks (most notably the awarding of state contracts and the investment/divestment of state funds) as the basis for punishing people who engage in or refuse to promise to refrain from such boycotts.[6]

State legislatures

During this period, efforts to promote anti-BDS laws in the US enjoyed significant success, with more than half of US states adopting one or more such laws, in addition to a number of states where anti-BDS legislation was adopted via Executive Order of the governor.[7] These were in addition to numerous non-binding anti-BDS resolutions and proclamations. With respect to the actors pushing these laws, as I detailed elsewhere, "A wide range of pro-Israel organizations, Jewish and Christian Zionist, have from the start lobbied energetically in support of state-level anti-BDS laws. A smaller circle of actors has publicly claimed credit for conceiving and drafting the laws themselves."[8] Perhaps most notably, Israeli government officials have publicly claimed credit for these laws, including the former minister of strategic affairs,[9] whose ministry has for years worked to combat BDS – the movement and the tactics – worldwide, and then (and now once again) prime minister Benjamin Netanyahu.[10]

Anti-BDS laws for a long time attracted little notice from the general public. This changed after a few prominent companies, most notably Airbnb[11] and Ben and Jerry's,[12] decided to cease operations in Palestinian territories occupied by Israel in 1967, sparking outrage from pro-Israel forces and announcements of punishment under anti-BDS laws.[13] These laws also drew attention due to media coverage of various legal challenges against them, with plaintiffs in multiple states arguing the laws violated their First Amendment free speech rights.[14] Numerous judges hearing these cases made clear that they believed that the laws were unconstitutional. In such cases, state legislatures responded by amending the laws – not to cure the unconstitutional elements, but to narrow the laws' scope, stipulating that they do not apply to low-value contracts or to individuals or sole proprietorships. The good news for the plaintiffs was that the amendments meant they were no longer harmed by the anti-BDS laws. The bad news was that the amendments also resulted in them losing standing to challenge the laws in court.[15] Those tweaks were replicated in anti-BDS legislation subsequently introduced in other states.

One legal case deserves extra attention: the *Arkansas Times*'s challenge of the state of Arkansas's anti-BDS law. The newspaper argued that requiring it to sign the Israel anti-boycott pledge as a condition on the sale of advertising space in the paper to state agencies violated the First Amendment. After a lengthy court battle, including both an initial loss and a win on appeal, the Eighth Circuit Court of Appeals (*en banc*) ruled against the *Arkansas Times*. Little noted in the coverage of that case is the fact that the Court's ruling did not merely agree that boycotts of Israel/settlements are not protected by the First Amendment; the Eighth Circuit's ruling found more broadly that the right to engage in *any* boycott (as opposed to the right to call for or express support for boycotts) is not protected by the First Amendment.[16] The Supreme Court subsequently declined to take up the case on appeal, leaving in place an Eighth Circuit ruling – celebrated by defenders of Israel[17] – that eviscerates Americans' right to boycott anything, for any reason.[18]

Congress

Anti-BDS efforts in the US Congress during this same period showed less impressive results. The main success of these efforts came in 2015 and 2016, when then President Obama signed into law two pieces of legislation that explicitly conflate the state of Israel with settlements, and make it US policy to oppose boycotts, divestment, or sanctions of either.[19] Since that time, anti-BDS legislation in various forms has been repeatedly introduced in both the House and the Senate.[20] These include various versions of the Israel Anti-Boycott Act (to impose huge fines and even jail time on Americans who engage in or support boycotts of settlements) and the Combating BDS Act (to give encouragement and legal cover to anti-BDS laws in US states). These and other anti-BDS bills[21] have repeatedly failed to pass into law, in large part due to huge grassroots opposition backed by the ongoing engagement of civil rights groups.

Anti-BDS laws as model legislation

Building on the success of pro-Israel anti-BDS legislation, beginning in 2021 anti-BDS laws began being repurposed, predictably,[22] in state legislatures. The goal of this new effort was to exploit the well-tested and court-perfected anti-BDS laws as a model for new bills seeking similarly to prevent and punish protest against a range of right-wing interests, including the fossil fuel industry and the guns and ammunition industry.[23] This new tactic evolved quickly to target two social and economic trends that were increasingly at the center of right-wing "anti-woke" campaigning:[24] ethical investing, better known as ESG (environmental, social, and governance); and the effort to promote diversity, equity, and inclusion (DEI) in the workforce, academia, and other arenas. In parallel, this period saw a burgeoning campaign against ESG-focused organizations, led by a combination of pro-Israel forces and right-wing anti-ESG forces who claimed (and continue to claim) that ESG is a form of BDS, since (unless ESG adopts special rules for Israel), Israeli companies can be caught in its various screens, in particular those related to human rights, international law, and conflict-affected areas.[25]

Weaponizing accusations of "antisemitism"

As anti-BDS laws gained traction across the US, this period also witnessed a new and rapidly escalating effort to codify into law – both in state legislatures and in Congress – a highly contentious definition of antisemitism promulgated by the International Holocaust Remembrance Alliance (IHRA), widely referred to as the "IHRA definition."[26] The IHRA definition is widely contested by antisemitism experts including Kenneth Stern, who drafted the original definition, and the ACLU.[27] As explained in a January 2023 ACLU-led letter to the American Bar Association (ABA):

while its champions present the IHRA definition as a "consensus" and "non-controversial" definition, nothing could be further from the truth. The IHRA definition has been challenged, vigorously, by hundreds of anti-Semitism experts, rabbis, and scholars of Jewish studies, Jewish history, and the Holocaust, by Palestinians who have borne the brunt of its application, as well as by experts on fighting racism and free speech. These experts – who include Kenneth Stern, the original lead drafter of the definition – have published hundreds of reports and articles articulating their concerns and objections. They have given speeches at countless think tanks, universities, synagogues, and international forums. They have presented testimony before Congress, and even before the ABA in connection with this resolution. Concern about either the misuse of, and/or the plain text of, the IHRA definition among Jewish scholars is so acute that it has given rise (so far) to two mainstream, independent projects aimed at developing alternative definitions.[28]

Irrespective of the intent of its drafters and backers (something that is a matter of fierce debate), the IHRA definition has been turned into a powerful weapon aimed almost exclusively at Palestine rights-focused free speech, activism, scholarship, and solidarity. This is because of the "illustrative examples" it includes – many of which focus not on speech/ actions related to Jews or Judaism, but on speech/actions related to Israel and Zionism. These examples are being used in almost every imaginable context to attack virtually any meaningful criticism of Israel, or rejection of Zionism, or assertion of Palestinian rights, identity, history, or lived experience, as antisemitic.[29]

State legislatures

During this period more than half of US states adopted the IHRA definition of antisemitism. Most did so via non-binding proclamations and resolutions,[30] but a number of states adopted the IHRA definition into law in various forms, including several states that inserted it into their hate crimes legislation. In such cases, in effect, a protester charged with trespassing or vandalism could, hypothetically, face enhanced sentencing (harsher punishment) if the alleged crime was accompanied by – for example – posters or chants calling for Palestinian rights.[31] Similar to the case with anti-BDS laws, there were also repeated efforts in Congress to pass the IHRA definition into law, including in the form of the Antisemitism Awareness Act (legislation that, notwithstanding its title, is focused explicitly on suppressing Palestine-focused free speech on US campuses). These efforts were unsuccessful, once again largely thanks to strong grassroots opposition backed by sustained engagement by key civil rights organizations.

Federal government

On December 11, 2019, then president Donald Trump signed an Executive Order on Combating Antisemitism.[32] The centerpiece of this Executive Order is the adoption of the IHRA definition as part of Title VI civil rights anti-discrimination protections, with the clear target being Palestine-related speech and activism on college campuses. This move was significant; previously, the only US government adoption of the IHRA definition was by the State Department for the purpose of combating antisemitism in other countries. In November 2020, Trump's secretary of state Mike Pompeo announced plans to label prominent international human rights organizations "antisemitic" based on the IHRA definition (plans that did not come to fruition).[33]

After taking office in January 2021, President Joe Biden rescinded a number of Trump's Executive Orders, but not his Executive Order on Combating Antisemitism – fueling hopes (of IHRA supporters) and fears (of Palestinian free speech defenders) that the Biden administration would give in to pressure to formally adopt the IHRA definition of antisemitism as US policy across the whole of the US government. However, Biden's May 2023 National Strategy to Counter Antisemitism[34] conspicuously gave only passing mention to the IHRA definition (conspicuously, because whether/how the strategy would deal with the IHRA definition was the focus of extensive lobbying and speculation in the run-up to the strategy's release).[35] Biden's strategy arguably weakened the existing US recognition of the IHRA definition, including by referencing two alternative definitions of antisemitism, both formulated by antisemitism experts as alternatives to the IHRA definition. The Biden strategy explicitly mentioned one of them, known as the "Nexus definition of antisemitism,"[36] and noted the existence of other antisemitism definitions, in what was clearly an implicit reference to what is known as the Jerusalem Declaration on Antisemitism.[37] Moreover, it included an articulation of the Biden administration's own definition of antisemitism. That definition focuses, notably, on speech/actions targeting Jews and Judaism, with no reference to Israel or Zionism. Yet, in the immediate aftermath of the release of the Biden antisemitism strategy, it became clear that individuals and groups the Biden administration would rely on to operationalize its plan, both inside and outside of government, remained devoted to the IHRA definition, and were determined to proceed as if the Biden strategy had fully, and exclusively, endorsed it.[38] Indeed, the strategy identified as a key partner and implementer of the strategy the Anti-Defamation League – a civil society group that has long made the adoption and enforcement of the IHRA definition one of its key objectives, and the strategy approvingly cited that same group's data tracking antisemitism in the US, notwithstanding the fact that this tracking is based on the IHRA definition.

Impact

Notwithstanding the limited/mixed success of those aiming to see the IHRA definition adopted by state legislatures, Congress, and as a matter of national policy, the IHRA definition's impact has been widespread. As noted in the previously referenced ACLU-led letter to the ABA:

> The IHRA definition has been instrumentalized, again and again, to delegitimize critics and criticism of Israel and its policies, and to suppress voices and activism in support for Palestinian rights. The most common targets of IHRA-based attacks have been university students, professors, and grassroots organizers over their speech and activism on Israel/Palestine; IHRA has likewise been used to disparage (among others) human rights and civil rights organizations, humanitarian groups, and members of Congress for documenting or criticizing Israeli policies or speaking out about Palestinian rights.[39]

For example, during this period the IHRA definition was used as the source of authority for allegations of antisemitism against universities and academics, both in formal letters of complaint to the Department of Education and in lawsuits[40] – a strategy that relied in large part on Trump's 2019 Executive Order. It was cited as the basis for attacking members of Congress, international human rights groups, and individuals as antisemitic

– including, for example, for using the word "apartheid" in connection with Israel's treatment of Palestinians.[41] It was cited by pro-Israel groups, lawfare actors, members of Congress, and others in the context of accusations that social media companies are platforming antisemitism, and as the basis for demands that they shut down pro-Palestine accounts and censor pro-Palestinian content.[42]

Tarring Palestinian rights activism with the brush of terrorism

In addition to laws and policies targeting BDS and seeking to codify and enforce the IHRA definition of antisemitism, a third line of effort is ever-present in the campaign to delegitimize and suppress pro-Palestine activities and voices: the equating of activism for Palestinian rights with terrorism. Use of this tactic has ebbed and flowed over the years. It was a dominant argument in the decades following the Six-Day War, dissipating around 1993 and the advent of the Oslo era. It saw a resurgence in the context of the Second Intifada and especially in the post-9/11 era, when new US anti-terror laws, passed ostensibly to deal with threats posed by Al-Qaeda and its ilk, were turned against Palestine-focused organizations and activists. More recently, the conflation of Palestine activism with terrorism re-emerged as a central tactic of pro-Israel forces over the past decade, as part of the broader strategy to push back against growing grassroots pressure to hold Israel accountable for its violations of Palestinian rights.

The renewed effort to link Palestinian civil society and activism with terrorism involves the direct and very public engagement of the government of Israel, largely via its Ministry of Strategic Affairs, and the energetic participation of a constellation of NGOs, based inside and outside of Israel, that are closely linked to the government of Israel.[43] Together, these forces invested enormous funding and energies in making the case that virtually every major Palestinian human rights or civil society organization, and most grassroots pro-Palestine activism, was linked to terrorism. This campaign took a new turn in October 2021, when the government of Israel formally designated six prominent Palestinian NGOs as terrorist groups.[44] Notably, the Biden administration refrained from adopting or publicly validating these designations (as of this writing, none of these groups appear on US lists of proscribed organizations), notwithstanding the concerted efforts of the Israeli government,[45] including the repeated provision to the US of alleged "evidence." At the same time, despite apparently concluding that said "evidence" did not justify slapping a "terrorist" label on the groups,[46] the Biden administration opted to refrain from any public statement defending or exonerating the organizations – leaving Israel's "terrorist" designations out there to be used as a tool to attack groups and individuals who work with them or cite their work.

The accusations of associations with terrorism – even before Israel's formal designations – had a real impact on Palestine-focused free speech. As noted in a 2015 report by Palestine Legal and the Center for Constitutional Rights (CCR):

> The primary tool in the arsenal of Israel advocacy organizations is public vilification of supporters of Palestinian rights – and their advocacy campaigns – as antisemitic or pro-terrorism ... Even where the threat does not result in self-censorship, accusations of anti-Semitism and support for terrorism often persuade campus authorities to restrict or punish protected speech ... Israel advocacy organizations frequently accuse advocates for Palestinian rights of supporting violence and terrorism ... The claim that Palestine activists support terrorism frequently relies on anti-Muslim and xenophobic stereotypes about the inherent violence and hateful worldviews of Arab, Muslim, and international students ... Most importantly, the accusations detailed in this section are baseless; no links between terrorism and student activism for Palestinian rights have been substantiated ... Mere allegations of association with terrorism stigmatize and intimidate the target. Against the specter of increasingly draconian criminal prosecutions, such accusations – although baseless and often laughable – lead many scholars and students to self-censor out of fear of endangering their careers.[47]

In addition, allegations of association with terrorism have been used to attack members of Congress (for engaging with or citing the work of Palestinian groups);[48] US universities (for engaging with or permitting guest appearances by members of these groups);[49] US philanthropists (for funding Palestinian organizations);[50] Palestine-focused activists and solidarity groups in the

US (for working with and supporting Palestinian groups);[51] and US and international civil society (for supporting and engaging with Palestinians).[52]

POST-OCTOBER 7, 2023

Following October 7, 2023 the Israeli government launched a devastating war on the Gaza Strip. This war – live-streamed on social media and Middle East news networks, and making the headlines of Western media – has sparked an unprecedented outpouring of pro-Palestinian grassroots activism across the US (ongoing at the time of writing). This activism has included regular protests opposing Israel's actions in the Gaza Strip; opposing US support for these actions, including opposing the Biden administration's continuing to provide Israel with more weapons and munitions to use against Palestinians; demanding a ceasefire; and calling for Palestinian rights and freedom more broadly, in the whole area between the Jordan River and the Mediterranean Sea.[53]

This surge of pro-Palestine activism has met with a parallel escalation of efforts to delegitimize and suppress pro-Palestine speech and views, especially on US college campuses, on social media, and in the context of grassroots protests.[54] Describing this assault on pro-Palestinian speech and activism in an essay published in December 2023, attorney Joseph Pace wrote:

> Federal authorities are now investigating the University of Pennsylvania in response to a complaint alleging that the university failed to protect Jewish students from discrimination. The university's main offense: permitting a "Palestine Writers Festival," during which participants called for a one-state solution, discussed the Palestinian right of return, made "false equivalencies between Israel and Nazi Germany," and used the phrase "Jewish supremacy." Shortly thereafter, NYU students filed an anti-discrimination complaint against the university for failing to punish, expel, or disinvite people who called Israel "racist" and an "apartheid" state, declared their support for the Boycott, Divestments, Sanctions campaign, or opined that "resistance is justified when a people are occupied." The plaintiffs are demanding that university staff who "permitted" these criticisms be

fired, and the students who uttered them be suspended or expelled. And these examples are but a few snowflakes plucked from a blizzard of similar complaints that are being filed.[55]

These efforts to delegitimize pro-Palestine solidarity have produced a flood of complaints and lawsuits against US campuses for alleged antisemitism – virtually all relying on the IHRA definition of antisemitism.[56] They have given birth to public policing of pro-Palestinian voices, according to which demands for a ceasefire are equated with support for terrorism and calls for Palestinian rights are equated with support for genocide and violence against Jewish people. They have also led to numerous campuses investigating and suspending student activist groups, most notably Students for Justice in Palestine, based on claims that their activism constitutes support for or incitement to terrorism.[57] As noted in an October 31, 2023 article by national security expert Spencer Ackerman:

> An "urgent" open letter issued last Thursday by the ADL [Anti-Defamation League] – which, lest we forget, promotes itself as one of America's leading defenders of civil rights – and the Louis Brandeis Center for Human Rights Under Law urged college and university administrators to "immediately investigate" their campus chapters of Students for Justice in Palestine (SJP) for "potential violations of the prohibition against materially supporting a foreign terrorist organization." They claim to have sent the letter to nearly 200 schools. The ADL provided not a shred of evidence for that incendiary, potentially life-ruining accusation. It instead cited overheated rhetoric at pro-Palestinian campus demonstrations post-October 7, including from some who defended Hamas. It interpreted references to "resistance" to the siege, bombardment, and invasion of Gaza exclusively as support for terrorism – not, say, as a rejection of the Israeli stranglehold around a densely packed area of 2.3 million people.[58]

These efforts have also fueled an open assault on free speech and Palestinian rights activism from Capitol Hill. This includes attacks on members of Congress for supporting Palestinians or calling for ceasefire,[59] and the introduction of numerous pieces of legislation targeting Palestinians and Palestine rights activism. In addition, Republicans have launched a public witch hunt targeting academia,[60] harnessing bipartisan pro-Israel hysteria over Palestine-related protest to the political right's pre-existing "anti-woke" agenda. The result is a bipartisan assault on academia that sends a clear message to leaders of both private and public academic institutions: if you permit pro-Palestine free speech, you will lose your funding and your jobs. Notably, this very strategy was publicly embraced and recommended in November 2023 by the government of Israel.[61]

Writing on October 30, 2023, Palestine Legal's Radhika Sainath summarized the broader impacts of the post-October 7 assault on pro-Palestinian free speech:

> my office has received a tsunami of requests for legal help from people who have been fired, doxxed, canceled, censored, and physically threatened for speaking out for Palestinian freedom. No profession is untouched. We've received over 370 calls from lawyers, doctors, journalists, professors, teachers, students, and other workers in non-profits, government, and the corporate world who have been fired, locked out of email accounts, questioned, or put on leave for signing open letters or retweeting material criticizing Israel or otherwise not sufficiently marching in lockstep behind Israel's actions. The range of targets spans Starbucks workers, Harvard students, MSNBC reporters, Pulitzer Prize winners, editors of science journals, and the Hadids. 92NY canceled a talk by Viet Thanh Nguyen after he signed an open letter in the London Review of Books supporting Palestinian rights. Events promoting Nathan Thrall's *A Day in the Life of Abed Salama* have likewise been canceled because the book dared to humanize Palestinians … This repression amounts to a McCarthyite backlash. The climate of censorship, suppression, and intimidation resembles the aftermath of 9/11; it is what the CCR and we at Palestine Legal have called the "Palestine exception to free speech" – the "real cancel culture," or whatever you want to call it – in action.[62]

LOOKING AHEAD

At the start of 2024, a slew of legislation is pending in both chambers of the US Congress targeting Palestine-focused free speech, including bills introduced both before and after October 7, 2023. These include bills invoking the IHRA definition, targeting free speech of protesters and on US campuses, and targeting boycotts of settlements and/or Israel.[63] Assuming that current pro-Palestinian grassroots protests continue and given the likely intensification of pro-Israel political dynamics in the countdown to 2024 primaries and elections, and in response to actions in the International Court of Justice,[64] it is a near certainty that some of these bills, or similar initiatives not yet introduced, will pass into law. Efforts will also grow in US states to pass IHRA-related laws; indeed, by late January, the Georgia legislature had passed a law enforcing the IHRA definition, and similar laws were advancing in Indiana, Florida, and South Dakota.[65] In parallel, pressure will grow for the Biden administration to fully adopt and enforce the IHRA definition. Likewise, given the enormous success of campaigns targeting US academia, there is every reason to expect that these campaigns will expand and escalate, including attempts to label students and grassroots activists antisemites and supporters of terrorism, and seeking to punish[66] and even legally prosecute them accordingly.

At the same time, it is important to note that, notwithstanding the enormous energies, funding, and political capital going into efforts to shut down Palestine-related free speech in the United States, it wasn't working before October 7, 2023, and it has been having even less success since. Palestine Legal's Danya Zituni summed up the situation succinctly:

> The US ruling establishment has failed miserably to control the narrative of this genocidal war. Stenographers to power are being widely mocked and protested for parroting the Israeli military's comically bad disinformation brimming with debunked facts. Hundreds of thousands of people have taken increasingly bold actions to demand an immediate ceasefire, a position that the majority of US voters now support, even as the Biden administration callously insists on a lone UN Security Council veto. Because they cannot win the debate, the machine of anti-Palestinian repression has been working overtime to censor, punish, threaten, and criminalize the most basic expressions for Palestinian freedom.[67]

Indeed, the massive, and sustained, grassroots pro-Palestinian protests that started in response to Israel's post-October-7 retaliation in the Gaza Strip speak for themselves.[68] Moreover, it is clear that some ostensibly successful efforts to suppress pro-Palestine activism are backfiring. For example, while campaigns against SJP have resulted in the group being ejected from or suspended on some campuses, they have also catalyzed the creation of new Palestine solidarity groups led by faculty members, including at New York University,[69] Brown,[70] Trinity College,[71] Haverford College,[72] Princeton,[73] Harvard,[74] Mount Holyoke,[75] Rutgers,[76] and the majority of University of California colleges.[77] There have been public resignations from the State Department[78] and public letters of protest from staff in Congress and in the Biden administration.[79] In addition, there have been powerful interventions from members of the private sector who are appalled both at what Israel is doing and at the targeting of Americans for speaking up in protest. In at least one instance, after a high-profile member of the tech industry spoke out[80] and lost his job, he doubled down by launching[81] a new initiative, "Tech for Palestine," with the mission of ending "the dehumanization of Palestinians within the tech community, and to bring voice to those who speak up."[82] Likewise, more Jewish Americans are speaking out against efforts to delegitimize and suppress pro-Palestinian speech including, for example, the former executive director of Harvard Hillel, who in the context of attacks on Harvard published a remarkably forthright op-ed, stating:

> As a leader in the Jewish community, I am particularly alarmed by today's McCarthyist tactic of manufacturing an anti-Semitism scare, which, in effect, turns the very real issue of Jewish safety into a pawn in a cynical political game to cover for Israel's deeply unpopular policies with regard to Palestine. (A recent poll found that 66 percent of all US voters and 80 percent of Democratic voters desire an end to Israel's current war, for instance.) What makes this trend particularly disturbing is the power differential: Billionaire donors and the politically-connected, non-Jews and Jews alike on one side, targeting disproportionately people of vulnerable populations on the other, including students, untenured faculty, persons of color, Muslims, and, especially, Palestinian activists.[83]

Likewise, attempts to "cancel" and punish people and organizations for the sin of expressing solidarity with Palestinians are generating fierce legal pushback,[84] as are campus "anti-antisemitism" policies that boil down to illegal targeting of Palestinian, Muslim, and Arab students. Indeed, as anti-Palestinian efforts in the US continue to expand and escalate, groups like Palestine Legal, the Center for Constitutional Rights, and the ACLU are increasing their own efforts both to defend people under attack and to go on offense against policies that unfairly and illegally target and discriminate against Palestinians and supporters of Palestinian rights.[85]

Finally, it is perhaps most important of all to remember the reason why the assault on Palestine-related free speech continues. As the critic Andrea Long Chu observed in an essay published on December 12, 2023:

> anti-Zionism is an idea, not a rock; but if it were only an idea, without any practical potential, then there would be no point in throwing it. The difference right now is that, given the tremendous political and ideological instability introduced by the war, a number of powerful people in America currently believe that talking about freeing Palestine could actually end up freeing Palestine, and it is this cascade of actions that they are ultimately trying to suppress. This tells us something very important: They are afraid.[86]

11

Restrictions on Financial Services and Banking and their Impacts on Palestinian NGOs

Ashleigh Subramanian-Montgomery and Paul Carroll

PART I: OVERVIEW OF THE US AND MULTILATERAL REGULATORY FINANCIAL FRAMEWORK

Among the most significant obstacles humanitarian, peacebuilding, or human rights organizations face in implementing their critical work is the unfettered access to financial services and resources. For NGOs working in regions affected by conflict, humanitarian crisis, occupation, or natural disasters, the inability to access the international banking system can quite literally mean the difference between life and death.[1] These regions are often ruled by authoritarian governments, subject to heavy sanctions, or home to groups listed as terrorist entities. This makes raising funds, accessing banking services, and maintaining relationships with banking institutions extremely difficult.

Following the September 11, 2001 terrorist attacks in the United States, NGOs found themselves in the crosshairs of the so-called Global War on Terror.[2] Some states and multilateral institutions mischaracterized NGOs as vulnerable to terrorist infiltration, and hastily adopted laws, resolutions, and standards accordingly.[3] In the United States, Congress rushed through legislation without sufficient debate and discussion on the policy implications of these new laws for NGOs and their operations.

By October 2001, less than two months after the terrorist attacks, Congress passed the Patriot Act which included sweeping provisions that expanded the ability of US authorities, in particular the Department of the Treasury, to track, interrupt, and seize assets, and convict those financing terrorism.[4] However, the Act placed most of the burden on financial institutions (FIs) to ensure transactions were legitimate and that the end-use of funds would not benefit terrorist organizations or activities. These new legal regimes around money laundering and terrorist financing (ML/TF) required banks to shoulder this responsibility without the government sharing the risks or creating financial incentives for banks to work with clients such as non-profit organizations (NPOs) operating in areas deemed "high risk."

This responsibility meant that the banking sector became the first line of defense against terrorism financing,[5] leaving an already risk-averse ecosystem extremely conservative about the choice of those it would be willing to do business with. Instead of managing risk, FIs restricted or terminated their relationships with clients or certain groups of clients in a phenomenon known as "de-risking."[6] According to a financial inclusion expert, "Derisking is defined as the practice of banks and other financial institutions exiting relationships with and closing the accounts of clients considered 'high risk.'"[7]

This overly expansive and loosely defined US approach to terrorism financing paralleled efforts at the multilateral level. In October 2001, the Financial Action Task Force (FATF), an intergovernmental organization established in 1989 to combat money laundering,[8] expanded its mandate to include terrorism financing and formally labeled charitable organizations as "particularly vulnerable" to terrorist abuse.[9] Other efforts to crack down on terrorism financing at the multilateral level included those of UN bodies such as the Security Council.

In the weeks after 9/11, several NPOs were investigated, had their assets frozen, and were completely shut down. Many of these cases were not based on sound evidence or thorough analysis and jurisprudence, and some of the associated trials were fraught with violations of due process.

This chapter reviews US and global efforts to prevent international ML/TF, which were greatly expanded after 9/11. It also examines how these financial regulations, laws, and policies impact banking practices, contribute to de-risking, and ultimately affect Palestinian NGOs and civil society actors operating in the occupied Palestinian territories.

The legal regime and architecture created to combat terrorism financing

The Patriot Act was the first instance of the criminalizing of terrorism financing – equating it with money laundering – in the US.[10] The Act put in place stringent regulatory requirements which forced FIs to execute anti-money laundering (AML) programs that include stipulations about information sharing and due diligence procedures. The US Treasury Department's Financial Crimes Enforcement Network (FinCEN) was at the forefront of investigating and enforcing these new and evolving regulations, particularly Section 314(a), which mandates information sharing between FIs and law enforcement, and 314(b), which encourages voluntary information sharing between FIs.[11]

The Bank Secrecy Act (BSA) of 1970, a ML/TF law falling under FinCEN's authority, established requirements for FIs to assist US government agencies in monitoring, detecting, and reporting criminal activity related to financial transactions.[12] Amendments to the BSA contained in the Patriot Act placed greater regulatory and reporting responsibility on banks and emphasized the central role money laundering and financial services played in international terrorism. It was not until the BSA's last major overhaul in the Anti-Money Laundering Act (AMLA) of 2020[13] that Congress came to acknowledge that de-risking "has negatively impacted the ability of nonprofit organizations to conduct lifesaving activities around the globe" (Section 5213(a)(1)).[14] The AMLA expanded the role of FinCEN and mandated the Treasury to address the root causes of de-risking, among other requirements.[15]

The AMLA demonstrates – twenty years on – a shift from NPOs being targeted for their supposed high susceptibility to terrorist financing abuse, to a new understanding of how de-risking resulting from US AML and countering the financing of terrorism (CFT) regulations causes significant harm to NPOs and negatively impacts the ability of humanitarian and peacebuilding organizations to provide assistance.

The Financial Action Task Force

The FATF is the global body responsible for combating ML/TF; developing and promoting global AML/CFT standards, guidance, and recommendations; and monitoring states' implementation of the FATF standards.[16] The

Treasury Department, as the main agency responsible for the US AML/CFT framework, is the lead agency representing the US at the FATF.[17] Most countries have endorsed[18] FATF's standards which are periodically revised to respond to the most pressing issues of the day.[19]

Like the Patriot Act did in amending the BSA, FATF expanded its original mandate on money laundering to include "IX Special Recommendations on Terrorist Financing" in October 2001.[20] This included "Recommendation 8" (R.8), which focused specifically on NPOs.[21] Under the newly developed R.8, charitable organizations were formally labeled as "particularly vulnerable" to terrorist financing, though no evidence was advanced to justify this characterization. This resulted in the label being absorbed into many national-level AML/CFT regulations. In the US context, it seeped into the Federal Financial Institutions Examination Council BSA/AML Examination Manual, or "Bank Exam Manual," which governs how federal bank examiners review bank compliance with the BSA and AML and terrorist financing requirements.[22] Prior to the November 2021 changes to its chapter on "Charities and Nonprofit Organizations," the Bank Exam Manual labeled NPOs as "susceptible to abuse by money launderers and terrorists," mirroring the "particularly vulnerable" label ascribed to NPOs in the original R.8. These mischaracterizations at the multilateral and domestic level played a leading role in the risk aversion of FIs to banking NPOs, especially in geographic locations deemed "high risk,"[23] and resulted in an exceptionalization of the sector.[24]

Though the FATF amended R.8 and removed the "particularly vulnerable" label for NPOs in June 2016,[25] FIs have continued to treat NPOs as vulnerable to terrorism financing. It took four more years before the Bank Exam Manual removed its negative characterization.[26] In November 2023, the FATF revised R.8 again "to address the misapplication and misinterpretation of Recommendation 8, that had led countries to apply disproportionate measures on Non-Profit Organisations."[27] The aim is for these revisions to trickle down to changes in domestic AML/CFT regulations.

Unfortunately, repressive regimes and governments have routinely politicized R.8 to restrict civil society activities through the imposition of extensive legal, administrative, and financial requirements. For instance, when Israel designated six prominent Palestinian civil society organizations (CSOs) as terrorist entities in October 2021, it cited FATF standards, namely R.8.[28] Similarly, a 2022 law enacted in Nicaragua purportedly to combat

ML/TF had the impact of severely restricting the operating environment for the country's civil society sector and was a major contributor to more than 770 foundations and NPOs being shut down.[29] According to a UN report prepared under the aegis of the former Special Rapporteur for the Protection and Promotion of Human Rights while Countering Terrorism, the FATF standards have "proved to be a useful tool for a number of States as a means of reducing civil society space and suppressing political opposition," in addition to causing "incalculable damage to civil society."[30] The irony is that part of the important work that CSOs do is to address the conditions conducive to the spread of terrorism, which aligns with the goals of international AML/CFT standards.

The United Nations Security Council

In parallel with the US and the FATF, the UN greatly expanded its counterterrorism and CFT efforts in the wake of 9/11 by creating a number of new entities and policy initiatives to address terrorism and terrorism financing. The Security Council adopted two key resolutions that have shaped efforts to combat terrorism financing: Resolution 1373 (2001)[31] and 2462 (2019).[32]

Led by the US,[33] Resolution 1373 requires member states to freeze the funds of persons and entities who engage in or support acts of terrorism; adopt national legislation to criminalize acts of terrorism; establish strong information-sharing channels on terrorist activity; prevent recruitment efforts among terrorist groups; and impose travel bans.[34] The resolution also called for the creation of the UN Counter-Terrorism Committee.[35]

Resolution 2462 reaffirmed existing UN Security Council Resolutions and member state anti-terrorism financing obligations and the close ties between the UN's CFT agenda and the FATF.[36] It went much further,[37] however, by making it a terrorism financing offense to "directly or indirectly" provide funds, financial assets, or other related services for any purpose for the benefit of terrorist organizations or individual terrorists – "even in the absence of a link to a specific terrorist act."[38] Resolution 2462 fills in gaps left by Resolution 1373 by calling on member states to give due consideration to their international legal obligations including under human rights, humanitarian, and refugee law when implementing CFT measures, thus attempting to mitigate the potential harm caused to NGOs.[39]

The UN's counterterrorism architecture – and its budget – continue to grow at an exponential pace, with increasing concerns about the need for more oversight, transparency, and accountability.[40]

PART II: IMPACT ON PALESTINIAN NGOS AND CIVIL SOCIETY

Closing civic space

Civic space is rapidly deteriorating on a global scale; according to CIVICUS, "only 3.2% of the world's population lives in countries with open civic space."[41] Defined by Civic Space Watch as "the political, legislative, social and economic environment which enables citizens to come together, share their interests and concerns and act individually and collectively to influence and shape their societies,"[42] civic space encompasses fundamental rights such as freedom of peaceful assembly, expression, and association.[43] The increasing closure of civic space comes in many forms; this section will demonstrate how this includes restrictions on access to banking and financial services, and the resulting harms caused to Palestinian NGOs and civil society.

There are few places in the world where restrictions on civic space and access to banking services are more acute than Palestine. Consider that when Israel declared its independent statehood on May 15, 1948 after the British Mandatory administration withdrew, one of the first things it did was order all banks to freeze Palestinian Arab customers' accounts.[44] If the banks failed to obey the order, they were threatened with revocation of their licenses. All Palestinian Arabs lost access to their funds and personal property housed in the lockboxes of the banks.

Controlling the funds of an individual or entity can be weaponized to restrict access to civic space. And today, in maintaining the occupation of Gaza and the West Bank, including East Jerusalem, Israel's control of access to banking is deployed to limit the activities of Palestinian NGOs and civil society.

The October 7 Hamas attack, and Israel's subsequent relentless assault on Gaza, has both significantly changed the landscape and exacerbated the existing challenges of financial exclusion, de-risking, and access to banking services for Palestinian civil society actors. Palestinian civil society and those wishing to support them in rights-promotion or for humanitarian concerns have come under even greater scrutiny and are facing new allegations of supporting terrorism and smear campaigns. Though such allegations have been leveled many times over the decades,[45] they have not been substantiated. While Israel perpetrates the most catastrophic military assault on Palestinians in Gaza not witnessed since World War II,[46] allegations – even unsubstantiated ones – could result in the immediate drying up of funds and the cutting off of financial services to a targeted NGO or civil society actor.

The weaponization of counterterrorism measures

The case of UNRWA: unfounded terrorism accusations and allegations

In late January 2024,[47] Israel accused twelve United Nations Relief and Works Agency for Palestine Refugees (UNRWA) staff of involvement in the October 7 Hamas attack, claiming it had "evidence highlighting UNRWA's ties to terrorism."[48] The announcement of these allegations coincided with the day the International Court of Justice released its findings that Israel's actions in Gaza amount to "plausibly genocidal."[49] The allegations led to sixteen countries suspending their voluntary contributions to UNRWA, causing the organization to lose an estimated $440 million in revenue and to be at severe risk of terminating their operations.[50] UNRWA took immediate steps in response to the Israeli allegations, firing nine accused staff and opening two investigations into the claims. In early March, Israel made additional accusations that UNRWA was employing 450 Hamas and other armed militants.[51] Save the US, all countries have since resumed funding to UNRWA;[52] the US funding, which provides one-third of the agency's budget,[53] has been prohibited by Congress until March 2025 through the Further Consolidated Appropriations Act, 2024.[54] With this, UNRWA is facing its most difficult period since it was established in 1949.[55]

At the time of writing an investigation into Israel's allegations by the UN Office of Internal Oversight Services (OIOS), the UN's equivalent of an attorney general's office, is ongoing at the time of writing. However, Israel still has not provided the investigators with any evidence to support their initial claims.[56] As of March 14, 2024, top humanitarian officials at the European Commission and the European Union (EU) stated that neither they nor "any other UNRWA donor had been presented with evidence by Israel."[57] Additionally, UNRWA staff who were detained by Israel reported that they were pressured and coerced into falsely stating that UNRWA staff participated in the attacks on October 7 and have ties to Hamas.[58] As of April 26, some cases within the OIOS investigation were closed or suspended due to a lack of sufficient evidence from Israel.[59] In April, a finalized UN secretary-general-appointed investigation into the allegations against UNRWA, carried out by a UN Independent Review Group, found that "Israel made public claims that a significant number of UNRWA employees are members of terrorist organizations. However, Israel has yet to provide supporting evidence of this."[60]

UNRWA employs a total of 13,000 staff in Gaza. The organization's closure – which remains a real possibility – would be a complete disaster, as UNRWA constitutes the vast majority of Gaza's humanitarian infrastructure, while also being responsible for millions of Palestinian refugee populations in other host countries and in the occupied West Bank, including East Jerusalem.[61]

Israel has long campaigned to dismantle UNRWA due to its symbolism and mandate around the right of return for Palestinian refugees,[62] as enshrined under UN General Assembly Resolution 194.[63] In 2017, Israeli prime minister Benjamin Netanyahu stated that "It is time UNRWA be dismantled"[64] and echoed these calls in February 2024, declaring that "UNRWA's mission has to end."[65] Israel's ambassador to the UN, Gilad Erdan, stated recently that "UNRWA will never again operate in Gaza as it has prior to October 7 … Its role in Gaza is finished … UNRWA must be defunded and dismantled."[66] Israel's latest accusations against UNRWA build on their long-standing efforts to shut the agency down, employing equally long-standing tactics of tying agencies and organizations they want dismantled to terrorism.[67]

The case of the six Palestinian CSOs: instrumentalizing counterterrorism laws

In October 2021, Israel invoked its Counter-Terrorism Law of 2016 to label six Palestinian CSOs as terrorist entities without producing evidence to support their allegations.[68] As mentioned previously, Israel claims the designations are due to, *inter alia*, the six CSOs playing a central role in financing the Popular Front for the Liberation of Palestine.[69] The designations against the six organizations permit Israel to conduct asset seizures, charge their staff and leadership with terrorism offenses, shut their offices, and stop their work.[70] These designations have come under serious scrutiny from the international community.[71] And despite Israel's attempt to justify the designations to US officials,[72] the Central Intelligence Agency could not find evidence to substantiate them.[73]

None of this stopped Israeli security forces from raiding the offices of the six designated CSOs, plus a seventh, in August 2022.[74] During the raid, Israeli security forces issued closure orders, confiscated property, and seized assets. According to many of the targeted Palestinian organizations, the primary goal of the designations and raids was to smear and hamper the organizations in order to reduce external funding to them and force them to close down.[75] Indeed, research shows this is the primary goal of the majority of these types of designations, politically motivated attacks, and terrorist financing allegations.[76] In the case of two of the designated CSOs, the European Commission suspended funding for thirteen months before resuming support in June 2022.[77] One of these CSOs, Al-Haq, noted the wider negative impacts of this temporary funding suspension: "The fact that [Al-Haq] has been suspected of financing terrorism for over a year on the basis of information that has no factual basis, is in itself damaging to its reputation."[78]

These designations restrict civic space for Palestinian CSOs and the communities they support, disrupting not only immediate funding, but making potential donors reluctant to fund these organizations, and causing reputational harm. Further, banks may refuse to transfer funds to designated groups to avoid future legal complications.[79] Likewise, they serve to redirect focus away from these organizations' work to fighting the allegations. It wastes the organizations' valuable time, is resource-intensive, and creates "a chilling effect on all organizations that work in Palestine, or that wish to do so."[80]

The case of the Holy Land Foundation: sham trials and sham due process

The misuse of counterterrorism measures (CTMs) is nothing new. Since 9/11, the US has had an outsized influence on the global counterterrorism architecture and agenda which has trickled down to the national level where similar CTMs have been adopted. In September 2001, the Bush administration made swift, discriminatory, and baseless accusations in the name of fighting terrorist financing to assert that NGOs were being used by terrorist entities as a front for their operations and activities.[81] Muslim NGOs were at particular risk of falling prey to these accusations and perhaps none so much as those whose work supported communities in Palestine, or that were Palestinian-led. In December 2001, the Bush administration conducted an asset freeze of the three biggest Muslim charities in the US, forcing them to close down.

The largest of these charities, the Holy Land Foundation for Relief and Development (HLF), not only had its assets frozen, but was also listed by the US as a Specially Designated Global Terrorist (SDGT).[82] HLF's mission, prior to being shut down, was to provide humanitarian aid and relief in Palestine[83] and for Palestinian refugees in Jordan and Lebanon. It was run mostly by Palestinian-American Muslims.[84] Following HLF's unsuccessful federal court challenge regarding the SDGT designation, HLF and seven associated individuals were indicted by the US and charged with various material support for terrorism (to Hamas) crimes and other associated charges.[85]

The accusation of providing material support to Hamas is especially significant due to the October 1997 US designation of Hamas as a Foreign Terrorist Organization (FTO).[86] Most engagement with an FTO is proscribed under the material support to terrorism statutes.[87] The penalties for running afoul of the material support law are severe, including exorbitant fines and strict criminal liability.[88] Thus, material support allegations can mean a death sentence for accused organizations, irrespective of whether the allegations are true.

HLF became a casualty of the Bush administration's so-called Global War on Terror, and the largest major terrorist financing "victory" post-9/11.[89] The case has been widely criticized.[90] The trials were fraught with questionable and prejudicial admissions of evidence, including "secret evidence" that the defense was not able to review for "national security reasons."[91] The jury instructions did not include a sufficient "knowledge" requirement for the defendants, which violated the defendants' rights to due process under the Fifth Amendment.[92] Further, HLF funds were sent to the same charities in the occupied Palestinian territories that the US government had also supported.[93] These problematic and controversial aspects of the trial contributed to the convictions of the defendants, some of whom remain in prison to this day.[94] The trial itself has been called a "sham"[95] and unprecedented because up until then the constitutional principles would not support the conviction of a person based on anonymous accusations.[96] However, all five of the HLF defendants were convicted without facing their accusers.

The rise of material support charges

Following the October 7 Hamas attack, donors became afraid of providing support to individuals or entities in Palestine or doing advocacy in the US in support of Palestinian rights. One reason for this is that material support accusations against US-based Palestinian organizations have increased. For instance, in late October 2023, material support allegations were brought against American Muslims for Palestine, a grassroots organization that has one Washington DC-based national office and ten chapters throughout the US,[97] and National Students for Justice in Palestine, a grassroots campus organization that has nearly 300 chapters across the US and Canada.[98] In May 2024, both groups were sued by survivors of the October 7 attack over allegations of providing material support to Hamas.[99] As with the aforementioned terrorist designations, research organization Arab Center Washington DC (ACW) cites the goal of these accusations as "put[ting] the targets on the defensive, [and] hav[ing] them expend time, energy and resources in a legal defence."[100] Additionally, these allegations create a chilling effect whereby donors are hesitant to fund groups associated with Palestine due to the reputational risk of being linked to an organization that has been accused of supporting terrorism.

One of the most devastating examples of this type of chilling effect was when Al-Shabaab, a Somalia-based al-Qaeda-affiliated insurgent group,[101] was designated as an FTO in 2008.[102] Fears of violating its own US material support law prompted the US to scale back its aid to Somalia by nearly 88%, from $237 million in 2008 to only $20 million in 2011. This also forced many international aid organizations to curtail humanitarian operations in areas where Al-Shabaab was present. Prior to this, the US had been the largest humanitarian aid donor in Somalia. Those who work in spaces that support Palestinian organizations and rights activists have noted that often this chilling effect on donors is the intention behind these types of allegations.[103] The ACW explains that "Reputational damage – putting stress and intimidation on the organizations – is the point. It's not really to win."[104]

Palestine's banking sector

The banking sector's development in the occupied Palestinian territories was positively impacted by the Oslo Accords in 1993 and 1995.[105] Following the creation of the Palestine Monetary Authority, a public, independent institution that develops and implements banking and financial policies to ensure growth and stability,[106] Palestine's banking sector flourished.[107] During this time, new FIs were authorized to open branches and to operate. In late 2009, Palestine had 209 branches under twenty licensed FIs, with three Islamic and ten foreign banks.

However, this era of prosperity was severely disrupted by the 2006 Palestinian Legislative Council elections.[108] After Hamas won the majority of seats in the parliament, Canada and the Middle East Quartet, a multilateral group composed of the EU, the UN, Russia, and the US, imposed an aid suspension on the then Hamas-led Palestinian Authority (PA).[109] According to a case study on "Humanitarian Action in the Occupied Palestinian Territory," during this time, Israel withheld "between $50 and $60 million in VAT customs and duties that it collects on behalf of the PA every month."[110] Further disruptions to financial flows were caused by Israel's imposition of a blockade on Gaza to force Hamas out of governance, coupled with the cuts to aid from international donors. The PA was unable to pay the salaries of its nearly 160,000 civil servants.[111] The impact on the PA and the Palestinian financial system resulted in dire hardships for Palestinians.[112] Eventually, the EU established a "Temporary International Mechanism" to provide some PA employees with salaries and basic services.

Further disruptions came under the former US president Donald Trump's administration. In 2019, then president Trump requested that international banks stop transfers to the Fatah-ruled PA in an attempt to force Palestinian leadership based in the occupied West Bank to acquiesce to President Trump's new "peace plan"[113] (the administration denied it told banks this at the time).[114] As a result, Palestinians and Palestinian entities still face limitations on the number of international banks to which they have access.[115] As a workaround, Palestinians have tried to turn to cryptocurrencies such as bitcoin "to bypass Israeli control" and to support making and receiving international transfers.[116] Policies and actions since October 7 notwithstanding, after taking office in January 2021, US president Joe Biden reversed many of the Trump administration's policies toward Palestine, and resumed many diplomatic ties and relationships, including with the PA.[117]

In late June 2024, Israel renewed a waiver providing indemnification to Israeli banks working with Palestinian banks in the occupied West Bank,[118] which would have expired had the four-month extension not been granted.[119] This waiver temporarily prevents the PA's financial collapse, with the International Crisis Group warning that "Without it, the Palestinian economy could face a liquidity crisis and a meltdown with dire consequences for West Bank Palestinians."[120] In a "quid-pro-quo" exchange,[121] Israel's finance minister Bezalel Smotrich extended the waiver and released some of the PA's frozen funds – demanding authorization of five illegal Israeli-occupied West Bank settlements in return.[122] Prior to this exchange, Smotrich was "with[holding] hundreds of millions in funding for the Palestinian Authority."[123] This comes amidst an economic crisis in the occupied West Bank that is described by regional experts as "the most difficult yet."[124]

Financial exclusion: discriminatory banking practices and de-risking

The case of the Co-operative Bank: de-risking and defamation

Palestinian NGOs and civil society actors face many banking challenges and financial restrictions in the occupied West Bank and Gaza, outside of weaponized CTMs. Account closures are another form of exclusion from financial services and relationships. The case of the Palestine Solidarity Campaign (PSC), the UK's largest organization committed to ensuring human rights and freedom for Palestinians, is illustrative.[125] The organization's bank account with the Co-operative Bank (the Co-op) was closed in October 2015, along with those of fellow PSC chapters and other organizations supporting Palestine.[126] These organizations met the Bank's compliance standards and shared requested information with the Co-op.[127] Despite this, according to the Bank, PSC's account closure was due to the Co-op's "risk appetite." PSC sought legal advice which yielded findings that the Co-op's decision both violated the UK's

Equality Act 2010 and was discriminatory due to PSC's "cogent belief in Palestinian rights." The Co-op made public statements to multiple media outlets citing an inability to complete due diligence inspections to their satisfaction "to ensure that funds do not 'inadvertently fund illegal or other proscribed activities'."[128]

The Co-op statements implying that PSC activities are linked to international terrorism had damning consequences for the organization and arguably contravened the Co-op's commitment to treat customers "fairly, promote human rights, and act with honesty and transparency."[129] PSC was added to World Check's database, which houses news, data, and information on "high risk" organizations, individuals, and politically exposed persons, to support entities undertaking compliance checks in understanding regulatory, reputational, and financial risks.[130] Being listed in the database means PSC is labeled as a "high compliance risk" throughout the financial sector.

The case of PayPal: financial exclusion and inequality

In addition to account closures, some payment platforms refuse to provide services to Palestinians altogether. For example, PayPal, a virtual payment platform (digital wallet) that enables users to transfer and receive money across the globe,[131] operates in illegal Israeli settlements in the occupied West Bank, but does not allow Palestinian residents there or in Gaza to use its platform, despite Palestinians and Israelis using the same currency, the Israeli shekel.[132] Palestinian tech companies, Palestinian and international organizations, and members of Congress have called on PayPal to end these exclusionary practices.[133] According to 7amleh, the Arab Center for the Advancement of Social Media, they amount to "inequality in access to financial services ... mak[ing] it difficult for many Palestinians to participate in the global market."[134]

Payment platforms also operate in discriminatory ways that prevent or delay transactions to Palestinian organizations and causes. In Israel's May 2021 bombardment of Gaza, PayPal subsidiary Venmo delayed transactions that involved combinations of key words such as "Palestinian," "Palestine," or "emergency fund."[135] Venmo claimed the delays were due to upholding the Treasury Department's Office of Foreign Assets Control's (OFAC) regulatory measures on Palestine. However, nothing in OFAC's regulatory regimes prevents donations in support of humanitarian aid or emergency relief in Palestine, provided they do not support a proscribed entity.[136]

Further funding and banking challenges

Banking hurdles and restrictions on Palestinian CSOs greatly impede their ability to access and deposit funds.[137] Banks often ask intrusive questions about what the organization's work entails, especially for those operating in Gaza. One Palestinian CSO noted that something as simple as a project title or a word in a contract has led banks to return transfers and to request that the wording be revised so that it is "less controversial."[138] Findings from a March 2022 "Scoping study on operating conditions of civil society in the Occupied Palestinian Territory" highlight that despite CSOs having stringent risk mitigation and due diligence measures to prevent aid diversion, donor compliance is especially complicated in Palestine due to grant contracts having restrictive clauses that "place the entire responsibility on implementing partners to comply with unreasonable anti-terrorism/aid diversion measures that are not reflective of the reality of the situation on the ground."[139]

Funding challenges are particularly pronounced for Palestinian CSOs that operate in Gaza, that have been the victim of Israeli smear campaigns, or that operate in specific parts of the occupied West Bank which the Israeli government has designated for illegal Israeli settlements.[140] Projects in Gaza are also more resource- and time-intensive, as they have heightened reporting requirements. The ruling authority in Gaza, Hamas, must approve CSO projects, while some donors prohibit CSOs they fund from any cooperation whatsoever with Hamas. This leaves CSOs in a protracted predicament without a feasible solution and deprives Palestinian communities of vital services and aid.

The Humanitarian Policy Group working paper, "A humanitarian sector in debt," reported that financial access impediments in Palestine occur in a variety of ways.[141] One occurs locally, with administrative procedures, taxes, and registration fees required by Hamas differing from the NGO fees and burdensome approval processes for transfers required by the PA's Ministry of the Interior. Another occurs regionally, with Israeli occupation authorities and governments in the region restricting funds transfers in an attempt to avoid engaging with Hamas.[142] A third occurs internationally, with the global financial system, where funds transfers to NGOs in the occupied

Palestinian territories face heavy restrictions due to AML/CFT regulations that require expensive compliance costs. One of the main challenges at the international level is de-risking, which creates barriers in funds being transferred to and from Palestinian NGOs, individuals, and organizations. This, in turn, creates further challenges, as de-risking leads to donor reluctance in providing funding to Palestinian NGOs in Gaza due to the reputational risks associated with working in a Hamas-controlled area. De-risking has reputational repercussions for Palestinian NGOs, as transaction delays or account closures result in funders being hesitant to work with organizations that have experienced this, potentially impacting further funding opportunities.[143] These constraints have led to financial exclusion from the international financial system for much of the Palestinian population.[144]

FIs deem almost every area where an FTO operates, such as Hamas in Gaza, as falling into the "high risk" category, making them *less likely* to develop and maintain banking relationships in these areas, and *more likely* to de-risk clients operating in these areas. Gaza also faces financial isolation due to Israel's ongoing blockade. Additionally, the Tahrir Institute for Middle East Policy highlights how Israel's ongoing occupation also means it "can freeze or close bank accounts at any moment for any individual or organization it accuses of being affiliated with Hamas."[145] Since October 7, Palestinian NGOs have faced intensified restrictions on funding by European countries, including for some of their most essential programs, which are needed now more than ever.[146]

Finally, the legal and compliance complexities of Treasury Department counterterrorism sanctions and regulations[147] on Palestine create bank hesitancy in conducting transactions with Palestinian NGOs and civil society, in addition to creating donor hesitancy in funding organizations and projects in Palestine.[148]

As a plausible case of genocide has been unfolding in Gaza,[149] and the UN has deemed northern Gaza to be facing a "full-blown famine,"[150] Palestinians' bank accounts are being frozen or blocked. For example, Neobanks Payoneer and Wise started blocking Palestinians' bank accounts in late October 2023 without providing warnings beforehand or reasons as to why, and only a limited number of account holders have had their accounts restored.[151] Some of the reasons Payoneer and Wise cited for these closures included the need to conduct due diligence checks, compliance requirements and regulatory policies and obligations, and elevated risk levels associated with terrorism financing.¹⁵² Compliance with terrorism financing laws and worries about running afoul of financial regulations play a continued leading role in decision making within FIs.

CONCLUSION

Measures targeting cashflow and banking access have been used to obstruct Palestinian NGOs and civil society from 1948 onward. The immediate aftermath of 9/11 exacerbated these challenges, with a flurry of new terrorist financing regulations that mischaracterized NPOs and did not account for the negative impacts these regulations might have on NPO operations. These include the implementation of global AML/CFT regulations, the expansion of overbroad domestic legal regimes, the weaponization of CTMs, discriminatory banking practices, donor hesitancy, smear campaigns, terrorist allegations, de-risking, and fifty-seven years of Israeli occupation.¹⁵³ Palestinian NGOs and civil society deserve equitable access to the global financial system and free and open civic space; this can be achieved through political will, regulatory and policy change, and stable banking relationships and services. Palestinians have been asked to wait too long for change – they quite simply cannot afford to wait any longer.

PART THREE

TRANSNATIONAL REPRESSION AND THE IMPACT ON ARAB CONSTITUENCIES IN THE US AND ABROAD

12

Closing Spaces Beyond Borders: Israel's Transnational Repression Network

Yousef Munayyer

Over the last decade, advocates for Palestinian rights in Western democracies have become targets of smear campaigns, lawfare, and legislation aimed at curtailing their civil liberties and ability to organize and engage in advocacy. This is a product of a calculated Israeli government strategy to silence critics. This chapter details the genesis and evolution of this strategy and describes the increasingly aggressive tactics deployed to restrict speech and activism in support of Palestinian rights beyond Israel's borders. In addition, it examines the infrastructure, policies, and international networks of non-governmental and quasi-governmental actors established since 2005 that have been working with Israeli authorities – either in tandem or in partnership – to suppress Palestinian solidarity advocacy.

THROWING THE BOOMERANG

Over the last two decades, criticism of Israel's treatment of Palestinians has grown significantly around the world. Three key moments contributed disproportionately to this phenomenon: the apparent collapse of Palestinian–Israeli negotiations in the early 2000s, the International Court of Justice's advisory opinion on Israel's separation wall as contrary to international law in the occupied West Bank in 2004, and the Palestinian civil society call to boycott, divest from, and sanction Israel in 2005.

Israel's treatment of Palestinians and rule over Arab territories over decades has led to several regional wars, military occupation of territory, mounting human rights abuses and humanitarian crises, and varied multilateral and international efforts at peace-making. Following the end of the Cold War, the Palestine Liberation Organization (PLO) and Israel signed the Oslo Accords, which appeared to many as an opportunity to reach a comprehensive Palestinian–Israeli settlement. As peace talks collapsed in 2000, after no agreement could be reached on Jerusalem or Palestinian refugees' right of return, the Second Intifada broke out.

By 2004, in a seminal advisory opinion,[1] the International Court of Justice ruled Israel's wall of separation built inside the occupied West Bank illegal under international law, raising hopes among some for the prospects for internationalizing a solution to the Israel–Palestine conflict. As the situation on the ground in the occupied territories worsened and political leaders and processes failed to advance just outcomes, Palestinians looked to develop new avenues to advance their search for rights and security. With the vacuum of leadership left by states, Palestinians increasingly turned to international institutions and global civil society actors to put pressure on state authorities to act – a phenomenon Keck and Sikkink labeled the "boomerang pattern" in their seminal work on transnational activism.[2]

As Israel continued to entrench its occupation and expand its wall of separation, apartheid road system, and settlements in the West Bank, Palestinian civil society organizations sought a greater role for global civil society in the effort to confront the occupation and advance the goal of a just peace for the Palestinian people. A year after the International Court of Justice advisory opinion, Palestinian civil society organizations issued a call to "international civil society organizations and people of conscience all over the world to impose broad boycotts and implement divestment initiatives against Israel similar to those applied to South Africa in the apartheid era."[3] Endorsed by 170 different Palestinian civil society organizations, the boomerang had been thrown.

In the years immediately after the call for Boycott, Divestment, and Sanctions (BDS), the Israeli state was largely ambivalent about the potential of global civil society to successfully generate pressure on the Israeli state regarding its treatment of Palestinians. Over the next five years, however, ambivalence gave way to growing concern within the Israeli government about the increase in international criticism of its policies toward Palestinians, particularly following the 2008–2009 Israeli war on the Gaza Strip. The brutality of that military campaign led to a series of international human rights reports examining whether Israel's use of force against Palestinians violated international humanitarian law and the laws of war, most notable among them being the Report of the United Nations Fact Finding Mission on the Gaza Conflict. In what came to be referred to as the "Goldstone Report," a commission of three factfinders found credible evidence of war crimes and potential crimes against humanity perpetrated by Israel and Palestinian militant groups. The Report, along with the highly publicized 2010 Israeli naval attack on a flotilla composed of international solidarity activists, in which nine people were killed, raised growing questions about the legitimacy of Israeli policies. As international civil society answered the Palestinian call to adopt BDS tactics, the legitimacy of Israel's policies toward Palestinians faced increased scrutiny. According to Ronnie Olesker, during this period, the Israeli government experienced a "moment of rupture which catalyzed a securitized Israeli government response."[4]

ATTACKING THE BOOMERANG

The initial Israeli response to this, according to Olesker, came in 2007 at the relaunch of Palestinian–Israeli peace talks. For the first time, Israel elevated the demand that the PLO recognize Israel as a Jewish state as part of a comprehensive peace deal.[5] The PLO, as the internationally recognized representative of the Palestinian people, had already recognized the state of Israel in 1993 in the Oslo I Accord. This new Israeli demand aimed to obtain Palestinian acceptance of, and international legitimacy for, Israel's majoritarian system, privileging Jews over non-Jews. Palestinian leaders rejected this demand, asserting it would undermine the status of Palestinian citizens of Israel and prejudice the claims of Palestinian refugees for return and reparations. As this approach to bolster Israel's legitimacy through concessions in the negotiation process failed, members of the Israeli policy community were also pointing out the failures of existing government agencies in responding to the "threat" posed to Israel by growing global civil society activism.

The earliest and most extensive critique of the Israeli government's shortcomings in confronting international civil society campaigns in solidarity with Palestinians came from the Reut Institute, an Israeli think tank that was "established to serve Israeli government agencies and decision makers."[6] Its

2010 conceptual framework entitled "Building a political firewall against Israel's delegitimization" made several key policy recommendations that would end up shaping the Israeli government response in the years to come.[7] Reut argued that it was insufficient to defend Israeli policy from global dissenters; instead Israel had to go on the offense against the dissenters themselves. To do so, it proposed the adoption of a network-based strategy that would rely on the development of a series of catalysts and hubs throughout the world. These hubs, which would have great sensitivity to their own local contexts and nuances, would be used to "exchange information, coordinate, brand, create a sense of urgency."[8]

Reut warned that the Ministry of Foreign Affairs and other state agencies were ill-equipped to respond effectively to the new challenge presented by the "delegitimization" campaign, maintaining that it was new in both structure and scope and unlike anything Israel had experienced before. It asserted that it was vital to organize an effective response because "it takes a network to fight a network." Five years later, the state comptroller of Israel came to a similar conclusion in a report concerning the failure of the Ministry of Foreign Affairs to combat the "threat" of BDS.[9]

Late in 2015, the Israeli government took significant action to shift course. It handed a mandate to a single government ministry, the Ministry of Strategic Affairs (MSA), "to act against the delegitimization and boycott campaigns against the state of Israel." The responsibilities of the ministry included "the formation, inclusion, and coordination of government efforts to deal with the phenomenon in all its aspects." The Ministry was mandated to work with "non-governmental organizations in Israel and around the world" to "advance the objectives of the campaign and its strategies" including through "diplomacy, consciousness, academic, economic, cultural, and legal activity." This single ministry would act as "the leading government agency for all the relevant ministries and governmental bodies"[10] and would be in contact with pro-Israel organizations fighting in this campaign in countries across the world.

Immediately after its formation, the MSA drew heavily on the conclusions and recommendations of Reut's 2010 report, particularly when it came to creating a network-based approach and going on the offensive. In fact, the phrases "it takes a network to fight a network" and shifting "from defense to offense" come directly from Reut and were used regularly by ministry officials to describe their work. The MSA understood its responsibilities and became the central agency coordinating the Israeli government's global effort to attack the work of activists and the organizations involved in boycotts and criticism of Israel. In 2016, the first full year of operation, the Ministry spent time building up staff and offices. One year later, its work became more robust.[11] According to its 2017 annual report, the Ministry "builds the infrastructure required for the operation of pro-Israel organizations as an organized network." It described the pro-Israel network as an "array of NGOs deployed around the world that engage in pro-Israel activities."[12]

The Ministry's annual reports offer more insight into the network it sought to coordinate. The 2018 report discussed ongoing efforts "to create the necessary infrastructure for the operation of pro-Israel organizations as an organized network" which included convening "3 professional networks: the main pro-Israel organizations, the network of lawyers and the network of social media influencers."[13] The 2019 report identified these three sub-networks as the Global Coalition for Israel (GC4I), the Legal Network Initiative (LNI), and the DigiTell Network.[14]

Jonathan Neuberger, the director of international cooperation at the Ministry at the time, said during a panel event that those "best-equipped to fight delegitimization and BDS" are "civil society together with the government." He went on to explain that his office "empowers and coordinates the work" of three sub-networks, the "GC4I, LNI and DigiTell."[15]

At another MSA network conference in 2019, Tzachi Gabrieli, the director general of the Ministry at the time, explained the natural evolution of the unified network concept. Standing before a presentation slide depicting network actors across the globe, he said:

> We understood that unless we would have unity, unless we would have all these blue dots representing different organizations doing tremendous, tremendous work, long before the state of Israel has done … You were there from the start. Long before we came along as enforcement, *heavy enforcement*. And we understood that the only thing that could really change the paradigm is this – is having the unity, is having the synergetic network. Everybody is working together in a professional manner.[16]

Gabrieli went on to describe a "network of networks," where each sub-network would be responsible for different areas. Members from the GC4I, the LNI, and the DigiTell Network were all seated in the room. He thanked them for their work, stating: "The GC4I, the LNI, the DigiTell ... safeguard the state of Israel and the Jewish people. 500 people safeguard the future of the state of Israel. You are the Iron Dome of Israel's legitimacy."[17]

THE IMPORTANCE OF SECRECY

From the beginning the MSA sought to be secretive about its activities, particularly in the early years after it was handed the mandate to fight activists around the globe. Speaking before the Special Committee for the Transparency and Accessibility of Government Information[18] in the Knesset in 2016, the director general of the Ministry, Sima Vaknin-Gil, asserted: "We want most of the work ... to be classified. There is a lot of sensitivity and I cannot even explain in a public forum why there is sensitivity ... A lot of what we do is under the radar."[19]

Transparency was not a value at the MSA, especially not early on. In fact, not only did the Ministry claim it was exempt from complying with public disclosure laws, but it also sought to advance Knesset legislation that would legally grant it an exception. In support of such legislation at the time, the minister of strategic affairs, Gilad Erdan, stated: "One of the principles for success is keeping our methods of action secret ... Since most of the ministry's actions are not of the ministry, but through bodies around the world who do not want to expose their connection with the state, we must protect the information whose exposure could harm the battle."[20]

After several years of pressure for greater transparency from Israeli advocacy groups – as well personnel changes at the MSA in 2020 – the Ministry began responding to public disclosure requests, albeit with some redactions. In the months that followed these personnel changes, the shift to greater transparency allowed for greater insight into the inner workings of the MSA and its valued networks. Financial transactions, meeting logs, and agreements between the Ministry and third parties all began to seep into the public sphere. In addition to this significant data trove, open-source information from the MSA's social media account, and those of its officials and actors in its networks, shed important light on the MSA's activities, its partners, and the conduct of their joint operations.

One slide depicting the Ministry's "main efforts and activities" summarized a presentation by Ron Brummer, then MSA director of operations. The slide identified five operational goals: creating reputational harm for BDS activists by equating them with terror and antisemitism; cutting off the money trail by targeting platforms and state funding; dealing with the "centers of gravity"; responding to real-time events; and combating leading delegitimization campaigns. The Israeli government, together with its networked NGO partners, sought to carry out this repressive activity to target critics in countries around the world with a specific emphasis on the United States and Europe.

The MSA has declined to give details about its relationship with specific network actors pursuant to public requests. Though lacking specificity, the Ministry's response does provide important insights into its activities. In one such response,[21] the MSA categorized the groups it works with accordingly:

Relationship type	"Professional engagements, open or confidential, based on an agreement."	"Ongoing working relationships with pro-Israel organizations, not within the framework of the transfer of funds."	"Organizations that are not included in sections 1 or 2, but nevertheless receive information/updates from the office and/or send updates/information to the office from time to time."
Explanation	"Contract based engagements where the Ministry pays for a service provided by the organization. These engagements go through a government tender process and some have been made public while others remain redacted."	"This relationship is characterized by the participation of the organizations in the conferences of the office and vice versa, the distribution of professional information to the organizations (such as the reports produced by the ministry) and sending mutual updates from time to time."	"Regarding these organizations, the MSA sends updates, distributes information and consults on various issues with varying frequency with different parties."

Reason for not revealing names	"The publication of the names of these organizations may harm the work of the Ministry, the organizations with which the Ministry has contracted, and will also help the adversary learn about the ways in which Israel is fighting the phenomenon of delegitimization."	"Some of the organizations with which the ministry is in contact, including the organizations that participate in the ministry's conferences, do so on the assumption that their connection to the ministry is not visible, among other things for the reasons detailed above. Therefore, the delivery of the organizations' details may disrupt the proper functioning of the office and its ability to perform its duties, as well as harm the organizations themselves."	"Tracking all of these factors constitutes an unreasonable allocation of resources."

CONCEALING PARTNER FUNDING

The MSA took extensive measures to conceal its funding of some of these actors. It did this in a number of different ways, including by passing the money through to a separate entity which would aggregate it with donations from private philanthropists. The separate entity contracted by the MSA, a public benefit corporation which went through a series of name changes (originally "Kela Shlomo," then "Concert: Together for Israel," and finally "Voices for Israel"), would then transfer the money to the network organizations. The appeal of this non-transparent approach was that government funding could get funneled to actors who may not have wanted it known that they received financial support from the Israeli government. For some actors, exposure of a financial relationship with the Israeli government could trigger regulatory oversight and/or threaten a group's reputation or independence. Alternatively, donors who wanted to partner with the government but did not want to be seen as doing so could send money to the public benefit corporation, which would then pass it on to select network actors. This rationale was described by the Israeli minister of strategic affairs as well as the head of the public benefit corporation before the Knesset transparency committee.[22]

In addition to funding that was passed through this public benefit corporation, the MSA also sought to hide information on funding that it sent directly to actors through its classification process. Dozens of transactions which were partially released via public disclosure requests have the recipients' names redacted. The dates of transactions, amounts involved, and currency are all visible, but the recipient of the funds is blacked out. In some cases, references to "exemptions" from public disclosure laws are listed as well. These explanations for why names of recipients were not shared include "Fear of harm to national security," "Information that is a trade secret or a professional secret or constitutes an infringement of an all-important interest," and "Information that may disrupt the functioning or capabilities of the ministry."[23]

IDENTIFYING NETWORK ACTORS

While the MSA refused to release a detailed roster of the network they regularly boasted about, the categories and details that they did offer, along with other information they were compelled to release as a result of public disclosure requests, provided sufficient information to identify a number of the key actors working with the Ministry in its transnational repression efforts. According to the response provided by the MSA to a public disclosure request concerning the network, the Ministry engaged in three categories of relationships with outside actors: financial/contractual ties; ongoing working relationships; and information collaboration. Documents released by the MSA which detail financial transactions, contractual agreements, and meeting schedules, along with a plethora of images and video from MSA events, provide crucial information on the identity of these actors.

Contractual agreements, tender exemptions, and rosters of financial transactions which the MSA was compelled to release publicly helped to identify ties to network actors who sustained financial or contractual relationships with the MSA during the period examined. For example, the MSA contracted the group Aish HaTorah, a right-wing Orthodox organization, for the purpose of fighting boycotts on college campuses in the United States. In their tender exemption justification, the MSA writes that "delegitimization organizations see university students and faculty in the US as a target to influence and invest in, because they will be the leaders of the world's greatest power and will be setting policy in the coming decades." Thus, they argue, "[t]he campus arena, especially in the US, is a main focus of the campaign against delegitimization."[24]

In addition to contracts and tender exemptions, the MSA also released a lengthy roster of financial transactions for every quarter of the year over multiple years. These transactions include everything from expenses for office supplies, to large grants or payments to organizations outside of Israel with which the government had a contractual relationship and others with which it did not. For example, the transaction roster includes transfers to groups like the Zionist Federation in the UK; the Czech branch of the International Christian Embassy Jerusalem; the US-based organizations Institute for the Study of Global Antisemitism and Policy, Hatzad Hasheni, and Proclaiming Justice to the Nations; the French-based CRIF (France Israel Foundation); and the Belgian Friends of Israel, among others.

In addition to a record of financial transactions with these entities, participation in the Ministry's conferences and meetings with MSA officials produced a paper trail. The MSA released the meeting diaries of the minister and director general of the Ministry, as well as conference materials, including agendas, presentations, videos, and images. These materials identify a number of event participants including groups like StandWithUs,[25] which can be seen in attendance at the conferences, along with the Anti-Defamation League, Shurat HaDin, the Lawfare Project,[26] NGO Monitor,[27] the Brandeis Center,[28] and many others. While the exact number of entities engaged in this network is unknown, for their part, MSA officials have, on multiple occasions, referred to there being somewhere between 400 and 500 actors, including organizations represented by their leaders as well as individuals in their own capacity, in different sub-networks.

REPRESSING AND DELEGITIMIZING CRITICS: AVENUES OF ATTACK

Speaking before an MSA conference for network members in 2019,[29] Gilad Erdan, the head of the MSA, heralded the Ministry's progress, along with that of "all of the relevant bodies in the Israeli government" in combating the threat presented by international civil society activism. These accomplishments included passage of anti-BDS laws in "27 US states, Congress and the UK," initiation of "more than 50 lawsuits" against civil society activists, successful court decisions against BDS activists in Spain and France, the closure of numerous "BDS bank accounts," deportation and the denial of visas for activists seeking entry to third countries, growing success in the adoption and use of the International Holocaust Remembrance Alliance (IHRA) definition of antisemitism, and the production and circulation of Ministry resources on antisemitism to "assist the pro-Israel network to convince universities" to crack down on BDS. On multiple occasions during his remarks, Erdan drew linkages between the work of his Ministry and the success of network partners in achieving repressive outcomes against international civil society organizations and actors in a number of areas, which we now examine in turn.

Shutting down bank accounts

In 2019, the German SozialBank (then the Bank für Sozialwirtschaft) shut down the account of a local Jewish organization that had advocated for the rights of Palestinians. The account of Jewish Voice for a Just Peace was closed after a letter to the bank from the group Shurat HaDin alleged the Jewish peace group was antisemitic and had ties to terrorism. The letter warned the bank that its willingness to host this account exposed it "and its officers to potential criminal and civil liability under the United States Anti-Terrorism Act."[30] Shurat HaDin works closely with the Israeli government and participated in the MSA-convened network conferences. Speaking at a Shurat HaDin event in 2019, Erdan lauded their joint success, saying "[w]e are working together with legal experts all around the world, including of course Shurat HaDin ... to close down BDS financial accounts and outlaw some of the BDS organizations ... We just had another success in closing down the bank account of, unfortunately, a Jewish BDS group in Germany."[31]

Cutting funding to Palestinian civil society

In 2016, NGO Monitor, an Israel-based organization and part of the MSA network, launched a campaign to press several European governments to end their funding for several Palestinian civil society groups critical of Israel's treatment of Palestinians and supportive of efforts to hold Israel accountable for its human rights abuses. Israeli officials and NGOs working in parallel with the Israeli government campaigned to stop European government funding to the human rights organizations.[32] In response, several of these governments announced shifts in funding policies in 2017 and 2018, resulting in cuts to the financial support they had been providing to several Palestinian human rights groups. The director general of the MSA spoke of this achievement in a speech given at a convening of the network in 2019, stating that "along with the work – amazing work being done from these tables, Denmark, Norway, Sweden, Holland, and other states that we will not reveal yet, are, in fact, canceling their allocations, budgets, grants to BDS organizations. This is groundbreaking, friends. No money? No activity. We will continue to do this because when there are no resources, there is no activity."[33]

Passing anti-BDS laws

Legislation targeting the right to boycott, divest from, or sanction Israel to hold it to account for its human rights abuses began to proliferate in the United States in 2014/2015. As of this writing some thirty different US states have adopted anti-BDS laws, several of which have been challenged successfully in US courts for violating free speech rights guaranteed under the US Constitution. MSA network entities played important roles in producing these outcomes. Some of the central players included former South Carolina state representative Alan Clemmons and the Israel Allies Foundation (IAF).[34] The author of an early anti-BDS bill in his home state, Clemmons would become closely affiliated with the IAF as well as assuming the position of national chairman of the American Legislative Exchange Council (ALEC) – a right-wing organization that brings together state legislators from around the United States to advance a common political agenda in state legislatures. Clemmons credited the IAF for its support in making the anti-BDS legislation possible. The IAF, which has received funding from the MSA's proxy funding vehicle Concert, also claimed credit for creating a model policy for attacking BDS advocates which could be replicated across states. Meeting logs indicate that the IAF's leadership has met with MSA officials on several occasions.

In 2016, ALEC also adopted a "model policy"[35] with respect to anti-BDS legislation which became a blueprint for its members who wanted to introduce and pass the laws in their state legislatures. "The goal of the resulting model policy," ALEC noted on its webpage, "will be to create disincentives to engaging in (and prohibit to the extent possible) secondary boycott activities (specifically coordinated activities, rather than individual consumer behavior) that target specific commercial entities (i.e., those that do business with Israel/and or Jews) with the intention of creating significant economic harm to Israeli or Jewish entities by exerting coercive economic pressure on those doing business with them."[36]

According to reports from a South Carolina newspaper, the *Post and Courier*,[37] Alan Clemmons caught the attention of Israeli officials after he authored legislation objecting to 2011 statements made by the Obama administration suggesting that Israel was carrying out an occupation. After these reports, Israeli officials courted Clemmons and invited him to Israel on a trip that appears to have been transformative in launching his personal engagement with the BDS issue. In 2018, Clemmons attended the MSA's Legal Network Initiative conference in Israel.[38] The agenda for this Israeli government-convened conference included sessions entitled "US state level legislation: where do we go now?" and "Legislation at the federal level in the US."[39] By 2019, Clemmons was the national chairman of ALEC and attended another MSA conference at that time.[40]

Several other MSA-linked organizations have promoted anti-BDS legislation, including the Anti-Defamation League (ADL). The ADL, which regularly appeared in the meeting logs of MSA officials and often attended MSA conferences,[41] pushed for federal anti-boycott legislation with members of Congress. The Israel Action Network, another group with links to the MSA through its parent organization, the Jewish Federations of North America,[42] claims to be "the primary organization helping communities fight municipal BDS" according to the organization's 2019 annual report.[43]

Lawfare

Several MSA network actors have been involved in the use of lawfare to repress and intimidate global civil society actors seeking to demand accountability for

Israel's human rights abuses. This activism can take multiple forms, including by sending letters threatening legal action like the ones sent to SozialBank, or submitting regulatory complaints targeting registered charities in criminal and civil proceedings. According to the *Jerusalem Post*, the MSA contracted with[44] and significantly funded an entity called the International Legal Forum (ILF) to "establish an international legal network to fight the Boycott, Divestment and Sanctions movement."[45] The ILF "would help administer grants of up to NIS 600,000 [approximately $160,000 in 2018] to members of the network, which could include jurists, lawyers and other legal professionals or organizations, to fight BDS on the legal battleground."[46]

The ILF was also a co-convenor of the 2018 LNI conference alongside the MSA and the Israeli Bar Association. A session entitled "BDS & criminal law, where, how, when?" was listed on the conference meeting agenda.[47] During this session, the president of the American Zionist Federation, Washington-based attorney Richard Heideman,[48] urged participants:

> give us a court of law where we can take an aggrieved plaintiff as a result of a discriminatory boycott, give us a jury where we can argue the discrimination, where we can argue the violation, where we can argue the damages, combine that with the court of public opinion, and combine that with the confluence of power of the congress, the administration, the court system, the victims, their families and those who wish to stand up strongly and proudly for Israel, give us a chance in the courts in the United States to make a difference.[49]

In the year that followed this conference, the US Campaign for Palestinian Rights (USCPR), the largest coalition supporting Palestinian rights advocacy in the United States, was sued by the Jewish National Fund and other plaintiffs for its advocacy. The suit alleged that the USCPR was liable for upwards of $90 million in damages to the plaintiffs under anti-terror laws. Richard Heideman's firm represented the plaintiffs. The ILF claimed to have recruited the plaintiffs and amassed the research for the suit.[50] After the trial court dismissed the spurious claims, the plaintiffs appealed with the help of the MSA's legal network and LNI conference participant attorney Alyza Lewin.[51] The appellants lost their appeal in the DC circuit and the Supreme Court declined to review the matter. Despite the failure of the legal case, it may have achieved the plaintiffs' objectives: to distract and intimidate effective critics of Israeli policy by jeopardizing their reputations and raising the cost of their advocacy.

The USCPR case is but one example of lawfare initiated by participants in the MSA's legal network. Representatives from many other organizations which have engaged in lawfare to intimidate and silence dissent have been linked to the MSA through their presence and participation in network events identified in material secured through the public disclosure requests.

Redefining antisemitism

Another tactic to silence critics of Israeli policy that has become popular since 2019 concerns efforts to redefine antisemitism. By conflating criticism of Israel with antisemitism, a new set of repressive tools and practices became available in the MSA's strategy. Anti-discrimination laws have been weaponized to repress pro-Palestinian rights speech and expressions of Palestinian narratives and national identity. This new tactic came at a very specific and pivotal moment. Between 2015 and 2018, anti-BDS laws were successfully challenged on free speech grounds in some US courts. In January of 2018, an injunction was granted against a Kansas anti-BDS law.[52] In September of that year, a similar ruling in Arizona[53] was announced. And in April 2019, a court in the conservative state of Texas found[54] an anti-BDS law violated free speech protections guaranteed under the US Constitution. The message from all of this was clear: anti-BDS legislation would continue to clash with the First Amendment and, even worse for the planners of this repressive strategy, the approach was counterproductive as it created common cause between BDS advocates and free speech defenders who had not previously been active on Palestine issues.

By redefining BDS as antisemitism, the MSA and its allies sought to circumvent free speech protections and hijack anti-discrimination law for repressive purposes. This shift is also notable in the material published by the MSA over this period. This included several significant reports aimed at branding the BDS effort in a negative light in the hopes of pushing countries and institutions to sever ties with or sanction dissenters engaged in these efforts. In a forty-page May 2018 report entitled "The money trail,"[55] aimed at convincing EU institutions to cut funding ties to Palestinian and international civil society organizations based on their support for non-violent BDS efforts, the word "antisemitism" does not appear at all. Instead, it describes several groups described as "anti-Israel." The next major output of the MSA was a report entitled "Terrorists in suits,"[56] alleging ties between NGOs promoting BDS and perpetrators or supporters of terrorism. In this seventy-six-page MSA report issued in February 2019, "antisemitism" or "antisemitic" appears twice, in passing, while the preferred adjective applied to groups the MSA was seeking to smear is "anti-Israel" – a term that appears nineteen times in the report. A new MSA report issued a few months later, however, adopts a very different approach which is aimed squarely at branding BDS as "antisemitic." The September 2019 "Behind the mask" report is ninety-four pages long and includes a striking 287 references to "antisemitic" or "antisemitism." This development represents a clear and significant messaging shift on the part of the MSA. And, lest there be any doubt, the foreword to the report, which is written in part by Alan Dershowitz, is entitled "BDS discrimination is not freedom of speech."

Alyza Lewin, the head of the Brandeis Center for Human Rights Law and participant in the MSA's LNI network, has outlined the strategic logic behind this shift toward near-exclusive emphasis on opposition to the political ideology of Zionism, or criticism of Israel, as a form of discrimination. In an address delivered to a meeting of the LNI convened by the MSA in 2019, Lewin asks: "Why is it so important that you be able to articulate how Zionism is a key component of Jewish identity and how pro-Israel Zionists are being discriminated against on the basis of this shared ethnic characteristic?"[57] Her response to the audience of lawyers gathered by the MSA left little doubt about the strategy being adopted:

> The answer, my friends, lies in the law. Our laws are designed to protect individuals from harassment and discrimination. The law does not protect you from an opinion you find offensive. In the United States, even hate speech is protected speech. So, if we want to be able to effectively utilize our legal tools, we must act – accurately articulate what is happening as harassment and discrimination. If we fail to do this, we won't be able to use the tools in our toolbox. If we permit administrators on university campuses, representatives on Capitol Hill, and the public to perceive the situation as merely a political disagreement where each side takes offense at the other side's position, then we neuter the most important weapons in our arsenal. So, I implore you for several reasons: articulate what is happening using the language of discrimination.[58]

Similarly, the director general of the MSA made clear that the agenda was to use the IHRA definition of antisemitism as a weapon against "BDS organizations" because "this is exactly what they fear." He went on to tell the audience of network actors convened by the MSA in its 2019 meeting that BDS organizations are vulnerable to "being portrayed, being called as antisemites" and that it is incumbent upon all those gathered in the room to work so that "the IHRA definition will be accepted in more and more countries, more and more municipalities, more and more universities."[59] From the same dais, a video was played to the audience promoting the use of the IHRA definition as a weapon against BDS. It lays out a process of hegemonizing the IHRA definition in Western countries, and then demanding its enforcement against BDS, as a strategy for conveniently circumventing free expression protections. It ends with a simple message: "if you accept IHRA you can't accept BDS," and a graphic showing the letters BDS stamped out by the logo of the IHRA.

There have been several cases of the IHRA being deployed to stifle criticism of Israel. One example reported by the *Guardian* involved a class being taught at an American college on apartheid in Israel–Palestine. A representative of the Israeli government, through its consulate, tried to persuade the college to cancel the course "on the grounds that it breached the controversial International Holocaust Remembrance Alliance (IHRA) definition of anti-Semitism." Along with pressure from the Israeli government, the college also came under pressure from the ADL, a participant in the GC4I network, as well as from a significant donor to the school who had ties to the ADL. This case demonstrates how both state and non-state actors can come together to push for a repressive outcome, in this case canceling a college class on a topic they don't want discussed. The college didn't yield but, in the process, lost a significant donor and suffered a degree of reputational damage as it was smeared for tolerating "antisemitism."

A FUTURE OF INTENSIFYING REPRESSION

Israeli elections in 2021 finally dislodged Benjamin Netanyahu from the office of prime minister after multiple election cycles, bringing about some changes to the Israeli government. One of those shifts was the dissolution of the MSA and the relocation of its portfolio – including its anti-BDS activity

– and much of its staff to the Ministry of Foreign Affairs. When Netanyahu regained the premiership in 2023, however, he charged a new ministry, the Ministry of Diaspora Affairs (MDA), with the same responsibilities that the MSA had from 2015 to 2021. Led by Netanyahu confidant Amichai Chikli, the MDA, which added "and Combating Antisemitism" to its title, would be empowered to continue with the same agenda as the MSA.[60] While the machinery of government agencies has evolved somewhat over the years, the commitment of the government to partner with a network of like-minded non-governmental actors for the purpose of combating international criticism of Israeli policies has remained consistent. In early 2023, Chikli presented his proposals for the continuation of this transnational mission before the Israeli Knesset, and in the wake of the October 7 Hamas attack and the 2023 Israeli war on Gaza, the international coordination to repress human rights defenders and Israel's critics only intensified.[61]

During the first months of the post-October 7 period, as this chapter was being completed, growing criticism of Israel's military campaign and siege in Gaza and the humanitarian disaster that engulfed the 2.3 million men, women, and children there presented a massive public relations challenge for the Netanyahu coalition, particularly among young people and on college campuses globally. The MDA along with the Ministry of Foreign Affairs quickly "formulated an action plan aimed at inflicting economic and employment consequences on protesting students and compelling universities to distance them from their campuses," according to a news report in the Israeli newspaper *Ynet*.[62] This campaign reportedly seeks "Personal, economic and employment repercussions for the distributors of 'anti-Semitism'" and will "examine options against civil society organizations active in the United States and in general."[63]

This transnational repression strategy is a response to global dissent against Israeli violations of Palestinian human rights and it was well underway prior to October 7, 2023. The Israel war on Gaza that followed October 7, however, has already led to a dramatic escalation in these types of repressive efforts. Israel's conduct in Gaza has provoked massive mobilizations around the world, as well as charges of genocide before the International Court of Justice and a second case at the World Court challenging Israel's prolonged occupation of Palestinian land is pending. The stage is being set for a new era of intensified global dissent against Israeli policy. Israel's wars on Gaza in 2008–2009 and 2014 led to significant increases in international criticism and immediately preceded the shift in Israeli government strategy toward a transnational repression response. This most recent war is of a categorically different magnitude, as are the degree of violations of human rights and international law inherent in it, and it logically follows that the scale of dissent and civil society challenges to Israeli policy around the world will follow suit. In turn, Israel is likely to depend even more on its transnational repression efforts and as it does it will build upon the foundation laid during the crucial and formative period covered in this chapter. As this book was going to press, in late August 2024, the Israeli war on Gaza that followed October 7, however, has already led to a dramatic escalation in these types of repressive efforts.[64]

13

From Exclusion to Erasure: The Attempt to Silence Arab Americans on Palestine

Maya Berry

ROOTED IN PALESTINIAN HUMAN RIGHTS

There are an estimated 3.7 million Arab Americans in the United States today.[1] As a collective, they are not, nor have they been, a single-issue constituency.[2] Yet the majority of Arab Americans have consistently identified with and advocated for Palestinian human rights. Much of the scholarship marks the period after the 1967 Arab–Israeli War, when most of the community's institutions were founded, as a critical moment in Arab American political empowerment. It was then that the community adopted a distinctly political focus that went beyond village associations, or the religious, social and cultural organizations formed in the earlier years of Arab immigration to the United States.[3] However, support for Palestinian self-determination arguably predates the formation of the Arab American identity as generally understood.[4]

In 1915, two years before the Balfour Declaration would proclaim the British government's intentions concerning "the establishment in Palestine of a national home for the Jewish people,"[5] prominent Lebanese writer Mikhail Naimy rejected political Zionism, and the notion that Palestine was "an empty land devoid of inhabitants."[6] Naimy and Kahlil Gibran, who together with other prominent writers formed the historic Pen League in New York City in 1920, were leading voices among the recent immigrants. This group of intellectuals, who first considered themselves Syrian, and then later, Arab nationalists, wrote in defense of Palestine.⁷ After World War I, they helped create a vibrant literary scene and founded many newspapers which advocated for Palestinian self-determination and opposed British and French colonial rule, and Anglo-Zionist plans for Palestine.⁸

Another co-founder of the Pen League, Lebanese poet and writer Ameen Rihani, along with Palestinian doctor Fuad Shatara, who were both members of the Palestine National League, played a significant role in Arab American engagement on Palestine.⁹ Shatara testified as an American citizen before the US House of Representatives Foreign Affairs Committee at a hearing about the Balfour Declaration in April 1922, stating:

> This [Palestine] is our national home, the national home of the Palestinians and I think those people are entitled to priority as the national home of the Palestinians and not aliens who have come in and have gradually become a majority.¹⁰

Rihani's countless contributions ranged from attending the Paris Peace Conference in 1919 to meeting with secretary of state Henry Stimson and British prime minister James Ramsay MacDonald during his visit to the United States in 1929.¹¹ This engagement with elected officials was undertaken on behalf of an Arab American community and its associated organizations that represented community interests before elected officials. Besides their advocacy efforts with policymakers, they also worked to address the anti-Arab bias in media coverage about Palestine. Like contemporary attempts to give context to unfolding events in Palestine/Israel that refer to the seventy-six years of Palestinian dispossession or the fifty-seven years of Israeli military occupation, they attempted to provide background on the violence in the region during their time.

> This effort first drew the attention of the press on August 29, 1929 when *The New York Times* reported that "a group of Arabian citizens [sic] and sympathizers living in or near New York met yesterday afternoon [August 28] to protest against the unfairness [of press reports] dealing with the present Palestine rioting."¹²

While perhaps not unusual for 1929, Arab Americans were not acknowledged as American citizens and were instead presented as foreign, "Arabian citizens." This other-ization of Americans of Arab descent world persists today and contributes to bias against and the marginalization of the Arab American community – and sometimes their "sympathizers."

PALESTINE AND THE POLITICS OF EXCLUSION

In the decades that followed, the size of the Arab American community would grow, and its efforts to build power would continue to meet roadblocks related to advocacy on behalf of Palestine and Palestinian rights. Like other constituencies, Arab Americans had to organize, increase their voter rolls, and join interest groups, value coalitions, and political parties, to name but a few paths to finding their place in electoral politics. However, unlike most other ethnic constituencies, they faced a unique challenge: their seat at the civic engagement table was restricted by a zero-sum mindset that viewed Arab American access as directly oppositional to Jewish Americans. The fact that many of the most prominent organizations of the Jewish American community, including some whose mission was to combat hate and discrimination, were actively pushing back against Arab American inroads in politics, media, and academia enabled that thinking, or, at best, simply reinforced it.[13]

The effort to restrict the involvement of Arab Americans in politics and to prevent their engagement as a constituency on the issue of Palestine was first dubbed the "politics of exclusion," and included "Arab-baiting,"[14] where the political involvement of Arab Americans is restricted so as to prevent their engagement as a constituency on the issue of Palestine. According to community advocate Helen Samhan: "This form of political racism consists primarily of harassing candidates for being affiliated with any sort of organized Arab American effort."[15] The basis for the exclusion is not only rooted in the constituency's ethnic origin, but also in the nature of their political activity, which "takes prejudice and exclusion out of the arena of personal relations into the arena of public information and public policy."[16]

In a discussion lamenting the nature of anti-Arab bias prevalent in America, historian Michael Suleiman relayed the following conversation he had with Ibrahim Abu-Lughod, a co-founder of the Association of Arab-American University Graduates, and a person Edward Said would call "Palestine's foremost academic and intellectual":[17]

As Ibrahim Abu-Lughod once said to me in almost utter despair: "We thought the problem was lack of organization, so we organized; then we thought it was the absence of factual and objective information, so we provided it through lectures and conferences; then we thought it was the fact that publishers refused to publish our manuscripts, so we set up our own press; now we find that distribution of our publications is blocked. Will there ever come a time when we can present our viewpoint to the general public without it being deflected, distorted or blocked?"[18]

The entire enterprise of an ethnic constituency organizing to represent, protect, or advocate for its interests was deemed outside of the margin of acceptable political discourse or engagement because it challenged the American political establishment orthodoxy of unconditional support for the state of Israel. By speaking out in support of Palestinian human rights or advocating to change US policy that enabled Israeli oppression and occupation, community leaders would be targeted, its academics defamed, and its institutions maligned. The impact has been profound, and has included candidates rejecting endorsements or returning campaign contributions, and the exclusion of Arab American presence as an organized constituency from civic spaces.[19]

BREAKTHROUGHS FOR PROGRESS

Undaunted by their circumstances, or perhaps motivated by them, Arab Americans continued to engage politically and participate in various political campaigns, but usually not as *Arab* Americans. The presidential campaign of Richard Nixon had a "Lebanese Americans for Nixon" effort, and the campaigns of President Jimmy Carter and Ronald Reagan in 1980 also organized under the "Lebanese American" identity.

Arab American participation in American democracy as an organized constituency would see its breakthrough moment in the 1984 presidential campaigns of Reverend Jesse Jackson and Ronald Reagan. Prior to that, the "Arab" part of the identity remained a political liability. That significant breakthrough led to the formation of the Arab American Institute in 1985 with its exclusive focus on the American political process.

The next breakthrough came in the aftermath of the signing of the Oslo Accords on the White House lawn in September 1993. While the Accords proved incapable of advancing peace or creating meaningful improvements in the lives of Palestinians suffering under Israeli occupation, it did have a transformative effect on Arab American political organizing, generally bringing Arab political exclusion to an end. Washington officialdom acknowledged that Palestinian rights existed, as part of a framework to achieve a two-state solution. The Clinton White House engaged in outreach to Arab Americans, and in 1998, President Bill Clinton became the first sitting president to address an Arab American audience.[20] He would also be the last.

A fair reading of the history of Arab American organizing would suggest a less difficult journey for the community were advocacy on Palestinian human rights not part of its political agenda. Excluding Palestine was never an option, however. US policy has tended to view Arab Americans through a securitized lens. They were assumed to pose a potential national security threat – both before and after the attacks of 9/11 – precisely because of their real or perceived political views on events in the Middle East *and* due to their criticism of US policy toward Palestine/Israel. The mere fact of their Arab national origin or ethnicity proved to be sufficient to warrant US government scrutiny, profiling, and discrimination.[21] As demonstrated earlier, Arab Americans' emergence as a constituency is shaped by concerns about or connections to their individual countries of origin or that of their ancestors, and to Palestine.

ARAB AMERICAN PUBLIC OPINION

Before American attitudes began to shift toward a better understanding of, and empathy for, the Palestinian cause,[22] Arab American opinion polls consistently showed strong concern among the community about US policy toward Palestine/Israel and support for Palestinian human rights. In a 2000 poll, 79% of Arab Americans responded that "a candidate's position on the conflict is important to their vote."[23] More than a decade later, 83% of Arab Americans indicated that the conflict was important in their vote for president.[24] As early as 2007, almost 90% of Arab Americans said they believed "an end to the occupation is in the interests of both Palestinians and Israelis."[25] The vast majority of Arab Americans (81%) indicated in a 2023 poll that they were "concerned that policies targeting those boycotting Israel violate Americans' rights to freedom of speech."[26]

While a transformation in how Americans understand the situation in Palestine/Israel had been underway well before Hamas launched its brutal attack on Israel on October 7, 2023 and Israel began its genocidal campaign against Gaza,[27] Arab American support for Palestine has been a consistent fixture. A special poll conducted to get a snapshot of Arab American opinion just after the 2023 Israel–Gaza war is illustrative of how that support translates into voting preferences. Asked about who they would vote for "if the election were held today," only 17% of Arab Americans said they would vote for the Democrat incumbent, President Joe Biden, a remarkable 42% decrease from the 59% who said they would vote for him in 2020. His approval dropped from 74% in 2020 to just 29%. And for the first time in twenty-six years of polling Arab American voters, fewer people identified as Democrats (23%) than Republicans (32%). The reason for the dramatic change in the incumbent president's numbers? Two-thirds said they had a negative view of his "response to the current violence in Palestine and Israel," with 68% saying the US "should not send weapons and military supplies to Israel."[28]

FROM JESSE JACKSON TO JOE BIDEN: HOW PRESIDENTIAL CAMPAIGNS IMPACTED ARAB AMERICANS

The emergence of Arab Americans as a political force in presidential politics took place during the 1984 and 1988 campaigns of Reverend Jesse Jackson. Jackson did not merely ally with the Arab American community; he took on key parts of their political agenda as his own, including the demand to center Palestinian rights in US policy. His run for the presidency created a movement – the Rainbow Coalition – that empowered many who had been marginalized by counterproductive federal policies, racism, neglect, and, in the case of Arab Americans, exclusion. Jackson approached politics with a moral compass that included opening the door to an Arab American campaign staffer to raise the issue of Palestine at the main podium of the Democratic National Convention stage.[29]

The 2016 presidential run of Senator Bernie Sanders was another milestone in a new era that saw candidates lean into support for Palestinian rights. Not only did Sanders not pay a political price for his position, it proved to benefit his campaign. Sanders showed the moral clarity of Jackson, while also building a national movement that broke taboos on Palestine. And in the campaigns of both Jackson and Sanders, Arab Americans were instrumental to making those breakthroughs happen.

Building on lessons learned during prior Democratic campaigns, Arab American engagement with the Biden presidential campaign was organized and effective, with the overwhelming community support contributing to his election in 2020. However, Biden's position on Palestine/Israel quickly soured the community against him and his reelection, particularly after his expression of unconditional support for Israel even while the Palestinian death toll mounted during the Israel–Gaza war. The dramatic drop in Arab American support for Biden since October 7, 2023 underscores the importance of Palestinian rights to the Arab American community. The problem is not simply President Biden's staunch support for Israel; it is the domestic implications of that support: the provision of billions of dollars-worth of weapons to Israel during the months of the killing of Palestinian civilians on an unprecedented scale, and the harm done to democratic norms and institutions in the United States. These harms include restrictions on First Amendment-protected speech[30] (the comparisons with McCarthy-era suppression have been rampant), disregard for federal laws related to weapons transfers,[31] violent state police power unleashed on peaceful student protestors,[32] White House press officials regularly redefining what hate speech is or defaming people they disagree with,[33] amplification of disinformation or misinformation from White House officials,[34] and a failure to maintain basic constituent outreach standards that have been the norm for presidential administrations for decades. The administration's apparent acquiescence to and support for the unprecedented actions being taken since October 7 to suppress dissent and undermine freedom of expression – a fundamental American value – appears to have been deemed an acceptable trade-off necessary to shut down pro-Palestinian activism.[35]

The approach to outreach to the Arab American community by successive US administrations is worthy of some examination. Each administration determines its own priorities and the best staff structures to implement them. Outreach to interest groups, including community-based constituencies, is typically managed by the White House Office of Public Liaison. The first administration to create an official public engagement office was President Gerald Ford's White House and, coincidentally, the first person to lead it was an Arab American named William Baroody.[36] The office today is referred to as the Office of Public Engagement (OPE).

While not all constituency groups have official designated liaisons, the White House and federal agencies prioritize community engagement because it aids them in the effective execution of their responsibilities in the service of the president's policies. Arab Americans do not have a specific official dedicated to engaging with them exclusively, but are assigned to different administration officials to add to their respective outreach portfolios. Thus, the Arab American community has been incorporated into the portfolios of the various officials responsible for ethnic, faith-based, or other community outreach.

Though OPE outreach varies in effectiveness from one administration to another, hopes were high for the Biden administration as President Biden had issued a thoughtful and meaningful agenda for Arab American outreach during his campaign that spoke to many community concerns. On the issue of Palestine, in particular, it said:

> Joe Biden believes in the worth and value of every Palestinian and every Israeli. He will work to ensure that Palestinians and Israelis enjoy equal measures of freedom, security, prosperity, and democracy. His policies will be grounded in a commitment to a two-state solution, where Israel and the future viable state of Palestine will live together in peace, security, and mutual recognition. Biden opposes any unilateral steps by either side that undermine a two-state solution. He opposes annexation and settlement expansion and will continue to oppose both as President. As President, Biden will take immediate steps to restore economic and humanitarian assistance to the Palestinian people, consistent with US law, including assistance to refugees, work to address the ongoing humanitarian crisis in Gaza, reopen the US consulate in East Jerusalem, and work to reopen the PLO mission in Washington.[37]

Acknowledging an organized constituency, President Biden also issued the first presidential proclamation designating April as Arab American Heritage Month in 2023 and again in 2024.

Recognition of the value of engaging with a particular constituency becomes especially important when policy disagreements arise with the White House. The value of OPE staff in such circumstances "lies in their intimate familiarity with the nuances of a constituency – the players, the internal politics, the policy positions, and the group's particular sensitivities."[38] Arab Americans found themselves without such nuanced understanding from the administration during the Israel–Gaza war. The OPE did not engage with Arab Americans *as Arab Americans*; instead, they approached the issues arising during the Israel–Gaza war through a religious frame that subsumes Arab Americans under the umbrella of American Muslims. An approach like this fails to acknowledge how the Arab American community, including its leadership and institutions, is organized, and risks sowing community divisions along religious lines that harken back to a century ago when the first wave of immigrants had to overcome religious divisions. For example, a request for an Arab American leadership meeting with the president was not honored, though such a meeting was held for five American Muslim individuals on the same subject.[39] When an Arab American (who happened to be Christian) asked about the status of the meeting with President Biden, they were advised to put in a request for a meeting through a "non-Arab Christian group."[40] For a community that had to fight to create its own institutions to protect its identity and that has faced political exclusion for decades, the marginalization of the ethnic identity of its members is effectively the erasure of the community as a political force and undermines Arab American political participation.

THE AGENDA OF WIELDING ISLAM IN PALESTINE/ISRAEL DISCOURSE

Organizations representing Arab American interests have long taken issue with how government officials have tended to prioritize religious identity over the ethnic origin of the members of their community. If officials only engage with Arab Americans as Muslims (even as most Arab Americans are Christian), then that engagement will center around issues related to religious-based discrimination or what some refer to as "Islamophobia." And when Arab Americans engage with officials on the violence in Palestine/Israel, officials will tend to cast the matter as a religious conflict rather than a military occupation involving gross violation of Palestinian rights. The "conflict" can then be ameliorated, in their view, through interfaith dialogue rather than an end to Israeli occupation of Palestinian land.

To be clear, like anti-Arab racism, anti-Muslim animus is prevalent in America. Both lead to acts of hate and bias and unlike most other forms of discrimination, they often emanate from policy makers and the media alike, including in policy deliberations about Palestine. However, anti-Muslim bigotry is not at the foundation of Palestine/Israel discourse that denies Palestinians their self-determination or Americans the right to express support for it. It is the dehumanization of Arabs, and specifically, Palestinians. Framing Palestine/Israel as a religious conflict at its core also allows ardent pro-Israel advocates to espouse seemingly centrist views on religious liberty while simultaneously making anti-Arab statements. Indeed, this narrative is why the same member of Congress can sponsor a resolution "denouncing the rise of Islamophobia and anti-Semitism" while also proclaiming that the liberatory slogan "'from the river to the sea, Palestine will be free' is outrightly antisemitic and must be strongly condemned."[41]

It is important to note that the use of religion as the lens through which to understand the situation in Palestine/Israel is not exclusively advanced by supporters of Israel. Some writers who recognize that "the conflict between Palestinians and Israelis is rooted in a settler-colonial project ... that is erroneously portrayed as a conflict between Judaism and Islam"[42] will still use "Islamophobia" broadly to describe "both anti-Arab and anti-Palestinian racism."[43] However, doing so obscures the nature of what Arab Americans experience as an ethnic group and contributes to the community's erasure.

While many Americans fail to distinguish between Muslims as a religious group and Arabs as an ethnic community, the work of scholars, advocates, and certainly policy makers ought to avoid such a conflation. American Muslims are among the most diverse religious communities in America. Black Muslims had comprised a plurality historically.[44] Those originating from or having family backgrounds in Arab countries or the Middle East do not constitute the majority of Muslims in America.[45] The majority of Arab

Americans are in fact Christian.[46] When people conflate religious identity and ethnicity and use imprecise language, they are not usually referring to Arabs *and* Muslims but rather *Arab American Muslims*, which ignores the diversity of American Muslims and the ethnic Arab identity uniquely constructed in America. The label "Muslim" is not a proxy for "Arab," just as "Islamophobia" is not the same as anti-Arab racism. Use of the terms interchangeably misconstrues the nature of the challenges Arab Americans face in the United States and the possible remedies.

Just as political Zionism advanced narratives that erased Palestinian identity, denying the existence of Palestinians as a people, Arab Americans, in particular Palestinian Americans, risk being effectively erased from the policy debates concerning Palestine/Israel. This is despite the fact that it is this particular community that is intrinsically linked to the region and impacted by US policy designed to address the conflict abroad.

CONCLUSION

The experience of Arab Americans today – the repression of their advocacy in support of Palestinians and the failure to recognize them as an *ethnic* community as they attempt to engage with policymakers on the Israel–Gaza war – is reminiscent of America in the 1930s. At that time, Ameen Rihani commanded large audiences, including Arab Americans and policymakers interested in the Middle East. When a June 5, 1937 speech of his at a townhall in New York City concerning the situation in Palestine was aired on municipal radio station WNYC, "a storm of protest broke out."[47] Following the uproar, a city official held a hearing with the commissioner responsible for the station. After reviewing the recording of Rihani's speech and finding no basis for the allegations of "anti-Semitism and racial hatred"[48] made against Rihani, the matter was dropped (though the person responsible for broadcasting his speech was dismissed by the radio station).[49] In a declaration as applicable today as it was in 1937, the US-based Arab National League stated: "In a country which sanctifies freedom of speech and freedom of the press, such acts of censorship should not be tolerated, because they are definitely un-American."[50]

James Zogby, president of the Arab American Institute, has said that "Palestine – its history and the agony of its people – is the wound that will not heal."[51] For the reasons discussed in this chapter, until that wound heals, Arab American civic engagement and empowerment will remain intrinsically linked to the rights and freedom of the Palestinian people. The challenge for American democracy is whether it is strong enough to uphold constitutionally protected freedoms, pluralism, and civil rights and liberties for *all*, including those who advocate for Palestinians and Palestine.

14

Shrinking Civic Space in the Arab World and its Relationship to Palestine/Israel

Marwan Muasher and Rafiah Al Talei

In the Arab world, the restrictions imposed on civil society take various forms depending on the country involved. Nevertheless, they do share some common features, particularly when the matter concerns Palestine and Israel. In this chapter, we share reflections from two different vantage points: one from the Arab political elite, a former foreign minister; and one from Arab civil society, a former journalist. Their perspectives on how civil society has evolved – and in some cases, devolved – offer us greater understanding about the challenges ahead.

—Editors' note

PART I: MARWAN MUASHER: 'CIVIL SOCIETY' ACTIVITY, WHEN SOME DON'T EVEN RECOGNIZE THE TERM

In 2004, when I was foreign minister of Jordan, I attended a meeting with my Arab counterparts in Tunis in advance of a summit meeting. On the agenda was a discussion of various reform initiatives we were considering. Before the meeting could get very far, however, one foreign minister objected to use of the term "civil society" in the collective document, explaining that his government didn't recognize it. While not all Arab states have the same draconian attitude toward civil society as this particular foreign minister, most have traditionally resisted civil society organizing in support of political or social change, as the stringent regulations imposed on community-based and non-governmental organizations (NGOs) in Arab countries makes evident. Governments tend to tolerate civil society efforts when they align with their agenda. Activism for Palestinian rights highlights this dynamic.

Civil society organizations' ability to operate in the Arab Middle East is further complicated by burgeoning Arab–Israeli normalization and security cooperation, including reliance on Israeli spyware technologies, as they can facilitate repression of activism and engagement perceived as a threat to state authority. The deeply unpopular trend toward Arab–Israeli normalization has also been accompanied by government crackdowns on speech and protest. Given the interconnectedness between threats to civic freedoms and warming bilateral relations with Israel, the future does not bode well for those who believe civic engagement with institutions is critical to representative governance.

Civil society in the Arab Middle East: perceptions and its instrumentalization

Most Arab governments tend to view "legitimate" civil society organizations (CSOs, including NGOs) as strictly charitable endeavors, limited to social development work.[1] Groups engaged in advocacy are either totally banned or severely restricted by legal or regulatory regimes. When advocacy groups have been allowed to exist, they operate in a kind of grey zone, vulnerable at any time to an order from the government to close or cease operations. And because the concept of issue-specific advocacy or NGO monitoring and documentation of governmental functions has been relatively alien to Arab states, in many cases these entities are required to register with the relevant ministries of social development, trade, or industry, and are likely to face severe restrictions on their operations. These restrictions include prohibitions on lobbying and almost any other form of political, social, or economic activity.[2]

The Arab uprisings of 2010–2012 only temporarily changed matters. For example, Egypt, Tunisia, and Syria witnessed a mushrooming of civil society work during this period. As the process of transitioning to new political systems and writing new constitutions in Egypt and Tunisia began, it was accompanied by serious NGO documentation and monitoring, advocacy efforts, and lobbying on issues such as gender equality and political inclusion, and in support of enshrining certain civic freedoms in the new constitutions.³ In war-ravaged Syria, NGOs often stood in place of the Syrian government to provide essential services to the population in areas outside government control.⁴

Notably, advocacy and protest relating to the Palestinian issue is one area where state authorities have granted civil society greater latitude. It is still, however, heavily contingent on whether the activities and message involved align with the regime's interests. In certain countries, such as Jordan, Syria, and Morocco, demonstrations against the Israeli occupation are often allowed as a way for citizens to let off steam. When the protesters begin to challenge the government's position vis-à-vis Israel, the tolerance runs out.

Since the signing of the Abraham Accords between Israel, Bahrain, and the United Arab Emirates (UAE), with Morocco later formally joining thereafter, the chasm between Arab publics and their state authorities on the Palestine issue has grown. A poll conducted by the Washington Institute for Near East Policy reveals that as of July 2022, around 80% of people in Bahrain, the UAE, Saudi Arabia, Kuwait, Egypt, and Jordan view the Abraham Accords negatively, even as plans for increasing regional cooperation are developing.⁵ As indicated in the chart below from Arab Barometer polling conducted from 2020 to 2022, overall regional support for normalization with Israel has remained low.

To what extent do you favor or oppose the normalization of relations between Arab states and Israel, % saying that they strongly favor/favor

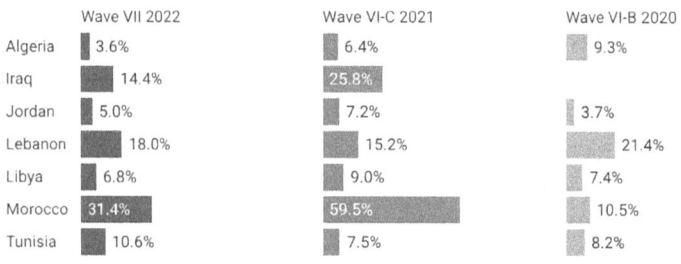

	Wave VII 2022	Wave VI-C 2021	Wave VI-B 2020
Algeria	3.6%	6.4%	9.3%
Iraq	14.4%	25.8%	
Jordan	5.0%	7.2%	3.7%
Lebanon	18.0%	15.2%	21.4%
Libya	6.8%	9.0%	7.4%
Morocco	31.4%	59.5%	10.5%
Tunisia	10.6%	7.5%	8.2%

In 2021, the question was about the normalization of relations between Morocco and Israel; in 2020, it was about the normalization of relations between the UAE and Israel, and Bahrain and Israel.
Chart: Rain Ji • Source: Arab Barometer • Created with Datawrapper

The graph illustrates the extent of support for the normalization of relations between Arab states and Israel, measured across different waves of surveys conducted in 2020, 2021, and 2022 by the Arab Barometer. The data indicate varying levels of favorability among seven Arab countries: Algeria, Iraq, Jordan, Lebanon, Libya, Morocco, and Tunisia. Notably, Morocco consistently shows the highest support, with a significant peak in 2021 at 59.5%, reflecting a favorable public response to its formal normalization of relations with Israel. In contrast, other countries exhibit lower and more fluctuating levels of support. For instance, Iraq shows a marked decline from 25.8% in 2021 to 14.4% in 2022, while Lebanon and Libya display moderate favorability without significant changes over the three waves. These data suggest that public opinion on normalization varies considerably across the region, influenced by specific geopolitical contexts and developments.

Speech or protests against Arab–Israeli normalization, particularly initiatives associated with the Abraham Accords, have not only been prevented in the countries that signed the agreements, but have also faced restrictions in those countries that feared such public opposition might strain relations with the signatory countries. In countries that had previously signed peace agreements with Israel but have maintained cold people-to-people relations, such as Egypt and Jordan, protests have also been quelled[6] in part to avoid angering Arab Gulf states that provide them with economic aid or employ significant numbers of their citizens as foreign workers.[7] Concern about public opposition to normalization is why Abraham Accords countries marketed them as supportive of Palestinian rights, even though pursuit of Palestinian–Israeli peace is hardly mentioned in the text of the agreements. Arab–Israeli normalization has been motivated much more by less savory realities, such as the desire of Arab states to acquire Israeli spyware.[8]

Protests against Israel's 2023–2024 bombardment of Gaza, and blockade of its food, water, and essential supplies, produced different reactions from Arab states. In Egypt and Jordan, both bordering Israel and concerned about the mass transfer of Palestinians into their territory, protests were tolerated temporarily, perhaps even encouraged at times, while tightly controlled.[9] However, in the Gulf, public reaction was severely discouraged. There were almost no protests against Israel or in support of Palestinians in any of the Gulf countries, with the exception of quickly shut down protests in Bahrain and Kuwait, despite clear evidence that public opinion remains highly critical of the war on Gaza.[10]

The state of civil society in the Arab Middle East and Palestine/Israel: two Mashriqi and two Maghrebi case studies

Tunisia

Tunisia presents the most encouraging, if brief, example of Arab state support for civil society. Following the 2011 revolution, a decree was issued that guaranteed NGOs freedom to operate.[11] As a result, tens of thousands of new NGOs emerged as Tunisians were able to freely establish civil society groups and receive foreign funding without excessive governmental oversight or permissions. These organizations were critical in drafting the 2014 Tunisian Constitution. In fact, a group of Tunisian civil society organizations was awarded the Nobel Peace Prize in 2015 for their role in advancing peaceful political transition.[12]

Since President Kais Saied came to power in 2019, however, the situation has deteriorated.[13] He has accused civil society of serving foreign interests – a common tactic in the Arab world – and has placed severe restrictions on the operations of NGOs.[14] With regard to Arab normalization with Israel, Saied has been an outspoken critic, positioning himself as a champion of Palestinian rights in line with popular sentiment. However, he has so far opposed a bill prepared after Israel's latest war on Gaza, which would have criminalized the normalization of relations with Israel,[15] while permitting mass protests throughout Tunisia calling for a ceasefire. Most recently, the government prevented a Tunisian lawyer from leaving the country to represent Palestine in the International Court of Justice to file a complaint against Israel.[16]

Egypt

Whether under the presidency of Hosni Mubarak, Mohamed Morsi, or Abdel Fattah El-Sisi, Egypt has maintained strict control over associations and NGOs. Under Mubarak, NGOs were required to register with the Ministry of Social Affairs and swear never to engage in political activities.[17] The Morsi government did very little to alleviate NGO restrictions, only slightly revising the NGO law. Restrictions worsened again under el-Sisi.[18] Campaigns have been carried out to delegitimize civil society by claiming that NGOs are associated with terrorist networks and work as foreign agents.[19] In 2019, the government passed a law giving authorities sole discretion and power to oversee the registration, activities, funding, and dissolution of NGOs.[20]

Though Egypt maintains a cold peace with Israel since the signing of the 1979 peace treaty between the two countries, security and intelligence ties are strong. Egypt uses Israeli spyware technologies. In fact, in the last presidential elections in 2023, Israeli Predator spyware was found on the phones of two candidates opposing el-Sisi, Ayman Nour and Ahmed al-Tantawi.[21] The government also often suppresses activism in support of Palestinian rights. For example, Ramy Shaath, an Egyptian-Palestinian activist who campaigned in support of a boycott of Israel and who drew comparisons between Israel's occupation and Arab dictators, was held in Egyptian prison for over two-and-a-half years before being deported abroad.[22] However, when it came to shows of solidarity with Palestinians in Gaza since October 7, 2023, the Egyptian regime has used state-controlled media to call on people to congregate in designated areas for mass protests, while refraining from recalling its ambassador in Tel Aviv.[23] The freedom to protest was short-lived: dozens of peaceful protestors have been detained and prosecuted since.[24]

Jordan

In the 1990s and early 2000s, the Kingdom began to allow greater space for civil society organizations to grow, though NGOs operated in a grey area, left uncertain what activities might go too far and trigger authorities.[25] During this period, NGOs had little influence on government policies; they existed as a liberal facade for regime-initiated reforms. Today, local and international NGOs are strictly controlled, and subjected to various laws restricting their political and financial activities.[26]

The Palestinian issue has been at the center of many Jordanian protests. Support for normalization between Arab states and Israel is low in the country, standing at about 5%.[27] The Kingdom allows pro-Palestine activism as long as it does not challenge its rule; however, they also have gone forward with Jordanian–Israeli energy projects despite popular sentiment in support of Palestinians. Such agreements are hugely unpopular and have sparked protests against Jordanian policies.[28]

Since the outbreak of war on Gaza in 2023, there has been a change in Jordanian thinking; they are less interested in bilateral cooperation with Israel and more concerned about how Israel's campaign in Gaza might create conditions to effect a mass transfer of Palestinians into Jordan. Public criticism of Israel in Jordan has reached unprecedented levels and Jordan has recalled its ambassador to Israel.[29] Public protests are given wider latitude within certain red lines, including allowing sanctioned protests in areas farther away from the border.[30] These protests continued as the war dragged on.

Morocco

Under King Mohammed VI, there has been limited liberalization for civil society. In 2002, the country liberalized the legal environment for NGOs, but the Kingdom still maintains control over the sector and those working on sensitive issues still face repression.[31] After the February 20 protest movement in 2011, the regime reacted by allowing constitutional reform, giving slightly more civic space to NGOs. Today, there are approximately 116,000 such organizations in the country.[32] However, efforts to promote agendas seen as controversial, such as calls for democracy, are repressed.

The normalization deal between the Kingdom and Israel was met with objections from pro-Palestinian civil groups, but tangible opposition is difficult, as a result of the linkage between the Abraham Accords, and recognition by the United States and Israel of Moroccan sovereignty over the Western Sahara.[33] This garners support for the normalization process because public sentiment is in support of sovereignty over the Western Sahara. Support for normalization is reportedly the second-highest in the Arab world, trailing just after Sudan. However, support for the Accords has since fallen, to about 31% in 2022.[34]

In 2019, Amnesty International revealed that Israeli spyware had been used against two Moroccan human rights defenders.[35] There have also been media reports that Morocco deployed Pegasus spyware against top French officials.[36]

Since October 7, 2023, Morocco has witnessed hundreds of public protests in support of Palestinians. The majority of these protests have called for canceling the normalization deal with Israel;[37] no such move has been made. According to the Doha Institute, in December 2023, 29% of Moroccans supported suspending normalization with Israel to stop the war.[38] The Foreign Ministry has denounced Israeli actions as contradictory to international law and criticized the UN Security Council for not stopping the war.[39]

PART II: RAFIAH AL TALEI: RESTRICTIONS ON FREEDOM OF EXPRESSION IN THE GULF

I started as a journalist in Oman in 1994 at the country's state-owned media company, Oman Newspaper. It was a time of some hope in the Middle East. The Palestine Liberation Organization and Israel had just signed the Declaration of Principles, an instrument of mutual recognition that was supposed to be the first step toward a comprehensive Israeli–Palestinian peace agreement and a sovereign Palestinian state. It was also a pivotal year for Omani–Israeli rapprochement and a unique moment when the Omani press and public opinion were in sync on Palestinian–Israeli affairs, foreign policy, and the notion of warming relations with Israel. Of course, this was also before the advent of social media networks, and at a time when Arab governments could shape popular opinion and the public discourse on foreign policy matters. In the case of Oman, the public only had access to state-owned media and a few private local outlets that were also subject to government influence and restrictions. Most journalists and commentators refrained from voicing dissent publicly, choosing instead to self-censor to stay within the parameters set by the authorities.

With the rise of social media, Arab regimes lost some of their ability to control unwanted ideas from spreading within their countries. Omanis and Arab publics in the Gulf had an opportunity to express their opinions without fear of repercussion from the regime – at least for a while. As Gulf states have normalized relations with Israel and benefited from security cooperation and growing ties, the latent fissures between Arab publics and state authorities have become more apparent and pronounced. The rest of this chapter examines the limits of freedom of expression and the press in Arab Gulf states amid the normalization of relations with Israel and the recent Israeli war on Gaza. Since the unprecedented violence against Palestinian civilians that began following the October 7, 2023 Hamas attacks, Arab publics have expressed even greater online opposition to normalization with Israel if it is not part of a comprehensive plan for a just political solution for Palestinians. This has set the popular will and the regime on a collision course.

Restrictions on freedom of expression: drivers and mechanisms

Restrictions on media organizations

Gulf states wield substantial control over both the domestic and international media outlets that operate within their borders. While private media outlets exist, they typically receive government subsidies, engage in self-censorship, and risk punitive measures if they cross certain red lines.

Al Jazeera, the privately owned international Arab media conglomerate based in Doha, is an important example in this regard. As arguably the most recognized Gulf media company, it boasts several of the most popular presenters in the Arab world. Yet it is not free from government restrictions. The Qatari government has reportedly provided financial support for Al Jazeera's operating costs since its establishment in 1996, prominent Qatari families heavily influence the content of both the print and broadcast media in Qatar, and the editorial stance is tied to the prevailing political climate.[40] Coverage of domestic political issues in Qatar poses a formidable challenge for journalists in particular. For example, the situation of the two million foreign workers in the country (around 4% of the population)[41] generally does not receive any media exposure.[42]

Things are not much better elsewhere in the Gulf. A 2023 Freedom House report indicates that the Omani government instructed media organizations to refrain from covering the 2021 demonstrations protesting about the economy, shrinking job opportunities, and unemployment among youth.[43] Even in Kuwait, a country known as the least restrictive in the Gulf, the government exerts substantial control over news and the dissemination of information. The 2023 Reporters without Borders Index notes that the Kuwaiti government's control over information remains significant, despite democratizing trends in the country and the emergence of some independent digital media platforms.[44] Like in Qatar, most Kuwaiti media companies are owned by well-connected and prominent families. To obtain the permissions needed to operate, media companies must go through prohibitive, costly, and tedious processes. Even if they manage to overcome the obstacles, media outlets must stay in line. While a 2020 law[45] ostensibly guarantees journalists the freedom to work in Kuwait, some journalists have been compelled to flee to avoid arrest.[46] One Kuwaiti media company, Al-Watan TV, faced closure in 2015 for making "anti-government" comments.[47] In Saudi Arabia, according to Freedom House, internet freedom remains highly restricted. Saudi Arabia also sees media restrictions as part of its comprehensive security approach, balancing internal dynamics, geopolitical considerations, and regional rivalries.[48] The government's monopoly on power is utilized to severely limit individuals' online activities and control access to information. Censorship and advanced surveillance systems persist, with authorities increasingly relying on global spyware providers to monitor the online presence of residents.[49]

Restrictions on social media networks and usage

Because of the challenges faced by journalists and traditional media organizations, social media networks have come to play a crucial role in facilitating public discourse and debate on both domestic and international issues, including the Israel–Palestine conflict. In recent years, Arab Gulf regimes have sought ways to control content on different platforms and to limit freedom of expression. To this end, Saudi law requires social media influencers to obtain licenses.[50] The apparent aim of the regime in monitoring content is to help shape the public discourse in a way that is favorable toward governmental policies, including on issues impacting the regime's foreign policy; for example, normalization with Israel and the latest Israeli war on Gaza.

Other Gulf Arab states have enacted social media laws that criminalize certain types of criticism of the regime if authorities determine it might jeopardize the national interest, security, or diplomatic relations. A 2022 Freedom House report notes that internet freedom remains significantly constrained in the UAE, Saudi Arabia, and Bahrain. In Kuwait[51] and Oman,[52] there are restrictions on critique of the government's regional policies. Other legislation in the UAE and Qatar imposes criminal penalties on social media users for sharing "fake news." In other countries, including Kuwait and Oman, dissemination of material deemed insulting to Islam or the ruling family is criminalized.

Surveillance of activists

Multiple Gulf governments have used surveillance technologies to monitor online activists and journalists, heightening the likelihood of self-censorship online. Both the UAE and Saudi Arabia are known clients of NSO Group, an Israeli spyware company. The technology has been used to target anti-regime activists, journalists, and rival members of the UAE royal families. A Reuters investigation published in January 2019 revealed that former US intelligence employees had joined a team to help the UAE government surveil perceived government opponents and pro-democracy activists.[53] Qatari security forces have also reportedly monitored personal communications in the country.[54]

Through this combination of legal restrictions and widespread surveillance, Gulf regimes have been able to effectively restrict online expression. In Oman, Bahrain, and the UAE, security forces have fined, arrested, and imprisoned social media users for their posts.[55] Some Gulf governments have pressured social media companies to remove content critical of its foreign policy or have asked for accounts to be suspended.[56] In Saudi Arabia and Kuwait, dissenting voices on social media have faced online trolls and bots that disseminate government propaganda. They have also been subjected to state-sponsored smear campaigns.[57] In these repressive contexts, individuals and organizations have adopted pseudonyms to engage in online discussions on the Israeli–Palestinian conflict and normalization in order to reduce the risk of government reprisals.[58]

In the Gulf countries, the risk of government reprisals leads many individuals and civil society organizations to engage in self-censorship on the Israel–Palestine issue. In authoritarian regimes, expressing dissent on sensitive international matters like the Israeli–Palestinian conflict may be construed as a direct challenge to the government's foreign policy or a catalyst for domestic unrest. Such reprisals include arrests, harassment, censorship, and legal actions against dissenting individuals and organizations. They also extend to economic and professional ramifications, such as job loss or business closures, and critics may face social ostracization for speaking out. Some governments even pursue critics beyond their borders, raising concerns about personal safety and interference with their activities abroad, exemplified by the case of Jamal Khashoggi.[59]

How four Arab Gulf countries – the UAE, Bahrain, Saudi Arabia, and Oman – differ from their citizens' views on normalization with Israel and the war on Gaza is examined in the following section, with a focus on how restrictions on social media and limitations on freedom of expression and the press are imposed to hide these differences from public view.

Normalization with Israel: shaping the narrative
While Arab Gulf countries have historically supported Palestinian national aspirations, they tightly control pro-Palestinian activism inside their respective countries to ensure that it is in alignment with their interests. In recent years, Arab normalization with Israel and associated shifting regional alliances have tended to result in restrictions on civic space and the press, particularly at times of escalating violence in Palestine/Israel.[60]

The Israel–Gaza war in 2023 has increased government restrictions on speech in the Arab Gulf states. According to the Euro-Med Human Rights Monitor, Bahraini, Emirati, and Saudi authorities arrested activists for their expression of solidarity with Palestinians despite obligations they owe under international human rights treaties, including the International Covenant on Civil and Political Rights.[61] Bahrain detained at least fifty-seven citizens for participating in pro-Gaza protests, with some facing extended detentions.[62] In the UAE, activist Mansour al-Ahmadi was arrested in 2017 without charge and without being permitted legal representation. Mansour, an advocate for human rights in his country and the Middle East and North Africa, was arrested after a decade of activism. Previous government attempts to silence him included a six-month detention in 2011, a travel ban, and multiple sophisticated spyware hacking attempts on his devices orchestrated by UAE authorities.[63] UAE authorities also summoned academics for questioning after they posted opinions about Gaza online.[64] In Saudi Arabia, visitors to the Kingdom have been arrested for showing solidarity with Gaza, including a British Muslim actor wearing a Palestinian scarf known as the keffiyeh.[65]

The UAE and Bahrain
The UAE[66] and Bahrain[67] are original signatories to the Abraham Accords and both have been active in promoting the benefits of normalization with Israel. While some in the Gulf states view the Accords as fostering regional stability and economic development, most of the public have been critical of establishing diplomatic relations with Israel, because doing so is seen

as compromising Palestinian rights and sidestepping core issues between Israelis and Palestinians.[68] In Bahrain, twenty-four political societies and civil society organizations published a joint statement declaring that the Accords do not represent the popular will, nor will they bring peace or restore the usurped rights of the Palestinian people. Instead, they say, normalization of the "Zionist enemy" has allowed it to commit more crimes against Palestine and the sanctities of Arabs and Muslims in Jerusalem.[69]

Because of domestic opposition in the UAE and Bahrain, authorities have taken measures to curtail criticism of the Abraham Accords, particularly that expressed over social media, where the issue has been a leading concern and topic. Immediately after the announcement of the Accords, a number of hashtags began trending on Twitter (now X) in the region and in the Gulf, in particular, including "Normalization is betrayal" and "Gulf people against normalization."[70] Users published recordings and archival photos of King Faisal bin Abdulaziz of Saudi Arabia, recalling his five-decades-long position on Israel.[71] Most social media posts during this period expressed opposition to the Abraham Accords.[72]

The UAE increased its control over the media after the events of the Arab Spring in 2011,[73] and its regulatory landscape has further tightened with the enactment of two laws. The 2012 cybercrime law, to which in January 2022 the UAE implemented amendments, with ambiguous language, imposes criminal penalties for sharing "fake news" online, posing a potential threat to freedom of expression. Simultaneously, a new data protection law introduced in 2021, despite its stated purpose, contains exemptions that may compromise online privacy and reinforce government surveillance practices.[74]

A 2023 Freedom House report noted that internet freedom in the UAE remains significantly constrained, characterized by widespread online censorship and a lack of diversity in the online media landscape. Social media users have been fined or even arrested for their posts, and the government routinely surveils online activists and journalists. Complicating matters, three former US intelligence employees faced fines for providing hacking software to the UAE government, which was deployed against perceived government opponents and pro-democracy activists. A Reuters investigation published in January 2019 revealed that a group of former US intelligence agents participated in Project Raven, a hacking project that was managed by the security company DarkMatter beginning in 2016 and was used for the purpose of systematic surveillance.[75] The former US agents associated with the project entered an agreement with US federal prosecutors to pay $1.7 million in fines for violating export control regulations after furnishing the UAE government with zero-click software. According to the Freedom House report, the UAE government is a known client of NSO Group and authorities have used spyware technologies such as remote zero-click surveillance – a technique that could compromise a device without any action by the target – of smartphones to target anti-regime activists, journalists, and royal family members.[76]

Despite that, dissenting voices and activism challenging normalization have surfaced.[77] The Emirati Anti-Normalization Association[78] was founded in 2020. And well-known Emirati figures such as Rafia Ghubash[79] and Abdulkhalek Abdullah[80] who are academics and active on social media, mainly on the platform X, showed their support for Palestinians and Gaza during the war. Nevertheless, both figures are close to and loyal to the UAE government. Their social media posts demand aid for Gaza and criticize the continued killing of civilians, but they do not criticize the UAE's policy toward Israel and do not call for an end to normalization as Bahrainis did. Although Emiratis popularized anti-normalization hashtags[81] to show their opposition, demonstrations or protests did not take place in the country, even during Israel's invasion of Gaza in 2023. The Emirati government justified banning pro-Palestine protest by saying that the ban will actually benefit the Palestinians.[82]

The 28th Conference of the Parties of the UN Framework Convention on Climate Change (COP28) hosted by UAE, however, offered a rare opportunity for activists to hold pro-Palestinian demonstrations. Some activists challenged the UAE over its restrictions on protest, called for a ceasefire in Gaza,[83] and chanted "free, free Palestine." Protestors also challenged the UAE government's use of intrusive surveillance technologies.[84]

Opposition within Bahrain to Israeli normalization has also grown and found avenues for expression despite restrictions. After the Bahraini president of the Authority for Culture and Antiquities, Mai Al Khalifa, was forced to resign from her post in 2022 for refusing to shake the hand of an Israeli official at a funeral at the residence of the US ambassador to Bahrain, the hashtag #Shukran-Mai ("Thank you, Mai") began trending online.[85] And when in April 2023, Israeli security forces attacked worshipers in Al-Aqsa Mosque Compound in Jerusalem and violent escalations ensued in other parts of the occupied Palestinian territories and elsewhere in the region,[86] the hashtag "Bahrainis against normalization" again topped the platform X in Bahrain. Bahraini social media users confirmed online that Palestine is their "first cause," with some users publishing photos from a protest that included twenty-five civil society organizations under the umbrella of the Bahraini National Initiative Against Normalization. Bahraini civil society opposition to normalization has led Israel's Institute for National Security Studies to conclude that initiatives between Bahrain and Israel are impracticable.[87] This should not be mistaken for Bahrain protecting civic space. Even after Bahrain withdrew its ambassador from Tel Aviv following Israel's war on Gaza, authorities have shown little tolerance for protestors. Pro-Palestinian activists faced arrest and their protests were not allowed.[88] Even the grandson of Bahrain's top Shia cleric was arrested,[89] as were other well-known activists.[90]

Bahrain's government faces criticism for online surveillance, particularly in the wake of the Arab Spring, with activists who challenge the government's foreign policy and relations with Israel being subjected to harassment and legal action. According to Freedom House, internet freedom in Bahrain remains constrained, with ongoing instances of website blocking and forced removal of online content, particularly social media posts critical of the government.[91]

Bahraini security forces have interrogated, arrested, and imprisoned social media users for their posts, and the Ministry of Interior actively discourages discussions on sensitive topics. Journalists and online activists encounter extralegal intimidation, cyberattacks, and surveillance from state authorities, which all help to cement a general atmosphere of online self-censorship.[92]

Saudi Arabia

Saudi Arabia's flirtation with normalizing relations with Israel under Crown Prince Mohammed bin Salman has evoked a complex and mixed response within the Kingdom.[93] Supporters of the government's approach emphasize economic gains, viewing closer ties as opportunities for trade, investment, and technological cooperation that could contribute to Saudi Arabia's development and diversification. Another perspective sees improved relations with Israel in more strategic terms, as a way to counter common adversaries like Iran and enhance regional security alliances.[94] According to a Doha Institute poll published in January 2024, 95% of the Saudi public see the Palestinian cause as an Arab issue, and not exclusively a Palestinian issue. This result regarding Saudi Arabia had gone up from 69% in 2011, a statistically significant increase that represents a fundamental shift in the opinions of Saudi citizens.[95]

Those segments of the Saudi population that view normalization as a betrayal of Palestinian rights have taken to the platform X to express their views. Some base their disapproval on religious or ideological concerns, perceiving it as incongruent with Saudi Arabia's custodianship of Islamic holy sites and undermining the Islamic world's stance on Jerusalem. Other critics question the government's priorities, pointing to human rights concerns and restrictions on political activism that should be addressed before fostering closer ties with Israel.[96]

When a Saudi delegation visited Israel in 2016, an online group called "Boycott Israel Movement in the Gulf" published a statement denouncing the visit.[97] In the same year, an independent group that claimed to be working to amplify the voices of Saudis who reject normalization launched the viral hashtag #Saudis_against_normalization to push back against signs that the Kingdom might be considering open diplomatic relations with Israel.[98] Even though the Palestinian cause is popular among Saudis, authorities in the Kingdom have a long history of persecuting Palestinian residents.[99] In 2020, a group of Palestinians were put on trial on vague charges of having links to an unnamed "terrorist organization."[100]

Media restrictions have increased following Israel's war on Gaza. Saudi authorities have sought to clamp down on popular anti-war sentiment, which has created a perception among Arab observers that the government's position is unfavorable to Palestinians since it has not declared a position that rejects normalization with Israel. The Saudis believe that their government should adopt a stronger stance of denunciation and should reject all forms of normalization with Israel in the future. These views intensified after statements by Saudi officials that Saudi Arabia will not stop normalization with Israel after the Gaza war, despite the massacres of Palestinians.[101]

When some Saudis expressed support for the government's approach toward the Israel–Gaza violence, others expressed online criticism of their religious authorities for ignoring the situation, failing to offer prayers for Palestinians in the occupied territories, and not voicing sufficient opposition to Israel's campaign in Gaza.[102] In response to such criticism, Saudi state news outlets felt compelled to highlight instances of sheikhs offering prayers for Palestinians in Gaza, emphasizing the duration and intensity of the supplications in the reporting.[103]

According to the Freedom House report, the Saudi authorities used spyware from NSO Group to target activists and journalists, and it revealed that Saudi authorities had likely purchased Predator spyware from Cytrox, a North Macedonia-based spyware company.[104] Saudi Arabia mandates government licenses for social media influencers, aiming to control and monitor platform content to shape the narrative favorably toward governmental policies, including those on normalization and the Gaza war.

A new online phenomenon since Israel's war on Gaza has been social media users doxing other users as "Arab Zionists."[105] The "List of Shame"[106] includes influencers[107] such as writers, novelists, media professionals, researchers, sheikhs, and celebrities.[108] Almost half of the influencers identified were Saudi, holding around a third of the followers. The second-highest number of influencers came from the UAE at 15%, with 76% of the followers.[109]

According to an article published by Al Jazeera in November 2023,[110] the phenomenon of "Arab Zionists" transcends mere political animosity, or ideological divergence with the Palestinian resistance, evolving into a strategic paradigm shift within the Arab elite. This transformation suggests the emergence of a novel movement characterized by a well-defined agenda, garnering local, regional, and international support.

This movement encourages select intellectuals and elite media members to advocate for normalization with Israel and acceptance of coexistence before securing a comprehensive agreement safeguarding the legitimate rights of Palestinians. This trend particularly gained momentum following the recent wave of normalization with Israel undertaken by the UAE, Bahrain, and Morocco. The Gaza war made this phenomenon obvious.

Oman

During the early days of the Oslo peace process and up until the Second Intifada in 2000, Oman and Israel enjoyed improved relations. In 1994, Israel's prime minister Yitzhak Rabin visited Oman, the first Gulf Arab country to host an Israeli leader. Two years later, the two countries signed an agreement to establish commercial offices in their respective countries. The Omani office closed amid the Second Intifada, reflecting public opposition in Oman, though diplomatic relations continued discreetly.[111]

Omani state television prominently featured the meeting between Sultan Qaboos and Israeli prime minister Benjamin Netanyahu on October 27, 2018, as did Omani newspapers. The media largely echoed the government's official position, emphasizing the visit's objective of advancing the peace process and fostering stability in the Middle East. Accompanying Netanyahu were high-ranking officials, including his wife, the head of Mossad, his national security advisor, the director general of the Foreign Ministry, and officials from the Ministry of Defense. During the visit, Omanis took to social media to express their discontent using a method that was previously unavailable to them.[112]

Oman's approach to Israel is marked by cautious engagement rather than full normalization. The Sultan has had diplomatic interactions with Israeli officials without establishing formal relations. Historically positioned as a neutral mediator in regional conflicts, Oman has facilitated talks between Israel and other actors to promote stability and peace. The government's lack of transparency on diplomatic activities with Israel can fuel public speculation about the extent of the bilateral relations taking place away from public view, but official narratives influence perceptions. For example, after the Second Intifada, Oman officially announced the cessation of trade relations with Israel, but nevertheless continued relations in secret. Therefore, Omanis do not always trust what the government announces, especially regarding its foreign relations.[113]

Oman's political culture generally allows for the expression of diverse opinions so long as respect is shown for the Sultan's authority.[114] Public sentiment on normalization varies: while some support diplomatic engagement to support regional stability, most Omanis are concerned about the impact on Palestinian rights. Prior to 2018, there were no reported incidents of individuals being arrested in Oman for supporting the Palestinian cause. This changed, however, following Netanyahu's 2018 visit, when authorities detained two internet activists for their involvement in promoting pro-Palestine content.[115]

Following Sultan Haitham's ascension to the throne in Oman in January 2021, a discernible shift in the country's foreign policy toward Israel has become apparent. The minister of foreign affairs asserted in an interview only months after Haitham came to power that Oman would not be the third Gulf state to normalize relations with Israel – despite the Omani ambassador's attendance at the signing ceremony for the Abraham Accords and speculation surrounding Saudi Arabia following suit.[116] The Omani minister of foreign affairs has consistently conveyed the country's official position on social media, aligning with the sentiments of the Omani populace.[117] The Sultan has permitted pro-Palestinian demonstrations, particularly in universities, and has allowed a greater degree of freedom of speech online – a marked departure from previous restrictions on expressions of solidarity with Palestinians.

The Grand Mufti of Oman, Ahmed bin Hamad Al-Khalili, has emerged as a prominent figure condemning Israel's practices in the occupied territories.[118] Al-Khalili's active engagement on social media, particularly after UAE and Bahraini normalization, included written statements and video clips, garnering notable popularity not only among Omanis and Gulf Arabs but also resonating with a broader Arab audience. Remarkably, Omani authorities took no action signaling tacit approval. Al-Khalili's firm and popularly received positions diverge from more flexible discourses by Saudi clerics, making him the sole Omani official, if not the sole Gulf religious affairs official, adopting such a bold stance.

The Omani government has adopted a robust stance against the bombing of civilians in Gaza and has advocated for a ceasefire. The alignment observed among official, popular, and religious stances concerning the Gaza conflict in Oman is noteworthy,[119] as evidenced by the absence of reported arrests, website restrictions, or content removal. This consensus not only contributes to social harmony but also serves as a strategic means to redirect public focus away from the socio-economic challenges confronting the Omani population.[120]

CONCLUSION

Although the outbreak of the Arab Spring in 2010 raised hopes for a broader and more free civic space, progress has not been linear. Revolutionary reforms in Egypt and Tunisia, particularly related to civic space, were largely rolled back, and in some respects the situation worsened, starting in the mid-to-late 2010s. Today, CSOs in these countries, as well as in countries still suffering from civil wars like Syria, Yemen, and Libya, are often forced to operate from the outside. And while the concept of advocacy has started to creep its way into many Arab countries, governments have countered it through "legal" means by tightening their laws governing civil society work, placing severe restrictions on their ability to operate freely, or often by "illegal" interference by security agencies to stifle free speech. The increased use by several Arab governments of Israeli spyware technologies such as Pegasus, to spy illegally on their citizens, is particularly problematic. These technologies have been banned in several countries including the US, but no Arab government has followed suit. The result has been an overall shrinking of civic space in most of the region, with governments keen not to repeat the wave of massive protests across the Arab world in 2011–2013, demanding better economic governance and more political inclusion. Although initially the Arab uprisings seemed to promise a more open civic space for Arab societies, the result has often been the opposite. Arab civil society is thriving only outside the borders of the countries they cover. As long as this situation prevails, the transition to pluralistic and democratic societies in the region will be more difficult.

Arab public opinion on normalization agreements with Israel, particularly in the absence of a Palestinian–Israeli agreement to end the occupation, remains largely unsupportive. But the space to express those sentiments, especially in Gulf states, remains almost non-existent. Even during the latest war on Gaza, public protests in the Gulf were not allowed, and public expressions of solidarity with Palestinians were also stifled. The governments' claim, repeated by several policymakers in the West, that the Arab–Israeli conflict no longer commands the attention of an Arab public with more pressing priorities, is not supported by evidence. Gulf governments find themselves increasingly at odds with the wishes and expectations of their people. Whether it is their support for normalization with Israel or their failure to work actively for a ceasefire in Gaza to prevent further death and destruction there, Arab public sentiment has diverged markedly from the position of Gulf regimes. Given these states' restrictions on dissent, domestic repression of civil society is expected to continue and will likely increase.

In certain Gulf states, specifically Oman, Qatar, and Kuwait, social media and general media confrontations between the governments and citizens appear less intense than in other Gulf states such as the UAE, Bahrain, and Saudi Arabia. This disparity is attributed to their shared positions on the Palestinian issue, where governments and citizens in the first group express support for Palestine, condemn Israel, and are critical of its primary supporter, the United States. Conversely, the second group experiences more heated confrontations and discussions due to discrepancies in government positions and support, contrasting with a general population that stands in favor of the Palestinian cause. During the ongoing Gaza conflict, Gulf citizens have demonstrated a strong commitment to expressing their opinions, even if they run the risk of arrest or detention due to state repression.

The Palestinian issue has historically influenced the popularity of Arab/Gulf governments, with some Gulf states consistently supporting Palestinians. Examples include Kuwait's longstanding support for the Palestinian Liberation Organization and Oman's restriction of Israeli airplanes from its airspace during the Gaza war. Qatar plays a central role in mediating between Hamas and Israel, providing aid and medical treatment. Conversely, Saudi Arabia faced criticism for hosting the Riyadh Festival amid the Gaza crisis, diverting attention from wider issues. Arab governments employ Israeli-made technologies for citizen surveillance, using them to deter and punish dissenting voices. Normalization with Israel may perpetuate access to advanced spy technologies, leading to increased repression and strict measures against citizens. This pattern could extend to other Arab countries, fueling citizen frustration due to their pro-Israel stance and the suppression of freedom of expression. The expectation is that normalization without addressing the Palestinian issue and without public consent may lead to societal unrest similar to the Arab Spring revolts.

The examination of the Palestine issue as a gauge for permissible civic space and dissent within the Middle East underscores a critical nexus between regional geopolitics and the state of civil liberties. As Arab governments navigate their relationships with Israel, including covert security collaborations and normalization efforts, the scope for civil society engagement and dissent, particularly concerning Palestinian self-determination and resistance to the occupation, becomes increasingly restricted. This dynamic not only reflects the regimes' efforts to align domestic discourse with foreign policy shifts, but also highlights the instrumentalization of civil society as a tool for political control. The resulting landscape presents a stark reality where the expression of solidarity with Palestinians often serves as a litmus test for the boundaries of civic freedom and dissent in the Arab world, revealing a complex interplay of regional politics, human rights, and governmental control over public discourse.

Conclusion: Rules, Dissent, and National Security

H.A. Hellyer

Nations have lost their freedom while preparing to defend it, and if we in this country confuse dissent with disloyalty, we deny the right to be wrong.

EDWARD R. MURROW, AMERICAN JOURNALIST, 1953[1]

Here in America we are descended from revolutionists and rebels – men and women who dare to dissent from accepted doctrine. As their heirs, we may never confuse honest dissent with disloyal subversion.

DWIGHT D. EISENHOWER, US PRESIDENT, 1954[2]

When our project looking at civil society space began in 2022, the space to engage in public discourse pertaining to Palestine/Israel was already "shrinking." The scholars and practitioners in this collection have detailed many of the different methods at play in circumscribing the ability of civil society institutions in the region and further afield to advocate for social and political change. Some of those approaches were old, others were new; some involved "hard" measures with the use of force, others involved "soft" ones with procedural manipulations; but all had their own significant and substantial impacts on civil society in the region, as well as the corollary, the shutting down of discourse on Israel/Palestine in the United States.

Yet, if the ability to work for political and social change and engage in discourse on this subject was challenging in 2022, the situation in

2024 is even more so. The Hamas-led attacks of October 7, 2023 and the ensuing Israeli bombardment of Gaza that is ongoing at the time of writing has dramatically transformed the landscape. It is difficult to properly account for all those consequences, and what they will mean in the years and decades to come, but we should not shut our eyes to the importance of understanding them. The intensification of events in Palestine/Israel in 2023 will have long-lasting repercussions for the prospects of a negotiated political solution between Palestinians and Israelis. It may also influence the relationship between various Arab populations in the broader region, and the various types of regimes they live under, as many of those governments have declared their intentions to normalize political relations with Israel eventually. Even further afield, it will have a bearing on relationships and understandings in liberal societies about space for dissent and civil liberties far away from Israel/Palestine, including the United States. It has already shaped how the United States and other Western states justify their policy approach on matters concerning Palestinians and Israelis. Those who invoked the importance of upholding the "rules-based order" in responding to the Russian invasion of Ukraine in 2022 are notably reluctant to apply the same framework to Palestine.[3]

A formidable group of scholars from a broad variety of backgrounds and disciplines came together for this book to help policymakers, academics, and the wider public better understand how civil society space is shrinking in the region. Moreover, they examined how the same thing is occurring in the United States with regards to the topic of Palestine/Israel, and what that means for the future of Israelis, Palestinians, and civil society globally, but in the United States especially.

As Nathan J. Brown and Dana El Kurd explore in their respective chapters, the consequences of shrinking civic space are severe, affecting how ordinary Palestinians can access essential services. Brown examines how Palestinian civil society was, once upon a time, almost a substitute for a Palestinian state, and then tracks how the end of the Oslo process, along with the deepening of Israel's occupation, led to incredible constraints on that same civil society. El Kurd, looking at Palestinian civil society from another angle, shows how an indigenous form of authoritarianism arose as a direct consequence of the Oslo Accords, and the empowering of a particular type of governance within the occupied territories. Both Brown and El Kurd note the direct relationship between constraints on Palestinian civil society, and the Israeli occupation.

In their chapter, Zaha Hassan and Layla Gantus show how Palestinian community-based organizations, humanitarian workers, and human rights defenders have all been criminalized with the entrenchment of occupation, and what this has meant in terms of their ability to fulfill their remits. They also show how the Palestinian Authority's security cooperation arrangements with Israel have created new layers of restrictions on the operations of this important segment of Palestinian society.

Israelis and Palestinians might be two different, segregated populations, but they also overlap in a variety of ways: there is an indigenous Palestinian population in Israel that constitutes 20% of all Israeli citizens, and Israeli occupation authorities have transferred hundreds of thousands of Jewish Israeli settlers into East Jerusalem and the West Bank. Dahlia Scheindlin, Jessica Buxbaum and Katherine Wilkens, in their chapters, examine the nature of Israeli civil society. Scheindlin focuses more on how it has gone through certain permutations, as Israel struggles with questions around its identity, while Buxbaum and Wilkens look at the growing political power of Jewish supremacists in Israeli society and its implications for how Israelis see their future in relation to Palestinians.

Yael Berda looks at a wider structural issue, identifying a major inspiration for the legal regime that characterizes Israel's rule over Palestinians that limits their ability to organize and challenge the restrictions on virtually every aspect of their lives, not only in the occupied territories, but also in Israel's pre-June 1967 borders. Her chapter focuses on a long history of emergency security laws, including some that were held over from British colonial rule over Mandatory Palestine, but were then developed and repurposed. Matt Mahmoudi delves into how surveillance and communication technologies, some using artificial intelligence, have been deployed by Israel as a means to deepen the occupation. Moreover, technologies "trialed" in the occupied territories are exported to local administrations in the West. Marwa Fatafta examines the technological dimension of shrinking space through investigating how online platforms algorithmically censor Palestinian voices and expressions of solidarity for Palestinians.

But in neither Israel nor Palestine are conditions determined simply by Israeli government policy, or indeed, that of the Palestinian administrations. The United States, as the most important supporter and ally of Israel, plays a major role in setting the boundaries of civic space within the occupied Palestinian territories, and internationally when it comes to pro-Palestine activism. Nour Soubani and Diala Shamas, in their chapter on US counter-terrorism policy, explore how the securitization of Palestinian activism has severely curtailed its development. Lara Friedman looks at the "shutting down" of Palestinian voices and their supporters in the US via legal measures aimed at the Boycott, Divestment and Sanctions movement, as well as wider attempts to govern how language is used around the Israel/Palestine question through the use of definitions of antisemitism.

Ashleigh Subramanian-Montgomery and Paul Carroll explore a key tool in constraining NGO operations in Palestine/Israel and the United States, particularly via financial and banking restrictions, as a direct consequence of the "Global War on Terror" that began in 2001. But those NGOs – largely Palestinian solidarity groups and humanitarian organizations – existed due to a long history of American activity domestically. Maya Berry elaborates the history of pro-Palestine activism in the United States, starting in the early twentieth century, and generally spearheaded by the Arab American community. Berry argues that this community is presumed to be overly concerned with the question of Palestine, and its access to policymakers and influence on state policy have suffered as a result. Yousef Munayyer investigates how Israeli state actors have been deployed internationally to constrain activism beyond Israel's borders, particularly within the United States, amounting to the transnational repression of civic space.

Yet, closer to home in the Arab world, there are civil society formations that have also been circumscribed in recent years. Marwan Muasher and Rafiah Al Talei assess the changes in attitude toward pro-Palestine advocacy in a broad array of Arab countries from complementary perspectives, describing the impact on civil society organizations more widely, as well as providing specific observations about individual countries.

As work on this volume was being completed, Washington, DC was managing the public relations fallout from a steady, if small, stream of resignations from the Biden administration, and dissent expressed by serving officials. One dissent memo was signed by 100 State Department and US Agency for International Development (USAID) employees, urging the US to reassess its policy toward Israel and demand a ceasefire in Gaza.[4] Over 800 officials in the US and Europe signed another letter protesting Israeli policies,[5] while more than 1,000 employees of USAID endorsed an open letter urging the administration to call for an immediate end to Israel's bombardment, as early as November 2023.

A USAID official said, "The silence from leadership on the internal letter is frustrating and disappointing,"[6] while "a growing storm of dissent was brewing in the diplomatic corps," due to what was termed Washington's "de facto blank check" for Israel.[7] One of those who resigned due to disagreements over the administration's policy,[8] Josh Paul, a State Department official, declared he'd been told by others in the State Department that "as soon as any hard policy discussions come up, they are told, 'This is coming from the top. There's no room for any discussion'."[9]

The "shrinking of space" that these former US officials alluded to in discussions around Israel/Palestine has consequences. In this crisis, the United States has already been drawn into wider conflicts. American weaponry has been used in Gaza by the Israel Defense Forces throughout; in April of 2024, the prospect of all-out war between Iran and Israel threatened a situation where the United States could enter into direct confrontation with Iran; and in June 2024, the United States assured[10] Israel that in the event of an open war breaking out between Israel and Lebanon, following months of saber rattling across the border, the US would be fully prepared to back their ally.

If the ability to freely discuss Palestine/Israel continues to shrink, the US could end up being dragged into costly wars without the agreement of much of its population, with all the heightened national security risks that entails. Expanding civic space should hence be treated as a national security interest first and foremost, especially in the case of discussing Israel/Palestine. Moreover, if there is a change of course, in the United States and more generally, and civic space expands, policy regarding Palestine/Israel can become more democratic and more representative of citizens' views. This can only be a healthy development.

List of Contributors

Rafiah Al Talei serves as the editor-in-chief of Sada, a platform for emerging voices from the Middle East published by the Carnegie Endowment for International Peace. Previously, Rafiah was a senior producer at Al Jazeera Media Network's Public Liberties and Human Rights Center. She received her PhD from Qatar University in Gulf Studies and has received fellowships from Stanford University, Syracuse University, and the National Endowment for Democracy. She has been a candidate for the Omani parliament (Majlis Al-Shura) and is a frequent speaker on press freedom and female empowerment in the Gulf including at the inaugural Arabic-language TED Talk Summit in Doha in March 2023.

Yael Berda is an associate professor of sociology and anthropology at Hebrew University and a nonresident fellow with the Middle East Initiative at the Harvard Kennedy School. Her research focuses on the way bureaucracy shapes politics and how mundane and routine practices of the state determine citizenship, sovereignty, and social power, with a focus on states that succeeded British colonial rule. Berda was a practicing human rights lawyer, representing in military and district courts as well as the Supreme Court in Israel.

Maya Berry is executive director of the Arab American Institute (AAI), a non-profit, non-partisan, national civil rights advocacy organization. She previously worked at AAI, establishing its first government relations department, which she led for five years before becoming legislative director for House Minority Whip David Bonior, where she managed the congressman's legislative strategy and developed policies on international relations, human rights, immigration, civil rights and liberties, and trade. With a deep knowledge of public policy making, she helped expand AAI's work on combatting hate crime, protecting the rights of securitized communities, strengthening democracy, and advocating for data equity, including the creation of a new Middle East and North Africa (MENA) category. In her personal capacity, Berry served as a member of the 2016 Democratic National Convention's Platform Standing Committee and has attended all but two previous Democratic National Conventions as a delegate, alternate, or standing committee member since 1992.

Nathan J. Brown is professor of political science and international affairs at George Washington University and nonresident fellow at the Carnegie Endowment for International Peace. He has served as a Guggenheim fellow, a Fulbright scholar, a Carnegie scholar, and a fellow at the Woodrow Wilson International Center for Scholars. He serves on the board of trustees at the American University in Cairo. His most recent co-authored books are *Autocrats Don't Always Get What They Want* (University of Michigan Press, 2024) and *Lumbering State, Restless Society: Egypt in the Modern Era* (Columbia University Press, 2022). He is sole author of six other books, including *Palestinian Politics after the Oslo Accords: Resuming Arab Palestine* (University of California Press, 2002). He is currently completing a book on religion and politics entitled *Religion in State*.

Jessica Buxbaum is an independent journalist based in Jerusalem, covering Israel's occupation of Palestine and the Syrian Golan. She primarily reports on Israeli state and settler violence, governmental policy, land rights, and the right-wing agenda, and investigates the Israeli settler movement and its network of support. Her work has been featured in *Mondoweiss*, *Middle East Eye*, and Al Jazeera English, among others. She is a frequent contributor to the *New Arab*, Jerusalem Story and MintPress News. South Africa cited her article on Israel's genocidal rhetoric, which was published in the *New Arab*, in its genocide case against Israel at the International Court of Justice. She holds a Master's degree in International Journalism specializing in the Middle East from City, University of London.

Paul Carroll is the managing director of Charity & Security Network where he is responsible for overall organizational management of the network, its staff, and strategy setting with respect to its issues and policy advocacy. Paul spent seventeen years at the Ploughshares Fund, a public foundation that works to eliminate the risks from nuclear weapons. More recently, Paul served as the director of nuclear security partnerships at N Square, a funders collaborative that seeks to foster innovation and collaboration in the nuclear security sector. Paul provided content expertise to members of this growing network and facilitated introductions and connections across different professional sectors to spark partnerships and creative ideas to reduce nuclear threats.

Dana El Kurd is an assistant professor at the University of Richmond in the Department of Political Science, and a senior non-resident fellow at Arab Center Washington DC. She specializes in Palestinian and Arab politics, particularly on topics related to mobilization, public opinion, and international intervention. Her work has been published in academic journals such as *Global Studies Quarterly*, *PS Political Science & Politics*, and *Democratization*, as well as media outlets such as the *Nation*, *Foreign Affairs*, the *Financial Times*, and more. El Kurd is author of *Polarized and Demobilized: Legacies of Authoritarianism in Palestine*, published with Oxford University Press in 2020.

Marwa Fatafta is a Palestinian digital rights advocate and tech policy expert based in Berlin. She leads Access Now's work on digital rights in the Middle East and North Africa region as the MENA Policy and Advocacy director. Her work spans a number of issues at the nexus of human rights and technology including content governance and platform accountability, online censorship, surveillance tech, and transnational repression. She has written extensively on the digital occupation in Palestine and is particularly interested in the role of new technologies in armed conflicts and humanitarian contexts. Marwa is also a policy analyst at Al-Shabaka: the Palestinian Policy Network, and an advisory board member of the Tahrir Institute for Middle East Policy. Marwa was a Fulbright scholar, and holds an MA in International Relations from Maxwell School of Citizenship and Public Affairs at Syracuse University.

LIST OF CONTRIBUTORS | 247

Lara Friedman is the president of the Foundation for Middle East Peace (FMEP). She is a leading authority on the Middle East, with particular expertise on US foreign policy in the region, on Israel/Palestine, and on the way Middle East and Israel/Palestine-related issues play out in Congress and in US domestic politics, policies, and legislation. Lara is also a preeminent subject-matter expert in the area of anti-Palestinian legislation and "lawfare," including the weaponization and instrumentalization of the definition of, and concerns about, antisemitism. Lara's research on lawfare- and antisemitism-related topics – which she makes available to the public – is widely cited and widely recognized as the authoritative data in the field. Lara is a former officer in the US Foreign Service, with diplomatic postings in Jerusalem, Washington, Tunis, and Beirut. She also served previously as the director of policy and government relations at Americans for Peace Now. In addition to her work with FMEP, Lara is a non-resident fellow at the US/Middle East Project (USMEP).

Layla Gantus is a researcher in the Middle East Program at the Carnegie Endowment for International Peace. Previously, she was the international advocacy coordinator at Mossawa Center, a Haifa-based NGO that advocates for the equal citizenship of the Palestinian minority in Israel. She holds a Master's in human rights and public policy from University College London.

Zaha Hassan is a human rights attorney and policy analyst. Her legal work has included a landmark case challenging the George W. Bush administration's warrantless surveillance program targeting American attorneys of a US-based Muslim charity, a program which was found illegal in a decision by a federal trial court before being reversed by the Ninth Circuit Court of Appeals under the "State Secrets Doctrine." As a fellow at the Carnegie Endowment for International Peace, Hassan's research focus is on Palestine–Israel, the use of international legal mechanisms by political movements, and the interplay between US foreign policy and domestic politics as it relates to the US–Palestinian bilateral relationship. Previously, she was the coordinator and senior legal advisor to the Palestinian negotiating team during Palestine's bid for UN membership, and a member of the Palestinian delegation to Quartet-sponsored exploratory talks between 2011 and 2012.

H. A. Hellyer has more than twenty years of experience in governmental, corporate advisory, and academic environments in the West, the Middle East, and Southeast Asia, specializing in geopolitics, security studies, and political economy. A scholar at the Carnegie Endowment for International Peace (USA), he simultaneously serves as senior associate fellow in International Security Studies at the Royal United Services Institute for Defence and Security (UK). Designated as deputy convenor of the UK government's taskforce on tackling radicalization, he was appointed as the first Economic and Social Research Council fellow in the Foreign & Commonwealth Office. He has held senior positions at policy institutes such as Brookings (USA), the Atlantic Council (USA), and the Institute for Strategic and International Studies (Malaysia); and academic posts at Warwick University (UK), Harvard University (USA), Cambridge University (UK), and the American University (Egypt). His insights on current events are regularly sought by the international media networks such as CNN and the BBC, with op-eds for publications like the *Washington Post*, *Foreign Policy*, the *New York Times*, the *Guardian*, *Politico*, and the *Financial Times*. His publications in his specialist subject areas include eight books, and more than twenty book chapters, journal articles and monographs for various academic presses.

Matt Mahmoudi is an assistant professor at the University of Cambridge, working on racialized borders in digital cities. He has led Amnesty International's research on biometric surveillance from New York City to the occupied Palestinian territories. He was the inaugural Jo Cox PhD scholar at the University of Cambridge, studying digital urban infrastructures as new frontiers for racial capitalism, where he remains an affiliated lecturer in Sociology. He helped to initiate and organize the No Tech for Tyrants (NT4T) collective to interrupt Silicon Valley entanglements with the UK government and challenge the hostile immigration environment. Matt is a co-editor of *Resisting Borders & Technologies of Violence* (Haymarket, 2024), and further appears in the journal *International Political Sociology*, and *Digital Witness* (Oxford University Press, 2020). His forthcoming book is *Migrants in the Digital Periphery: New Urban Frontiers of Control* (University of California Press, 2025).

Marwan Muasher is vice president for studies at the Carnegie Endowment, where he oversees the Endowment's research in Washington and Beirut on the Middle East. Muasher served as foreign minister (2002–2004) and deputy prime minister (2004–2005) of Jordan, and his career has spanned the areas of diplomacy, development, civil society, and communications. He was also a senior fellow at Yale University in 2010–2011. He was senior vice president of external affairs at the World Bank from 2007 to 2010. He is the author of *The Arab Center: The Promise of Moderation* (Yale University Press, 2008) and *The Second Arab Awakening and the Battle for Pluralism* (Yale University Press, 2014). He was a member of the American University of Beirut Board of Trustees (2007–2024), and is chair of an international jury for the Global Pluralism Award, given bi-annually by the Global Centre on Pluralism in Canada, an ex-member of the Global Centre for Pluralism Board of Directors, and a member of the Asfari Foundation Board of Trustees.

Yousef Munayyer is co-director of the Transnational Repression Project, a research initiative on transnational repression housed at the University of Michigan's Center for Political Studies. He also serves as head of the Palestine/Israel Program and senior fellow at Arab Center Washington DC. Munayyer is a member of the editorial committee of the *Journal of Palestine Studies*. Some of his published articles can be found in the *New York Times*, *Foreign Affairs*, the *Washington Post*, the *New Yorker*, *Foreign Policy*, the *Journal of Palestine Studies*, *Middle East Policy*, and others. Dr. Munayyer holds a PhD in International Relations and Comparative Politics from the University of Maryland. He has taught on Palestine as well as Repression and Dissent in the Middle East at Georgetown University and George Mason University.

Dahlia Scheindlin is a political strategist and a public opinion researcher who has advised on nine national campaigns in Israel and worked on elections, referendums, and public affairs campaigns in fifteen other countries over the last twenty-five years. In addition to Israel, she has regional expertise in the Balkans and Eastern Europe, the South Caucasus, and Cyprus. Dahlia conducts extensive public opinion research for civil society organizations, including joint Israeli-Palestinian surveys. She holds a PhD in Political Science from Tel Aviv University and a Master's degree from Harvard Divinity School. Dahlia is a regular columnist for *Haaretz* (English) and a policy fellow at Century International. Her writing has appeared in the *New York Times*, the *Guardian*, *Foreign Affairs*, *Foreign Policy*, the *New York Review of Books*, and the *New Statesman*, among other publications, and she has co-hosted several podcasts, including the Tel Aviv Review and the Election Overdose podcast at *Haaretz*. Her new book, *The Crooked Timber of Democracy in Israel: Promise Unfulfilled*, was published in September 2023.

Diala Shamas is a senior staff attorney at the Center for Constitutional Rights (CCR), where she works on challenging government and law enforcement abuses perpetrated under the guise of national security, both in the US and abroad. Prior to joining the CCR, Diala was a clinical supervising attorney and lecturer in Law at Stanford Law School, and a senior staff attorney supervising the Creating Law Enforcement Accountability and Responsibility project at CUNY School of Law.

Nour Soubani is a Root-Tilden-Kern scholar and Institute for International Law and Justice scholar at New York University School of Law. She holds a Master's degree in Middle East Studies from Harvard University. Nour has worked as a grassroots organizer in Dearborn, Michigan, using community education, storytelling, and advocacy to challenge War on Terror surveillance policies that profile Arab and Muslim communities. She also has experience working as a research analyst supporting human rights litigation and the legal defense of Muslim charities targeted by material support laws. While at NYU, Nour has worked on issues related to international law and Palestine at the Al Quds University Human Rights Clinic and the Center for Constitutional Rights, as well as indigenous land rights and criminal defense.

Ashleigh Subramanian-Montgomery is the Senior Director, Policy & Advocacy with the Charity & Security Network, where she leads the organization's policy goals and is head of the DC office. Her work supports protecting civil society from the harmful impacts of counter-terrorism measures worldwide. Ashleigh is experienced in working on policy, gender, and research, and has worked on peacebuilding across a number of contexts and conflicts. She integrates intersectional gender perspectives and human rights-based approaches across her areas of expertise. She started her career in social service roles supporting women experiencing homelessness and children experiencing abuse in the US, which developed her drive to close the gaps between policy and those most impacted by policy. She has since had the privilege of working in Botswana, Burundi, the Golan Heights, Israel, Nigeria, Palestine, Timor-Leste, and the US, and on Afghanistan,

Iraq, Namibia, South Sudan, and Syria. Ashleigh has been published in *Responsible Statecraft*, *Truthout*, and *Inkstick*. She studied at Columbia University's School of International and Public Affairs and the University of California, San Diego. Though she's been told repeatedly it can't be done, Ashleigh's ultimate goal is to work herself out of a job through partnering in community to achieve collective liberation.

Katherine Wilkens is a foreign policy professional and policy analyst. She is currently a non-resident fellow at the Carnegie Endowment for International Peace where she formerly served as deputy director of the Middle East Program. Previously, she was vice president of AMIDEAST, staff director of the House Foreign Affairs Subcommittee on Europe and the Middle East, and senior advisor on the Middle East at the National Democratic Institute.

Acknowledgements

The idea for this book arose out of conversations that took place after the publication of an April 2021 report by the Carnegie Endowment for International Peace (CEIP) and the US/Middle East Project (US/MEP) titled "Breaking the Israel/Palestine status quo: a rights-based approach."[1] The report set out policy prescriptions toward ending the Israeli military occupation over Palestinians, and argued that laying the foundation for a durable and just peace between Palestinians and Israelis required centering rights and human security in US foreign policy. Weeks after the release of the report, Human Rights Watch published "A Threshold Crossed,"[2] a groundbreaking legal assessment of Israel's policies and practices toward Palestinians which confirmed those of Palestinian and Israeli human rights organizations and various UN experts that Israel's regime over Palestinians is one of apartheid. Then in May 2021, high-intensity violence erupted in the region. It began with an Israeli attempt to evict Palestinian refugees from their home in occupied East Jerusalem and assaults on Muslim worshipers in Al-Aqsa Mosque during Ramadan. It quickly spread to Gaza and inside Israel with Hamas firing rockets at Israeli towns and around Jerusalem, and Jewish Israelis attacking Palestinian citizens in the few mixed Arab-Jewish cities inside Israel. During this period between April and May and in the months that followed, human rights activists, legal experts, humanitarian workers, and NGOs were subjected to various attacks, reports documented how social media platforms had engaged in over-moderation of pro-Palestinian viewpoints on their platforms and deactivated accounts, and invasive surveillance technologies were discovered to have been used against activists inside the occupied Palestinian territories and abroad.

Concerned about these developments and how they might impact dissent and discourse in the United States and the prospects for a just and durable peace between Palestinians and Israelis, the editors of this book convened a study group of experts from the United States and the region at the Carnegie Endowment for International Peace. This collection came out of the convenings of the study group and constitutes an effort to make sense of trends that have been in play for many years now. Our hope is that this book will support more informed US policy toward Palestine/Israel and elucidate how the troubling trends identified by the contributors threaten to become a blueprint for shutting down debate and discussion on other important policy concerns.

Our thanks and appreciation go to our publisher, Oneworld, and to Novin Doostdar, who understood the importance of this topic immediately. He and his team of editors at Oneworld, particularly Rida Vaquas, have been incredibly patient with our many rounds of edits; we appreciate how quickly they moved the manuscript through their internal processes to get us to publication on time.

We wish to acknowledge the work of Layla Gantus, Carnegie researcher and manager of the project and the editing process. Special thanks also go to our Carnegie colleague Nathan J. Brown who helped launch the project and reviewed some of the contributions with such care. Finally, we wish to express our deep gratitude to Marwan Muasher, Carnegie's vice president of studies, and the other members of the study group who shared their time and expertise.

This book would not have been possible without the generous support of the Carnegie Endowment for International Peace and Open Society Foundation. The editors and contributors alone, however, are responsible for this book's final content. Carnegie does not take institutional positions on public policy issues; the views represented herein do not necessarily reflect the views of Carnegie, its staff, or its trustees. Likewise, the views represented herein are not necessarily those of the Open Society, its board, staff or advisors.

Notes

Introduction

1. Natanson, Hannah, and Emmanuel Felton. "Business titans privately urged NYC mayor to use police on Columbia protesters, chats show." Washington Post, May 16, 2024.
2. Zwelivelile, Nkosi. "My grandfather Nelson Mandela fought apartheid. I see the parallels with Israel." Guardian, October 11, 2018. https://www.theguardian.com/commentisfree/2018/oct/11/grandfather-nelson-mandela-apartheid-parallels-israel-palestinian; Miller, Aaron David. "I was in Ann Arbor during Vietnam. But since then, never have I seen any foreign policy issue roil domestic waters like the Israel-Hamas war..." https://twitter.com/aarondmiller2/status/1784697324213604535?t=8XHNwZ9Mt9Ah7nudaRlhdQ&s=08.
3. As this book goes to press, the International Court of Justice, the principal judicial arm of the United Nations, issued an advisory opinion finding that Israel's regime in the occupied Palestinian territories is consistent with the legal definition of apartheid. See, "Legal Consequences arising from the Policies and Practices of Israel in the Occupied Palestinian Territory, including East Jerusalem, Advisory Opinion." July 19, 2024. https://www.icj-cij.org/sites/default/files/case-related/186/186-20240719-adv-01-00-en.pdf, 65.
4. Shakir, Omar. "Israeli apartheid: 'a threshold crossed'." Human Rights Watch, July 19, 2021. https://www.hrw.org/news/2021/07/19/israeli-apartheid-threshold-crossed; Amnesty International. "Israel's apartheid against Palestinians," February 1, 2022. https://www.amnesty.org/en/latest/campaigns/2022/02/israels-system-of-apartheid/.
5. Menand, Louis. "Academic freedom under fire." New Yorker, April 29, 2024. https://www.newyorker.com/magazine/2024/05/06/academic-freedom-under-fire.
6. Kaleem, Jaweed. "USC's valedictorian speech cancelled: 'The university has betrayed me.'" LA Times, April 16, 2024. https://www.latimes.com/california/story/2024-04-16/usc-valedictorian-banned-graduation-speech.

7   Maruf, Ramishah. "Students are lawyering up in the wake of Israel-Hamas war." CNN, November 28, 2024. https://www.cnn.com/2023/11/28/business/students-lawsuits-israel-hamas-war/index.html.
8   Davidoff Solomon, Steven. "Don't hire my anti-semitic law students." Wall Street Journal, October 15, 2023. https://www.wsj.com/articles/dont-hire-my-anti-semitic-law-students-protests-colleges-universities-jews-palestine-6ad86ad5.
9   Hamid, Shadi, Brett Max Kaufman, Yousef Munayyer and Natasha Roth-Rowland. "Is a new McCarthyism punishing pro-Palestine speech on US universities? Our panel reacts." Guardian, December 13, 2023. https://www.theguardian.com/commentisfree/2023/dec/13/israel-gaza-us-universities-free-speech.
10 Bedi, Neil, Bora Erden, Marco Hernandez, Ishaan Jhaveri, Arijeta Lajka, Natalie Reneau, Helmuth Rosales and Aric Toler. "How Counterprotesters at UCLA Provoked Violence, Unchecked for Hours." New York Times, May 3, 2024. https://www.nytimes.com/interactive/2024/05/03/us/ucla-protests-encampment-violence.html.
11 See, "Israel defying ICJ ruling to prevent genocide by failing to allow adequate humanitarian aid to reach Gaza." Amnesty International, February 26, 2024. https://www.amnesty.org/en/latest/news/2024/02/israel-defying-icj-ruling-to-prevent-genocide-by-failing-to-allow-adequate-humanitarian-aid-to-reach-gaza/. On May 20, 2024, the Prosecutor of the International Criminal Court, Karim Khan, announced the filing of applications for warrants of arrest before the court's Pre-Trial Chamber for Israeli Prime Minister Benjamin Netanyahu and Defense Minister Yoav Gallant on the basis of various acts including using "[s]tarvation of civilians as a method of warfare". Warrants were also issued against leaders of Hamas. See, "Statement of ICC Prosecutor Karim A.A. Khan KC: Applications for arrest warrants in the situation in the State of Palestine." May 20, 2024. https://www.icc-cpi.int/news/statement-icc-prosecutor-karim-aa-khan-kc-applications-arrest-warrants-situation-state.
12 Beckett, Lois. "'They're sending a message': harsh police tactics questioned amid US campus protest crackdowns." Guardian, May 4, 2024. https://www.theguardian.com/us-news/article/2024/may/04/police-tactics-us-campus-protest-crackdowns.
13 "Israeli forces' conduct in Gaza." Human Rights Watch, March 19, 2024, last accessed April 5, 2024. https://www.hrw.org/news/2024/03/19/israeli-forces-conduct-gaza.
14 H. Res. 845, 118th Congress (2023–2024), passed November 7, 2023. https://www.congress.gov/bill/118th-congress/house-resolution/845/text.
15 UN Security Council Briefing, SC/15487, "World Health Organization Chief, briefing Security Council on war in Gaza, joins calls for an immediate ceasefire, unfettered humanitarian access." November 10, 2023. https://press.un.org/en/2023/sc15487.doc.htm; Abi-Rached, Joel M. "The war on hospitals." Boston Review, December 20, 2023. https://www.bostonreview.net/articles/the-war-on-hospitals/; Polglaze, Katie, Gianluca Mezzofiore, Eliza Mackintosh, Livvy Doherty, Henrik Petterson, Byron Manley and Lou Robinson. "How Gaza's hospital became battlegrounds." CNN, January 12, 2024. https://www.cnn.com/interactive/2024/01/middleeast/gaza-hospitals-destruction-investigation-intl-cmd/.
16 Wade, Peter. "Graham: Israel should do 'whatever' they want to Palestinians like when US nuked Japan." Rolling Stone (blog), May 12, 2024. https://www.rollingstone.com/politics/politics-news/graham-israel-bomb-palestinians-hiroshima-nagasaki-1235019216/; Vargas, Ramon Antonio. "Congressman rebuked for call to bomb Gaza 'like Nagasaki and Hiroshima.'" Guardian, March 31, 2024. https://www.theguardian.com/us-news/2024/mar/31/tim-walberg-republican-congressman-gaza; Reid, Scotty T. "US congressman Andy Ogles stirs outrage

256 | SUPPRESSING DISSENT

with Gaza comment – 'Kill them all.'" Al Jazeera, February 21, 2024. https://www.aljazeera.com/news/2024/2/21/us-congressman-andy-ogles-stirs-outrage-with-gaza-comment-kill-them-all.

17 Gross, Judah Ari. "One every hour: ADL records 8,873 antisemitic incidents in 2023." EJewish Philanthropy, April 16, 2024. https://ejewishphilanthropy.com/one-every-hour-adl-records-8873-antisemitic-incidents-in-2023-more-than-double-the-previous-record/.

18 See this report for a definition of anti-Palestinian racism formulated in the Canadian context: *Anti-Palestinian Racism: Naming, Framing and Manifestations.* Canadian-Arab Lawyers Association, April 25, 2022. https://static1.squarespace.com/static/61db30d12e169a5c45950345/t/627dcf83fa17ad41ff217964/1652412292220/Anti-Palestinian+Racism-+Naming%2C+Framing+and+Manifestations.pdf.

19 "CAIR received 1,283 complaints over past month, an unprecedented increase in complaints of Islamophobia and anti-Arab bias." CAIR, November 9, 2023. https://ca.cair.com/sfba/news/cair-received-1283-complaints-over-past-month-an-unprecedented-increase-in-complaints-of-islamophobia-anti-arab-bias/.

20 Llamas, Tom and Mirna Alsharif. "Palestinian student shot in Vermont say the suspected waited for and targeted them." NBC News, January 17, 2024. https://www.nbcnews.com/news/us-news/palestinian-students-shot-burlington-vermont-interview-hospital-recove-rcna133822.

21 "Chicago area landlord indicted for murder, hate crime in stabbing death of 6-year-old Palestinian boy." CBS News, October 26, 2024. https://www.cbsnews.com/chicago/news/joseph-czuba-indicted-murder-hate-crime-wadee-alfayoumi-plainfield/.

22 "University professors testify on college campus antisemitism, Parts I." CSPAN, December 5, 2023. https://www.c-span.org/video/?c5096365/user-clip-rep-elise-stefanik-v-harvard-pres.

23 Ibid.

24 Menand, "Academic freedom under fire."

25 Svrluga, Susan. "Harvard president resigns amid plagiarism allegations, testimony backlash." Washington Post, January 3, 2024. https://www.washingtonpost.com/education/2024/01/02/claudine-gay-resigns-harvard/.

26 Snyder, Susan. "Penn leadership upheaval could have a 'chilling effect' on college presidencies and university operations nationally." Inquirer, December 10, 2023, last accessed May 19, 2024. https://www.inquirer.com/education/penn-president-resignation-university-donors-antisemitism-20231210.html.

27 Blinkley, Collin, and Moriah Balingit, "How conservative outrage and plagiarism charges led to resignation of Harvard's president." PBS NewsHour, January 3, 2024. https://www.pbs.org/newshour/education/how-conservative-outrage-and-plagiarism-charges-led-to-resignation-of-harvards-president.

28 "Pro-Palestine student protests nearly triple in April." ACLED Brief, May 2, 2024. https://acleddata.com/2024/05/02/pro-palestine-us-student-protests-nearly-triple-in-april-acled-brief/.

29 "Columbia students not representing Jewish and pro-Palestinian sides speak about protests." NBC News, April 24, 2024. https://www.nbcnews.com/now/video/columbia-students-representing-jewish-and-pro-palestinian-sides-speak-about-protests-209610309512.

30 Silva, Manuela. "'I am the Jewish future': detained Jewish Columbia students hold press conference outside president's house." Columbia Daily Spectator, April 24, 2024. https://www.columbiaspectator.com/city-news/2024/04/24/i-am-the-

jewish-future-detained-jewish-columbia-students-hold-press-conference-outside-presidents-house/.
31 Kaur, Harmeet. "Examining the history of the 'outside agitator' narrative." CNN, April 29, 2024. https://www.cnn.com/2024/04/27/us/campus-protests-palestine-outside-agitator-cec/index.html.
32 Myscofski, Megan. "Pro-Palestinian protestors are calling for UNM to 'disclose and divest' from its investments in Israel, but what would that look like?" KUNM 98.9 FM, May 2, 2024. https://www.kunm.org/local-news/2024-05-02/pro-palestinian-protestors-are-calling-for-unm-to-disclose-and-divest-from-its-investments-in-israel-but-what-would-that-look-like.
33 "ICJ ruling: key takeaways from the court decision in Israel genocide case." Reuters, January 26, 2024. https://www.reuters.com/world/middle-east/key-takeaways-world-court-decision-israei-genocide-case-2024-01-26/.
34 The first university to reach an agreement was UC Riverside. See Rajikumar, Shruti. "UC Riverside becomes first UC campus to reach deal with pro-Palestine protestors." HuffPost, May 4, 2024. https://www.huffpost.com/entry/uc-riverside-reaches-agreement-with-pro-palestine-student-protestors_n_663681a2e4b00b1eab537589.
35 Latham, Angele. "Vanderbilt University students protest, arrested at sit-in: what to know." MSN, March 28, 2024. https://www.msn.com/en-us/news/us/vanderbilt-university-students-protest-arrested-at-sit-in-what-to-know/ar-BB1kI0e5.
36 See Palestine Legal. "List of legislation targeting Palestinian advocacy." https://legislation.palestinelegal.org/#states-list.
37 SB 1993 and HB 2050, effective March 13, 2022. https://wapp.capitol.tn.gov/apps/Billinfo/default.aspx?BillNumber=SB1993&ga=112; see Palestine Legal. Legislation/Tennessee. https://legislation.palestinelegal.org/location/tennessee/.
38 Franke, Katherine. "Columbia is waging a war on dissent." Nation, April 1, 2024. https://www.thenation.com/article/society/columbia-lawsuit-israel-antisemitism/.
39 "University policies: a growing catalogue of Columbia-wide policies." Columbia University website. https://universitypolicies.columbia.edu/content/rules-university-conduct.
40 Lynch, Mark, and Shibley Telhami. "Scholars who study the Middle East are afraid to speak out." Chronicle of Higher Education, December 5, 2023. https://www.chronicle.com/article/scholars-who-study-the-middle-east-are-afraid-to-speak-out.
41 University of Maryland. "Critical Issues poll, Middle East Scholar Barometer." November 10–17, 2023. https://criticalissues.umd.edu/middle-east-scholar-barometer.
42 University of Maryland. "Critical Issues poll with IPSOS." January 29–February 5, 2024. https://criticalissues.umd.edu/sites/criticalissues.umd.edu/files/UMCIP_February2024_Israel-Palestine_Results.pdf.
43 Ibid.
44 Pietsch, Bryan. "Most Americans oppose Israel's war in Gaza, poll finds." Washington Post, March 27, 2024. https://www.washingtonpost.com/world/2024/03/27/us-poll-israel-gaza/; Data for Progress. "Voters call for a permanent ceasefire." February 27, 2024. https://www.dataforprogress.org/blog/2024/2/27/voters-support-the-us-calling-for-permanent-ceasefire-in-gaza-and-conditioning-military-aid-to-israel; Institute for Social Policy and Understanding. "Majority of Muslim and Jewish Democrats favor a ceasefire." February 12, 2024. https://www.ispu.org/ceasefire-poll/; Data for Progress. "Voters want the US to call for a permanent ceasefire in Gaza and to prioritize diplomacy." December 27, 2023. https://www.

dataforprogress.org/blog/2023/12/5/voters-want-the-us-to-call-for-a-permanent-ceasefire-in-gaza-and-to-prioritize-diplomacy.

45 Long, Collen, and Aamer Madhani. "Biden takes tougher stance on Israel's 'indiscriminate bombing' of Gaza." AP News, December 12, 2023. https://apnews.com/article/biden-israel-hamas-oct-7-44c4229d4c1270d9cfa484b664a22071.

46 Ebrahim, Nadine, and Abbas Lawati. "The US allowed a Gaza ceasefire resolution to pass at the UN. What does that mean for the war?" CNN, March 27, 2024. https://www.cnn.com/2024/03/26/middleeast/israel-gaza-ceasefire-un-resolution-war-impact-intl/index.html. The United States blocked three UN Security Council resolutions calling for an immediate ceasefire before abstaining from the resolution adopted in March. However, following the adoption of Resolution 2728 it declared that it viewed the resolution as non-binding.

47 "More Americans are getting news on Tiktok, bucking the trend on other social media sites." Pew Research Center, November 15, 2023. https://www.pewresearch.org/short-reads/2023/11/15/more-americans-are-getting-news-on-tiktok-bucking-the-trend-seen-on-most-other-social-media-sites/.

48 Drew, Harwell, and Taylor Lorenz. "TikTok again at center of debate over Israel, Hamas war." Washington Post. November 2, 2023. https://www.washingtonpost.com/technology/2023/11/02/tiktok-israel-hamas-video-brainwash/.

49 "The Journal." Wall Street Journal Podcast, March 13, 2024. https://www.wsj.com/podcasts/the-journal/house-passes-bill-to-ban-tiktok/dff6dbdc-76bb-4076-b116-302d32246f70.

50 US State Department. "Secretary Blinken participates in keynote conversation at McCain Institute." US State Department YouTube Channel, May 4, 2024. https://www.youtube.com/watch?v=V92PzA6eEyM.

51 Zeldin, Jeff. "Efforts by US to crack down on TikTok spark backlash against Israel." VOA, March 20, 2024. https://www.voanews.com/a/efforts-by-us-to-crack-down-on-tiktok-spark-backlash-against-israel/7535577.html.

52 Gallop Polling. "Most Important Problem." https://news.gallup.com/poll/1675/most-important-problem.aspx.

53 University of Maryland. "Critical Issues poll, American attitudes toward the Israeli-Palestinian conflict: part I." May 6–16, 2022. https://criticalissues.umd.edu/sites/criticalissues.umd.edu/files/May_BDS_Questionnaire%20with%20results.pdf.

54 Data for Progress. "Voters want the United States to call for a permanent ceasefire in Gaza and to prioritize diplomacy." December 5, 2023. https://www.dataforprogress.org/blog/2023/12/5/voters-want-the-us-to-call-for-a-permanent-ceasefire-in-gaza-and-to-prioritize-diplomacy.

55 Data for Progress. "Voters support the US calling for permanent ceasefire in Gaza and conditioning military aid to Israel." February 27, 2024. https://www.dataforprogress.org/blog/2024/2/27/voters-support-the-us-calling-for-permanent-ceasefire-in-gaza-and-conditioning-military-aid-to-israel.

56 Reuters and Israel Hayom staff. "Biden dogged by Democrats' anger over Israel, poll finds." Israel Hayom, February 29, 2024. https://www.israelhayom.com/2024/02/29/biden-dogged-by-democrats-anger-over-israel-poll-finds/.

57 Gallup. "Americans' views of both Israel and Palestinian Authority down." March 4, 2024. https://news.gallup.com/poll/611375/americans-views-israel-palestinian-authority-down.aspx#:~:text=A%20separate%20question%20in%20the,have%20an%20opinion%20(8%25).

58 University of Maryland. "Critical Issues poll with Ipsos, American public attitudes on Israel/Palestine." June 21–27, 2023. https://criticalissues.umd.edu/sites/criticalissues.umd.edu/files/UMCIP_Israel_Results_June2023.pdf.
59 B'tselem. "A regime of Jewish supremacy from the Jordan River to the Mediterranean Sea: this is apartheid." January 12, 2021. https://www.btselem.org/publications/fulltext/202101_this_is_apartheid; Human Rights Watch. "A threshold crossed: Israeli authorities and the crimes of apartheid and persecution." April 27, 2021. https://www.hrw.org/report/2021/04/27/threshold-crossed/israeli-authorities-and-crimes-apartheid-and-persecution; Amnesty International. "Israel's apartheid against Palestinians: a look into decades of oppression and domination." February 1, 2022. https://www.amnesty.org/en/latest/campaigns/2022/02/israels-system-of-apartheid/.
60 Harvard Kennedy School Institute of Politics. "Harvard Youth Poll, 47th edition, Spring 2024." https://iop.harvard.edu/youth-poll/47th-edition-spring-2024.
61 Axelrod, Tax, and Gabriella Abdul-Hakim. "Israel's war in Gaza became a political flashpoint. Will it risk Biden's coalition for reelection?" ABC News, April 8, 2024. https://abcnews.go.com/Politics/israels-war-gaza-political-flashpoint-risk-bidens-coalition/story?id=108962662.
62 "Let it go to voicemail: Democrats reportedly ignoring calls for cease-fire." New Republic, November 10, 2023. https://newrepublic.com/post/176873/let-go-voicemail-democrats-reportedly-ignoring-calls-ceasefire-gaza; Guo, Kayla. "Democratic aides in Congress break with their bosses on Israel-Hamas War." New York Times, November 13, 2023. https://www.nytimes.com/2023/11/13/us/politics/democratic-aides-congress-israel-hamas.html.
63 Wolf, Zachary B. "Biden's younger voter problem keeps getting worse." CNN, April 29, 2024. https://www.cnn.com/2024/04/29/politics/biden-young-voters-what-matters/index.html.
64 Nate Cohn, "Trump leads in 5 key states as young and nonwhite voters express discontent with Biden." May 13, 2024. https://www.nytimes.com/2024/05/13/us/politics/biden-trump-battleground-poll.html.
65 Yerushalmi, Shalom. "Israel in talks with Congo and other countries on Gaza 'voluntary migration' plan." The Times of Israel, January 3, 2024. https://www.timesofisrael.com/israel-in-talks-with-congo-and-other-countries-on-gaza-voluntary-migration-plan/.
66 McKernan, Bethan. "Israeli ministers attend conference calling for 'voluntary migration' of Palestinians." Guardian, January 29, 2024. https://www.theguardian.com/world/2024/jan/29/israeli-ministers-attend-conference-calling-for-voluntary-migration-of-palestinians.
67 See Chotiner, Isaac. "Biden's increasingly contradictory Israel policy." New Yorker, April 2, 2024. https://www.newyorker.com/news/q-and-a/bidens-increasingly-contradictory-israel-policy.
68 See Monrad, Phillip. "Ideological exclusion, plenary power, and the PLO." California Law Review 77 (1989): 828–9.
69 Democracy Now! "The case of the LA 8: US drops 20-year effort to deport Arab Americans for supporting Palestinian national rights." November 2, 2007. http://www.democracynow.org/2007/11/2/the_case_of_the_la8_u.
70 *Palestine Information Office v. Shultz*, 853 F.2d 932 (DC Cir. 1988). https://www.congress.gov/bill/118th-congress/house-resolution/845/text.
71 Gwertzman, Bernard. "Reagan administration held 9-month talks with PLO." New York Times, February 19, 1984. https://www.nytimes.com/1984/02/19/world/reagan-administration-held-9-month-talks-with-plo.html.

72 Section 901 of the Foreign Relations Authorization Act for fiscal years 1988 and 1989 ended ideological exclusion providing that no immigrant or nonimmigrant may be excluded or deported on the basis of "past, current, or expected beliefs, statements, or associations which, if engaged in by a United States citizen would be protected under the Constitution of the United States." However, Section 901 excepted PLO officials and spokespersons from the benefits of the Act. Public L. 100-204, 101 Stat. 1331, 1399-1400 (1987).
73 Immigration Act of 1990, Pub.L. 101-649, 104 Stat. 4978 (1990).
74 8 US Code Section 1182(a)(3)(B)(i).
75 Ibid.
76 22 US Code Section 1501. https://uscode.house.gov/view.xhtml?path=/prelim@title22/chapter61&edition=prelim.
77 Ragson, Adam. "Palestinians reject explanation for threatened closure of DC PLO office." Jerusalem Post, November 19, 2017. https://www.jpost.com/Arab-Israeli-Conflict/Palestinians-reject-Trump-teams-reasons-for-threatening-closure-of-DC-PLO-office-514633.
78 Mostafa, Amr. "Palestinian foreign minister reportedly barred from speaking to the media in Washington." National News, December 9, 2023. https://www.thenationalnews.com/mena/palestine-israel/2023/12/09/us-denies-barring-palestinian-minister-from-speaking-to-media-in-washington/.
79 Romo, Vanessa. "Reps. Omar and Tlaib barred from visiting Israel after Trump supports a ban." NPR, August 15, 2019. https://www.npr.org/2019/08/15/751430877/reps-omar-and-tlaib-barred-from-visiting-israel-after-trump-insists-on-ban.
80 Private roundtable with designated organizations conducted in Ramallah, July 19, 2022.
81 Interview with Shawan Jabarin in Ramallah, June 19, 2022; interview with Ubai Abboudi in Ramallah, June 9, 2022; interview with Khalid Quzmar in Al Bireh, June 19, 2022; interview with Sahar Francis in Ramallah, June 12, 2022.
82 Starr, Michael. "October 7 victims sue UNRWA USA for alleged financial support of Hamas." Jerusalem Post, March 10, 2024. https://www.jpost.com/israel-hamas-war/article-791159.
83 UNRWA USA. "Our commitment to refugees stands firm – UNRWA USA: showing Palestine refugees that Americans care." March 18, 2024. https://www.unrwausa.org/unrwa-usa-press-releases/our-commitment-to-refugees-stands-firm.
84 Peter Beinart, "The campaign to abolish UNRWA." Jewish Currents, February 13, 2024, https://jewishcurrents.org/the-campaign-to-abolish-unrwa.
85 Sinaz, Emine. "UNRWA staff accused by Israel sacked without evidence, chief admits." Guardian, February 9, 2024. https://www.theguardian.com/world/2024/feb/09/head-of-unwra-says-he-followed-reverse-due-process-in-sacking-accused-gaza-staff; Shifrin, Nick, Dan Sagalyn, Ethan Dodd and Nana Adwoa Antwi-Boasiako. "Israel accused UN agency of enabling and employing Hamas. Experts debate its future." PBS Newshour, February 21, 2024. https://www.pbs.org/newshour/show/experts-discuss-future-of-unrwa-in-gaza-and-allegations-some-employees-helped-hamas.
86 Brennan, Margaret and Richard Escobedo. "Government funding deal includes ban on US aid to UNRWA, a key relief agency in Gaza until 2025, sources say." CBS News, March 21, 2024. https://www.cbsnews.com/news/israel-gaza-government-funding-deal-includes-ban-on-u-s-aid-to-unrwa-until-2025-sources/.
87 "Integrated food security phase classification, food security analysis – the Gaza Strip." IPC Global Initiative Special Brief, March 18, 2024. IPC_Gaza_Strip_Acute_Food_Insecurity_Feb_July2024_Special_Brief.pdf.

88 "What they are saying: Ways and Means tax exempt charity legislation will combat tax breaks for terrorism." House Ways and Means, December 8, 2023. https://waysandmeans.house.gov/what-they-are-saying-ways-and-means-tax-exempt-charity-legislation-will-combat-tax-breaks-for-terrorism/.

89 Aronoff, Kate. "This bipartisan bill could give Trump huge power against his enemies." TNR, April 30, 2024. https://newrepublic.com/article/181087/treasury-pipelines-gaza-non-profit-terrorism.

90 "ADL says Palestinian scarf equals swastika." Breaking Points with Krystal and Saagar, April 1, 2024. https://www.youtube.com/watch?v=CGH95F8BiKM.

91 Markovitch, Ally. "A debate over Israel-Palestine curriculum flares at Berkeley schools." March 21, 2024. https://www.berkeleyside.org/2024/03/21/berkeley-unified-israel-palestine-curricul um-debate.

92 Stratford, Michael. "Trump administration adopts new definition of anti-Semitism in schools." Politico, September 11, 2018. https://www.politico.com/story/2018/09/11/trump-anti-semitism-schools-781917.

93 International Holocaust Remembrance Alliance. "Working definition of antisemitism." https://holocaustremembrance.com/resources/working-definition-antisemitism.

94 See, generally, Graber, Abigail A. "Religious discrimination at school: Application of Title VI of the Civil Rights Act of 1964, Legal Sidebar." Congressional Research Service, March 22, 2024. https://crsreports.congress.gov/product/pdf/LSB/LSB11129.

95 Barnett, Michael, and Nathan Brown. "Biden admin punts on defining antisemitism (opinion)." Inside Higher Ed, June 23, 2023. https://www.insidehighered.com/opinion/views/2023/06/23/biden-admin-punts-defining-antisemitism-opinion.

96 Tamkin, Emily. "The Anti-defamation League has abandoned some of the people it purports to protect." Slate, April 29, 2024. https://slate.com/news-and-politics/2024/04/antisemitism-adl-defamation-league-greenblatt-jews-israel-encampments-ceasefire.html; see also Goldman, David. "Wikipedia now labels the top Jewish civil rights group as an unreliable source." CNN, June 20, 2024. https://edition.cnn.com/2024/06/19/media/wikipedia-adl/index.html#:~:text=Wikipedia%20editors%20label%20the%20ADL,Israel%2DPalestine%20conflict%20%7C%20CNN%20Business.

97 H.R. 6090, The Antisemitism Awareness Act of 2023, 118th Congress, 2nd Session. govinfo.gov/content/pkg/BILLS-118hr6090eh/html/BILLS-118hr6090eh.htm.

98 Accorsi, Alessandro. "How Israel mastered information war in Gaza." Foreign Policy, March 11, 2024. https://foreignpolicy.com/2024/03/11/israel-gaza-hamas-netanyahu-warfare-misinformation/.

99 Ibid.

100 Ibid.

101 Goichman, Raphaela. "This anti-BDS effort failed. So Israel throws another $30 million at it." Haaretz, January 26, 2022. https://www.haaretz.com/israel-news/2022-01-26/ty-article-magazine/.premium/this-anti-bds-initiative-failed-so-israel-throws-another-100-million-nis-at-it/0000017f-db50-df9c-a17f-ff58b4110000.

102 Shabi, Rachel. "Special spin body gets media on message, says Israel." Guardian, January 1, 2009. https://www.theguardian.com/world/2009/jan/02/israel-palestine-pr-spin.

103 Benjakob, Omer. "Israeli influence operation targets US lawmakers on Hamas-UNRWA." Haaretz, March 19, 2024. https://www.haaretz.com/israel-news/security-aviation/2024-03-19/ty-article-magazine/.premium/israeli-influence-op-targets-u-s-lawmakers-on-hamas-unrwa/0000018e-5098-d282-a19f-7dd95cc70000.

104 "Human rights due diligence of Meta's impacts in Israel and Palestine." BSR, September 22, 2022. https://www.bsr.org/en/reports/meta-human-rights-israel-palestine.
105 Dwoskin, Elizabeth. "Outside audit says Facebook restricted Palestinian posts during Gaza War." Washington Post, September 23, 2022. https://www.washingtonpost.com/technology/2022/09/22/facebook-censorship-palestinians/.
106 Palestine Legal. "Legislation." https://legislation.palestinelegal.org/types-of-legislation/#antisemitism-redefinition.
107 Harb, Ali. "'Frightening': US appeals court upholds anti-BDS law." Al Jazeera, June 22, 2022. https://www.aljazeera.com/news/2022/6/22/frightening-us-appeals-court-upholds-arkansas-anti-bds-law.
108 Millhiser, Ian. "The Supreme Court effectively abolishes the right to mass protest in three US states." Vox, April 15, 2024. https://www.vox.com/scotus/24080080/supreme-court-mckesson-doe-first-amendment-protest-black-lives-matter.
109 "Pro-Palestinian protestors shut down Golden Gate Bridge, I-880 in Oakland, causing major delays." ABC 7 News, April 15, 2024. https://abc7news.com/pro-palestinian-protesters-shut-down-golden-gate-bridge-and-i-880-in-oakland/14668534/.
110 "Pro-Palestinian protestors block traffic into Chicago Airport, causing headaches for travelers." AP, April 15, 2024. https://www.usnews.com/news/best-states/illinois/articles/2024-04-15/pro-palestinian-demonstrators-block-traffic-into-chicago-airport-causing-headaches-for-travelers.
111 "United States Strategy to Combat Antisemitism." May 11, 2023. www.whitehouse.gov/wp-content/uploads/2023/05/US-National-Strategy-to-Counter-Antisemitism.pdf.
112 Civicus Monitor. "Global Findings 2023." https://monitor.civicus.org/globalfindings_2023/.
113 "Scoping study on operating conditions of civil society in the occupied Palestinian territory." International Civil Society Centre, March 2022. https://icscentre.org/wp-content/uploads/2022/04/ICSCentre_Scoping-Study-on-Operating-Conditions-of-Civil-Society-in-the-Occupied-Palestinian-Territory.pdf.
114 "Protections of space for civil society and human rights defenders: the case of Israel and Palestine." Act Alliance, February 2018. https://actalliance.org/documents/protection-of-space-for-civil-society-and-human-rights-defenders-the-case-of-israel-and-palestine/.
115 "Foreign influence: how Israel's Ministry of Strategic Affairs funded lobbying and extremism in the US" Foundation for Middle East Peace, Event, October 1, 2020. https://fmep.org/event/foreign-influence-how-israels-ministry-of-strategic-affairs-funded-lobbying-extremism-in-the-u-s/.
116 State Department. "State Department 2023 Country Report – Israel, the West Bank and Gaza." https://www.state.gov/reports/2023-country-reports-on-human-rights-practices/israel-west-bank-and-gaza/.
117 Gorokhovskia, Yana, and Grady Vaughan. "Addressing transnational repression on campuses in the United States." Freedom House, January 2024. https://freedomhouse.org/sites/default/files/2024-02/TNR_UniversityReport_2024F.pdf.
118 "Israel uses Canary Mission blacklist info to bar activists." Forward, October 4, 2018. https://forward.com/news/411453/israel-uses-canary-mission-blacklist-info-to-bar-activists/; see also Bamford, James. "Who is funding Canary Mission?

Inside the doxxing operation targeting anti-Zionist students and professors." Nation, December 22, 2023. https://www.thenation.com/article/world/canary-mission-israel-covert-operations/.
119 Human Rights Watch. "A threshold crossed." As noted in footnote 3, as this book goes to press, the International Court of Justice has confirmed in an advisory opinion that Israel's regime over Palestinians in the occupied Palestinian territories is consistent with the legal definition of apartheid. See, "Legal Consequences arising from the Policies and Practices," 65.
120 Freedom House. "Freedom in the World Report." 2024. https://freedomhouse.org/countries/freedom-world/scores.

1. Palestinian Civil Society in the Shadow of a One-State Reality: Managing the Terms of Subjugation After the Oslo Accords ... Resentfully and Ineffectively

1   All information comes from interviews conducted during periodic visits to the region since 1999.

2. The Oslo Framework and Palestinian Authoritarianism

1   Rapoport, Meron. "'I told Arafat: Israel will promise you an inch and not give you a millimeter.'" +972 Magazine, September 13, 2023. https://www.972mag.com/hanan-ashrawi-oslo-accords/.
2   The PLO had previously been routed from Jordan and Lebanon, before ending up in Tunisia.
3   "PM Rabin speech to Knesset on ratification of Oslo Peace Accords." October 5, 1995. https://www.jewishvirtuallibrary.org/pm-rabin-speech-to-knesset-on-ratification-of-oslo-peace-accords.
4   El Kurd, Dana. *Polarized and Demobilized: Legacies of Authoritarianism in Palestine* (Oxford and New York: Oxford University Press, 2020), 8.
5   Ali, Nijmeh, Marwa Fatafta, Dana El Kurd, Fadi Quran, and Belal Shobaki. "Reclaiming the PLO, re-engaging youth." Al-Shabaka (blog), August 13, 2020. https://al-shabaka.org/focuses/reclaiming-the-plo-re-engaging-youth/.
6   Cooptation can be defined as "giving certain segments of society a stake in the status quo by providing a variety of benefits. The most important aspect of this strategy is that it attempts to include certain segments of the population in the regime's institutions in a non-repressive manner." El Kurd, *Polarized and Demobilized*, 71.
7   Jamal, Manal A. "Western donor assistance and gender empowerment in the Palestinian territories and beyond." *International Feminist Journal of Politics* 17, no. 2 (2015): 232–52. https://doi.org/10.1080/14616742.2013.849966.
8   "On the state of security chaos and the weakness of the rule of law in the territories of the Palestinian National Authority." Palestinian Independent Commission for Citizens' Rights, 2005. https://www.ichr.ps/cached_uploads/download/ichr-files/files/000000436.pdf.

9. Pearlman, Wendy. "Precluding nonviolence, propelling violence: the effect of internal fragmentation on movement protest." *Studies in Comparative International Development* 47, no. 1 (2012), 23–46. https://doi.org/10.1007/s12116-012-9099-2.
10. Ibid., 41.
11. "Fatalities." B'tselem, n.d. https://statistics.btselem.org/en/stats/before-cast-lead/by-date-of-incident?section=participation&tab=overview.
12. El Kurd, *Polarized and Demobilized*, 32.
13. As the European Council on Foreign Relations notes, the 2006 PLC was dissolved by the Constitutional Court in 2018, in a move condemned by the PA's political rivals. PA official Saeb Erekat justified the move by saying a new constituent assembly would be formed to further the objective of statehood. No elections have been held for any new constituent assembly since that statement, however. For more details, see Wafa. "Erekat says decision to dissolve PLC goes in line with transition to statehood." December 23, 2018. https://english.wafa.ps/page.aspx?id=qOBEE8a107870733267aqOBEE8; ECFR. "Palestinian Legislative Council (PLC)." March 20, 2018. https://ecfr.eu/special/mapping_palestinian_politics/palestine_legislative_council/.
14. Sarsour, Shaker, Reem Nasser, and Mohammad Atallah. "The economic and social effects of foreign aid in Palestine." Palestine Monetary Authority, Research and Monetary Policy Department, November 2011, 13.
15. El Kurd, *Polarized and Demobilized*, 45–66.
16. Ibid., 113–22.
17. Ibid., 86–7.
18. Rabie, Kareem. *Palestine Is Throwing a Party and the Whole World Is Invited: Capital and State Building in the West Bank* (Durham: Duke University Press, 2021), 141.
19. See ibid., chapters 7 and 9, for more details.
20. Khalidi, Raja, and Sobhi Samour. "Neoliberalism as liberation: the statehood program and the remaking of the Palestinian national movement." *Journal of Palestine Studies* 40, no. 2 (2011): 6–25. https://doi.org/10.1525/jps.2011.XL.2.6.
21. "Palestine: reform restrictive cybercrime law." Human Rights Watch, December 20, 2017. https://www.hrw.org/news/2017/12/20/palestine-reform-restrictive-cybercrime-law.
22. Tartir, Alaa. "The PA's revolving door: a key policy in security coordination." Al-Shabaka (blog). August 27, 2023. https://al-shabaka.org/memos/the-pas-revolving-door-a-key-policy-in-security-coordination/.
23. "Palestine: impunity for arbitrary arrests, torture." Human Rights Watch, June 30, 2022. https://www.hrw.org/news/2022/06/30/palestine-impunity-arbitrary-arrests-torture.
24. United Nations Office for the Coordination of Humanitarian Affairs – Occupied Palestinian Territory. "Movement and access in the West Bank." August 25, 2023. http://www.ochaopt.org/2023-movement.
25. Reuters. "Israel advances peak number of West Bank settlement plans in 2023, watchdog says." July 13, 2023. https://www.reuters.com/world/middle-east/israel-advances-peak-number-west-bank-settlement-plans-2023-watchdog-2023-07-13/.
26. El Kurd, *Polarized and Demobilized*, 63–6.
27. Dana, Tariq. "Lost in transition: the Palestinian national movement after Oslo." In Mandy Turner (ed.), *From the River to the Sea: Palestine and Israel in the Shadow of "Peace"* (Lanham: Lexington Books, 2019).
28. Ibid., 64.
29. Ibid.

30 El Kurd, Dana. "The strengthening of Palestinian civil society activism, part II." New Lines Institute, October 7, 2021. https://newlinesinstitute.org/nonstate-actors/civil-society/the-strengthening-of-palestinian-civil-society-activism-part-ii/.
31 Ibid.
32 Hendrix, Steve, and Hazem Balousha. "Netanyahu and Hamas depended on each other. Both may be on the way out." Washington Post, November 27, 2023. https://www.washingtonpost.com/world/2023/11/26/netanyahu-hamas-israel-gaza/.
33 Middle East Eye. "Hamas in 2017: the document in full." May 2, 2017. https://www.middleeasteye.net/news/hamas-2017-document-full.
34 Baconi, Tareq. "What was Hamas thinking?" Foreign Policy (blog), January 12, 2024. https://foreignpolicy.com/2023/11/22/hamas-gaza-israel-netanyahu-palestine-apartheid-containment-resistance/.
35 Sen, Somdeep. *Decolonizing Palestine: Hamas between the Anticolonial and the Postcolonial* (Ithaca: Cornell University Press, 2020), 123.
36 Ibid., 223–4. The attack on October 7 was an attempt to break out of this "violent equilibrium," where both Hamas and Israel refuse to pursue a "sustainable resolution" and opt instead for "short-term victories."
37 Banafsheh, Keynoush. "Iran and Hamas beyond the borders of the Middle East." Middle East Institute, November 6, 2023. https://www.mei.edu/publications/iran-and-hamas-beyond-borders-middle-east. It is important to note that there was a disruption in Iran–Hamas relations as a result of Hamas's position during the 2011 Syrian uprising. However, these relations were restored in full by 2017.
38 Sen, *Decolonizing Palestine*, 104.
39 Ibid., 123.
40 "Public opinion poll no. 89." Palestinian Center for Policy and Survey Research, September 6, 2023.
41 "Thousands take to streets in Gaza in rare public display of discontent with Hamas." AP News, July 30, 2023. https://apnews.com/article/gaza-hamas-demonstration-israel-blockade-palestinians-306b19228f9dd21f1036386ce3709672.
42 Baconi, Tariq. "Under cover of war." Human Rights Watch, April 20, 2009. https://www.hrw.org/report/2009/04/20/under-cover-war/hamas-political-violence-gaza, 213.
43 "Six months on: Gaza's Great March of Return." Amnesty International, October 19, 2018. https://www.amnesty.org/en/latest/campaigns/2018/10/gaza-great-march-of-return/.
44 Sen, *Decolonizing Palestine*, 123.

3. Between a Rock and a Hard Place: The Impact of Israel's Occupation and Palestinian Authoritarianism on Community Organizing and NGOs

1 "'Not going anywhere': the Palestinian NGOs shut down by Israel." Al Jazeera, August 19, 2022. https://www.aljazeera.com/news/2022/8/19/what-are-the-palestinian-ngos-that-israel-shut-down.
2 Bensouda, Fatou. "Statement of ICC prosecutor, Fatou Bensouda, respecting an investigation of the situation in Palestine." March 2021. https://www.icc-cpi.int/news/statement-icc-prosecutor-fatou-bensouda-respecting-investigation-situation-palestine.

3 "ICC prosecutor opens war crimes probe in Palestinian territories." Al Jazeera, March 3, 2021. https://www.aljazeera.com/news/2021/3/3/icc-prosecutor-opens-war-crimes-probe-in-palestinian-territories.
4 "Experts: Pegasus spyware found in phones of Palestinian activists." November 8, 2021. https://www.occrp.org/en/daily/15450-experts-pegasus-spyware-found-in-phones-of-palestinian-activists.
5 "Israel outlaws Palestinian human rights groups, causing backlash from Israeli, international rights organizations." PBS NewsHour, October 22, 2021. https://www.pbs.org/newshour/world/israel-outlaws-palestinian-human-rights-groups-causing-backlash-from-israeli-international-rights-organizations.
6 "Open letter to the prosecutor of the International Criminal Court." Human Rights Watch, November 23, 2022. https://www.hrw.org/news/2022/11/23/open-letter-prosecutor-international-criminal-court.
7 "Adalah's expert opinion: Israel's 2016 Counter-Terrorism Law and 1945 Emergency Regulations regarding the outlawing of six Palestinian human rights and civil society groups." Adalah, November 23, 2021. https://www.adalah.org/uploads/uploads/Adalah_Expert_Opinion_Palestinian6_Nov2021.pdf.
8 "'Not going anywhere.'"
9 OHCHR. "UN experts condemn Israel's designation of Palestinian human rights defenders as terrorist organisations." October 25, 2021.
10 Interview with Shawan Jabarain in Ramallah, July 2022.
11 "Report of the Preliminary Examination Activities (2016)." Office of the Prosecutor, p. 32. https://www.icc-cpi.int/sites/default/files/iccdocs/otp/161114-otp-rep-PE_ENG.pdf.
12 "Experts: Pegasus spyware found."
13 Ibid.
14 Ibid.
15 "Christiane Amanpour interview with former State Department official, Josh Paul." CNN, December 4, 2023. https://www.cnn.com/videos/tv/2023/12/04/amanpour-state-epartment-official-resignation-josh-paul.cnn.
16 McKernan, Bethan. "Israeli forces raid offices of six Palestinian human rights groups." Guardian, August 18, 2022. https://www.theguardian.com/world/2022/aug/18/israeli-forces-raid-palestinian-human-rights-groups-offices.
17 Al Jazeera English. "Israeli forces close offices of six Palestinian rights organisation, 2022." https://www.youtube.com/watch?v=_wFQsKcX59I.
18 "Nine European nations condemn IDF's closure of Palestinian NGO offices." Jerusalem Post, August 20, 2022. https://www.jpost.com/israel-news/article-715153.
19 "Israel/Palestine: statement by High Representative Josep Borrell on the Israeli raids on six Palestinian civil society organisations." EEAS, August 22, 2022. https://www.eeas.europa.eu/eeas/israelpalestine-statement-high-representative-josep-borrell-israeli-raids-six-palestinian-civil_en?s=65.
20 Zaken, Ministerie van Buitenlandse. "Joint statement on the Israeli designation of six Palestinian civil society organisations as terrorist organisations." July 12, 2022. https://www.government.nl/documents/diplomatic-statements/2022/07/12/joint-statement-on-the-israeli-designation-of-palestinian-civil-society-organisations-as-terrorist-organisations.
21 "Adalah's expert opinion: Israel's 2016 Counter-Terrorism Law."
22 Ibid.

23 Munayyer, Yousef. "US silence enables Israel's crackdown on civil society organizations." Arab Center, Washington DC, April 30, 2024. https://arabcenterdc.org/resource/us-silence-enables-israels-crackdown-on-civil-society-organizations/.
24 "Scoping study on operating conditions," 13.
25 Ibid.
26 "Protection of space for civil society and human rights defenders: the case of Israel and Palestine." ACT Alliance, 2017. https://actalliance.org/wp-content/uploads/2018/03/AA_protection-of-space-web.pdf, 10.
27 "Scoping study on operating conditions," 13.
28 Ibid.
29 Ibid.
30 Ibid., 22.
31 Ibid., 15.
32 Ibid., 15.
33 Ibid.; confidential interview with Palestinian civil society organization, July 5, 2023.
34 Ibid.
35 "Letter from Israel's Unit 8200." New York Times, September 12, 2014. https://www.nytimes.com/interactive/2014/09/12/world/middleeast/13Israeldoc.html.
36 Amnesty International. "Devices of Palestinian human rights defenders hacked with NSO Group's Pegasus spyware." November 8, 2021. https://www.amnesty.org/en/latest/research/2021/11/devices-of-palestinian-human-rights-defenders-hacked-with-nso-groups-pegasus-spyware-2/.
37 "Scoping study on operating conditions," 19.
38 Ibid.
39 Ibid.
40 Ibid.
41 See executive summary of Amnesty International. "Human rights in Palestine (state of) 2023." 2024. https://www.amnesty.org/en/location/middle-east-and-north-africa/middle-east/palestine-state-of/report-palestine-state-of/.
42 Shalash, Fayha. "Palestinian student leader violently detained by the PA after election success." Middle East Eye, June 20, 2023. https://www.middleeasteye.net/news/palestine-student-leader-detained-after-election-success.
43 See "Freedom of assembly and expression, West Bank," in executive summary of Amnesty International, "Human rights in Palestine (state of) 2023."
44 DAWN. "Israel continues to violate rights of Palestinian-American human rights defender Ubai Al-Aboudi." DAWN (blog), September 7, 2023. https://dawnmena.org/israel-continues-to-violate-rights-of-palestinian-american-human-rights-defender-ubai-al-aboudi/.
45 Confidential interview with Palestinian civil society organization, July 5, 2023.
46 Roundtable discussion with Palestinian civil society organizations, July 19, 2022.
47 "Exclusive: Shaked urges Europeans she meets to quit funding pro-BDS groups." Jerusalem Post, October 14, 2015. https://www.jpost.com/israel-news/politics-and-diplomacy/exclusive-shaked-gives-european-ministers-lists-of-anti-israel-ngos-they-fund-424942.
48 "Protection of space for civil society," 11.
49 Ibid.
50 UNRWA. "Who we are." https://www.unrwa.org/who-we-are.

51 UNRWA. "Where we work." https://www.unrwa.org/where-we-work.
52 UNRWA. "Working at UNRWA." https://www.unrwa.org/careers/working-unrwa.
53 "'Insidious campaign' by Israel is denying lifesaving aid to Gaza says UNRWA chief." UN News, April 17, 2024. https://news.un.org/en/story/2024/04/1148676o.
54 Kingsley, Patrick, and Ronen Bergman. "The 8 days that roiled the U.N.'s top agency in Gaza." New York Times, February 3, 2024. https://www.nytimes.com/2024/02/03/world/middleeast/united-nations-gaza-unrwa.html.
55 See Beinart, Peter. "The campaign to abolish UNRWA." Jewish Currents, February 13, 2024. https://jewishcurrents.org/the-campaign-to-abolish-unrwa.
56 Al Kassab, Fatima. "A top U.N. court says Gaza genocide is 'plausible' but does not order cease-fire." NPR, January 26, 2024. https://www.npr.org/2024/01/26/1227078791/icj-israel-genocide-gaza-palestinians-south-africa.
57 Northam, Jackie. "Report on UNRWA concludes Israel has not provided evidence of employees' militancy." NPR, April 23, 2024. https://www.npr.org/2024/04/23/1246613547/unrwa-israel-hamas-gaza-war.
58 Hall, Richard, Bel Trew, and Andrew Feinberg. "Joe Biden has done more than arm Israel. He's complicit in Gaza's devastating famine." Independent (UK), May 14, 2024. https://www.independent.co.uk/news/world/americas/us-politics/gaza-famine-biden-israel-hamas-b2542961.html?s=08.
59 Ibid.
60 Harb, Ali. "'Moral failure': US House approves bill that would ban UNRWA funding." Al Jazeer, March 22, 2024. https://www.aljazeera.com/news/2024/3/22/moral-failure-us-house-approves-bill-that-would-ban-unrwa-funding.
61 Confidential interview with a Palestinian arts and culture organization, March 28, 2023 in Ramallah, and April 11, 2023 via Zoom.
62 Confidential interview with Palestinian civil society organization, June 19, 2023.
63 Confidential interview with Palestinian arts and culture organization, March 28, 2023.
64 Ibid.
65 "Scoping study on operating conditions," 18.
66 "Protection of space for civil society," 10.
67 "Scoping study on operating conditions," 15.
68 See Hassan, Zaha. "Neither here nor there: the shrinking physical space for Palestinians." DAWN (blog), May 12, 2023. https://dawnmena.org/neither-here-nor-there-the-shrinking-physical-space-for-palestinians/.
69 Scharf, Isaac, and Ami Bentov. "Israeli campaign raises funds for torched Palestinian town." AP, March 2, 2023. https://apnews.com/article/israel-palestinians-hawara-settlers-west-bank-234e49a04f712bab11aa236db0f784fb.
70 Mezzofiore, Gianluca, Celine Alkhaldi, Abeer Salman, and Nima Elbagdir. "Israel's military called the settler attack on this Palestinian town a 'pogrom.' Videos show soldiers did little to stop it." CNN, June 15, 2023. https://www.cnn.com/2023/06/15/middleeast/huwara-west-bank-settler-attack-cmd-intl/index.html.
71 Interview conducted with Huwara Village Council members, March 2023.
72 "Scoping study on operating conditions," 18.
73 Amnesty International. "Israel/Occupied Palestinian Territories: NGO director in administrative detention: Ubai Aboudi." November 22, 2019. https://www.amnesty.org/en/documents/mde15/1445/2019/en/; "Update on the detention of Bisan Center director and human rights activist, Ubai Aboudi by Israeli Shabak amidst ongoing travel ban." September 5, 2023. https://www.bisan.org/2023/09/

74 Amnesty International. "Israel/OPT: drop baseless charges against Palestinian human rights defender." November 22, 2016. https://www.amnesty.org/en/latest/news/2016/11/israel-opt-drop-baseless-charges-against-palestinian-human-rights-defender/.
75 See Khaled Quzmar speaking in: Foundation for Middle East Peace. "Israeli raids on Palestinian civil society organizations – the costs of international inaction." 2022. https://www.youtube.com/watch?v=3VlwYxWSgq0.
76 "Protection of space for civil society," 13.
77 Private Carnegie roundtable with Palestinian civil society activist on February 1, 2023; Tartir, Alaa. "The PA's revolving door: a key policy in security coordination." Al-Shabaka, August 27, 2023. https://al-shabaka.org/policy-memos/the-pas-revolving-door-a-key-policy-in-security-coordination/.
78 Ibid.
79 See Ubai Aboudi speaking in: Foundation for Middle East Peace. "Israeli Raids."
80 See chapter 2.
81 Carnegie Study Group virtual roundtable hosting representatives of Palestinian civil society organizations on July 5, 2023.
82 Ibid.
83 "Protection of space for civil society," 14.
84 Carnegie Study Group virtual roundtable hosting representatives of Palestinian civil society organizations on July 5, 2023.
85 Ibid.
86 Ibid.
87 Ibid.
88 ICNL. "Palestine." https://www.icnl.org/resources/civic-freedom-monitor/palestine.
89 Confidential interview with an executive director of a Palestinian research institute, July 5, 2023.
90 ICNL. "Palestine."
91 Freedom House. "West Bank: Freedom in the World 2024 Country Report." https://freedomhouse.org/country/west-bank/freedom-world/2024.
92 "Protection of space for civil society," 14.
93 Ibid.

4. The Rise, Weakening, and Resurgence of Civil Society in Israel

1 Scheindlin, Dahlia. *The Crooked Timber of Democracy in Israel: Promise Unfulfilled.* (Berlin and Boston: De Gruyter, 2023), 159–65.
2 On the twenty-first-century evolution of populist right-wing politics in the West and its roots, see Meindert, Fennema. "Populist Parties of the Right." In Jens Rydgren (ed.), *Movements of Exclusion: Radical Right-Wing Populism in the Western World* (New York: Nova Science Publishers, 2005).

3   Rogenhofer, Julius Maximilian, and Ayala Panievsky. "Antidemocratic populism in power: comparing Erdoğan's Turkey with Modi's India and Netanyahu's Israel." *Democratization* 27, no. 8 (2020): 1394–412.
4   Gidron, Noam, Michal Bar and Hagai Katz. *The Israeli Third Sector: Between Welfare State and Civil Society* (New York: Kluwer Academic/Plenum Publishers, 2004).
5   See, for example, Etzioni, Amitai. "Alternate ways to democracy: the example of Israel." *Political Science Quarterly* 74, no. 2 (1959): 198–201.
6   Meyers, Oren. "Israeli journalism during the state's formative era." *Journalism History* 31, no. 2 (2005): 88–97.
7   Meyers, Oren. "Expanding the scope of paradigmatic research in journalism studies: the case of early mainstream Israeli journalism and its discontents." *Journalism* 12, no. 3 (2011): 270.
8   Gidron et al., *Israeli Third Sector*, introduction.
9   Tzabag, Shmuel. "Co-operation in the shadow of a power struggle: Israel: the Likud governments and the Histadrut 1977–84." *Middle Eastern Studies* 31, no. 4 (1995), 849–88.
10 Gidron et al., *Israeli Third Sector*.
11 Scheindlin, *Crooked Timber*, chapter 11.
12 Ibid.
13 On the "forbidden Congress," see Jabareen, Yousef Tayseer. "The Emergency Regulations." In Nadim Rouhana and Areej Sabbagh-Khoury (eds), *The Palestinians in Israel: Readings in History, Politics, Society* (Haifa: Mada el Carmel – Arab Center for Applied Social Research, 2011), 70. For the original Clause 7a, see also: Basic Law: The Knesset (originally adopted in 5718/1958), Amendment 9 (1985).
14 Doron, Gideon. "The politics of mass communication in Israel." *Annals of the American Academy of Political and Social Science* 555, no. 1 (1998), 163–79.
15 See, for example, Aloni, Shulamit. *Democracy or Ethnocracy* (Tel Aviv: Am Oved, 2008), 188–9.
16 Yishai, Yael. "Civil society in transition: interest politics in Israel." *Annals of the American Academy of Political and Social Science* 555, no. 1 (1998): 147–62.
17 See, for example, Reichmann, Uriel, Baruch Bracha, Ariel Rosen-Zvi and Amos Shapira. "Draft constitution for the state of Israel." Public Committee for a Constitution for Israel, 1986.
18 "Israeli-Palestinian Interim Agreement on the West Bank and the Gaza Strip Washington, D.C., September 28, 1995," 180–7. https://peacemaker.un.org/israelopt-osloII95.
19 Scheindlin, Dahlia. "Strategic choices facing Israeli rights group during the current war." Open Global Rights, August 4, 2014. https://www.openglobalrights.org/strategic-choices-facing-israeli-rights-group-during-current-war/.
20 For a detailed summary of the role of international strategies alongside domestic activity, see Montell, Jessica. "Learning from what works: strategic analysis of the achievements of the Israel–Palestine human rights community." Sida Decentralized Evaluation, 2015.
21 Jamal, Amal. "The political ethos of Palestinian citizens of Israel: critical reading in the future vision documents." *Israel Studies Forum* 23, no. 2 (2008): 5.
22 Mudde, Cas. *Populist Radical Right Parties in Europe* (Cambridge: Cambridge University Press, 2007).
23 ACRI, Gisha, the Public Committee Against Torture in Israel, HaMoked: Center for the Defence of the Individual, Yesh Din, Adalah, and Physicians for Human Rights–Israel. "Submission of human rights organizations based in Israel to the

Goldstone Inquiry Delegation June 2009." *Adalah's Newsletter* 61 (June 2009). https://www.adalah.org/uploads/oldfiles/newsletter/eng/jun09/goldstone%20report_and_appendix%5B1%5D.pdf.

24 Fuchs, Amir, Dana Blander and Mordechai Kremnitzer. *Anti-Democratic Legislation in the 18th Knesset (2009–2013)*. Israel Democracy Institute, 2015.

25 Tibon, Amir, Noa Spigel and Ben Samuels. "New bill from Netanyahu's party targets foreign donations to Israeli NGOs, drawing sharp US criticism." Haaretz, May 24, 2023.

26 Scheindlin, Dahlia. "The logic behind Israel's democratic erosion." Century Foundation, May 29, 2019.

27 Ibid.

28 Scheindlin, Dahlia. "Ten years with Netanyahu." Friedrich Ebert Stiftung, January 2017.

29 Kashti, Or. "Im Tirtzu threatens boycott of Israeli university over 'anti-Zionist' bias." Haaretz, August 17, 2010.

30 Sadeh, Shuki. "The right-wing think tank that quietly 'runs the Knesset.'" Haaretz, October 5, 2018. https://www.haaretz.com/israel-news/.premium-the-right-wing-think-tank-that-quietly-runs-the-knesset-1.6514722.

31 Author's personal experience working as a consultant to human rights organizations in Israel.

32 Author's personal experience as a political analyst engaged with a range of organizations in the US advocating Israel-related affairs, both liberal and conservative.

33 Sharon, Jeremy. "Kohelet, right-wing think tank that inspired overhaul, calls for partial compromise." Times of Israel, March 14, 2023.

34 Lieber, Dov. "Israeli protest movement grapples with disagreements over stopping judicial overhaul." Wall Street Journal, September 1, 2023.

35 See, for example, Rudnitzky, Arik. "Survey among the Arab public in Israel." Moshe Dayan Center, June 26, 2023; Wattad, Mohammed S., Zhanyang Liu and Derek Lief. "What deters the Arab population from the protests." Institute for National Security Studies. INSS Insight, no. 1746, July 18, 2023.

36 Kremnitzer, Mordechai, and Amir Fuchs. "Bill to amend tax code." Israel Democracy Institute, May 28, 2023.

37 TOI Staff. "New communications minister says 'no place' for public broadcasting in Israel." Times of Israel, January 9, 2023.

38 Altshuler-Schwartz, Tehilla. "Kahri's broadcast legislation: reform or ruination." Israel Democracy Institute, August 3, 2023.

39 Marmor, Dror. "A political chief statistician? Too scary to think about." Globes, March 15, 2023.

40 Avriel, Eytan, "Spirit of Kaplan: the organizations and people behind the protest against the judicial overhaul." Marker, September 13, 2023.

41 Breiner, Josh. "Ben-Gvir's ministry runs 'like a crime organization has taken over.'" Haaretz, December 14, 2023.

42 Scheindlin, Dahlia. "Israelis should want to stop the war for their own sake, if not for Gaza's." Haaretz, January 4, 2024.

43 Douek, Roni. "Civil society saved Israel, and must lead its rehabilitation." Ynet, January 1, 2024.

44 Ibid.

45 Haaretz Editorial. "Israel is running out of time to rescue the hostages." Haaretz, December 4, 2023.

46 "Israel's Supreme Court rejects Adalah's petition to allow demonstrations in Palestinian towns." Adalah, November 8, 2023. https://www.adalah.org/en/content/view/10952.
47 Glazer, Hilo, and Itay Mashiah. "'Systematic witch hunt': what persecution of Arab-Israelis looks like amid Gaza war." Haaretz, November 2, 2023.
48 Sharon, Jeremy. "Gov't approves emergency regulations that could pave way to closing Al Jazeera offices." Times of Israel, October 20, 2023.
49 See, for example, a survey by the Israel Democracy Institute from July 2023, in which respondents were asked: "If elections are held in the foreseeable future and the leaders of the current protest movement establish a new party and run for the Knesset, would you consider voting for it?" One-third said they would likely or very likely vote for such a party. In informal conversations since October 7, some have speculated (or accused) the hostage release protests of having a political inclination. Survey: Hermann, Tamar, and Or Anabi. "Flash survey: most Israelis assess that the protest movement has delayed progression of the judicial overhaul." Israel Democracy Institute, July 17, 2023. https://en.idi.org.il/articles/50272; informal conversations based on author's observation.

5. Neo-Kahanism: The Growing Influence of a Violent, Jewish Supremacist Ideology

1 Kahane, Meir. "One Worlds." In *They Must Go* (New York: Grosset & Dunlap, 1981), 142.
2 Federman, Josef, and Joseph Krauss. "Radical rabbi's followers rise in Israel amid new violence." Associated Press, May 14, 2021. https://apnews.com/article/israel-middle-east-violence-religion-0dcc4073d660003f4e3fa8d4ed0a9a6a.
3 United States Department of State. "Country reports on terrorism 2017 – foreign terrorist organizations: Kahane Chai." September 19, 2018. https://www.refworld.org/reference/annualreport/usdos/2018/en/121958.
4 Jerusalem Story, s.v. "Betar." https://www.jerusalemstory.com/en/lexicon/betar.
5 Bruzonsky, Mark. "Opinion: the mentor who shaped Begin's thinking: Jabotinsky." *Washington Post*, December 23, 2023. https://www.washingtonpost.com/archive/opinions/1980/11/16/the-mentor-who-shaped-begins-thinking-jabotinsky/ceac5816-9feb-4766-93bb-c8ac65c80680/.
6 Green, David B. "Who was Meir Kahane." *Haaretz*, March 26, 2001. https://www.haaretz.com/israel-news/elections/2021-03-26/ty-article-magazine/.premium/israel-election-who-was-meir-kahane-and-why-is-his-racist-legacy-relevant-again/0000017f-db3c-df62-a9ff-dfffe2fa0000.
7 Southern Poverty Law Center. "Jewish Defense League." https://www.splcenter.org/fighting-hate/extremist-files/group/jewish-defense-league.
8 Kaufman, Elliot. "Meir Kahane: Review of American Militant." *The Wall Street Journal*, May 11, 2022. https://www.wsj.com/articles/meir-kahane-review-american-militant-11652306087.
9 ADL. "Jewish Defense League." https://www.adl.org/resources/profile/jewish-defense-league.
10 Ibid.
11 Magid, Shaul. *Meir Kahane* (Princeton: Princeton University Press, 2021), 15–52.

12 Likud. "An Arafat state will not be created!" https://digital.library.cornell.edu/catalog/ss:30593928/.
13 "This week in history: the Likud 'upheaval.'" *Jerusalem Post*, May 13, 2012. https://www.jpost.com/features/in-thespotlight/this-week-in-history-the-likud-upheaval.
14 "Intifada: history, meaning, cause, & significance." *Encyclopedia Britannica*. https://www.britannica.com/topic/intifada.
15 Green, "Who was Meir Kahane."
16 Council on Foreign Relations. "Kach, Kahane Chai (Israel, extremists)." 2008. https://www.cfr.org/backgrounder/kach-kahane-chai-israel-extremists.
17 Buxbaum, Jessica. "The Kahane Movement: a legacy of violence and racism in Israel." *New Arab*, 2022. https://www.newarab.com/analysis/kahanism-legacy-violence-and-racism-israel.
18 "Kach." Israel Democracy Institute. n.d. https://en.idi.org.il/israeli-elections-and-parties/parties/kach/.
19 Buxbaum, "Kahane Movement."
20 United States Department of State. "Country reports on terrorism 2017 – foreign terrorist organizations: Kahane Chai."
21 Council on Foreign Relations, "Kach."
22 United States Department of State. "Country reports on terrorism 2017 – foreign terrorist organizations: Kahane Chai."
23 Kingsley, Patrick. "As Violence Rises in the West Bank, Settler Attacks Raise Alarm." *The New York Times*, February 12, 2022. https://www.nytimes.com/2022/02/12/world/middleeast/settler-violence-west-bank.html.
24 Urquhart, Conal, and Rishon Letzion. "Gunman's Body to Lie near His Racist Hero." *The Observer*, August 7, 2005, sec. World news. https://www.theguardian.com/world/2005/aug/07/israel.
25 Breiner, Josh. "The Notorious Kahanist Facing Racism and Terror Charges Advising Israel's Far-Right Security Minister." *Haaretz*, June 8, 2023. https://www.haaretz.com/israel-news/2023-06-08/ty-article-magazine/.premium/far-right-israeli-ministers-adviser-is-kahanist-activist-facing-racism-and-terror-charges/00000188-9774-d3a7-adcf-b77f86910000.
26 Sprinzak, Ehud. "The politics of paralysis I: Netanyahu's safety belt." *Foreign Affairs*, July 1, 1998. https://www.foreignaffairs.com/articles/israel/politics-paralysis-netanyahus-safety-belt.
27 "At Rabin rally in Jerusalem, Labor chief rips Netanyahu, Ben Gvir over 1995 protest." *Times of Israel*, October 30, 2022. https://www.timesofisrael.com/at-rabin-rally-in-jerusalem-labor-chief-rips-netanyahu-ben-gvir-over-1995-protest/.
28 Sprinzak, "Politics of paralysis I."
29 "Total immigration to Israel from the former Soviet Union." Jewish Virtual Library. https://www.jewishvirtuallibrary.org/total-immigration-to-israel-from-former-soviet-union.
30 Sprinzak, "Politics of paralysis I."
31 Ibid.
32 Mitnick, Joshua. "The far-right rises in Israeli politics." *Christian Science Monitor*, December 10, 2008. https://www.csmonitor.com/World/Middle-East/2008/1210/p06s02-wome.html.
33 "The Platform of Otzma Yehudit." Jewish Virtual Library, 2024. www.jewishvirtuallibrary.org/jsource/Politics/Otzma_political_platform.pdf.

34. Keller-Lynn, Carrie. "Ben-Gvir: Security Forces Should Be Able to Shoot Anyone Holding Stones or Firebombs." *The Times of Israel*, November 27, 2022. https://www.timesofisrael.com/ben-gvir-security-forces-should-be-able-to-shoot-anyone-holding-stones-or-firebombs/.
35. "Likud party: original party platform." Jewish Virtual Library. https://www.jewishvirtuallibrary.org/original-party-platform-of-the-likud-party.
36. Cohen, Roger. "The incitement in Israel that killed Yitzhak Rabin." *New York Times*, December 4, 2019. https://www.nytimes.com/2019/12/04/opinion/incitement-movie.html.
37. Eldar, Shlomi. "Netanyahu quotes radical rabbi's racist invective." *Al-Monitor*, March 14, 2019. https://www.al-monitor.com/originals/2019/03/israel-benjamin-netanyahu-meir-kahane-arabs-incitement.html?token=eyJlbWFpbCI6ImpidXhiYXVtOTFAZ21haWwuY29tIiwibmlkIjoiMjEyMjkifQ%3D%3D&utm_medium=email&utm_campaign=Ungrouped%20transactional%20email&utm_content=Ungrouped%20transactional%20email+ID_43bc1e62-e519-11ee-88da-cf995bd60406&utm_source=campmgr&utm_term=Access%20Article.
38. Ibid.
39. Author interview with Shaul Magid in June 2022.
40. Ibid.
41. Gur, Haviv Rettig. "The Israeli left has lost more than an election." *Times of Israel*, November 7, 2022. https://www.timesofisrael.com/the-israeli-left-has-lost-more-than-an-election/.
42. Basic Law: Israel as the Nation State of the Jewish People. https://main.knesset.gov.il/EN/activity/documents/BasicLawsPDF/BasicLawNationState.pdf.
43. "'Admissions Committees Law' – Cooperative Societies Ordinance – Amendments No. 8 and 12." Adalah. https://www.adalah.org/en/law/view/494; "Amended bill to establish Admission Committees." *Jerusalem Post*, February 3, 2011. https://www.jpost.com/national-news/amended-bill-to-establish-admission-committees.
44. "Israel: Discriminatory Land Policies Hem in Palestinians | Human Rights Watch." May 12, 2020. https://www.hrw.org/news/2020/05/12/israel-discriminatory-land-policies-hem-palestinians.
45. Buxbaum, Jessica. "Israel's demographic battle for Jerusalem leaves Palestinians struggling to survive." *New Arab*, 2021. https://www.newarab.com/analysis/palestinians-jerusalem-face-struggle-survival.
46. "Document exposed by Akevot: Ariel Sharon instructed IDF to create training zone to Displace Palestinians." *Akevot*, August 9, 2020. https://www.akevot.org.il/en/news-item/document-revealed-by-akevot-ariel-sharon-instructed-idf-to-create-training-zone-to-displace-palestinians/.
47. Chacar, Henriette. "Largest Palestinian Displacement in Decades Looms after Israeli Court Ruling." Reuters, June 12, 2022. https://www.reuters.com/world/middle-east/largest-palestinian-displacement-decades-looms-after-israeli-court-ruling-2022-06-12/.
48. Smotrich, Bezalel. "Israel's Decisive Plan." Hashiloach, 2017. https://hashiloach.org.il/israels-decisive-plan/.
49. Kubovich, Yaniv, and Ben Samuels. "Far-right Israeli minister lays groundwork for doubling West Bank settler population." *Haaretz*, May 18, 2023. https://www.haaretz.com/israel-news/2023-05-18/ty-article/.premium/far-right-israeli-minister-lays-groundwork-for-doubling-west-bank-settler-population/00000188-2de6-d6e4-ab9d-ede74a3e0000.

50   Katz, Yaakov Ketzaleh. Rep. *West Bank Jewish Population Stats*, n.d., sent via personal correspondence.
51   United Nations High Commissioner for Human Rights and Reports of the Office of the High Commissioner and the Secretary-General. Report. *Israeli Settlements in the Occupied Palestinian Territory, Including East Jerusalem, and in the Occupied Syrian Golan*. 2024. https://documents.un.org/doc/undoc/gen/g24/008/94/pdf/g2400894.pdf?token=mYie9zfbpBBEfR8jqG&fe=true.
52   Peace Now. Report. "A good year for settlements; a bad year for Israel: summary of settlement activity in 2023." 2024. https://peacenow.org.il/wp-content/uploads/2024/02/A-Good-year-for-settlements-A-Bad-Year-for-Israel-Settlement-Watch-Peace-Now-Report-2023-February-2024-1.pdf.
53   Lurie-Pardes, Eyal. "Ben-Gvir is arming thousands of Israelis – and playing with fire." DAWN, November 3, 2023. https://dawnmena.org/ben-gvir-is-arming-thousands-of-israelis-and-playing-with-fire/.
54   "Israeli Knesset passes draconian amendment to the counter-terrorism law criminalizing 'consumption of terrorist publications.'" *Adalah*, November 8, 2023. https://www.adalah.org/en/content/view/10951.
55   Kadari-Ovadia, Shira. "Hebrew University suspends Palestinian scholar who doubted Hamas sexual violence, accused Israel of genocide in Gaza." *Haaretz*, March 12, 2024. https://www.haaretz.com/israel-news/2024-03-12/ty-article/.premium/hebrew-university-suspends-palestinian-scholar-who-denied-hamas-sexual-violence/0000018e-3350-d5ad-addf-7f5130b60000.
56   Buxbaum, Jessica. "'Erase Gaza': how genocidal rhetoric became normalised in Israel." *New Arab*, 2023. https://www.newarab.com/analysis/erase-gaza-how-genocidal-rhetoric-normalised-israel.
57   Gazit, Amitai. "Ha'atsaa shel Sharat HaModi'in: Transfer shel Toshvei Gaza le-Sinai | Calcalist." Calcalist, October 24, 2023. https://www.calcalist.co.il/local_news/article/rj2mplngp.
58   Buxbaum, Jessica. "In Israel, the resettlement of Gaza is no longer a fringe idea." *New Arab*, 2024. https://www.newarab.com/analysis/israeli-resettlement-gaza-no-longer-fringe-idea.
59   Freidson, Yael. "Israeli cab-hailing app Gett to compensate Arab drivers for discrimination." *Haaretz*, May 30, 2023. https://www.haaretz.com/israel-news/2023-05-30/ty-article/.premium/israeli-cab-hailing-app-gett-to-compensate-arab-drivers-for-discrimination/00000188-6cd5-de23-ad8d-fddd9ade0000.
60   Sharon, Jeremy. "Tempers flare in controversial Knesset hearing on West Bank civil rights activists." *Times of Israel*, March 12, 2024. https://www.timesofisrael.com/tempers-flare-in-controversial-knesset-hearing-on-west-bank-civil-rights-activists/.

6. US Counterterrorism Law and Policy: Its Role in Shutting Down Palestinian Activism and Agency

1   18 USC 2339A criminalizes the provision of material support for certain terrorist acts, while 18 USC 2339B prohibits the knowing provision of material support to FTOs designated by the secretary of state. The statutes define material support as "property, tangible or intangible, or service, including currency or monetary instruments or financial securities, financial services, lodging, training, expert advice

or assistance, safehouses, false documentation or identification, communications equipment, facilities, weapons, lethal substances, explosives, personnel (1 or more individuals who may be or include oneself), and transportation, except medicine or religious materials."

2   ADL and Brandeis Center letter to presidents of colleges and universities. October 25, 2023. https://www.adl.org/resources/letter/adl-and-brandeis-center-letter-presidents-colleges-and-universities.

3   Rizzo, Salvador. "Survivors of Oct. 7 attack sue pro-Palestinian groups in US" Washington Post, May 2, 2024. https://www.washingtonpost.com/dc-md-va/2024/05/02/lawsuit-students-palestinian-protests-hamas/.

4   Li, Darryl. "Anti-Palestinian at the core: the origins and growing dangers of US antiterrorism law." Briefing Paper, Center for Constitutional Rights, February 2024. https://ccrjustice.org/sites/default/files/attach/2024/02/AntiPalestinian%20at%20the%20Core_White%20Paper_0.pdf.

5   Said, E.W. "The essential terrorist: review of *Terrorism: How the West Can Win*, by B. Netanyahu." *Arab Studies Quarterly* 9, no. 2 (1987): 195–203. http://www.jstor.org/stable/41857908; Steaton, Matt. "The etymology of terror." New York Review of Books, November 17, 2023. https://www.nybooks.com/online/2021/11/17/the-etymology-of-terror/.

6   Bhungalia, Lisa. *Elastic Empire: Refashioning War through Aid in Palestine* (Stanford: Stanford University Press, 2024), 30–1.

7   Li, "Anti-Palestinian at the core," 6.

8   Bhungalia, *Elastic Empire*, 29.

9   Report of the National Lawyer's Guild Delegation to the Occupied Territories and Israel. "The Al Aqsa Intifada and Israel's apartheid: the US military and economic role in the violation of Palestinian human rights." January 2001. https://www.nlginternational.org/report/2001_Palestine_del_report.pdf; Clyde, R. Mark. Israeli-United States Relations, CRS, I.B. 82008, at 2 (updated Jan. 12, 2001)

10 Ibid.

11 Miller, Aaron David. "Why the Oslo peace process failed." Foreign Policy, September 13, 2023. https://foreignpolicy.com/2023/09/13/oslo-accords-1993-anniversary-israel-palestine-peace-process-lessons/.

12 Executive Order No. 12947, 60 Fed. Reg. 5079 (January 25, 1995).

13 Li, "Anti-Palestinian at the core," 13–14.

14 EO 12947 was "the first formal list of terrorist groups that triggered legal consequences. It drew on longstanding sanctions laws but broke ground in applying them to non-state actors." Li, "Anti-Palestinian at the core," 14.

15 Bhungalia, *Elastic Empire*, 35.

16 "The Oklahoma City bombing, 1995." *Encyclopedia Britannica*, last updated April 12, 2024. https://www.britannica.com/event/Oklahoma-City-bombing.

17 18 USC. § 2339B.

18 18 USC. § 2339A predated the AEDPA, but only criminalized provision of support for terrorism in service of specific terrorist acts. The AEDPA established USC. 2339B, which criminalizes provision of material support to an FTO, regardless of intent.

19 "Ambassador Philip Wilcox Jr., one of the key drafters of the proposed act, made a direct link to an ominous 'Islamic threat' seeking both to disrupt the Oslo Accords underway in Israel/Palestine and create 'turmoil' around the world … Similarly the Anti-Defamation League scripted Oklahoma City within the context of overseas-related terrorism, citing numerous terrorist acts it sutured distinctly to foreign actors,

such as the World Trade Center bombing of 1993, the death of an American student in a bombing in Gaza, and a plot to bomb American airliners in the Philippines, among others." Bhungalia, *Elastic Empire*, 35–40.
20 Ibid., 35.
21 Ibid., 46.
22 Shamas, Diala, and Tarek Ismail. "Calling the Capitol riot 'terrorism' will only hurt communities of color." Washington Post, January 10, 2021. https://www.washingtonpost.com/outlook/2021/01/10/capitol-invasion-terrorism-enforcement/.
23 Said, Wadie. *Crimes of Terror: The Legal and Political Implications of Federal Terrorism Prosecutions* (New York: Oxford University Press, 2015), 52–72.
24 Uniting and Strengthening America by Providing Appropriate Tools Required to Intercept and Obstruct Terrorism (USA Patriot Act) Act of 2001, Pub. L. No. 107-56 (2001).
25 Pub. L. No. 108-458, § 6603, 118 STAT. 3762 (codified at 18 USC. § 2339B(g)(4) (2006)). The amendments were made permanent in the USA Patriot Act Improvement and Reauthorization Act of 2005, Pub. L. No. 109-177, § 104, 120 STAT. 195 (2006).
26 Executive Order No. 13224, 66 Fed. Reg. 49079 (September 25, 2001).
27 Said, *Crimes of Terror*, 63–8.
28 The Ninth Circuit in *Humanitarian Law Project v. Reno*, 205 F.3d 1130, 1136 (9th Cir. 2000) cited the Anti-Defamation League's (ADL) amicus brief arguing that money is fungible, and funds sent for humanitarian aid could still be used indirectly to incentivize terrorism.
29 Due to space and time considerations, this chapter cannot cover all the ways in which US material support to terrorism laws and bars have disproportionate impact on Palestinians – including through the financial sector, social media and online platforms, and even US immigration enforcement.
30 Deutsch, Michael, and Emma Thompson. "Secrets and lies: the persecution of Muhammad Salah (part II)." *Journal of Palestine Studies* 38, no. 1 (2008): 25–53, esp. 27.
31 Ibid.
32 Bhungalia, *Elastic Empire*, 27–40.
33 Deutsch and Thompson, "Secrets and lies," 29.
34 Center for Constitutional Rights. *Salah v. US Department of Treasury*. https://ccrjustice.org/home/what-we-do/our-cases/salah-v-us-department-treasury.
35 Deutsch and Thompson, "Secrets and lies."
36 Allen, Mike, and Steven Mufsin. "US seizes assets of 3 Islamic groups." Washington Post, December 5, 2001. https://www.washingtonpost.com/archive/politics/2001/12/05/us-seizes-assets-of-3-islamic-groups/ad196eda-0bfc-4259-84f6-89d4ee60b888/.
37 Schumer, Charles E. "Terrorists fundraising in the United States." *Congressional Record* 142, no. 87 (June 13, 1996).
38 US Department of the Treasury. "Shutting Down the Terrorist Financial Network December 4, 2001." Press Release. https://home.treasury.gov/news/press-releases/po841.
39 Said, *Crimes of Terror*, 68–71.
40 Ibid., 69.
41 Schaper, David. "FBI targets peace activists for alleged terrorism support." NPR, October 2, 2010. https://www.npr.org/2010/10/02/130274688/fbi-targets-peace-activists-for-alleged-terrorism-support.

42 Silver, Charlotte. "Will Rasmea Odeh go to prison because of a confession obtained through torture?" Nation, November 4, 2104. https://www.thenation.com/article/archive/will-rasmeah-odeh-go-prison-because-confession-obtained-through-torture/.
43 *United States v. Rasmea Odeh*, 815 F.3d 969 at 975 (2016). https://scholar.google.com/scholar_case?case=6954439213867437073&hl=en&as_sdt=2006.
44 "US judge orders deportation of Palestinian activist." Al Jazeera, August 17, 2017. https://www.aljazeera.com/news/2017/8/17/us-judge-orders-deportation-of-palestinian-activist.
45 Palestine Legal. "The Palestine exception to free speech: a movement under attack in the US." https://palestinelegal.org/the-palestine-exception.
46 Thakker, Prem, and Daniel Boguslaw. "FBI targets Muslims and Palestinians in wake of Hamas attack, civil rights by President Biden on the terrorist attacks in Israel." October 10, 2023, https://www.whitehouse.gov/briefing-room/speeches-remarks/2023/10/10/remarks-by-president-biden-on-the-terrorist-attacks-in-israel-2/#:~:text=So%2C%20in%20this%20moment%2C%20we,is%20no%20justification%20for%20terrorism.
47 Kane, Alex. "The FBI is using unvetted, right-wing blacklists to question activists about their support for Palestine." Intercept, June 24, 2018. https://theintercept.com/2018/06/24/students-for-justice-in-palestine-fbi-sjp/.
48 Deutsch and Thompson, "Secrets and lies," 53.
49 Ibid., 54.
50 Antiterrorism Act, 18 USC. §§ 2331–2339D (1990).
51 Justice Against Sponsors of Terrorism Act (JASTA), Pub. L. No. 114-222, §4(a), 130 Stat.
52 See chapter 12.
53 Center for Constitutional Rights. "Jewish National Fund vs. US Campaign for Palestinian Rights." https://ccrjustice.org/home/what-we-do/our-cases/jewish-national-fund-v-us-campaign-palestinian-rights. See also "US Supreme Court dismisses lawsuit claiming Palestinian rights group supports terrorism." Middle East Monitor, January 23, 2024. https://www.middleeastmonitor.com/20240123-us-supreme-court-dismisses-lawsuit-claiming-palestinian-rights-group-supports-terrorism/.
54 Starr, Michael. "October 7 victims sue UNRWA USA for alleged financial support of Hamas." Jerusalem Post, March 10, 2024. https://www.jpost.com/israel-hamas-war/article-791159.
55 Brief amicus curiae of Anti-Defamation League, *Twitter v. Taamneh*, January 18, 2023. https://www.adl.org/sites/default/files/documents/2023-01/ADL-amicus-brief-Twitter-v-Taamneh-US-Sup-Ct-2023.pdf.
56 Human Rights Watch. "Meta's broken promises: systemic censorship of Palestine content on Instagram and Facebook." December 21, 2023. https://www.hrw.org/report/2023/12/21/metas-broken-promises/systemic-censorship-palestine-content-instagram-and; See also "Briefing on the Palestinian digital rights situation since October 7th." 7amleh: The Arab Center for the Advancement of Social Media. https://7amleh.org/storage/Briefing%20October%207th%20-6E.pdf.
57 Human Rights Watch, "Meta's broken promises." See also "Briefing on the Palestinian digital rights situation"; See also chapter 9.
58 Patel, Faiza, and Mary Pat Dwyer. "So, what does Facebook take down? The secret list of 'dangerous' individuals and organizations." Brennan Center for Justice,

November 4, 2021. https://www.brennancenter.org/our-work/analysis-opinion/so-what-does-facebook-take-down-secret-list-dangerous-individuals-and.
59 See chapter 10.
60 Shamas, Diala. "The downstream effects of Israel's terrorist designations on human rights defenders in the US" Just Security, November 4, 2021. https://www.justsecurity.org/78884/the-downstream-effects-of-israels-terrorist-designation-on-human-rights-defenders-in-the-us/.
61 Sullivan, Devin. "FOIA lawsuit reveals that the US State Department resisted pressure to censor Leila Khaled." Electronic Frontier Foundation, April 24, 2023. https://www.eff.org/deeplinks/2023/04/foia-lawsuit-reveals-us-state-department-resisted-pressure-censor-leila-khaled.
62 Guinane, Kay. "The alarming rise of lawfare to suppress civil society." Charity and Security Network, September 2021. https://charityandsecurity.org/wp-content/uploads/2021/09/The-Alarming-Rise-of-Lawfare-to-Suppress-Civil-Society.pdf.
63 Shamas, "Downstream effects."
64 Ibid.
65 Romero, Dennis, and Beatrice Guzzardi. "U.S., U.K. among 9 countries pausing funding to UNRWA amid allegations 12 employees were part of Oct. 7 attack." NBC News, January 28, 2024. https://www.nbcnews.com/news/world/us-uk-8-countries-pausing-funding-unrwa-allegations-12-employees-part-rcna136030.
66 H.R. 6408, To amend the Internal Revenue Code of 1986 to terminate the tax-exempt status of terrorist supporting organizations, 118th Congress (2023–2024).

7. Israeli Mechanisms to Restrict Civic Space: From Surveillance and Repression in the Occupied West Bank to Policing Israelis Writ Large

1 Gordon, Neve. *Israel's occupation* (University of California Press, 2008); Berda, Yael. *Living emergency: Israel's permit regime in the occupied West Bank* (Stanford University Press, 2017); Nashif, Nadim, and Marwa Fatafta. "Surveillance of Palestinians and the fight for digital rights." Policy Brief, Al Shabaka 23 (2017).
2 Handel, Ariel, and Hilla Dayan. "Multilayered surveillance in Israel/Palestine: dialectics of inclusive exclusion." *Surveillance & Society* 15, no. 3/4 (2017): 471–6.
3 Jabareen, Hassan. "Hobbesian citizenship: how the Palestinians became a minority in Israel." In Will Kymlicka and Eva Pföstl (eds), *Multiculturalism and minority rights in the Arab world* (Oxford University Press, 2014).
4 Shafir, Gershon, and Yoav Peled. "Citizenship and stratification in an ethnic democracy." *Ethnic and Racial Studies* 21, no. 3 (1998): 408–27; Smooha, Sammy. "The model of ethnic democracy: Israel as a Jewish and democratic state." *Nations and Nationalism* 8, no. 4 (2002): 475–503.
5 Robinson, Shira. *Citizen strangers: Palestinians and the birth of Israel's liberal settler state* (Stanford University Press, 2013); Tatour, Lana. "Citizenship as domination." *Arab Studies Journal* 27, no. 2 (2019): 8–39; Rouhana, Nadim N., and Areej Sabbagh-Khoury. "Settler-colonial citizenship: conceptualizing the relationship between Israel and its Palestinian citizens." *Settler Colonial Studies* 5, no. 3 (2015): 205–25.
6 Rouhana, Nadim N., and Nimer Sultany. "Redrawing the boundaries of citizenship: Israel's new hegemony." *Journal of Palestine Studies* 33, no. 1 (2003): 5–22.

7   See translation of Counter Terrorism Law 2016: https://www.gov.il/BlobFolder/dynamiccollectorresultitem/counter-terrorism-law-2016-english/he/legal-docs_counter_terrorism_law_2016_english.pdf.
8   Unofficial translation of Basic Law: Israel as the Nation-State of the Jewish People: chrome-extension://efaidnbmnnnibpcajpcglclefindmkaj/https://main.knesset.gov.il/EN/activity/documents/BasicLawsPDF/BasicLawNationState.pdf. For analysis of the law, see Jabareen, Hassan, and Suhad Bishara. "The Jewish nation-state law." *Journal of Palestine Studies* 48, no. 2 (2019), 43–57; Jamal, Amal. "Israel's new constitutional imagination: the nation state law and beyond." *Journal of Holy Land and Palestine Studies* 18, no. 2 (2019), 193–220.
9   For two prominent views on the relationship between citizenship and nationality from the perspective of rights and privileges, see Jamal, Amal. "Nationalizing states and the constitution of 'hollow citizenship': Israel and its Palestinian citizens." *Ethnopolitics* 6, no. 4 (2007): 471–93; Rosenhek, Zeev, and Michael Shalev. "The contradictions of Palestinian citizenship in Israel." In Nils A. Butenschon, Uri Davis, and Manuel Hassassian (eds), *Citizenship and the State in the Middle East: Approaches and Applications* (Syracuse University Press, 2000): 288–315.
10 For the sake of clarification: in the US, and other democracies, any focus on national origins would be perceived as illegal discrimination under the fundamental laws of the state in question.
11 Barnett, M., N.J. Brown, M. Lynch and S. Telhami (eds). *The one state reality: what is Israel/Palestine?* (Cornell University Press, 2023); Lustick, Ian S. *Paradigm lost: from two-state solution to one-state reality* (University of Pennsylvania Press, 2019).
12 Peled, Yoav. "The citizenship of minorities in ethnic democracies: Jewish citizens in the second Polish Republic (1918–1939); Catholic citizens in Northern Ireland (1921–1972) and Palestinian citizens in Israel." *Journal of Law, Society & Culture*, special issue on law, minority & national conflict (December 2016).
13 For a history of the use of emergency defence regulations 1945 and the transition to the counterterrorism law, see Berda, Yael. "Managing 'dangerous populations': how colonial emergency laws shape citizenship." *Security Dialogue* 51, no. 6 (2020): 557–78.
14 Administrative appeal 8277/17, *Alaa Zayoud v. Interior Minister* (Supreme Court). In its ruling, the Supreme Court noted that there was "no constitutional defect in the arrangement that allows the revocation of the citizenship of a person who committed an act that constitutes a breach of loyalty in the State of Israel," such as: an act of terrorism; an act of treason or serious espionage; or the acquisition of citizenship or the right of permanent residency in a hostile state or in hostile territory. This is so, even if as a result of the revocation of his citizenship, the individual becomes stateless, provided that if the individual becomes stateless, the Interior Minister must grant him a status of permanent residence in Israel or another designated status. For an extensive analysis of the case and its implications, see "Israeli Supreme Court upholds law authorizing the revocation of citizenship." Adalah, July 21, 2022. https://www.adalah.org/en/content/view/10661.
15 "Approved in final readings: Bill to revoke citizenship of a person convicted of terrorism who receives funds for his actions from the Palestinian Authority." Knesset News, February 15, 2023. https://main.knesset.gov.il/en/news/pressreleases/pages/press15223c.aspx.
16 Berda, "Managing 'dangerous populations,'" 577.
17 Kosti, Nir, and Yoav Mehozay, "The use of emergency regulations during Covid: a contemporary historical look 1948–2020." *Regulation Studies* 5 (2022): 211–45.

18. Who Profits report. "'Big Brother' in Jerusalem's old city: Israel's militarized visual surveillance system in occupied East Jerusalem November." 2018. https://www.whoprofits.org/writable/uploads/old/uploads/2018/11/surveil-final.pdf
19. Yadlin, Aya, and Avi Marciano. "COVID-19 surveillance in Israeli press: spatiality, mobility, and control." *Mobile Media & Communication* 10, no. 3 (2022): 421–47.
20. Cohen-Almagor, Raphael, and Eldar Haber. "Tracking and tracing in Israel during COVID-19: balancing between the need to protect public health and individual right to privacy." *Israel Studies Review* 38, no. 3 (2023): 29–50.
21. Altshuler, Tehila, and Rachel Aridor Hershkowitz. '"How Israel's COVID-19 mass surveillance operation works." Brookings Institute commentary, July 6, 2020. https://www.brookings.edu/articles/how-israels-covid-19-mass-surveillance-operation-works/.
22. The Association for Civil Rights in Israel appealed to the head of the Shin Bet, Israel's security service, to refrain from surveillance of leaders of the protest movement. ACRI, June 28, 2023. https://www.acri.org.il/post/__937.
23. See the designation of six organizations: NBCTF. "The Minister of Defense designated six organizations of the 'Popular Front for the Liberation of Palestine' as terror organizations." 2022. https://nbctf.mod.gov.il/en/Pages/211021EN.aspx.
24. Israel: Law No. 5712-1952, Entry into Israel Law, September 5, 1952. https://www.refworld.org/legal/legislation/natlegbod/1952/en/91344.
25. The term "the silent transfer" was coined in April 1997, as the title of a report of two Israeli human rights organizations, B'Tselem and HaMoked, about a policy that began in 1995 to revoke the residency status of Palestinians in Jerusalem by various legal and administrative means.
26. See article 49 of the Fourth Geneva Convention: https://ihl-databases.icrc.org/en/ihl-treaties/gciv-1949/article-47/commentary/1958.
27. "Law for Revocation of Citizenship or Residency of a Terrorist Who Receives Compensation for Carrying out a Terrorist Act." Adalah. https://www.adalah.org/en/law/view/608.
28. For information on the annexation through organizational and administrative changes, see Megiddo, Tamar, Ronit Levine-Schnur and Yael Berda. "Israel is annexing the West Bank, don't be misled by its gaslighting." Just Security, February 9, 2023. https://www.justsecurity.org/85093/israel-is-annexing-the-west-bank-dont-be-misled-by-its-gaslighting/
29. "Law for Revocation of Citizenship."
30. Berda, Yael. "The citizenship regime change behind Israel's rule-of-law crisis." *Current History* 122, no. 848 (2023).
31. Berda, "Managing 'dangerous populations," 557–78.
32. Rouhana, Nadim N., and Areej Sabbagh-Khoury. "Settler-colonial citizenship: conceptualizing the relationship between Israel and its Palestinian citizens." *Settler Colonial Studies* 5, no. 3 (2015): 205–25.
33. Margalit, L., and Makhon ha-Yiśre'eli le-demokratyah issuing body. *Mihu ṭerorisṭ? : 'al ha-manganon la-hakhrazah 'al irune ṭeror ba-ḥok ha-ma'avak ba-ṭeror [Who is a terrorist? : the framework for the designation of terrorist organizations in the counter-terrorism law]* (Jerusalem: ha-Makhon ha-Yiśre'eli le-demokratyah [Israel Democracy Institute], 2021).
34. This was first an emergency regulation on October 14, 2024, and then a primary law (temporary war provision) was promulgated on December 7, 2024. See Israeli Government. "Emergency regulations (authorization of the IDF to carry out an

35. "Hok Kiyum Diyunim Behiv'adot Chazutit Behishtatefut Atzurim, Asirim Ve'Kluyim (Hora'at Sha'a – Charvot Barzel), Tashpad-2023." https://www.nevo.co.il/law_html/law00/223278.htm.
36. Al Jazeera offices were physically shut down on May 6, 2024. See the emergency regulation: https://www.idi.org.il/media/22096/07-emergency-regulations-closing-foreign-media.pdf; and the proposal for the primary law from February 6, 2024: https://www.idi.org.il/media/23064/law-memorandum-of-07-closing-foreign-media-06022024.pdf.
37. "Emergency regulation to extend prevention for meeting with lawyers." https://www.idi.org.il/media/22097/08-emergency-regulations-security-offence-detainees-1.pdf; emergency regulation: https://www.idi.org.il/media/22098/09-emergency-regulations-security-offence-detainees-2.pdf.
38. "The Counter Terrorism Law (Amendment No. 9 Temporary Order) (Consumption of Terrorist Materials, 2023." Adalah. https://www.adalah.org/uploads/uploads/Consumption_Terrorist_Publications_Law.pdf.
39. Dwoskin, Elizabeth. "Israel escalates surveillance of Palestinians with facial recognition program in West Bank." *Washington Post*, November 8, 2021. https://www.washingtonpost.com/world/middle_east/israel-palestinians-surveillance-facial-recognition/2021/11/05/3787bf42-26b2-11ec-8739-5cb6aba30a30_story.html.
40. Amnesty International. "Automated apartheid: how facial recognition fragments, segregates and controls Palestinians in the OPT." May 2, 2023. https://www.amnesty.org/en/documents/mde15/6701/2023/en/. See also chapter 8.
41. See Amendment No. 40 to the police ordinance: https://www.law.co.il/media/computer-law/police_ordinance_amendment_40_law.pdf.
42. Ibid.
43. See Adalah report on cases of Palestinian citizens of Israel in academic institutions and disciplinary measures: "Israeli academic institutions persecute Palestinian students for social media posts amid offensive on Gaza." Adalah, October 22, 2023. https://www.adalah.org/en/content/view/10922.
44. Civil Service Commission. "Disciplinary measure against expression against the state of Israel at a time of war." Directive 20/2023, October 11, 2023. https://www.gov.il/BlobFolder/policy/directive-20-2023/he/directive-20-2023.pdf.
45. "Israeli academic institutions persecute Palestinian students."
46. "Crackdown on freedom of speech of Palestinian citizens of Israel." Adalah, October 23, 2024. https://www.adalah.org/en/content/view/10925.
47. Memorandum for Revocation of Citizenship or Residency for an Act Committed during a Special Situation on the Home Front (legislation amendments). 2023. https://moj.my.salesforce.com/sfc/dist/version/download/?oid=00D1t000000uX5h&ids=0683Y00000bkBhi&d=%2Fa%2F3Y000003dbjg%2FOH5.HcCgiVP7_wbIQBF72IdSxOpnsStffS_3upkpTEg&asPdf=false.
48. Ibid.
49. "Law for Revocation of Citizenship"; Berda, "Citizenship regime change," 342–7.

8. Made in Palestine: Repackaging Apartheid as "Smart" Cities

1. International Court of Justice. "Application of the Convention on the Prevention and Punishment of the Crime of Genocide in the Gaza Strip (South Africa v. Israel)."

January 26, 2024. https://www.icj-cij.org/sites/default/files/case-related/192/192-20240126-sum-01-00-en.pdf, 6–7.
2   Reiff, Ben. "'A mass assassination factory': inside Israel's calculated bombing of Gaza." +972 Magazine, November 30, 2023. https://www.972mag.com/mass-assassination-factory-israel-calculated-bombing-gaza/.
3   Iraqi, Amjad. "'Lavender': the AI machine directing Israel's bombing spree in Gaza." +972 Magazine, April 3, 2024. https://www.972mag.com/lavender-ai-israeli-army-gaza/.
4   Frenkel, Sheera. "Israel deploys expansive facial recognition program in Gaza." New York Times, March 27, 2024. https://www.nytimes.com/2024/03/27/technology/israel-facial-recognition-gaza.html.
5   7amleh. "Israel's surveillance industry and human rights: impacts on Palestinians and worldwide." December 2023. https://7amleh.org/storage/Israel%E2%80%99s%20Surveillance%20Industry%20english4.pdf.
6   Access Now. "Palestine unplugged: how Israel disrupts Gaza's internet." November 10, 2023. https://www.accessnow.org/publication/palestine-unplugged/.
7   Human Rights Watch. "Gaza: Israel's 'open-air prison' at 15." June 14, 2022. https://www.hrw.org/news/2022/06/14/gaza-israels-open-air-prison-15.
8   Cohen, Hillel. *Good Arabs: The Israeli Security Agencies and the Israeli Arabs, 1948–1967* (Berkeley: University of California Press, 2011).
9   National Action/Research on the Military-Industrial Complex and American Friends Service Committee (eds), *Automating Apartheid: US Computer Exports to South Africa and the Arms Embargo* (Philadelphia: NARMIC/America Friends Service Committee, 1982).
10 Grassiani, Erella. "Commercialised occupation skills: Israeli security experience as an international brand." In Matthias Leese and Stef Wittendorp (eds), *Security/Mobility: Politics of Movement* (Manchester: Manchester University Press, 2017), 57–73. https://www.jstor.org/stable/j.ctt1wn0s9r.9.
11 Goodfriend, Sophia. "How the occupation fuels Tel Aviv's booming AI sector." Foreign Policy, February 21, 2022, https://foreignpolicy.com/2022/02/21/palestine-israel-ai-surveillance-tech-hebron-occupation-privacy/.
12 Frenkel, "Israel deploys expansive facial recognition program."
13 Ibid.
14 Amnesty International, "Automated apartheid."
15 Dwoskin, "Israel escalates surveillance."
16 Amnesty International, "Automated apartheid."
17 Ibid.
18 Ibid.
19 Ibid.
20 OCHA Monthly Humanitarian Bulletin. "Twenty years since the division of Hebron." March 2017. https://www.ochaopt.org/content/isolation-palestinians-israeli-controlled-area-hebron-city-continues.
21 Amnesty International, "Automated apartheid."
22 Ibid.
23 Ibid.
24 Ibid.
25 Ibid.
26 "In environments subject to rampant illicit surveillance, the targeted communities know of or suspect such attempts at surveillance, which in turn shapes and restricts their capacity to exercise rights to freedom of expression [and] association." From Kaye, David. "Surveillance and human rights: report of the Special Rapporteur on

the promotion and protection of the right to freedom of opinion and expression." May 28, 2019, para. 21.
27 Amnesty International, "Automated apartheid."
28 "'Hebron Smart City': HaHam'alim HaHadashim bee'Ysh Nechashfim." April 12, 2024. https://www.israelhayom.co.il/article/807893.
29 Amnesty International, "Automated apartheid."
30 Ibid.
31 Ibid.
32 Ibid.
33 Caine, Ariel. "The ground of Palestine." Disegno Journal, September 2021. https://disegnojournal.com/newsfeed/ground-of-palestine-archaeology-architecture.
34 Amnesty International. "Israeli authorities using facial recognition to entrench apartheid." May 2, 2023. https://www.amnesty.org/en/latest/news/2023/05/israel-opt-israeli-authorities-are-using-facial-recognition-technology-to-entrench-apartheid/.
35 Grassiani, "Commercialised occupation skills."
36 Amnesty International, "Automated apartheid."
37 "We are Google and Amazon workers. we condemn Project Nimbus." Guardian, October 12, 2021. https://www.theguardian.com/commentisfree/2021/oct/12/google-amazon-workers-condemn-project-nimbus-israeli-military-contract.
38 Palantir is the controversial US company that empowered US Immigration Customs Enforcement (ICE) with software enabling some of the most aggressive immigration raids to date, with some 700 migrant workers in Mississippi detained, in broad daylight, in the fall of 2019. It has come under heavy scrutiny by several civil society organizations for its questionable human rights record. See, for instance, Mijente. "Breaking: Palantir's technology used in Mississippi raids where 680 were arrested." August 2019. https://mijente.net/wp-content/uploads/2019/08/Mijente-The-War-Against-Immigrants_-Trumps-Tech-Tools-Powered-by-Palantir_.pdf/.
39 "Palantir AIP for defense." Palantir. https://www.palantir.com/platforms/aip/defense/.
40 Newman, Marrisa. "Palantir supplying Israel with new tools since Hamas war started." Bloomberg, January 10, 2024. https://www.bloomberg.com/news/articles/2024-01-10/palantir-supplying-israel-with-new-tools-since-hamas-war-started.
41 Ahmed, Kaamil, and Lorenzo Tondo. "Fortress Europe: the millions spent on military-grade tech to deter refugees." Guardian, December 6, 2021. https://www.theguardian.com/global-development/2021/dec/06/fortress-europe-the-millions-spent-on-military-grade-tech-to-deter-refugees.
42 "Elbit America develops AI-based solutions for border and other security applications." Elbit Systems of America, June 17, 2020. https://www.elbitamerica.com/news/elbit-america-develops-ai-based-solutions-for-border-and-other-security-applications.
43 Oosto. "Oosto law enforcement datasheet." March 2023. https://oosto.com/wp-content/uploads/2023/03/oosto-law-enforcement-datasheet.pdf.
44 Dastin, Jeffery. "Microsoft to divest AnyVision stake, end face recognition investing." Reuters, March 28, 2020. https://www.reuters.com/article/us-microsoft-anyvision-idUSKBN21E3BA.
45 Halper, Jeff. *War against the People: Israel, the Palestinians and Global Pacification* (London: PlutoPress, 2015).
46 Loewenstein, Antony. *The Palestine Laboratory: How Israel Exports the Technology of Occupation around the World* (London and New York: Verso Books, 2023);

Fatafta, Marwa. "Apartheid tech: the use and expansion of biometric identification and surveillance technologies in the occupied West Bank." In Aizeki, Mizue, Matt Mahmoudi, and Coline Schupfer (eds). *Resisting Borders and Technologies of Violence* (Chicago: Haymarket Books, 2024).

47 Robinson, Cedric J. *Black Marxism: The Making of the Black Radical Tradition* (University of North Carolina Press, 1983).

48 Cath, Corrine. "Eaten by the internet: putting internet infrastructure power on your radar." Tech Policy Press, October 30, 2023. https://techpolicy.press/eaten-by-the-internet-putting-internet-infrastructure-power-on-your-radar.

49 Miller, Todd. "More than a wall: corporate profiteering and the militarization of US borders." Transnational Institute, September 2019.

50 Green, Ben. *The Smart Enough City: Putting Technology in Its Place to Reclaim Our Urban Future* (Cambridge: MIT Press, 2019).

51 Eubanks, Virginia. *Automating Inequality: How High-Tech Tools Profile, Police, and Punish the Poor* (St Martin's Press, 2018); Amnesty International. "Xenophobic machines: discrimination through unregulated use of algorithms in the Dutch childcare benefits scandal." October 25, 2021. https://www.amnesty.org/en/documents/eur35/4686/2021/en/; Amnesty International. "Trapped by automation: poverty and discrimination in Serbia's welfare state." December 4, 2023. https://www.amnesty.org/en/latest/research/2023/12/trapped-by-automation-poverty-and-discrimination-in-serbias-welfare-state/.

52 Benjamin, Ruha. "The shiny, high-tech wolf in sheep's clothing." Level (blog), October 23, 2020. https://level.medium.com/the-shiny-high-tech-wolf-in-sheeps-clothing-17d8db219b6d.

53 Cheesman, Margie. "Web3 and communities at risk: myths and problems with current experiments." Minderoo Centre for Technology and Democracy, November 1, 2022. https://doi.org/10.17863/CAM.90554.

54 Molnar, Petra. "Bots at the gate: a human rights analysis of automated decision-making in Canada's immigration and refugee system." Citizen Lab and International Human Rights Program (Faculty of Law, University of Toronto), September 2018. https://citizenlab.ca/wp-content/uploads/2018/09/IHRP-Automated-Systems-Report-Web-V2.pdf; Aizeki, Mahmoudi and Schupfer 2024.

55 Mahmoudi, Matt. *The Digital Periphery: New Urban Frontiers of Migration Control* (University of California Press, forthcoming).

56 Geraghty, Lena, Tina Lee, Julia Glickman and Brooks Rainwater. "Future of cities: cities and the metaverse." National League of Cities: Centre for City Solutions, 2022. https://www.nlc.org/wp-content/uploads/2022/04/CS-Cities-and-the-Metaverse_v4-Final-1.pdf.

57 Mozur, Paul. "One month, 500,000 face scans: how China is using AI to profile a minority." New York Times, April 14, 2019. https://www.nytimes.com/2019/04/14/technology/china-surveillance-artificial-intelligence-racial-profiling.html.

58 Amnesty International. "China: draconian repression of Muslims in Xinjiang amounts to crimes against humanity." June 10, 2021. https://www.amnesty.org/en/latest/news/2021/06/china-draconian-repression-of-muslims-in-xinjiang-amounts-to-crimes-against-humanity/.

59 Amnesty International. "Look inside the NYPD's surveillance machine." February 15, 2022. https://nypd-surveillance.amnesty.org.

60 Amnesty International. "USA: facial recognition technology reinforcing racist stop-and-frisk policing in New York – new research." February 15, 2022. https://

www.amnesty.org/en/latest/news/2022/02/usa-facial-recognition-technology-reinforcing-racist-stop-and-frisk-policing-in-new-york-new-research/.
61   Buolamwini, Joy, and Timnit Gebru. "Gender shades: intersectional accuracy disparities in commercial gender classification." In *Proceedings of the 1st Conference on Fairness, Accountability and Transparency* (PMLR, 2018), 77–91. https://proceedings.mlr.press/v81/buolamwini18a.html.
62   OHCHR. "Saudi Arabia: UN experts alarmed by imminent executions linked to NEOM Project." May 3, 2023, https://www.ohchr.org/en/press-releases/2023/05/saudi-arabia-un-experts-alarmed-imminent-executions-linked-neom-project.
63   Harris, Mark. "These exclusive satellite images show that Saudi Arabia's sci-fi megacity is well underway." MIT Technology Review, December 9, 2022. https://www.technologyreview.com/2022/12/09/1064544/satellite-images-line-megacity-google/.
64   Farouk, Menna A. "Feature: Saudi 'surveillance city': would you sell your data to the Line?" Reuters Foundation, August 23, 2022. https://www.reuters.com/article/idUSL8N2ZL0CM/.
65   Zukin, Sharon. *The Innovation Complex: Cities, Tech, and the New Economy* (Oxford University Press, 2020).
66   NYC Gov. "De Blasio administration announces NYCX technology leadership advisory council members." Official website of the City of New York, January 11, 2018. http://www1.nyc.gov/office-of-the-mayor/news/027-18/de-blasio-administration-nycx-technology-leadership-advisory-council-members.
67   Marcuse, Peter. "The enclave, the citadel, and the ghetto: what has changed in the post-Fordist US city." *Urban Affairs Review* 33, no. 2 (1997): 228–64, https://doi.org/10.1177/107808749703300206.
68   Shapiro, Aaron. *Design, Control, Predict: Logistical Governance in the Smart City* (University of Minnesota Press, 2020).
69   Ibid., 136.
70   Easterling, Keller. *Extrastatecraft: the Power of Infrastructure Space* (Verso, 2014).
71   Browne, Simone. *Dark Matters: on the Surveillance of Blackness* (Durham: Duke University Press, 2015).
72   Said, Edward W. *Orientalism* (London: Routledge and Kegan Paul, 1978).
73   Ibid., 1–9.
74   Amnesty International, "Automated Apartheid."
75   Shapiro, *Design, Control, Predict*.
76   Mahmoudi, *Digital Periphery*.

9. Digital Repression: How Palestinian Voices are Censored, Surveilled, and Threatened Online

1   Zeldin, Wendy. "U.N. Human Rights Council: First Resolution on Internet Free Speech." Library of Congress, July 12, 2012. https://www.loc.gov/item/global-legal-monitor/2012-07-12/u-n-human-rights-council-first-resolution-on-internet-free-speech/.
2   "The promotion, protection and enjoyment of human rights on the Internet (A/HRC/47/L.22)." U.N. Human Rights Council, July 7, 2021. https://documents-dds-ny.un.org/doc/UNDOC/LTD/G21/173/56/PDF/G2117356.pdf?OpenElement.

3 "UN rights chief issues call to protect and expand civic space." Press release, Office of the High Commissioner for Human Rights, May 26, 2023. https://www.ohchr.org/en/press-releases/2023/05/un-rights-chief-issues-call-protect-and-expand-civic-space.
4 "The rise of digital authoritarianism: fake news, data collection and the challenge to democracy." Press release, Freedom House, October 31, 2018, https://freedomhouse.org/article/rise-digital-authoritarianism-fake-news-data-collection-and-challenge-democracy.
5 Amnesty International. "Surveillance giants: how the business model of Google and Facebook threatens human rights." November 21, 2019. https://www.amnesty.org/en/documents/pol30/1404/2019/en/.
6 Feldstein, Steven, and Brian (Chun Hey) Kot. "Why does the global spyware industry continue to thrive? Trends, explanations, and responses." Carnegie Endowment for International Peace, March 14, 2023. https://carnegieendowment.org/2023/03/14/why-does-global-spyware-industry-continue-to-thrive-trends-explanations-and-responses-pub-89229.
7 Bajec, Alessandra. "Sheikh Jarrah: a new generation of activists lead the fight for Palestinian rights." New Arab, May 18, 2021. https://www.newarab.com/analysis/sheikh-jarrah-new-generation-palestinian-activism.
8 Hawari, Yara, host. "Palestinian resistance and shifting the media narrative with Marwa Fatafta." Rethinking Palestine (podcast), June 9, 2009. https://al-shabaka.org/podcasts/palestinian-resistance-and-shifting-the-media-narrative-with-marwa-fatafta/.
9 Vetch, Frankie. "Israel uses Palestine as a lab to test surveillance tech." Coda Story, October 4, 2022. https://www.codastory.com/newsletters/israel-ai-controlled-guns-palestine/.
10 Hodge, Nathan. "Gaza war's new front: Facebook." Wired, January 9, 2009. https://web.archive.org/web/20090328184614/http://blog.wired.com/defense/2009/01/facebook-fundra.html.
11 Lamont, Ian. "Twitter sees a furious debate over Gaza." Industry Standard, January 9, 2009. https://web.archive.org/web/20090421214601/http://www.thestandard.com/news/2009/01/09/twitter-sees-furious-debate-over-gaza.
12 Bhanoo, Sindya. "Gaza demonstrations turn virtual, as protestors converge on SL Israel." Industry Standard, January 7, 2009. https://web.archive.org/web/20090503144010/http://www.thestandard.com/news/2009/01/07/second-lifers-protest-gaza-attacks-sl-israel.
13 Perry Barlow, John. "A declaration of the independence of cyberspace." Electronic Frontier Foundation, February 8, 1996. https://www.eff.org/cyberspace-independence.
14 Aouragh, Miriyam. *Palestine Online: Transnationalism, the Internet and the Construction of Identity* (London: I.B. Tauris, 2011), 4.
15 Moore, Jack. "Israeli minister: Facebook's Zuckerberg has 'blood on his hands' over teenager's murder." Newsweek, July 4, 2016. https://www.newsweek.com/israel-minister-facebook-zuckerberg-blood-hands-over-teenager-settlement-477399.
16 Fatafta, Marwa. "Israel advances new 'Facebook bill', threatening free speech." Global Voices, January 13, 2017. https://globalvoices.org/2017/01/13/israel-advances-new-facebook-bill-threatening-free-speech/.
17 Fatafta, Marwa, and Nadim Nashif. "The Israeli algorithm criminalizing Palestinians for online dissent." OpenDemocracy, October 4, 2017. https://www.opendemocracy.net/en/north-africa-west-asia/israeli-algorithm-criminalizing-palestinians-for-o/.

18. "'Silenced net': the chilling effect among Palestinian youth in social media." 7amleh, October 20, 2019. https://7amleh.org/2019/10/20/silenced-net-the-chilling-effect-among-palestinian-youth-in-social-media.
19. Pulwer, Sharon, and Elihay Vidal. "Facebook complying with 95% of Israeli requests to remove inciting content, minister says." Haaretz, September 12, 2016. https://www.haaretz.com/israel-news/business/2016-09-12/ty-article/facebook-removes-inciting-content-at-israels-request-minister-says/0000017f-f37c-d497-a1ff-f3fc55240000.
20. Office of the State Attorney. "About the Cyber Unit." May 11, 2021. https://www.gov.il/en/Departments/General/cyber-about.
21. "Hundreds of inflammatory contents were removed from social networks." Ynet, May 20, 2021. https://www.ynet.co.il/digital/internet/article/SytSph7Fd.
22. "Fighting incitement online." Press release, Cyber Unit, November 26, 2023. https://www.gov.il/en/departments/news/news-26-11.
23. "Israel's 'Cyber Unit' operating illegally to censor social media content." Adalah, September 14, 2017. https://www.adalah.org/en/content/view/9228.
24. "Israeli Supreme Court green lights Israel's 'Cyber Unit' that works with social media giants to censor user content." Adalah, April 12, 2021. https://www.adalah.org/en/content/view/10292.
25. Nathan-Kazis, Josh. "Shadowy Israeli app turns American Jews into foot soldiers in online war." Forward, November 30, 2017. https://forward.com/news/388259/shadowy-israeli-app-turns-american-jews-into-foot-soldiers-in-online-war/.
26. Arria, Michael. "Israel pulls the plug on its anti-BDS app – 'a failure from the start.'" Mondoweiss, March 11, 2022. https://mondoweiss.net/2022/03/israel-pulls-the-plug-on-its-anti-bds-app-a-failure-from-the-start/.
27. Mac, Ryan. "Amid Israeli–Palestinian violence, Facebook employees are accusing their company of bias against Arabs and Muslims." Buzzfeed, May 27, 2021. https://www.buzzfeednews.com/article/ryanmac/facebook-employees-bias-arabs-muslims-palestine.
28. Ibid.
29. Biddle, Sam. "Israeli group claims it's working with big tech insiders to censor 'inflammatory' wartime content." Intercept, January 10, 2024. https://theintercept.com/2024/01/10/israel-disinformation-social-media-iron-truth/.
30. Human Rights Watch. "Meta: systemic censorship of Palestine content." December 20, 2023. https://www.hrw.org/news/2023/12/20/meta-systemic-censorship-palestine-content.
31. "Activists say Sheikh Jarrah posts 'deleted' by Instagram as Israel's forced evictions capture global attention." New Arab, May 7, 2021. https://www.newarab.com/news/activists-say-instagram-censoring-posts-israels-forced-evictions.
32. "Tell Facebook: stop silencing Palestine." 2021. https://stopsilencingpalestine.com/2021/.
33. Instagram Comms, X post, May 7, 2021, 3:57 a.m., https://twitter.com/InstagramComms/status/1390485897787883523?s=20.
34. "Global civil society coalition calls on Facebook to #StopSilencingPalestine." Access Now, June 10, 2021. https://www.accessnow.org/press-release/facebook-stop-silencing-palestine/.
35. Klonick, Kate. "The new governors: the people, rules, and processes governing online speech." *Harvard Law Review* 6 (2018). https://harvardlawreview.org/print/vol-131/the-new-governors-the-people-rules-and-processes-governing-online-speech/.

36 Pírková, Eliška, and Marwa Fatafta. "Content governance in times of crisis: how platforms can protect human rights." Access Now, November 29, 2022. https://www.accessnow.org/publication/new-content-governance-in-crises-declaration/.
37 Ohlheiser, A.W. "Why some Palestinians believe social media companies are suppressing their posts." Vox, October 29, 2023. https://www.vox.com/technology/23933846/shadowbanning-meta-israel-hamas-war-palestine.
38 "Social media stats in Palestinian territory – December 2023." Statscounter, 2023. https://gs.statcounter.com/social-media-stats/all/palestinian-territory.
39 Kemp, Simon. "Digital 2023: Palestine." DataReportal, February 13, 2023. https://datareportal.com/reports/digital-2023-palestine.
40 York, Jillian C. *Silicon Values: The Future of Free Speech under Surveillance Capitalism* (Verso Books, 2021), 45–6.
41 Ibid.
42 "Oversight Board announces a review of Meta's approach to the term 'shaheed.'" Oversight Board, March 2023. https://www.oversightboard.com/news/1299903163922108-oversight-board-announces-a-review-of-meta-s-approach-to-the-term-shaheed/.
43 Meta. "Dangerous organizations and individuals." August 29, 2023. https://transparency.fb.com/en-gb/policies/community-standards/dangerous-individuals-organizations/.
44 Ibid.
45 Biddle, Sam. "Revealed: Facebook's secret blacklist of "dangerous individuals and organizations." Intercept, October 12, 2021. https://theintercept.com/2021/10/12/facebook-secret-blacklist-dangerous/.
46 "Oversight Board announces a review."
47 "Human rights due diligence of Meta's impacts in Israel and Palestine." BSR, September 22, 2022. https://www.bsr.org/en/reports/meta-human-rights-israel-palestine.
48 Ibid.
49 Ibid.
50 Brynen, Rex. "Facebook blocks 'Palestinian?'" Palestinian Refugee ResearchNet Blog, July 25, 2010. https://prrnblog.wordpress.com/2010/07/25/facebook-blocks-palestinian/.
51 York, *Silicon Values*, 53.
52 Alsaafin, Linah. "Palestinians criticize social media censorship over Sheikh Jarrah." Al Jazeera, May 7, 2021. https://www.aljazeera.com/news/2021/5/7/palestinians-criticise-social-media-censorship-over-sheikh-jarrah.
53 Levenson, Michael. "Instagram blocked posts about the Aqsa Mosque in a terrorism screening error." New York Times, May 13, 2021. https://www.nytimes.com/2021/05/13/world/middleeast/instagram-aqsa-mosque.html#:~:text=Facebook%20said%20in%20the%20message,a%20foreign%20terrorist%20organization,%20and.
54 Taylor, Josh. "Instagram apologises for adding 'terrorist' to some Palestinian user profiles." Guardian, October 20, 2023. https://www.theguardian.com/technology/2023/oct/20/instagram-palestinian-user-profile-bios-terrorist-added-translation-meta-apology.
55 Bhuiyan, Johana. "WhatsApp's AI shows gun-wielding children when prompted with 'Palestine.'" Guardian, November 3, 2023. https://www.theguardian.com/technology/2023/nov/02/whatsapps-ai-palestine-kids-gun-gaza-bias-israel.
56 Human Rights Watch. "Meta: systemic censorship of Palestine content."

57 Meta. "Meta's ongoing efforts regarding the Israel-Hamas War." October 13, 2023. https://about.fb.com/news/2023/10/metas-efforts-regarding-israel-hamas-war/.
58 Shihab-Eldin, Ahmed. Facebook post, November 18, 2023, 7:12 p.m. https://m.facebook.com/ahmedshihabeldin/posts/895076695311292/?comment_id=637103655025019&reply_comment_id=1081570066206332.
59 Biddle, Sam. "Instagram hid a comment. It was just three Palestinian flag emojis." Intercept, October 28, 2023. https://theintercept.com/2023/10/28/instagram-palestinian-flag-emoji/.
60 Schechner, Sam, Jeff Horwitz and Newley Purnell. "Inside Meta, debate over what's fair in suppressing comments in the Palestinian territories." Wall Street Journal, October 21, 2023. https://www.wsj.com/tech/inside-meta-debate-over-whats-fair-in-suppressing-speech-in-the-palestinian-territories-6212aa58.
61 Ibid.
62 "Facebook Files: Facebook's manual on credible threats of violence." Guardian, May 21, 2017. https://www.theguardian.com/news/gallery/2017/may/21/facebooks-manual-on-credible-threats-of-violence.
63 "Thousands of human rights activists, scholars, and cultural figures call on Facebook to allow users to hold Israeli government accountable." Press release, Jewish Voice for Peace, January 27, 2021. https://www.jewishvoiceforpeace.org/2021/01/27/facebook-we-need-to-talk/; Biddle, Sam. "Facebook's secret rules about the word 'Zionist' impede criticism of Israel." Intercept, May 14, 2021. https://theintercept.com/2021/05/14/facebook-israel-zionist-moderation/.
64 "Palestinian Observatory of Digital Rights Violations (7or)s." 7amleh, 2023. https://7or.7amleh.org/charts.
65 "Human rights due diligence of Meta's impacts in Israel and Palestine."
66 Frenkel, Sheera. "Mob violence against Palestinians in Israel is fueled by groups on WhatsApp." New York Times, May 19, 2021. https://www.nytimes.com/2021/05/19/technology/israeli-clashes-pro-violence-groups-whatsapp.html.
67 Biddle, Sam. "Facebook approved an Israeli ad calling for assassination of pro-Palestine activist." Intercept, November 21, 2023. https://theintercept.com/2023/11/21/facebook-ad-israel-palestine-violence/.
68 "Al-Aqsa imam named as a target in far-right Israeli hit list on Telegram channel." Middle East Monitor, October 14, 2023. https://www.middleeastmonitor.com/20231014-al-aqsa-imam-named-as-a-target-in-far-right-israeli-hit-list-on-telegram-channel/.
69 Nazi Hunters 2023, Telegram channel, https://t.me/tsayadeyhanazim.
70 "Rise in intimidation, settler violence in the West Bank, warns OCHA." UN, November 2, 2023. https://palestine.un.org/en/251552-rise-intimidation-settler-violence-west-bank-warns-ocha.
71 Björksten, Gustaf. "A taxonomy of internet shutdowns: the technologies behind network interference." Access Now, June 1, 2022. https://www.accessnow.org/wp-content/uploads/2022/06/A-taxonomy-of-internet-shutdowns-the-technologies-behind-network-interference.pdf.
72 Rosson, Zach, Felicia Anthonio, and Carolyn Tackett. "Weapons of control, shields of impunity: internet shutdowns in 2022." February 28, 2023. https://www.accessnow.org/wp-content/uploads/2023/05/2022-KIO-Report-final.pdf.
73 "#KeepItOn: telecommunications blackout in the Gaza Strip is an attack on human rights." Press release, Access Now, October 13, 2023. https://www.accessnow.org/press-release/communications-blackout-gaza-strip/.

74 Martin, Liv, Clothilde Goujard and Hailey Fuchs. "Israel floods social media to shape opinion around the war." Politico, October 17, 2023. https://www.politico.eu/article/israel-social-media-opinion-hamas-war/?gad_source=1&gclid=CjwKCAiAs6-sBhBmEiwA1Nl8s-lXKAZXXkXOQskOepgbkG8_p_TlecAUBf79m8NBR6ic5Pi3RDj_hoC3dAQAvD_BwE.
75 Fusion. Facebook post, October 8, 2023, 3:24 p.m. https://www.facebook.com/photo?fbid=724655189687368&set=a.503024435183779.
76 Alfanet. Facebook post, October 8, 2023, 6:31 a.m. https://www.facebook.com/AlfaNetIT/posts/ pfbid02GSsU8PdChNktczmp4RT1k3RZZdY8vN9YZXf4UUVx2F7CutcWKzu4TcuYggZ2e67sl.
77 HiNet. Facebook post, October 9, 2023, 5:39 p.m. https://www.facebook.com/HiNet.Gaza/posts/pfbid02YKcy7r9ywaiqLYMZr5KEEWZDPvd3yoPUMKKzzNrFuDnApsMQhST2Q8nQBDuTV5Msl.
78 Shehada, Muhammed. X post, October 9, 2023, 5:47 p.m. https://twitter.com/muhammadshehad2/status/1711408136806969624.
79 "Hostilities in the Gaza Strip and Israel: flash update #4." OCHA, October 10, 2023. https://www.ochaopt.org/content/hostilities-gaza-strip-and-israel-flash-update-4.
80 Paltel. X post, November 12, 2023, 3:29 p.m. https://x.com/Paltelco/status/1723709517983035862?s=20.
81 Paltel. X post, November 16, 2023, 3:31 p.m. https://twitter.com/Paltelco/status/1725159705796821048?s=20.
82 Paltel. X post, November 17, 2023, 9:15 p.m. https://twitter.com/Paltelco/status/1725608660817109009.
83 McCarthy, Rory. "Gaza plunged into darkness as Israeli fuel blockade takes effect." Guardian, January 21, 2008. https://www.theguardian.com/world/2008/jan/21/israelandthepalestinians.international.
84 "Palestinians blame Israel for Gaza blackout." Al Jazeera, August 10, 2011. https://www.aljazeera.com/news/2011/8/10/palestinians-blame-israel-for-gaza-blackout.
85 "The telecommunication sector in the Palestinian territories: a missed opportunity for economic development." World Bank, February 1, 2016. https://documents1.worldbank.org/curated/en/993031473856114803/pdf/104263-REVISED-title-a-little-different-WP-P150798-NOW-OUO-9.pdf.
86 Sibai, Ali. "Israeli airstrikes destroyed internet infrastructure in Gaza." SMEX, May 28, 2021. https://smex.org/israeli-airstrikes-destroyed-internet-infrastructure-in-gaza-report/.
87 "Palestine unplugged: how Israel disrupts Gaza's internet." Access Now, November 10, 2023. https://www.accessnow.org/publication/palestine-unplugged/.
88 "Summary of the activities of the Ministry of Communications – ten days into the war." Press release, Ministry of Communications, October 23, 2023. https://www.gov.il/en/departments/news/17102023
89 Bashir, Abu Bakr, Iyad Abuheweila, Vivian Nereim and Yousur Al-Hlou. "34 hours of fear: the blackout that cut Gaza off from the world." New York Times, October 29, 2023. https://www.nytimes.com/2023/10/29/world/middleeast/gaza-blackout-internet-israel.html#:~:text=For%2034%20hours,%20the%20vast,Emergency%20phone%20lines%20stopped%20ringing.
90 Palestinian Red Crescent. X post, October 27, 2023, 7:17 p.m. https://twitter.com/PalestineRCS/status/1717953723605901373.

91 Ghebreyesus, Tedros Adhanom. X post, October 27, 2023, 9:41 p.m. https://twitter.com/DrTedros/status/1717989993577173013.
92 "Gaza experiences one-week communications blackout amid Israel-Hamas tensions." CNN, January 18, 2024. https://www.cnn.com/2024/01/18/middleeast/gaza-communications-blackout-one-week-israel-hamas-intl/index.html.
93 Fatafta, Marwa. "Internet freedoms in Palestine: mapping of digital rights violations and threats." 7amleh, January 23, 2018. https://www.apc.org/en/pubs/internet-freedoms-palestine-mapping-digital-rights-violations-and-threats.
94 See the Israeli-Palestinian Interim Agreement, Annex III: Protocol Concerning Civil Affairs, 1995. https://www.peaceagreements.org/viewmasterdocument/985.
95 Quintin, Cooper, and Andrés Arrieta. "Your phone is vulnerable because of 2G, but it doesn't have to be." Electronic Frontier Foundation, June 29, 2020. https://www.eff.org/deeplinks/2020/06/your-phone-vulnerable-because-2g-it-doesnt-have-be.
96 "Six Palestinian human rights defenders hacked with NSO Group's Pegasus spyware." Front Line Defenders, November 8, 2021. https://www.frontlinedefenders.org/en/statement-report/statement-targeting-palestinian-hrds-pegasus.
97 Kirchgaessner, Stephanie, and Michael Safi. "Palestinian activists' mobile phones hacked using NSO spyware, says report." Guardian, November 8, 2023. https://www.theguardian.com/world/2021/nov/08/palestinian-activists-mobile-phones-hacked-by-nso-says-report.
98 Ibid.
99 Hearst, Katherine. "Israel–Palestine war: Israel shut down NGO for reporting rape of teenager, ex-US official says." Middle East Eye, December 5, 2023. https://www.middleeasteye.net/news/israel-palestine-war-ngo-shut-down-reporting-sexual-assault-ex-us.
100 "Crackdown on freedom of speech of Palestinian citizens of Israel." Adalah, October 23, 2023. https://www.adalah.org/en/content/view/10925.
101 Ibid.
102 "Crackdown on freedom of speech."
103 Ibid.
104 Bisharat, Ghousoon, Oren Ziv, and Baker Zoubi "The crackdown has begun: Israel goes after critics of its Gaza war." Nation, October 18, 2023. https://www.thenation.com/article/world/israel-cracks-down-on-critics-of-gaza-war/.
105 Alo Boeirat, Amir. "Al-Jamieat Al-Isra'iliyyah Tastad'i 160 Taliban Arabiyyan Khalal Al-Harb Alaa Ghazzah: I'tiqaal Talibat Ba'd Asabi'a Min Dhalik." Arab 48, November 15, 2023, https://www.arab48.com/%D9%85%D8%AD%D9%84%D9%8A%D8%A7%D8%AA/%D8%AF%D8%B1%D8%A7%D8%B3%D8%A7%D8%AA-%D9%88%D8%AA%D9%82%D8%A7%D8%B1%D9%8A%D8%B1/2023/11/15/%D8%A7%D9%84%D8%AC%D8%A7%D9%85%D8%B9%D8%A7%D8%AA-%D8%AA%D8%B3%D8%AA%D8%AF%D8%B9%D9%8A-160-%D8%B7%D8%A7%D9%84%D8%A8%D8%A7-%D8%B9%D8%B1%D8%A8%D9%8A%D8%A7-%D8%AE%D9%8-4%D8%A7%D9%84-%D8%A7%D9%84%D8%AD%D8%B1%D8%A8-%D8%B9%D9%84%D9%89-%D8%BA%D8%B2%D8%A9-%D8%A7%D8%B9%D8%AA%D9%82%D8%A7%D9%84-%D8%B7%D9%84%D8%A8%D8%A9-%D8%A8%D8%B9%D8%AF-%D8%A3%D8%B3%D8%A8%D8%A7%D8%A8%D9%8A%D8%B9-%D9%85%D9%86-%D8%B0%D9%84%D9%83.
106 Shezaf, Hegar, and Jack Khoury. "Student at Israel's Technion arrested for 'victory shakshuka' social media post." Haaretz, October 30, 2023. https://www.haaretz.

107. "Arabs in Israel face reprisals over online solidarity with Gaza." Guardian, October 20, 2023. https://www.theguardian.com/world/2023/oct/20/israeli-arabs-reprisals-online-solidarity-gaza#:~:text=And%20an%20Arab%20teacher%20in,her%20go%20teach%20in%20Gaza.%E2%80%9D.
108. Schrader, Adam. "Israeli police arrest 'influencer' on terrorism charges amid crackdown on support of Hamas." UPI, October 29, 2023. https://www.upi.com/Top_News/World-News/2023/10/29/israeli-police-arrest-influencer-terrorism-charges/2431698594220/.
109. Morris, Loveday. "Israel's free speech crackdown: 'war inside of a war.'" Washington Post, November 12, 2023. https://www.washingtonpost.com/world/2023/11/12/israel-free-speech-arrests-hamas/.
110. "Israeli Knesset passes draconian amendment to the Counter-Terrorism Law criminalizing 'consumption of terrorist publications.'" Adalah, November 8, 2023. https://www.adalah.org/en/content/view/10951.
111. "'Raise your hands and give us your phones!' Palestinian Jerusalemites silenced in their private and public spaces." Jerusalem Story, October 22, 2023. https://www.jerusalemstory.com/en/blog/raise-your-hands-and-give-us-your-phones-palestinian-jerusalemites-silenced-their-private-and.
112. Good Shepherd Collective. X post, December 27, 2023, 5:24 p.m. https://twitter.com/Shepherds4Good/status/1740045915069796656.
113. Interview with UNRWA spokesperson Tamara Alrifai. CNN, November 2, 2023. https://www.unrwa.org/newsroom/videos/unrwa-spokesperson-tamara-alrifai-we-should-not-be-begging-fuel.
114. "ETC Palestine Situation Report #11." Emergency Telecommunications Cluster, January 11, 2024. https://www.etcluster.org/document/etc-palestine-sitrep-9-27-december-2023.

10. The How-to of Shutting Down Pro-Palestinian Speech and Protest in the US

1. Palestine Legal. "The Palestine exception." https://palestinelegal.org/the-palestine-exception.
2. Friedman, Lara. "Targeting free speech & redefining antisemitism: how pro-Israel actors are using US laws to attack Palestinian activism & solidarity." *University of the Pacific Law Review* 54, no. 4 (2023): 612. https://scholarlycommons.pacific.edu/uoplawreview/vol54/iss4/7.
3. Grim, Ryan, and Glenn Greenwald. "US lawmakers seek to criminally outlaw support for boycott campaign against Israel." Intercept, July 19, 2017. https://theintercept.com/2017/07/19/u-s-lawmakers-seek-to-criminally-outlaw-support-for-boycott-campaign-against-israel/.
4. "Marsha Blackburn's free-speech resolution is a step in the right direction, but doesn't go far enough." Washington Examiner, June 24, 2019. https://www.washingtonexaminer.com/red-alert-politics/1962602/marsha-blackburns-free-speech-resolution-is-a-step-in-the-right-direction-but-doesnt-go-far-enough/.

5   Blackburn, Marsha. "Marsha Blackburn: not one dime from US taxpayers should go to antisemitic universities." Commercial Appeal, December 26, 2023. https://www.commercialappeal.com/story/opinion/contributors/2023/12/26/marsha-blackburn-antisemitism-on-college-campuses-must-be-punished/71991114007/.
6   Friedman, "Targeting free speech."
7   Friedman, Lara. "Anti-boycott legislation – Israel/Palestine." FMEP. https://lawfare.fmep.org/resources/anti-boycott-legislation-israel-palestine/.
8   Friedman, "Targeting free speech."
9   Weiss, Philip. "Israeli government minister takes credit for 27 US states passing anti-BDS laws." Mondoweiss, July 2, 2019. https://mondoweiss.net/2019/07/israeli-government-minister/.
10 X (formerly Twitter). Prime Minister of Israel. February 12, 2020. https://twitter.com/IsraeliPM/status/1227660066700042242.
11 Human Rights Watch. "US: states use anti-boycott laws to punish responsible businesses." April 23, 2019. https://www.hrw.org/news/2019/04/23/us-states-use-anti-boycott-laws-punish-responsible-businesses.
12 Bailey, Kristian. "The right to boycott Israel: yours, mine and Ben & Jerry's." Palestine Legal, August 17, 2021. https://palestinelegal.org/news/2021/8/17/ben-and-jerrys-bds-right-to-boycott.
13 Adely, Hannan. "Israeli leaders are asking states to sanction Ben & Jerry's after Palestinian boycott." USA Today, July 23, 2021. https://www.usatoday.com/story/money/food/2021/07/23/ben-jerrys-ice-cream-new-jersey-law-israeli-leaders/8071530002/. In response to this outrage and legal pressure, Airbnb notably backtracked on this policy, and Ben and Jerry's parent company, Unilever, ended up selling off the Ben and Jerry's business in Israel to an Israeli company.
14 Friedman, Lara. "US politicians are backing a free speech exception for Israel – & creating a template for broader assault on the First Amendment." Medium (blog), March 19, 2018. https://medium.com/@LFriedman_FMEP/u-s-politicians-are-backing-a-free-speech-exception-for-israel-creating-a-template-for-broader-ebe406fdf3b7.
15 American Civil Liberties Union. "After court defeat, Kansas changes law aimed at boycotts of Israel." June 29, 2018. https://www.aclu.org/press-releases/after-court-defeat-kansas-changes-law-aimed-boycotts-israel.
16 *Arkansas Times LP v. Mark Waldrip*, No. 19-1378 (8th Circuit 2022).
17 Kredo, Adam. "Anti-semites lose: Arkansas court upholds anti-BDS law." *Washington Free Beacon* (blog), June 22, 2022. https://freebeacon.com/latest-news/anti-semites-lose-federal-court-upholds-arkansas-anti-bds-law/.
18 Harb, Ali. "'Frightening': US Appeals Court upholds Arkansas anti-BDS law." Al Jazeera, June 22, 2024. https://www.aljazeera.com/news/2022/6/22/frightening-us-appeals-court-upholds-arkansas-anti-bds-law.
19 Gorenberg, Gershom. "Why are Democrats voting for Israeli settlements?" American Prospect, January 7, 2016. https://prospect.org/api/content/e8f8b623-8322-5c3d-94a7-f78169b85ffa/. It is important to note that President Obama issued a non-legally binding signing statement that rejected the conflation of Israel with Israeli settlements in the West Bank. See JTA and Jared Cortellessa, "Signing law to defend Israel from boycott, Obama excludes settlements." Times of Israel, February 25, 2016. https://www.timesofisrael.com/signing-law-to-defend-israel-from-boycott-obama-excludes-settlements/.
20 Friedman, "Anti-boycott legislation."

21 See, generally, FMEP Resources on anti-BDS bills here: https://lawfare.fmep.org/resources/anti-boycott-legislation-israel-palestine/.
22 Friedman, "US politicians are backing a free speech exception."
23 Aronoff, Kate. "Conservatives have a new bogeyman: critical energy theory." New Republic, December 7, 2021. https://newrepublic.com/article/164641/conservatives-new-bogeyman-critical-energy-theory; McGreal, Chris. "Rightwing group pushing US states for law blocking 'political boycott' of firms." Guardian, November 11, 2022. https://www.theguardian.com/us-news/2022/nov/11/alec-anti-political-boycott-state-legislation; Armiak, David. "ALEC doubles down on punishing ESG firms." EXPOSEDbyCMD (blog), December 9, 2022. https://www.exposedbycmd.org/2022/12/09/alec-doubles-down-on-punishing-esg-firms/.
24 Friedman, Lara. "Free speech-quashing laws based on Israel-focused anti-boycott laws + related articles." Foundation for Middle East Peace, n.d. https://fmep.org/wp/wp-content/uploads/BDS-Laws-as-Template-for-Laws-on-Other-Issues.pdf.
25 Friedman, Lara, and Tara Van Ho. "Promoting risk & undermining rights: Morningstar's betrayal of Palestine & ESG." Occupied Thoughts, December 6, 2022. https://fmep.org/resource/promoting-risk-undermining-rights-morningstars-betrayal-of-palestine-esg/. For example, see Cruz, Ted, and Marsha Blackburn. "Letter to Secretary of Commerce Raimondo." September 28, 2022. https://www.cruz.senate.gov/imo/media/doc/letter_to_raimondo_on_morningstar_inc1.pdf.
26 IHRA. "What Is Antisemitism?" https://holocaustremembrance.com/resources/working-definition-antisemitism.
27 American Civil Liberties Union. "Letter to co-sponsors of proposed American Bar Association Resolution 514 on Antisemitism." January 19, 2023. https://www.aclu.org/documents/letter-co-sponsors-proposed-american-bar-association-resolution-514-antisemitism.
28 Ibid.
29 See, generally, FMEP Resources on IHRA critiques here: https://lawfare.fmep.org/resources/challenging-the-ihra-definition-of-antisemitism-expert-views-and-resources/.
30 Friedman, "Anti-boycott legislation."
31 Friedman, Lara. "States are moving to class criticism of Israel as antisemitism." Jewish Currents, January 31, 2024. https://jewishcurrents.org/states-are-moving-to-class-criticism-of-israel-as-antisemitism.
32 "Executive Order on Combating Anti-Semitism – The White House." December 11, 2019. https://trumpwhitehouse.archives.gov/presidential-actions/executive-order-combating-anti-semitism/.
33 Friedman, Lara. "Weaponizing anti-semitism, State Department delegitimizes human rights groups." American Prospect, November 12, 2020. https://prospect.org/api/content/10d535be-245b-11eb-b8c8-1244d5f7c7c6/.
34 "The US National Strategy to Counter Antisemitism." White House, May 2023. https://www.whitehouse.gov/wp-content/uploads/2023/05/US-National-Strategy-to-Counter-Antisemitism.pd.
35 Kampeas, Ron. "Biden administration set to roll out antisemitism strategy on Thursday." Jewish Telegraphic Agency (blog), May 24, 2023. https://www.jta.org/2023/05/24/politics/biden-administration-set-to-roll-out-antisemitism-strategy-on-thursday.
36 Nexus Taskforce. "The Nexus Document." Israel & Antisemitism, February 24, 2021. https://israelandantisemitism.com/the-nexus-document/.

37 JDA. "The Jerusalem Declaration on Antisemitism." https://jerusalemdeclaration.org/.
38 Bandler, Aaron. "ADL CEO Jonathan Greenblatt, Special Envoy Deborah Lipstadt discuss Biden antisemitism plan in webinar." Jewish Journal, June 2, 2023. https://jewishjournal.com/news/united-states/359372/adl-ceo-jonathan-greenblatt-special-envoy-deborah-lipstadt-discuss-biden-antisemitism-plan-in-webinar/.
39 American Civil Liberties Union. "Letter to co-sponsors."
40 Friedman, Lara. "Lawfare/IHRA – targeting academia." FMEP. https://lawfare.fmep.org/resources/lawfare-ihra-targeting-academia/.
41 "Amnesty's outrageous lie, its big problem with Jews, and the truth about Israel." AJC, February 1, 2022. https://www.ajc.org/news/amnestys-outrageous-lie-its-big-problem-with-jews-and-the-truth-about-israel.
42 Klien, Zvika. "180 NGOs call on Elon Musk to adopt IHRA definition of antisemitism." Jerusalem Post, November 16, 2022. https://www.jpost.com/diaspora/antisemitism/article-722555; Kavaler, Tara. "128 organizations call on Facebook to adopt anti-semitism definition." Media Line, August 10, 2020. https://themedialine.org/people/128-organizations-call-on-facebook-to-adopt-anti-semitism-definition/.
43 See chapter 12.
44 Associated Press. "Israel designates 6 Palestinian human right groups as terrorist organizations." NPR, October 23, 2021. https://www.npr.org/2021/10/23/1048690050/israel-palestinian-human-right-groups.
45 Barak, Ravid. "Israel to designate six Palestinian NGOs as terrorist organizations." Axios, September 13, 2022. https://www.axios.com/2022/09/13/israel-palestinian-ngos-terrorist-designation-state.
46 Scher, Isaac. "CIA unable to corroborate Israel's 'terror' label for Palestinian rights groups." Guardian, August 22, 2022. https://www.theguardian.com/world/2022/aug/22/cia-report-israel-palestinian-rights-groups.
47 Palestine Legal. "Palestine exception."
48 Harkov, Lahav. "US lawmaker touts terror-linked orgs' support to condition Israel aid." Jerusalem Post, May 7, 2023. https://www.jpost.com/american-politics/article-742313; Schiffmiller, Yona. "Human rights, Palestinian terror and congressional lobbying." Hill (blog), December 12, 2016. https://thehill.com/blogs/congress-blog/foreign-policy/309746-human-rights-palestinian-terror-and-congressional-lobbying/; Schiff, David. "Why do congressional Democrats support terror-designated NGOs?" Washington Examiner, November 18, 2021. https://www.washingtonexaminer.com/restoring-america/courage-strength-optimism/why-do-congressional-democrats-support-terror-designated-ngos.
49 Touré, Madina. "CUNY investigates allegations that partner group is tied to terrorism." Politico, March 3, 2019. https://www.politico.com/states/new-york/city-hall/story/2019/03/03/cuny-investigates-allegations-that-partner-group-is-tied-to-terrorism-885061.
50 "Palestinian terror-tied group booted from new online fundraising platform." Zachor Legal Institute (blog), October 18, 2023. https://zachorlegal.org/2023/10/18/palestinian-terror-tied-group-booted-new-online-fundraising-platform/; Kaminsky, Gabe. "Palestinian terrorists 'exploit loopholes' for taxpayer dollars, watchdog tells Congress." Washington Examiner, November 7, 2023. https://www.washingtonexaminer.com/news/2444288/palestinian-terrorists-exploit-loopholes-for-taxpayer-dollars-watchdog-tells-congress/.

51 Center for Constitutional Rights. "US Palestinian rights group prevails as D.C. Circuit Court tosses out lawsuit that targeted advocacy." https://ccrjustice.org/node/9886.
52 Guinane, "Alarming rise of lawfare."
53 "A global day of protests draws thousands in Washington and other cities in pro-Palestinian marches." AP News, January 13, 2024. https://apnews.com/article/protest-gaza-israel-palestinians-london-29d5cd664c81654283344d1874691a4f.
54 See chapter 9.
55 Pace, Joseph. "Congress hauled in college presidents over anti-Israel speech. That's not the worst of it." Slate, December 6, 2023. https://slate.com/news-and-politics/2023/12/congress-harvard-president-israel-speech-code.html.
56 Friedman, "Lawfare/IHRA."
57 Kane, Alex. "The push to deactivate Students for Justice in Palestine (SJP)." Jewish Currents, November, 23, 2023. https://jewishcurrents.org/the-push-to-deactivate-students-for-justice-in-palestine-sjp; Khalili, Zoha. "DeSantis' Order to Deactivate National SJP in Florida." Palestine Legal, October 25, 2023. https://palestinelegal.org/news/2023/10/25/desantis-order-to-deactivate-national-sjp-in-florida; Cohen, Haley. "Columbia University temporarily suspends anti-Israel groups from campus." Jewish Insider, November 10, 2023. https://jewishinsider.com/2023/11/columbia-university-temporarily-suspends-anti-israel-groups-from-campus/.
58 Ackerman, Spencer. "The ADL is defaming Palestinian students as terrorist supporters." October 31, 2023. https://www.thenation.com/article/society/adl-palestine-terrorism-letter/.
59 Dicker, Ron. "Karine Jean-Pierre says House members' comments on Israel are 'repugnant.'" Huffington Post, October 11, 2023. https://news.yahoo.com/karine-jean-pierre-says-house-203819124.html; Green, Justin, Andrew Solender, and Eugene Scott. "Deep split erupts between Democrats on Israel-Hamas war." Axios, November 1, 2023. https://www.axios.com/2023/11/01/israel-hamas-war-congress-democrats-bid. See also "House votes to censure Rep. Rashida Tlaib over her Israel-Hamas rhetoric in a stunning rebuke." AP, November 8, 2023. https://apnews.com/article/congress-house-censure-resolution-tlaib-8085189047a4c40f2d44ada4604aa076.
60 Michaelson, Jay. "Elise Stefanik's calculated demagoguery on antisemitism and free speech." Daily Beast, December 7, 2023. https://www.thedailybeast.com/elise-stefaniks-calculated-demagoguery-on-antisemitism-and-free-speech.
61 Eichner, Itamar. "Shaming and pressuring donors: Israel's strategy against antisemitism on US campuses." Ynetnews, November 26, 2023. https://www.ynetnews.com/article/rk5ppryht.
62 Sainath, Radhika. "The free speech exception – support for Palestinian rights is facing a McCarthyite backlash," Boston Review, October 30, 2023. https://www.bostonreview.net/articles/the-free-speech-exception/.
63 For a weekly tracking of Palestine-related legislation in the US Congress, see Friedman, Lara. "The weekly legislative round-up." FMEP. https://fmep.org/resources/?rsearch=&rcat%5B%5D=345.
64 "Top UN court orders Israel to prevent genocide in Gaza but stops short of ordering cease-fire." AP News, January 26, 2024. https://apnews.com/article/israel-gaza-genocide-court-south-africa-27cf84e16082cde798395a95e9143c06.
65 Friedman, Lara. "Research publication: targeting free speech & redefining antisemitism." FMEP. https://lawfare.fmep.org/resources/targeting-free-speech-and-redefining-antisemitism/.

66 Moore, Paul. "All colleges should be banning Students for Justice in Palestine." Hill, November 14, 2023. https://thehill.com/opinion/education/4306667-all-colleges-should-be-banning-students-for-justice-in-palestine/; Griffith, Joel. "Defund SJP and deport Hamas-supporting visitors." Heritage Foundation, November 3, 2023, https://www.heritage.org/middle-east/commentary/defund-sjp-and-deport-hamas-supporting-visitors; "7 things to know about campus support for Hamas and antisemitism." Foundation for Defense of Democracies, December 4, 2023. https://www.fdd.org/analysis/2023/12/04/7-things-to-know-about-campus-support-for-hamas-and-antisemitism/.

67 Zituni, Danya. "Silencing of Pro-Palestinian voices is proof that Israel is losing." Daily Beast, December 20, 2023. https://www.thedailybeast.com/silencing-of-pro-palestinian-voices-is-proof-that-israel-is-losing.

68 "Global day of protests draws thousands."

69 Nehme, Adrianna, and Krish Dev. "Faculty form group in support of Palestinian students at protest." Washington Square News, October 19, 2023. https://nyunews.com/news/2023/10/19/faculty-forms-group-to-support-palestinians/.

70 Brown University Faculty Members. "Brown faculty call for a ceasefire in Israel-Palestine and the protection of academic freedom and student activism." Brown Daily Herald, November 7, 2023. https://www.browndailyherald.com/article/2023/11/brown-faculty-call-for-a-ceasefire-in-israel-palestine-and-the-protection-of-academic-freedom-and-student-activism.

71 "Statement by Trinity Coalition for Justice in Palestine." Trinity Tripod, November 10, 2023. https://trinitytripod.com/opinion/statement-by-trinity-coalition-for-justice-in-palestine/.

72 Haverford Faculty for Justice in Palestine. "Haverford Faculty for Justice in Palestine releases statement supporting pro-Palestinian students." Left Voice, November 27, 2023. https://www.leftvoice.org/haverford-faculty-for-justice-in-palestine/.

73 "An open letter from Faculty for Justice in Palestine." Daily Princetonian, November 29, 2023. https://www.dailyprincetonian.com/article/2023/11/princeton-opinion-opguest-faculty-for-justice-in-palestine-demand-free-speech-protection-divestment.

74 Harvard Faculty and Staff for Justice in Palestine. "Statement in support of Harvard student Elom Tettey-Tamaklo." Medium, December 5, 2023. https://medium.com/@harvardfsjp/statement-in-support-of-harvard-student-elom-tettey-tamaklo-cdb164760bf3.

75 MHC Faculty for Justice in Palestine. "Mount Holyoke Faculty – call to action." Medium, December 5, 2023. https://medium.com/@mhc-fjp/mount-holyoke-faculty-call-to-action-46c2bca3a1f7.

76 Faculty for Justice in Palestine. "Letter to the editor: Rutgers Faculty for Justice in Palestine releases statement." Daily Targum, December 13, 2023. https://dailytargum.com/article/2023/12/letter-to-the-editor-rutgers-faculty-for-justice-in-palestine-releases.

77 Watanabe, Teresa. "Pro-Palestinian UC students feel they are not supported. Some on the faculty are organizing to change that." Los Angeles Times, December 21, 2023. https://www.latimes.com/california/story/2023-12-21/uc-faculty-launch-unprecedented-organizing-drive-to-aid-campus-supporters-of-palestinians.

78 Treisman, Rachel. "A former State Dept. official explains why he resigned over US arms sent to Israel." National Public Radio, October 19, 2023. https://www.npr.org/2023/10/19/1207037984/josh-paul-resign-state-department-military-

assistance-israel-gaza; Falconer, Rebecca. "2nd Biden admin official resigns over president's response to Gaza war." Axios. January 4, 2024. https://www.axios.com/2024/01/04/gaza-war-education-official-resigns-biden-israel-policy.
79 Abi-Habib, Maria, Michael Crowley and Edward Wong. "More than 500 US officials sign letter protesting Biden's Israel policy." New York Times, November 14, 2023. https://www.nytimes.com/2023/11/14/us/politics/israel-biden-letter-gaza-ceasefire.html; Johansen, Ben. "Biden campaign staff issue anonymous letter protesting approach to Israel-Hamas war." Politico, January 3, 2024. https://www.politico.com/news/2024/01/03/biden-campaign-anonymous-letter-israel-hamas-00133705; Hayssem, Sophie. "Congressional interns send open letter calling for Gaza ceasefire." Mother Jones, December 12, 2023. https://www.motherjones.com/politics/2023/12/congressional-interns-ceasefire-letter/; Harb, Ali. "More than 1,000 USAID employees sign letter backing Israel–Gaza ceasefire." Al Jazeera, November 8, 2024. https://www.aljazeera.com/news/2023/11/8/more-than-1000-usaid-employees-sign-letter-backing-gaza-ceasefire; Suter, Tara. "Hundreds of Jewish organization staffers press Biden on Gaza cease-fire." Hill, December 7, 2023. https://thehill.com/homenews/administration/4347585-jewish-organizations-staffers-letter-gaza-cease-fire/.
80 Biggar, Paul. "I can't sleep." Paul Biggar Blog, December 14, 2023. https://blog.paulbiggar.com/i-cant-sleep/.
81 Davis, Dominic-Madori. "Tech for Palestine launches to provide tools to help support Palestinians." TechCrunch, January 1, 2024. https://techcrunch.com/2024/01/02/tech-for-palestine-launches-to-provide-tools-and-projects-to-help-advocate-for-palestinians/.
82 Tech for Palestine. https://techforpalestine.org/.
83 Steinberg, Bernie. "For the safety of Jews and Palestinians, stop weaponizing antisemitism." Harvard Crimson, December 29, 2023. https://www.thecrimson.com/article/2023/12/29/steinberg-weaponizing-antisemitism/.
84 "Media roundup: Palestine Legal and ACLU file lawsuit challenging DeSantis' deactivation order against SJPs." Palestine Legal, December 14, 2023. https://palestinelegal.org/news/media-fl-lawsuit.
85 "Joint letter to universities: protect essential student activism for Palestinian human rights." Palestine Legal et al., November 14, 2023. https://palestinelegal.org/news/letter-to-ocr; "Our letter to the Dept. of Education: address rise of anti-Palestinian and Islamophobic racism." Palestine Legal, November 3, 2023. https://palestinelegal.org/news/joint-letter-to-unis.
86 Long Chu, Andrea. "The free-speech debate is a trap." New York Magazine, December 22, 2023. https://nymag.com/intelligencer/article/free-speech-debate-free-palestine.html.

11. Restrictions on Financial Services and Banking and their Impacts on Palestinian NGOs

1 World Bank. "Brief: de-risking in the financial sector." October 7, 2016. https://www.worldbank.org/en/topic/financialsector/brief/de-risking-in-the-financial-sector; Norwegian Refugee Council. "Life and death: NGO access to financial services in Afghanistan." January 2022. https://www.nrc.no/globalassets/pdf/reports/life-and-death/financial-access-in-afghanistan_nrc_jan-2022.pdf.

2   Eckert, Sue E., Kay Guinane and Andrea Hall. "Financial access for US nonprofits." Charity & Security Network, February 2017, 1. https://www.charityandsecurity.org/system/files/FinancialAccessFullReport_2.21%20(2).pdf.
3   Broekhoven, Lia, Sangeeta Goswami, Thalia Malmberg and Floor Knoote. "The future of FATF Recommendation 8: a foresight piece." Human Security Collective, November 2023. https://www.hscollective.org/assets/Final_R8-Foresight_.pdf.
4   Authenticated US Government Information, GPO, Public Law-107-56. "Uniting and Strengthening America by Providing Appropriate Tools Required to Intercept and Obstruct Terrorism (USA Patriot Act) Act of 2001." October 26, 2001. https://www.govinfo.gov/content/pkg/PLAW-107publ56/pdf/PLAW-107publ56.pdf.
5   Office of the Comptroller. "Counter Terrorist Financing." https://www.occ.treas.gov/topics/supervision-and-examination/bsa/counter-terrorist-financing/index-counter-terrorist-financing.html.
6   US Department of State. "De-risking." https://www.state.gov/de-risking/#:~:text=De-risking%20refers%20to%20the%20phenomenon%20of%20financial%20institutions,of%20clients%20to%20avoid%2C%20rather%20than%20manage%2C%20risk.
7   van Broekhoven, Lia. "Article – derisking and civil society: drivers, impact and solutions." Human Security Collective. https://www.hscollective.org/news/timeline/article-derisking-and-civil-society-drivers-impact-and-solutions/.
8   FATF. "History of the FATF." https://www.fatf-gafi.org/en/the-fatf/history-of-the-fatf.html#:~:text=The%20Financial%20Action%20Task%20Force,Commission%20and%20eight%20other%20countries.
9   Ibid.; FATF/OECD. "FATF Standards: FATF 40 recommendations." October 2003, 2. https://www.fatf-gafi.org/content/dam/fatf-gafi/recommendations/FATF%20Standards%20-%2040%20Recommendations%20rc.pdf.
10 Luttrell, Terri. "Remembering 9/11 – a pivotal day for BSA/AML professionals," Abrigo, September 10, 2021, 3. https://www.abrigo.com/blog/remembering-9-11-a-pivotal-day-for-bsa-aml-professionals/.
11 Wilejto-Rieken, Monika. "USA Patriot Act, Section 314(a) and 314 (b) – Information Sharing: beneficial and detrimental effects of the Act." ACAMS, 5, 10. https://www.acams.org/sites/default/files/2020-08/USA%20PATRIOT%20Act%2C%20Section%20314%28a%29%20and%20314%28b%29%20Information%20Sharing-%20Beneficial%20and%20Detrimental%20Effects%20of%20the%20Act.pdf.
12 Alessa. "The Bank Secrecy Act: understanding US AML regulations and laws." April 9, 2021. https://alessa.com/blog/compliance-with-bank-secrecy-act-aml-requirements/.
13 Arnold and Porter. "Overview of BSA/AML reform under the AML Act of 2020." https://www.arnoldporter.com/-/media/files/perspectives/publications/2022/06/amla-overview.pdf.
14 Through the AMLA, Congress also acknowledges that "Without access to timely and predictable banking services, non-profit organizations cannot carry out essential humanitarian activities that can mean life or death to those in affected communities" (Sec. 5213(a)(1)); that "providing vital humanitarian and development assistance and protecting the integrity of the international financial system are complementary goals" (Sec. 5213(b)(1)); and that "Congress supports anti-money laundering and countering the financing of terrorism and sanctions policies that do not unduly hinder or delay the efforts of legitimate humanitarian organizations" (Sec. 5213(b)

15. (2)(B)). 116th Congress, S.4909. "Division E-Anti-Money Laundering." https://charityandsecurity.org/wp-content/uploads/2020/07/Brown-Crapo-amendment-to-NDAA-2020.pdf.
15. These additional requirements include: reviewing regulations and guidance that do not adhere to the risk-based approach (RBA), which is designed "to ensure that measures to prevent or mitigate money laundering and terrorist financing are commensurate with the risks identified"; making any needed changes including with regard to overly burdensome reporting requirements demanded of FIs; and providing training for regulators. Charity & Security Network. "Congress passes AML Act of 2020." January 8, 2021. https://charityandsecurity.org/financial-access/language-on-charities-and-derisking-in-ndaa/.
16. FATF. "What we do." https://www.fatf-gafi.org/en/the-fatf/what-we-do.html. The FATF is comprised of 40 "Members" (countries) (FATF. "Outcomes FATF Plenary, 25–27 October 2023." https://www.fatf-gafi.org/en/publications/Fatfgeneral/outcomes-fatf-plenary-october-2023.html); over 20 entities with observer status, including the World Bank, the Organisation for Economic Co-operation and Development (OECD), the International Monetary Fund (IMF), and a host of law enforcement bodies at the UN level; nine FATF-Style Regional Bodies (FSRBs); and two regional organizations, the European Commission (EC) and the Gulf Cooperation Council (GCC) (Global NPO Coalition on FATF. "FATF explained." https://fatfplatform.org/context/fatf-explained).
17. FATF. "United States: head of delegation." https://www.fatf-gafi.org/en/countries/detail/United-States.html.
18. Global NPO Coalition on FATF. "FATF explained."
19. For example, the standards were expanded to include financing for weapons of mass destruction in FATF. "History of the FATF." https://www.fatf-gafi.org/en/the-fatf/history-of-the-fatf.html#:~:text=The%20Financial%20Action%20Task%20Force,Commission%20and%20eight%20other%20countries.
20. Ibid.; FATF-GAFI. *FATF Standards, FATF IX Special Recommendations*. October 2001, 20–4. https://www.fatf-gafi.org/content/dam/fatf-gafi/recommendations/FATF%20Standards%20-%20IX%20Special%20Recommendations%20and%20IN%20rc.pdf.coredownload.pdf.
21. Ibid.
22. The Bank Exam Manual has been described as the "Bible" of bank examinations. Charity & Security Network. "Federal Bank Examination Manual chapter on nonprofit customers updated to reflect a risk-based approach." December 9, 2021. https://charityandsecurity.org/news/federal-bank-examination-manual-chapter-on-nonprofit-customers-updated-to-reflect-a-risk-based-approach/.
23. Charity & Security Network. "Event summary: the future of FATF Recommendation 8: for financial integrity and for civil society." October 26, 2023. https://charityandsecurity.org/news/event-summary-the-future-of-fatf-recommendation-8-for-financial-integrity-and-for-civil-society/.
24. FATF/OECD. "FATF Standards: FATF 40 Recommendations." October 2003, 2. https://www.fatf-gafi.org/content/dam/fatf-gafi/recommendations/FATF%20Standards%20-%2040%20Recommendations%20rc.pdf; Broekhoven et al., "Future of FATF Recommendation 8."
25. Charity & Security Network. "Revision of FATF Recommendation 8 applauded by NPO sector." June 29, 2016. https://charityandsecurity.org/financial-action-task-force/npos_hail_r8_revision/.

26 Charity & Security Network, "Federal Bank Examination Manual chapter."
27 FATF. "Protecting non-profits from abuse for terrorist financing through the risk-based implementation of revised FATF Recommendation 8." November 16, 2023. https://www.fatf-gafi.org/en/publications/Fatfrecommendations/protecting-non-profits-abuse-implementation-R8.html.
28 United Nations Security Council, S/2021/915. "Identical letters dated 1 November 2021 from the Permanent Representative of Israel to the United Nations addressed to the Secretary-General and the President of the Security Council." November 11, 2021. https://www.un.org/unispal/wp-content/uploads/2021/11/ISRAELLETTER.S.2021.915_011121.pdf. For a critique of the Israeli position, see "Letter of the Global NPO Coalition on FATF to the President and Executive Secretary of the FATF." November 11, 2021. https://fatfplatform.org/assets/Global-Coalition-Response-re-Israel-UN-Letter-Citing-FATF.pdf.
29 United Nations. "Nicaragua: new law heralds damaging crackdown on civil society, UN warns." May 9, 2022. https://news.un.org/en/story/2022/05/1117802. See also Human Rights Watch. "Nicaragua: government dismantles civil society – arbitrary closures of groups impede rights, humanitarian work." July 19, 2022. https://www.hrw.org/news/2022/07/19/nicaragua-government-dismantles-civil-society.
30 Charbord, Anne, and Fionnuala Ní Aoláin. "The role of measures to address terrorism and violent extremism on closing civic space." 2019. https://www.icnl.org/wp-content/uploads/civil_society_report_-_final_april_2019.pdf.
31 United Nations Security Council, S/RES/1373 (2001). "Resolution 1373 (2001): adopted by the Security Council at its 4385th meeting, on 28 September 2001." September 28, 2001. https://www.unodc.org/pdf/crime/terrorism/res_1373_english.pdf.
32 United Nations Security Council, S/RES/2462(2019). https://www.un.org/securitycouncil/content/sres24622019.
33 United States Mission to the United Nations. "Remarks at a UN Security Council Open Debate on the 20th anniversary of Resolution 1373 (via VTC)." January 12, 2021. https://usun.usmission.gov/remarks-at-a-un-security-council-open-debate-on-the-20th-anniversary-of-resolution-1373-via-vtc/.
34 United Nations Security Council, S/RES/1373 (2001). "Resolution 1373 (2001)."
35 United Nations, Security Council – Counter-Terrorism Committee (CTC), Counter-Terrorism Committee Executive Directorate (CTED). "Our mandate: the Counter-Terrorism Committee (CTC)." https://www.un.org/securitycouncil/ctc/content/our-mandate.
36 FATF. "New UN resolution reaffirms the close collaboration between the FATF and the United Nations in the fight against terrorist fighting." March 28, 2019. https://www.fatf-gafi.org/en/publications/Fatfgeneral/Un-fatf-2019.html.
37 United Nations Office of Counter-Terrorism. "Countering the financing of terrorism: new avenues to address terrorist financing." https://www.un.org/counterterrorism/cct/countering-the-financing-of-terrorism.
38 Weizmann, Nathalie. "Respecting international humanitarian law and safeguarding humanitarian action in counterterrorism measures: United Nations Security Council Resolutions 2462 and 2482 point the way." International Review of the Red Cross, no. 916–17, February 2022. https://international-review.icrc.org/articles/respecting-international-humanitarian-law-safeguarding-humanitarian-action-916.
39 Charity & Security Network. "Summary of UN Security Council Resolution 2462 on Counter Terrorist Financing." April 15, 2019. https://charityandsecurity.org/humanitarian-safeguards/summary_unscr_2462/.

40. United Nations Human Rights Special Procedures, Special Rapporteurs, Independent Experts & Working Groups. "Global study on the impact of counter-terrorism on civil society & civic space." https://defendcivicspace.com/wp-content/uploads/2024/01/SRCT_GlobalStudy-1.pdf.
41. CIVICUS Monitor: Tracking Civic Space. "Civic space in numbers." March 16, 2023. https://monitor.civicus.org/facts/.
42. Civic Space Watch. "About civic space: what is civic space?" https://civicspacewatch.eu/what-is-civic-space/.
43. CIVICUS. "What is civic space?" https://www.civicus.org/documents/reports-and-publications/reporting-civic-space/Reporting-Civic-Space-Infographic.pdf.
44. Bascunan-Wiley, Nick. "The Jerusalem Fund for Education and Community Development." May 23, 2014. https://thejerusalemfund.org/2014/05/a-history-of-money-in-palestine-the-case-of-the-frozen-bank-accounts-of-1948/.
45. Charity & Security Network. "Material support allegations against Palestinian groups lack evidence: old tactics, new situation." November 30, 2023. https://charityandsecurity.org/news/material-support-allegations-against-palestinian-groups-lack-evidence-old-tactics-new-situation/.
46. Frankel, Julia. "Israeli military campaign in Gaza among deadliest in history, experts say." Associated Press, January 11, 2024. https://apnews.com/article/israel-gaza-bombs-destruction-death-toll-scope-419488c511f83c85baea224458472a796.
47. Lazzarini, Philippe. "Serious allegations against UNRWA staff in the Gaza Strip." UNRWA, January 26, 2024. https://www.unrwa.org/newsroom/official-statements/serious-allegations-against-unrwa-staff-gaza-strip.
48. "UN chief appoints independent panel to assess UNRWA." Al Jazeera, February 5, 2024. https://www.aljazeera.com/news/2024/2/5/un-chief-appoints-independent-panel-to-assess-unrwa.
49. Adler, Jonathan. "UNRWA and the day after in Gaza." Carnegie Endowment for International Peace, February 21, 2024. https://carnegieendowment.org/sada/91682.
50. "UN chief appoints independent panel to assess UNRWA"; Adler, "UNRWA and the day after in Gaza."
51. "UNRWA report says Israel coerced some agency employees to falsely admit Hamas links." Reuters, March 8, 2024. https://www.reuters.com/world/middle-east/unrwa-report-says-israel-coerced-some-agency-employees-falsely-admit-hamas-links-2024-03-08/.
52. "UK to resume funding to UN Gaza aid agency." BBC News, July 19, 2024. https://www.bbc.com/news/articles/cjm9row71g80.
53. "US looks for alternatives as Congress mulls making UNRWA funding freeze permanent." Times of Israel, March 13, 2024. https://www.timesofisrael.com/us-looks-for-alternatives-as-congress-mulls-making-unrwa-funding-freeze-permanent/.
54. "The United Nations Relief and Works Agency for Palestine Refugees in the Near East (UNRWA): overview and US funding prohibition." Congressional Research Service, June 14, 2024. https://crsreports.congress.gov/product/pdf/IN/IN12316#:~:text=In%20March%202024%20(in%20Division,%2C%20until%20March%2025%2C%2025.
55. UNRWA. "Who we are – establishment." https://www.unrwa.org/who-we-are.
56. Borger, Julian. "Israel yet to provide evidence to back UNRWA 7 October attack claims – UN." Guardian, March 1, 2024. https://www.theguardian.com/world/2024/

mar/01/unrwa-funding-pause-employees-october-7-hamas-attack-claims-no-evidence-un.

57 Baczynska, Gabriela, and Nette Noestlinger. "No evidence from Israel to back UNRWA accusations, says EU humanitarian chief." Reuters, March 14, 2024. https://www.reuters.com/world/no-evidence-israel-back-unrwa-accusations-says-eu-humanitarian-chief-2024-03-14/.

58 "UNRWA report says Israel coerced some agency employees."

59 "Statement from the spokesperson of the UN secretary-general on the OIOS investigation regarding allegations against UNRWA staff." UNRWA, April 26, 2024. https://www.unrwa.org/newsroom/official-statements/statement-spokesperson-un-secretary-general-oios-investigation.

60 "Final report for the United Nations Secretary-General: independent review of mechanisms and procedures to ensure adherence by UNRWA to the humanitarian principle of neutrality." UNRWA. April 20, 2024. https://www.unrwa.org/sites/default/files/content/resources/unrwa_independent_review_on_neutrality.pdf.

61 UNRWA. "Palestine refugees." https://www.unrwa.org/palestine-refugees.

62 Nashed, Mat. "What's behind Israel's decision to target UNRWA? – Israel has long tried to eliminate the UN agency, which enshrines the right of Palestinian refugees to return home." Al Jazeera, January 31, 2024. https://www.aljazeera.com/features/2024/1/31/israels-allegations-unrwa-effort-eliminate-agency.

63 UNRWA. "Frequently asked questions – protracted displacement & solutions: what is the agency's stance on UN General Assembly Resolution 194 (III) and the 'right of return'?" https://www.unrwa.org/who-we-are/frequently-asked-questions.

64 "Israel calls for end of UN Palestinian refugee agency – Prime Minister Netanyahu calls for total shut down of UNRWA, saying it is responsible for incitement against Israel." Al Jazeera, June 11, 2017. https://www.aljazeera.com/news/2017/6/11/israel-calls-for-end-of-un-palestinian-refugee-agency.

65 Adler, "UNRWA and the day after in Gaza."

66 Besheer, Margret. "UNRWA chief: Israel conducting campaign to eliminate Palestinian aid agency." VOA, March 4, 2024. https://www.voanews.com/a/unrwa-chief-israel-conducting-campaign-to-eliminate-palestinian-aid-agency/7514033.html. In late February 2024, pro-Israel group UN Watch went as far as hosting the International Summit for a Future Beyond UNRWA, with an aim to "formulate a plan for a future beyond UNRWA, a failed agency with deep and widespread ties to Hamas and Islamic Jihad." UN Watch. "Summit for a Future Beyond UNRWA opens at United Nations on Monday." February 22, 2024. https://unwatch.org/summit-on-replacing-unrwa-opens-at-united-nations-on-monday-in-geneva/.

67 Guinane, "Alarming rise of lawfare."

68 Front Line Defenders. "Statement – OPT/Israel: Front Line Defenders strongly condemns Israeli security force raids and closures of the offices of seven Palestinian human rights organisations." August 19, 2022. https://www.frontlinedefenders.org/en/statement-report/statement-opt-israel-raids-and-closures-seven-palestinian-human-rights-organisations.

69 In October 1997, the Popular Front for the Liberation of Palestine was designated as an FTO by the US. And in October 2001, the group was also designated as a Specially Designated Global Terrorist (SDGT) by the US "Outcry as Israel labels Palestinian rights groups 'terrorists.'" *Al Jazeera*, October 22, 2021. https://www.aljazeera.com/news/2021/10/22/israel-palestinian-human-rights-groups-terrorism.

70 United Nations Human Rights Office of the High Commissioner. "Israel/Palestine: UN experts call on governments to resume funding for six Palestinian CSOs designated by Israel as 'terrorist organisations.'" April 25, 2022. https://www.ohchr.org/en/press-releases/2022/04/israelpalestine-un-experts-call-governments-resume-funding-six-palestinian#:~:text=In%20October%202021%2C%20the%20UN,Agricultural%20Work%20Committees%20and%20the.

71 During her tenure as the UN High Commissioner for Human Rights, Michelle Bachelet stated that "Without adequate substantive evidence, these decisions appear arbitrary, and further erode the civic and humanitarian space in the Occupied Palestinian Territory" (United Nations, Meetings Coverage and Press Releases. "Outraged over Israel's designation of six civil society groups as terrorists, speakers tell Palestinian Rights Committee harassment against human rights defenders must end." December 7, 2021. https://press.un.org/en/2021/gapal1443.doc.htm). Likewise, the designations were condemned by multiple human rights experts at the UN (United Nations Human Rights Office of the High Commissioner. "Israel/Palestine: UN experts call on governments to resume funding"), by leading international human rights organizations (Amnesty International. "Israel/OPT: designation of Palestinian civil society groups as terrorists a brazen attack on human rights." October 22, 2021. https://www.amnesty.org/en/latest/news/2021/10/israel-opt-designation-of-palestinian-civil-society-groups-as-terrorists-a-brazen-attack-on-human-rights), and by popular artists ("Artists denounce Israeli ban on Palestinian civil society groups." BBC News, November 17, 2021. https://www.bbc.com/news/world-middle-east-59297278), while international humanitarian organizations requested the US to make demands of Israel to rescind the designations (Norwegian Refugee Council. "Letter to the US secretary of state to urge Israel to stop repeated attacks on Palestinian human rights organisations." September 2, 2022. https://www.nrc.no/news/2022/september/letter-to-us-secretary-of-state-urge-israel-to-stop-repeated-attacks-on-palestinian-human-rights-organisations). Human rights experts at the UN outline that the designation "seems to indicate a politically-motivated attempt by Israel to silence some of its most effective critics in violation of their rights to freedom of association and of expression" and provides a timely reminder that counterterrorism laws "have to be rigorously consistent with international law and human rights protections, including the principles of legal certainty, necessity, proportionality, the rule of law and non-discrimination" (United Nations Human Rights Office of the High Commissioner. "Israel/Palestine: UN experts call on governments to resume funding"), while the Lawfare Institute states that the designation "demonstrates the current legal process' lack of due process and transparency" (Margalit, Lila, and Yuval Shany. "Israel's counterterrorism designation regime: a process in need of reform." Lawfare Institute in Cooperation with Brookings, January 10, 2022. https://www.lawfaremedia.org/article/israels-counterterrorism-designation-regime-process-need-reform).

72 Ravid, Barak. "Israeli officials in D.C. try to justify terrorist designation for 6 Palestinian NGOs." Axios, September 13, 2022. https://www.axios.com/2022/09/13/israel-palestinian-ngos-terrorist-designation-state.

73 Ibid.

74 Front Line Defenders, "Statement."

75 Kuttab, Jonathan. "An update on Israel's terrorist designation for Palestinian civil society organizations." Arab Center, Washington DC, August 3, 2021. https://

arabcenterdc.org/resource/an-update-on-israels-terrorist-designation-for-palestinian-civil-society-organizations/
76 Guinane, "Alarming rise of lawfare," 64.
77 "'Unfounded allegations': EU resumes funding of Palestinian NGOs." Al Jazeera, June 30, 2022. https://www.aljazeera.com/news/2022/6/30/no-suspicions-eu-resumes-funding-of-palestinian-ngos.
78 Ibid.
79 Guinane, Kay. "Israel's attack on Palestinian NGOs is a threat to civil society everywhere." Charity & Security Network, December 10, 2021. https://charityandsecurity.org/blog/israels-attack-on-palestinian-ngos-is-a-threat-to-civil-society-everywhere/.
80 Guinane, "Alarming rise of lawfare," vi.
81 Turner, Jennifer. "Blocking faith, freezing charity: chilling Muslim charitable giving in the 'war on terrorism financing.'" American Civil Liberties Union, June 2009. https://www.aclu.org/wp-content/uploads/legal-documents/blockingfaith.pdf.
82 "*USA v. Holy Land Foundation for Relief and Development.*" Charity & Security Network, August 24, 2020. https://charityandsecurity.org/litigation/holy-land-foundation/.
83 Ibid.
84 Bridge: a Georgetown University Initiative, Bridge Initiative Team. "Fact sheet: Holy Land Foundation." January 27, 2020. https://bridge.georgetown.edu/research/factsheet-holy-land-foundation/.
85 "*USA v. Holy Land Foundation for Relief and Development.*"
86 US Department of the Treasury. "Press releases: following terrorist attack on Israel, treasury sanctions Hamas operatives and financial facilitators." October 18, 2023. https://home.treasury.gov/news/press-releases/jy1816#:~:text=Hamas%2C%20and%20other%20Palestinian%20terrorist,Terrorist%20Organizations%20since%20October%201997.
87 "Issue brief: the prohibition on material support and its impacts on nonprofits." Charity & Security Network, July 2019. https://charityandsecurity.org/sites/default/files/material%20support%20issue%20brief%202019.pdf.
88 "Input to the Honorable Fionnuala D. Ní Aoláin, Special Rapporteur on the promotion and protection of human rights and fundamental freedoms while countering terrorism: report to the GA77 on the impact of counter-terrorism on peacemaking, peacebuilding, sustaining peace, conflict prevention and resolution, October 2022." Charity & Security Network, July 8, 2022. https://charityandsecurity.org/wp-content/uploads/2022/07/Submission-to-SR-on-CT-and-Peacebuilding_July-2022.pdf.
89 Federal Bureau of Investigation. "No cash for terror: convictions returned in Holy Land case." November 25, 2008. https://archives.fbi.gov/archives/news/stories/2008/november/hlf112508#:~:text=Guilty%20verdicts%20on%20all%20108,since%20the%209%2F11%20 attacks.
90 As Human Rights Watch notes, "The defendants in the Holy Land Foundation (HLF) case were never accused of directly funding terrorist organizations or terrorist attacks, nor were the Palestinian charities they funded accused of doing so" (Human Rights Watch. "After Israel's designation of human rights groups as 'terrorists,' Biden should release Palestinian-Americans imprisoned over similar claims: joint statement by US and international civil and human rights organizations and individuals." March 11,

2022. https://www.hrw.org/news/2022/03/11/after-israels-designation-human-rights-groups-terrorists-biden-should-release). Further criticisms include the use of falsified evidence that made up the foundation of the original charges, including glaring translation mistakes and multiple omissions that painted HLF in a damning light on the one hand and removed evidence that USAID provided support to one of the same hospitals that HLF had provided support to on the other hand (Bridge: A Georgetown University Initiative, Bridge Initiative Team. "Fact Sheet: Holy Land Foundation"). Additionally, evidence came via anonymous accusations by Israeli military witnesses (Human Rights Watch, "After Israel's designation").

91 Bridge: A Georgetown University Initiative, Bridge Initiative Team. "Fact sheet: Holy Land Foundation."

92 Kabat, Alan R. "Summary: the Fifth Circuit's Holy Land Foundation decision." Charity & Security Network, December 20, 2011. https://charityandsecurity.org/litigation/summary_fifth_circuit_hlf_decision/#HLF_was_Not_Represented_on_Appeal.

93 "USA v. Holy Land Foundation for Relief and Development."

94 Essa, Farooq. "Holy Land Five: rights groups, families demand release over 'miscarriage of justice.'" Middle East Eye, November 24, 2022. https://www.middleeasteye.net/news/holy-land-five-rights-groups-families-demand-release-over-miscarriage-justice.

95 Jamal, Hebh. "Justice for the Holy Land 5 and all Palestinian political prisoners." New Arab, December 12, 2022. https://www.newarab.com/opinion/justice-holy-land-5-and-all-palestinian-prisoners.

96 Glass, Charles. "The unjust prosecution of the Holy Land Foundation Five." Intercept, August 5, 2018. https://theintercept.com/2018/08/05/holy-land-foundation-trial-palestine-israel/.

97 American Muslims for Palestine. "Top 5 reasons to support AMP." https://www.ampalestine.org/.

98 National Students for Justice in Palestine. https://nationalsjp.org/; "Material support allegations against Palestinian groups lack evidence."

99 Osgood, Brian. "October 7 survivors are suing pro-Palestinian groups. But what is the aim?" Al Jazeera, May 31, 2024. https://www.aljazeera.com/news/2024/5/31/october-7-survivors-are-suing-pro-palestinian-groups-but-what-is-the-aim.

100 Ibid.

101 "Conflict with Al-Shabaab in Somalia." Council on Foreign Relations, June 12, 2024. https://www.cfr.org/global-conflict-tracker/conflict/al-shabab-somalia.

102 "Somalia: the 2011 famine and its response." Charity & Security Network, July 10, 2013. https://charityandsecurity.org/humanitarian-safeguards/somalia-2011-famine-and-its-response/.

103 Shamas, "Downstream effects."

104 Osgood, "October 7 survivors."

105 El Taraboulsi-McCarthy, Sherine. "'A humanitarian sector in debt': counter-terrorism, bank de-risking and financial access for NGOs in the West Bank and Gaza." Humanitarian Policy Group, August 2018, vii. https://cdn.odi.org/media/documents/12357.pdf.

106 Palestine Monetary Authority. "About PMA: Vision and Mission." https://www.pma.ps/en/AboutPMA/VisionandMission.

107 El Taraboulsi-McCarthy, "'Humanitarian sector in debt,'" 3–4.

108 Barron, Robert. "Palestinian politics timeline: since the 2006 election." United States Institute of Peace, June 25, 2019. https://www.usip.org/palestinian-politics-timeline-2006-election.
109 Fast, Larissa. "'Aid in a pressure cooker': humanitarian action in the occupied Palestinian territories." Feinstein International Center, November 2006, 9. https://dl.tufts.edu/pdfviewer/r781wt04r/c821gw56x.
110 Ibid.
111 "Human Rights Council Special Session on the Occupied Palestinian Territories, July 6, 2006." Human Rights Watch, July 6, 2006. https://www.hrw.org/news/2006/07/05/human-rights-council-special-session-occupied-palestinian-territories-july-6-2006.
112 Fast, "'Aid in a pressure cooker,'" 9.
113 "US has ordered banks not to send money to PA, official says." Times of Israel, February 11, 2019. https://www.timesofisrael.com/us-has-ordered-banks-not-to-send-money-to-pa-official-says/.
114 "US denies telling banks to stop working with Palestinians," Times of Israel, February 12, 2019. https://www.timesofisrael.com/us-denies-telling-banks-to-stop-working-with-palestinians/.
115 "When the giving gets tough: navigating risk in sanctioned locations." Charity & Security Network and CAF America, 9. https://www.cafamerica.org/wp-content/uploads/CAFAmerica_Sanctions_WP_FINAL-1.pdf.
116 Handagama, Sandali. "Why it's tough to send aid money to Palestine during the latest Israel-Hamas conflict." Yahoo, May 21, 2021. https://www.yahoo.com/now/why-tough-send-aid-money-160813170.html?guccounter=1&guce_referrer=aHR0cHM6Ly93d3cuZ29vZ2xlLmNvbS8&guce_referrer_sig=AQAAAKP5Y4w-fVhG57dpTw1Xzmi1AcDMH65dlp7YvppZzWnPhVcEGWK4st0nnBdRG9vw6RwvRSFymBA0-FsQjdCPn4KK7vbaH6BXjs10WlZ61-jvMC8L075gDPw5NsAftthyv4fqxec_BQblMnegwpLWC4hKDs6D_1pCP0ScxXO0dDef.
117 Gaouette, Roth. "US to resume diplomatic ties with Palestinians that were cut under Trump." CNN, March 25, 2021. https://www.cnn.com/2021/03/25/politics/us-palestinians-diplomatic-ties-two-states/index.html.
118 Scheer, Steven. "Israel extends cooperation between Israeli and Palestinian banks, official says." Reuters, June 30, 2024. https://www.reuters.com/world/middle-east/israel-extends-cooperation-between-israeli-palestinian-banks-official-says-2024-06-30/.
119 Boxerman, Aaron, and Rasgon, Adam. "Israeli minister will release palestinian funds if settlements are legalized, officials say." New York Times, June 28, 2024. https://www.nytimes.com/2024/06/29/world/middleeast/israel-funds-palestinian-authority-smotrich.html.
120 Wahid Hanna, Michael, and Rami Dajani. "Meltdown looms for the West Bank's financial lifelines." International Crisis Group, June 27, 2024. https://www.crisisgroup.org/united-states-israelpalestine/meltdown-looms-west-banks-financial-lifelines.
121 "Israel extends waiver for cooperation between Israeli and Palestinian banks." Times of Israel, June 30, 2024. https://www.timesofisrael.com/liveblog_entry/israel-extends-waiver-for-cooperation-between-israeli-and-palestinian-banks/.
122 Boxerman and Rasgon, "Israeli minister will release Palestinian funds."
123 Ibid.
124 Ibid.

125 Keatinge, Keen. "Study of the Co-operative Bank's closure of accounts of not-for-profit organisations." December 15, 2016. https://www.amnesty.org.uk/files/2017-04/Study%20into%20Co-op%20Bank%20Account%20Closures%20vFINAL.pdf?Jmkelh4z7XZslnDcuRiFAQNu0ZVp.Imk; Palestine Solidarity Campaign. "About." https://palestinecampaign.org/about/.
126 Palestine Solidarity Campaign. "Co-operative Bank closes PSC's account." November 24, 2015. https://palestinecampaign.org/co-operative-bank-close-pscs-account/.
127 Keatinge, "Study of the Co-operative Bank's closure of accounts."
128 Ibid.
129 Palestine Solidarity Campaign, "Co-operative Bank closes PSC's account."
130 "World-check screening: what is it and what is it used for." Reputation America. https://reputationamerica.org/world-check-screening/#how_does_the_world-check_database_work.
131 PayPal. "How PayPal works – what is PayPal?" https://www.paypal.com/us/digital-wallet/how-paypal-works.
132 Butcher, Mike. "PayPal brushes-off request from Palestinian tech firms to access the platform." TechCrunch, September 9, 2016. https://techcrunch.com/2016/09/09/paypal-brushes-off-request-from-palestinian-tech-firms-to-access-the-platform/.
133 Palestinian tech companies: ibid.; Palestinian and international organizations: 7amleh – The Arab Center for the Advancement of Social Media. "About." https://act.7amleh.org/about; Members of Congress: McGreal, Chris. "US Congress members demand that PayPal end ban on Palestinian business." Guardian, May 24, 2023. https://www.theguardian.com/technology/2023/may/24/paypal-palestine-ban-us-congress-.
134 Matsakis, Louise. "Venmo is halting some payments referring to Palestine." Rest of World, May 18, 2021. https://restofworld.org/2021/venmo-palestinian-relief/.
135 Ibid.
136 US Department of the Treasury, Office of Foreign Assets Control. "Counter terrorism sanctions." https://ofac.treasury.gov/sanctions-programs-and-country-information/counter-terrorism-sanctions#gls.
137 "Scoping study on operating conditions."
138 Ibid., 11.
139 Ibid., 11.
140 Ibid., 9.
141 El Taraboulsi-McCarthy, "'Humanitarian sector in debt'."
142 The working paper notes that financial exclusion for Palestinian NGOs is exacerbated at this level by barriers imposed by the Israeli government in the name of "money-laundering and terrorism financing concerns" and by banks through "terminat[ing] or limit[ing] correspondent banking services to Palestinian banks."
143 Ibid., 6–7.
144 Ibid., 1–3.
145 Ibid.
146 Muadi, Qassem. "'Soon they will ask us to become Zionist': Palestinian NGOs slam EU funding restrictions." New Arab, December 6, 2023. https://www.newarab.com/news/palestinian-ngos-eu-will-soon-ask-us-become-zionist.
147 US Department of the Treasury, Office of Foreign Assets Control, "Counter terrorism sanctions."
148 Alloush, Basma. "Overcoming the hurdles: the struggle of Palestinian humanitarian NGOs." Tahrir Institute for Middle East Policy, December 22, 2021. https://

timep.org/2021/12/22/overcoming-the-hurdles-the-struggle-of-palestinian-humanitarian-ngos/#:~:text=Daily%20manifestations%20of%20the%20Israeli,permits%20is%20unpredictable%20at%20best.
149	International Court of Justice. "Application of the Convention on the Prevention and Punishment of the Crime of Genocide in the Gaza Strip (South Africa v. Israel)"; United Nations Human Rights Office of the High Commissioner. "Gaza: ICJ ruling offers hope for protection of civilians enduring apocalyptic conditions, say UN experts." January 26, 2024. https://www.ohchr.org/en/press-releases/2024/01/gaza-icj-ruling-offers-hope-protection-civilians-enduring-apocalyptic.
150	Bynum, Russ, and Knickmeyer, Ellen. "A senior UN official says northern Gaza is now in 'full-blown famine.'" AP, May 3, 2024. https://apnews.com/article/gaza-israel-famine-humanitarian-aid-children-8a4cb5736c42caf50b6e204f40d83a91.
151	Shehadi, Sebastian. "Palestinians are having their bank accounts frozen. Their banks won't explain why." Novara Media, January 3, 2024. https://novaramedia.com/2024/01/03/palestinians-are-having-their-bank-accounts-frozen-their-banks-wont-explain-why/.
152	Ibid.
153	United Nations Human Rights Office of the High Commissioner. "Commission of Inquiry finds that the Israeli occupation is unlawful under international law." October 20, 2022. https://www.ohchr.org/en/press-releases/2022/10/commission-inquiry-finds-israeli-occupation-unlawful-under-international-law.

12. Closing Spaces Beyond Borders: Israel's Transnational Repression Network

1	ICJ. "Legal consequences of the construction of a wall in the occupied Palestinian territory." https://www.icj-cij.org/case/131.
2	Keck, Margaret E., and Kathryn Sikkink. *Activists beyond Borders: Advocacy Networks in International Politics* (Cornell University Press, 2014), 12–13.
3	"Palestinian civil society call for BDS." BDS Movement, July 9, 2005. https://bdsmovement.net/call.
4	Olesker, Ronnie. *Israel's Securitization Dilemma: BDS and the Battle for the Legitimacy of the Jewish State. Religion and International Security* (Abingdon and New York: Routledge, 2022).
5	Ibid., 111.
6	"About Reut – Reut Institute." March 3, 2011. https://web.archive.org/web/20110303205156/http://www.reut-institute.org/en/Content.aspx?Page=About.
7	Reut Institute. "Building a political firewall against Israel's delegitimization: conceptual framework." Reut Group, March 2010. https://www.reutgroup.org/_files/ugd/1bfcb5_d59cc682a61444439b12462b75e1fbb5.pdf.
8	Ibid.
9	Eichner, Itamar. "Comptroller's report highlights Israeli failure to fight BDS." Ynetnews, May 24, 2016, https://www.ynetnews.com/articles/0,7340,L-4807490,00.html.
10	"Ministry of Strategic Affairs and Public Diplomacy." August 14, 2020. https://web.archive.org/web/20200814053227/https://www.gov.il/en/departments/units/ministry_of_strategic_affairs_and_public_diplomacy.

11 State of Israel Ministry of Strategic Affairs. "Annual report: the Ministry of Strategic Affairs, 2016." December 2016. https://cdn.the7eye.org.il/uploads/2017/10/strategic-affairs-ministry-report2016.pdf.
12 State of Israel Ministry of Strategic Affairs. "Annual report – 2017." https://www.gov.il/BlobFolder/generalpage/strategy/he/strategic_affairs_doch2017.pptx.
13 State of Israel Ministry of Strategic Affairs. "Annual report: the Ministry of Strategic Affairs, 2018." December 2018. https://cdn.the7eye.org.il/uploads/2017/12/strategic-affairs-ministry-report2018.pdf.
14 State of Israel Ministry of Strategic Affairs. "Annual report for 2019." 2019. https://cdn.the7eye.org.il/uploads/2017/12/accountability220920.pptx.
15 Kontorovich, Eugene, et al. "Law & War Conference 2019 – panel: BDS defeat – achieving victory against delegitimization." July 11, 2019. https://ww.youtube.com/watch?v=t5RbXNpk6y4.
16 *Combating BDS – Opening Remarks, IHRA Promo, and Speeches*. Jerusalem, 2019. https://www.facebook.com/watch/live/?ref=watch_permalink&v=639294689919260.
17 Ibid.
18 "Special Committee for the Transparency and Accessibility of Government Information – historical makeup." https://www.knesset.gov.il/committees/eng/CommitteeHistoryByCommittee_eng.asp?com=571.
19 Winer, Stuart. "Israel seen as a 'pariah state,' says top strategy official." Times of Israel, August 7, 2006. http://www.timesofisrael.com/israel-seen-as-a-pariah-state-says-top-strategy-official/.
20 "Bill calling to keep Strategic Affairs Ministry's efforts to combat delegitimization secret passes first reading." June 29, 2019. https://web.archive.org/web/20190629002141/https://main.knesset.gov.il/EN/News/PressReleases/Pages/Pr13526_pg.aspx.
21 State of Israel Ministry of Strategic Affairs. "Response to the request of the movement for freedom of information regarding the Ministry's engagements." January 17, 2021.
22 Transparency Committee of Knesset. "Minutes of a meeting on the budget of the Ministry for Strategic Issues and 'Kela Shlomo.'" December 17, 2018. https://cdn.the7eye.org.il/uploads/2017/12/protocol17122018.pdf.
23 State of Israel Ministry of Strategic Affairs. "Report on sensitive engagements of the Ministry for Strategic Issues for the years 2015–2017." 2017. https://www.odata.org.il/dataset/strategic-secret-c; State of Israel Ministry of Strategic Affairs. "Sensitive engagements 2018 – the Ministry for Strategic Issues." 2018. https://www.odata.org.il/dataset/2f0ebeec-6b4a-4e7e-a4be-fbc6db0f27a3.
24 Tenders Committee. "Summaries of two meetings concerning the approval of a 'joint venture with the organization 'Yeshiva Ash-HaTorah' for training interpreters on campuses in the United States, 2016–2017." State of Israel Ministry of Strategic Affairs, February 19, 2017. https://cdn.the7eye.org.il/uploads/2017/10/233531-221913.pdf.
25 Dickson, Michael. "Conferencing! #gc4i2019." Instagram, June 19, 2019. https://www.instagram.com/p/By4vRg3lbls/.
26 Lawfare Project. "We were honored to join our dear friends and members of our attorney network, the world's top legal minds, who continue to dedicate their passion, expertise, and creativity to enforcing the rights of the Jewish people. #GC4I2019 From left: Pascal Markowicz, Benjamin Ryberg, Nathan Gelbart, Brooke Goldstein and Barbara Pontecorvo." Instagram, June 23, 2019. https://www.instagram.com/p/BzDzz7_F34c/.
27 Tapiero, Carlos Alberto. "GC4I 2019: Reuven Rivlin speech." June 20, 2019. https://www.facebook.com/share/fhfbpxGejEj3wgSv/?mibextid=xfxF2i.

28 Lewin, Alyza. "Remarks of Alyza D. Lewin at LNI Conference Jerusalem June 2019." July 29, 2019. https://www.youtube.com/watch?v=m80j9B8JoC4&list=PLSvvJrFl-9dyGWym18zCY_kbU7RJ7VKv2&index=3.
29 Erdan, Gilad. "The opening event of the largest international conference in the world to fight BDS." June 18, 2019. https://www.facebook.com/watch/live/?ref=watch_permalink&v=2243147089132061.
30 "Shurat HaDin shuts down German BDS bank account." Israel Law Center, June 12, 2019. https://israellawcenter.org/legal_actions/shurat-hadin-shuts-down-german-bds-bank-account/.
31 Erdan, Gilad. "Law & War Conference 2019 – keynote address: Gilad Erdan." July 10, 2019. https://www.youtube.com/watch?v=w8EyxmZSsDk.
32 Times of Israel Staff. "Norway said set to cut funding for pro-BDS Palestinian NGOs." Times of Israel, December 25, 2017. https://www.timesofisrael.com/norway-said-set-to-cut-funding-for-pro-bds-palestinian-ngos/.
33 *Combating BDS – Opening Remarks, IHRA Promo, and Speeches.*
34 "Pro-Israel statehouse lobbyists work behind the scenes to mute BDS." USA Today, May 1, 2019. https://www.usatoday.com/story/news/investigations/2019/05/01/statehouse-model-bills-bds-protest-bans/3575083002/.
35 "Draft Shell Model PEACE Israel Act – protection and enforcement against the Commercial Exclusion of Israel Act – American Legislative Exchange Council." July 20, 2016. https://web.archive.org/web/20160720150615/https:/alec.org/model-policy/draft-shell-model-peace-israel-act-protection-and-enforcement-against-the-commercial-exclusion-of-israel-act/.
36 Times of Israel Staff. "Norway said set to cut funding."
37 Brown, Andrew. "Myrtle Beach lawmaker Alan Clemmons, a Mormon, gains a national name as pro-Israel advocate." Post and Courier, April 1, 2017. https://www.postandcourier.com/news/myrtle-beach-lawmaker-alan-clemmons-a-mormon-gains-a-national-name-as-pro-israel-advocate/article_2b42d68e-131d-11e7-8329-d72b08a364a1.html.
38 LNI Conference 2018, https://www.youtube.com/watch?v=pdIwQTyaSqg.
39 Legal Network Initiative. "International Jurists' Conference on Boycotts and Delegitimization: Conference Agenda." January 2018.
40 Clemmons, Alan. "Alan Clemmons at GC4I Facebook Post." Facebook, June 19, 2019.
41 According to the meeting logs of MSA officials, ADL leaders met with ministry officials on multiple occasions including with Director General Sima Vaknin-Gil on January 28, 2018 and March 18, 2018 and with Director General Tzachi Gavrieli on May 23, 2019. Vaknin-Gil, Sima. "Diary of the Director General of the Ministry of Strategic Affairs, Sima Vaknin-Gil." February 11, 2019. https://www.odata.org.il/dataset/a67a8faf-6dbc-4beb-b7ed-0c19b176df08; State of Israel Ministry of Strategic Affairs. "The schedule of the CEOs of the Office for Strategic Issues: Sima Vaknin Gil, January–May 2019/Tzachi Gabrieli, May–December 2019." December 2019. https://cdn.the7eye.org.il/uploads/2017/12/zg2019.pdf.
42 European Jewish Congress. "EJC executive vice-president Raya Kalenova joins panel at GC4I Conference." June 20, 2018. https://eurojewcong.org/ejc-in-action/events-meetings/ejc-executive-vice-president-raya-kalenova-joins-panel-on-defending-israels-legitimacy/; Sima Vaknin Gil and Tzachi Gavrieli Diary 2019: State of Israel Ministry of Strategic Affairs. "The schedule of the CEO of the Office Tzachi Gabrieli, April–June 2020." July 2020. https://cdn.the7eye.org.il/uploads/2017/12/zg-april-june2020.pdf.

43 "Israel Action Network 2019 annual report." Israel Action Network, n.d. https://cdn.fedweb.org/fed-118/2/IAN%2520AR19spreads_FInal_For_Digital.pdf?v=1569247152.
44 State of Israel Ministry of Strategic Affairs. "Legal opinion on agreement with International Legal Forum." https://cdn.the7eye.org.il/uploads/2017/12/msa580622835-2018.pdf.
45 Jaffe-Hoffman, Maayan. "Strategic Affairs Ministry to form anti-BDS legal network." Jerusalem Post, December 20, 2018. https://www.jpost.com/arab-israeli-conflict/ministry-of-strategic-affairs-to-create-international-anti-bds-legal-team-574946.
46 Ibid.
47 Israeli Bar Association, International Legal Forum, and State of Israel Ministry of Strategic Affairs. International Jurists' Conference on Boycotts and De-legitimization. Jerusalem, 2018.
48 Heideman, Richard, and American Zionist Movement. "President of the American Zionist Movement Richard D. Heideman speaking at the Legal Network Initiative in Jerusalem, capital of Israel on BDS & criminal law." https://www.facebook.com/watch/?v=1675867515810956.
49 Ibid.
50 International Legal Forum. "Ground-breaking legal battle links BDS, terrorism and US-based human rights group." 2022. https://www.ilfngo.org/kkl-lawsuit.
51 Appeal by plaintiffs for reconsideration of dismissal. https://ccrjustice.org/sites/default/files/attach/2021/05/28-1_4-26-21_Memo-Pls-Motion-for-Reconsideration_w.pdf
52 American Civil Liberties Union. "In first, judge blocks Kansas law aimed at boycotts of Israel." January 30, 2018. https://www.aclu.org/press-releases/first-judge-blocks-kansas-law-aimed-boycotts-israel.
53 Greendorfer, Marc. "Brief of amicus curiae Zachor Legal Institute in support of the state of Arizona in case 3:17-Cv-08263-Djh *Jordahl et al. v. Brnovich*." SSRN Electronic Journal, 2018. https://doi.org/10.2139/ssrn.3127176.
54 *Amawi v. Pflugerville Independent School District*, No. 1:18-CV-1091-RP. https://www.aclutx.org/sites/default/files/4-25-19_bds_order.pdf
55 Israel State Ministry of Strategic Affairs. "The money trail." https://www.gov.il/BlobFolder/generalpage/money_trail/en/strategic_affairs_money_en.pdf.
56 Israel State Ministry of Strategic Affairs. "Terrorists in suits." https://www.gov.il/BlobFolder/generalpage/terrorists_in_suits/en/De-Legitimization%20Brochure.pdf.
57 Lewin. "Remarks of Alyza D. Lewin at LNI Conference."
58 Ibid
59 *Combating BDS – Opening Remarks, IHRA Promo, and Speeches.*
60 "Israel's Diaspora Affairs Ministry gets new name, director-general." Jerusalem Post, February 5, 2023. https://www.jpost.com/israel-news/politics-and-diplomacy/article-730692.
61 Ministry for Diaspora Affairs and Combating Antisemitism. "The Ministry for Diaspora Affairs and Combating Antisemitism in cooperation with the World Zionist Organization and the Jewish Agency for Israel, launched the 2023 Antisemitism Report." Gov.il, January 24, 2024. https://www.gov.il/en/pages/news-combatting180224.
62 Edelson, Daniel. "Fury in Wisconsin after neo-Nazis march in state capitol with swastika flags." Ynetnews, November 19, 2023. https://www.ynetnews.com/article/rjujmhw4t.
63 Eichner, "Shaming and pressuring donors."

64 In late August 2024, new reporting in the Israeli media, based on documents from the Israeli Ministry of Diaspora Affairs, revealed that the Ministry had surged financing of "Tens of millions of shekels" to a hundred entities through the public benefit company previously named Concert "to spread covert propaganda on behalf of the government." The same ministry reportedly sought to contract the services of private, Israeli-military linked intelligence firms to spy on student activists for Palestinian rights in the United States, as revealed by the Israeli newspaper *Haaretz*.

13. From Exclusion to Erasure: The Attempt to Silence Arab Americans on Palestine

1 "Demographics – Arab American Institute." Arab American Institute, n.d. https://www.aaiusa.org/demographics.
2 The Arab American Institute has conducted polling of Arab Americans since the mid-1990s. When asked about identifying their top issues of concern, not surprisingly, the issues that rank the highest generally include jobs and the economy, the budget deficit, gun violence, and the like. Foreign policy in general, and Palestine in particular, are often prioritized too. In one exception, a 2000 poll found 61% of Arab American immigrants said the Arab–Israeli conflict was the "single most important issue in determining their vote." See "Arab Americans: issues, attitudes, views." Arab American Institute, February 2000. https://www.aaiusa.org/library/arab-americans-poll-2000. While noteworthy, the majority of Arab Americans are native-born (55% based on 2022 American Community Survey one-year estimates; 58% at the time of the poll based on 2000 US Census, US Census Bureau).
3 Joseph, Suad. "Against the grain of the nation – the Arab." In Michael W. Suleiman (ed.), *Arabs in America: Building a New Future* (Temple University Press, 1999), 265–6.
4 Naff, Alixa. "The early Arab immigrant experience." In Ernest McCarus (ed.), *The Development of Arab American Identity* (University of Michigan Press, 1994), 23–36.
5 "The Avalon Project: Balfour Declaration November 2, 1917." https://avalon.law.yale.edu/20th_century/balfour.asp.
6 Ghareeb, Edmund, and Jenab Tutunji, "Arab American writers, the Mahjar Press, and the Palestine issue." *Arab Studies Quarterly* 38, no. 1 (2016): 424.
7 Ibid., 422.
8 Ibid., 424.
9 Davidson, Lawrence. "Debating Palestine: Arab-American challenges to Zionism 1917–1932." In Michael W. Suleiman (ed.), *Arabs in America: Building a New Future* (Temple University Press, 1999), 229.
10 Elgindy, Khaled. "The Balfour lens." In *Blind Spot: America and the Palestinians, from Balfour to Trump* (Brookings Institution Press, 2019), 16.
11 Davidson, "Debating Palestine," 234–5.
12 Ibid., 234.
13 Samhan, Helen Hatab. "Politics and exclusion: the Arab American experience," *Journal of Palestine Studies* 16, no. 2 (1987): 11–28.
14 Zogby, James, and Helen Hatab Samhan. "The politics of exclusion: a report on Arab-baiting in the 1986 elections." Arab American Institute, 1987. https://www.aaiusa.org/library/the-politics-of-exclusion-a-report-on-arab-baiting-in-the-1986-elections.
15 Samhan, "Politics and exclusion," 21.
16 Ibid., 16.

17 Said, Edward. "Ibrahim Abu-Lughod." Guardian, June 12, 2001. https://www.theguardian.com/news/2001/jun/12/guardianobituaries.internationaleducationnews.
18 Suleiman, Michael. "'I come to bury Caesar, not to praise him': an assessment of the AAUG as an example of an activist Arab-American Organization." *Arab Studies Quarterly* 29, no. 3/4 (2000): 78.
19 Zogby, James. "Before we bid farewell to Arab American Heritage Month." Nation, April 29, 2021. https://www.thenation.com/article/society/arab-american-heritage-discrimination/.
20 National Security Council, Speechwriting Office, and Edward (Ted) Widmer, "Arab-American Institute, May 7, 1998." *Clinton Digital Library*. https://clinton.presidentiallibraries.us/items/show/11378.
21 Examples include Operation Boulder under the Nixon administration, the persecution of the LA Eight, the use of secret evidence, the National Security Entry-Exit Registration System (NSEERS), and the extraordinary suggestion of deploying material support charges to go after the massive anti-war student movement.
22 See Saad, Lydia. "Democrats' sympathies in Middle East shift to Palestinians." Gallup, March 16, 2023. https://news.gallup.com/poll/472070/democrats-sympathies-middle-east-shift-palestinians.aspx; Mitchell, Travis. "Modest warming in US views on Israel and Palestinians." Pew Research Center, May 26, 2022. https://www.pewresearch.org/religion/2022/05/26/modest-warming-in-u-s-views-on-israel-and-palestinians/; Telhami, Sibley. "American public attitudes toward the Israeli-Palestinian conflict." Brookings, December 5, 2014. https://www.brookings.edu/articles/american-public-attitudes-toward-the-israeli-palestinian-conflict/. All polls conducted before the attacks of October 7, 2023.
23 "Arab Americans: issues, attitudes, views." Arab American Institute, February 23, 2000. https://www.aaiusa.org/library/arab-americans-poll-2000.
24 "The Arab American vote 2012." Arab American Institute, September 27, 2012. https://www.aaiusa.org/library/the-arab-american-vote-2012.
25 "Seeing eye to eye: a survey of Jewish American and Arab American public opinion." Arab American Institute, May 13, 2007. https://www.aaiusa.org/library/seeing-eye-to-eye-a-survey-of-jewish-american-and-arab-american-public-opinion.
26 "Poll of Arab Americans." Arab American Institute, April 28, 2023. https://www.aaiusa.org/library/the-arab-american-vote-2023-dm83t.
27 "Rights expert finds 'reasonable grounds' genocide is being committed in Gaza." UN News, March 26, 2024. https://news.un.org/en/story/2024/03/1147976.
28 "Arab Americans special poll: domestic implications of the most recent outbreak of violence in Palestine/Israel." Arab American Institute, October 31, 2023, https://www.aaiusa.org/library/arab-americans-special-poll-domestic-implications-of-the-most-recent-outbreak-of-violence-in-palestineisrael.
29 Zogby, James. "Jesse Jackson nominating speech." C-SPAN, July 14, 1984. https://www.c-span.org/video/?c4869531/user-clip-james-zogby.
30 Goldberg, Michelle. "Senators need to stop the Anti-Semitism Awareness Act." New York Times, May 7, 2024. https://www.nytimes.com/2024/05/06/opinion/antisemitism-act-free-speech.html.
31 Gedeon, Joseph. "Attorneys inside and outside the administration urge Biden to cut off arms to Israel." Politico, April 29, 2024. https://www.politico.com/news/2024/04/29/lawyers-israel-arm-sales-biden-00154958.

32 Skinner, Anna. "Police shoot at UCLA protesters as encampment cleared." Newsweek, May 2, 2024. https://www.newsweek.com/ucla-campus-protests-police-shoot-pro-palestinian-1896549.

33 McHardy, Martha. "White House slams Squad members' 'repugnant' comments on Israel attack." Independent, October 11, 2023. https://www.the-independent.com/news/world/americas/us-politics/israel-gaza-white-house-biden-rashida-tlaib-b2427831.html; Garrison, Joey. "White House condemns takeover of Columbia University building, use of 'intifada' at college protests." USA Today, April 30, 2024. https://www.usatoday.com/story/news/politics/2024/04/30/white-house-condemns-columbia-building-takeover-intifada-rhetoric/73512709007/.

34 Kessler, Glenn. "Biden yet again says Hamas beheaded babies. Has new evidence emerged?" Washington Post, November 22, 2023. https://www.washingtonpost.com/politics/2023/11/22/biden-yet-again-says-hamas-beheaded-babies-has-new-evidence-emerged/; Swann, Sara. "Archive: 'how politicians, media outlets amplified uncorroborated report of beheaded babies.'" PolitiFact, October 20, 2023. ("White House National Security Council spokesperson John Kirby said Oct. 12, 'I don't think we're in the business of having to validate or approve those kinds of images. They're from the prime minister of Israel and we have no reason to doubt their authenticity.'") https://www.politifact.com/archive-beheaded-babies-israel-hamas/.

35 Saba, Dylan. "A surge in suppression." N+1, October 19, 2023. https://www.nplusonemag.com/online-only/online-only/a-surge-in-suppression/.

36 Pika, Joseph. "The White House Office of Public Liaison." *Presidential Studies Quarterly* 39, no. 3 (2009): 552.

37 Biden, Joseph R. "Fact sheet: Biden campaign press release: Joe Biden and the Arab American Community: a plan of action." American Presidency Project, August 29, 2020. https://www.presidency.ucsb.edu/documents/biden-campaign-press-release-fact-sheet-joe-biden-and-the-arab-american-community-plan-for,

38 Pika, "White House Office of Public Liaison," 568.

39 Nicholas, Peter. "With no fanfare or acknowledgment, Biden hosts White House meeting with Muslim leaders." NBC News, October 27, 2023. https://www.nbcnews.com/politics/white-house/biden-hosts-meeting-muslim-leaders-rcna122433#.

40 Private conversation relayed to the author.

41 Gottheimer, Josh (D-NJ). "Text – H.Res.1114 – 118th Congress (2023–2024): Denouncing the rise of Islamophobia and antisemitism across the country." April 5, 2024. https://www.congress.gov/bill/118th-congress/house-resolution/1114/text; Congress.gov. "H.Res.883 – 118th Congress (2023–2024): Expressing the sense of the House of Representatives that the slogan, 'from the river to the sea, Palestine will be free' is antisemitic and its use must be condemned." April 16, 2024. https://www.congress.gov/bill/118th-congress/house-resolution/883.

42 Plitnick, Mitchell, and Sahar Aziz. "Presumptively antisemitic: Islamophobic tropes in the Palestine–Israel discourse." Rutgers University Law School, Center for Security, Race and Rights, November 2023. https://csrr.rutgers.edu/wp-content/uploads/2023/11/csrr-presumptively-antisemitic-report.pdf, 18.

43 Ibid., 7. In a simple introductory note on terminology, the reader is advised: "Although anti-Arab racism is separate from Islamophobia, the two forms of bias often overlap ... The considerable overlap between these two prejudices in the West, and especially in the United States, should be noted while acknowledging the two are not identical. For the sake of brevity and clarity, this report uses Islamophobia broadly to describe both anti-Arab and anti-Palestinian racism."

44 Younis, Mohamed. "Muslim Americans exemplify diversity, potential." Gallup, March 2, 2009. https://news.gallup.com/poll/116260/Muslim-Americans-Exemplify-Diversity-Potential.aspx; Mohamed, Besheer, and Jeff Diamant, "Black Muslims account for a fifth of all US Muslims, and about half are converts to Islam." Pew Research Center, January 17, 2019. https://www.pewresearch.org/short-reads/2019/01/17/black-muslims-account-for-a-fifth-of-all-u-s-muslims-and-about-half-are-converts-to-islam/.
45 "Demographic portrait of Muslim Americans." Pew Research Center, July 26, 2017, https://www.pewresearch.org/religion/2017/07/26/demographic-portrait-of-muslim-americans/#muslims-in-the-us.
46 A 2006 estimate has Arab Americans who identify as Christian at 63%. The Arab American Institute is in the process of updating a demographic profile of Arab Americans and the religious breakdown will be revised. While the majority of Arab Americans are Christian, the updated 2024 number will be less than 63%.
47 "Ameen Rihani." Khayrallah Center for Lebanese Diaspora Studies, n.d. https://lebanesestudies.ncsu.edu/explore/projects/ameen-rihani/.
48 "City probes use of its radio station for anti-Zionist program." Jewish Telegraphic Agency, June 10, 1937. https://www.jta.org/archive/city-probes-use-of-its-radio-station-for-anti-zionist-program.
49 "An appeal to American justice and fair play on behalf of the Palestine Arabs." Arab National League of America, 1938, 3. https://www.loc.gov/item/2017498665/.
50 Ibid.
51 Zogby, James. "Palestine: a wound in the heart." In *Arab Voices: What They Are Saying to Us, and Why It Matters* (Palgrave Macmillan, 2010), 158.

14. Shrinking Civic Space in the Arab World and its Relationship to Palestine/Israel

1 Derbal, Nora. *Charity in Saudi Arabia: Civil Society under Authoritarianism* (Cambridge: Cambridge University Press, 2022).
2 For example, in Bahrain, NGO services need to register under the Ministry of Social Development, as evident from its website; see Hamid, Shadi. "Civil society in the Arab world and the dilemma of funding." Brookings, October 21, 2010. https://www.brookings.edu/articles/civil-society-in-the-arab-world-and-the-dilemma-of-funding/.
3 Human Rights Watch. "Tunisia: looming curbs on civil society must be stopped, draft law could restore Ben Ali era restrictions." March 11, 2022. https://www.hrw.org/news/2022/03/11/tunisia-looming-curbs-civil-society-must-be-stopped.
4 Al Achi, Assad. "How Syrian civil society lost its independence in war of conflicting agendas." May 15, 2020. https://carnegie-mec.org/2020/05/15/how-syrian-civil-society-lost-its-independence-in-war-of-conflicting-agendas-pub-81802.
5 Kassin, Dylan, and David Pollock. "Arab public opinion, Arab-Israeli normalization, and the Abraham Accords." 2022. https://www.washingtoninstitute.org/policy-analysis/arab-public-opinion-arab-israeli-normalization-and-abraham-accords.
6 For Gulf aid to Egypt and Jordan, see Halawa, Hasfa. "Gulf investment in Egypt: a balance of mutual need." May 8, 2023. https://carnegie-mec.org/2023/05/08/gulf-investment-in-egypt-balance-of-mutual-need-pub-89641; Schielke, Joska

Samuli. *Migrant Dreams: Egyptian Workers in the Gulf States* (La Vergne: American University in Cairo Press, 2020).

7   See Muasher, Marwan. "Jordan: fallout from the end of an oil era." June 9, 2020. https://carnegieendowment.org/2020/06/09/jordan-fallout-from-end-of-oil-era-pub-82008.

8   US Government Accounting Office. "Human rights: agency actions needed to address harassment of dissents and other tactics of transnational repression in the United States." Report No. GAO-24-106183, October 3, 2023. https://www.gao.gov/products/gao-24-106183.

9   "Jordan arrests dozens planning to protest in support of Gaza." Middle East Eye, November 13, 2023. https://www.middleeasteye.net/news/israel-palestine-war-jordan-arrests-gaza-protests-planning; "Exploiting our anger: Egyptians denounce staged pro-Palestine protests." Al Jazeera, October 21, 2023. https://www.aljazeera.com/features/2023/10/21/exploiting-our-anger-egyptians-denounce-staged-pro-palestine-protests; Human Rights Watch. "Egypt: dozens of peaceful protesters detained." November 1, 2023. https://www.hrw.org/news/2023/11/01/egypt-dozens-peaceful-protesters-detained.

10 Human Rights Watch. "Bahrain: repression of pro-Palestine protests." December 22, 2023. https://www.hrw.org/news/2023/12/22/bahrain-repression-pro-palestine-protests; Said, Summer. "Protests take place across Middle East following Gaza hospital blast." Wall Street Journal, October 19, 2023. https://www.wsj.com/livecoverage/israel-hamas-war-biden/card/watch-protests-spread-across-middle-east-after-gaza-hospital-blast-dvOOAmOKxJhh5ozRy4dI.

11 International Center for Not-for-Profit Law. Translated version of Decree-Law 2011-88. https://www.icnl.org/wp-content/uploads/Tunisia_88-2011-Eng.pdf.

12 "The Norwegian Nobel Committee has decided to award the Nobel Peace Prize for 2011." October 7, 2011. https://www.royalcourt.no/nyhet.html?tid=130885&sek=27262.

13 "Droit d'association: le projet liberticide du gouvernement Bouden." February 8, 2022. https://nawaat.org/2022/02/08/droit-dassociation-le-projet-liberticide-du-gouvernement-bouden/.

14 "Tunisia's Saied will bar foreign funding for civil society." Reuters, February 24, 2022. https://www.reuters.com/world/africa/tunisias-saied-will-bar-foreign-funding-civil-society-2022-02-24/.

15 "Tunisian President Kais Saied objects proposed law criminalizing normalization with Israel." Le Monde, November 3, 2023. https://www.lemonde.fr/en/international/article/2023/11/03/tunisian-president-kais-saied-objects-proposed-law-criminalizing-normalization-with-israel_6225783_4.html.

16 El Atti, Basma. "Tunisia travel bans lawyer representing Palestine in ICJ." New Arab, January 18, 2024. https://www.newarab.com/news/tunisia-travel-bans-lawyer-representing-palestine-icj.

17 Al-Sayyid, Mustapha. "A civil society in Egypt?" *Middle East Journal* 47, no. 2 (1993): 228. https://ceip.idm.oclc.org/login?url=https://www.proquest.com/scholarly-journals/civil-society-egypt/docview/218484691/se-2.

18 Ibid.

19 "Under threat: rules and practice of NGO registration, legal status and reporting in ten countries." March 2015. https://www.europarl.europa.eu/meetdocs/2014_2019/documents/droi/dv/55_underthreat_/55_underthreat_en.pdf.

20 Amnesty International. "Egypt's National Human Rights Strategy covers up human rights crisis." 2022. https://www.amnesty.org/en/documents/mde12/6014/2022/en/.

21 "Two Israeli spyware firms hacked dissidents' phones in Egypt, India." Haaretz, December 17, 2021. https://www.haaretz.com/israel-news/2021-12-17/ty-article/two-israeli-spyware-fi,rms-hacked-dissidents-phones-in-egypt-india/0000017f-ed9b-d639-af7f-eddf0b8f0000; "Investigation: how Israeli spyware was sold to Egypt and pitched to Qatar and Saudi Arabia." Haaretz, October 5, 2023. https://www.haaretz.com/israel-news/security-aviation/2023-10-05/ty-article/.premium/investigation-how-israeli-spyware-was-sold-to-egypt-and-pitched-to-qatar-and-saudi-arabia/0000018a-ff33-d037-a9ae-ffffdb00000.
22 "Activist jailed by Egypt sees wider struggle for rights." AP News, February 15, 2022. https://apnews.com/article/middle-east-africa-israel-egypt-west-bank-d9b480864df0b38c897ce9e2737f32fc.
23 Human Rights Watch. "Egypt: dozens of peaceful protesters detained." November 1, 2023. https://www.hrw.org/news/2023/11/01/egypt-dozens-peaceful-protesters-detained.
24 Ibid.
25 Wiktorowicz, Quintan. "Civil society as social control: state power in Jordan." *Comparative Politics* 33, no. 1 (2000): 43–61. https://doi.org/10.2307/422423.
26 Abdel-samad, Mounah. "Legislative advocacy under competitive authoritarian regimes: the case of civil society in Jordan." *Voluntas* 28, no. 3 (2017): 1035–53. https://ceip.idm.oclc.org/login?url=https://www.proquest.com/scholarly-journals/legislative-advocacy-under-competitive/docview/1899628702/se-2.
27 Duggal, Hanna. "Map: which MENA countries have diplomatic ties with Israel?" Al Jazeera, September 15, 2023. https://www.aljazeera.com/news/2023/9/15/map-which-mena-countries-have-diplomatic-ties-with-israel.
28 "Youth activism and protest: Jordan's movement against Israeli gas." POMEPS, https://pomeps.org/youth-activism-and-protest-jordans-movement-against-israeli-gas.
29 "Jordan recalls envoy to Israel over Gaza bombardment." Reuters, November 1, 2023. https://www.reuters.com/world/middle-east/jordan-recalls-envoy-israel-over-gaza-bombardment-2023-11-01/.
30 "Jordan disperses pro-Palestinian protesters heading for border with West Bank." Reuters, October 13, 2023. https://www.reuters.com/world/middle-east/jordan-disperses-pro-palestinian-protesters-heading-border-with-west-bank-2023-10-13/.
31 Atia, Mona, and Catherine E. Herrold. "Governing through patronage: the rise of NGOs and the fall of civil society in Palestine and Morocco." *Voluntas* 29, no. 5 (2018): 1044–54. http://www.jstor.org/stable/45105514.
32 Ibid.
33 "Where do Morocco and Sudan relations stand with Israel." Al Jazeera, September 18, 2023. https://www.aljazeera.com/news/2023/9/18/where-do-morocco-and-sudan-relations-stand-with-israel.
34 "How do MENA citizens view normalization with Israel?" Arab Barometer, 2022. https://www.arabbarometer.org/2022/09/how-do-mena-citizens-view-normalization-with-israel/.
35 "Moroccan human rights defenders targeted using malicious NSO Israeli spyware." Amnesty International, October 10, 2019. https://www.amnesty.org/en/latest/press-release/2019/10/moroccan-human-rights-defenders-targeted-using-malicious-nso-israeli-spyware/.
36 "Le Monde: France increasingly suspects Morocco used NSO spyware against it." Haaretz, July 28, 2021. https://www.haaretz.com/world-news/europe/2021-07-28/

ty-article/le-monde-france-increasingly-suspects-morocco-used-nso-spyware-use-against-it/0000017f-e705-df2c-a1ff-ff5555920000.

37 For detailed data on pro-Palestine and anti-normalization protests in Morocco since the Israel–Hamas war, please see ACLED. "Infographic: global demonstrations in response to the Israel-Palestine conflict." November 7, 2023. https://acleddata.com/2023/11/07/infographic-global-demonstrations-in-response-to-the-israel-palestine-conflict/.

38 Doha Institute. "Arab public opinion about the Israeli war on Gaza." January 10, 2024. https://www.dohainstitute.org/en/News/Pages/arab-public-opinion-about-the-israeli-war-on-gaza.aspx.

39 Metz, Sam. "Opposition mounts in Arab countries that normalized relations with Israel." AP News, November 2, 2023. https://apnews.com/article/israel-palestinians-arab-normalization-agreements-0c4707ff246c0c25d1ca001f8b1e734a.

40 Abdul-Nabi, Zainab. "Based on the peace journalism model: analysis of Al-Jazeera's coverage of Bahrain's uprising and Syria's chemical attack." *Global Media and Communication* 11, no. 3 (2015): 271–302. https://doi.org/10.1177/1742766515606300. Also see McGann, James G. "Qatar: an overview." In James G. McGann (ed.), *Think Tanks, Foreign Policy and the Emerging Powers* (Cham: Springer International Publishing, 2019), 377–81. https://doi.org/10.1007/978-3-319-60312-4_26; Boyce, Sir Graham. "Qatar's foreign policy." *Asian Affairs* 44, no. 3 (2013): 365–77. https://doi.org/10.1080/03068374.2013.826003.

41 "What has changed for migrant workers in Qatar?" ILO, November 2022. https://www.ilo.org/infostories/en-GB/Stories/Country-Focus/world-cup-qatar#intro/who-are.

42 RSF. "Qatar." November 20, 2022. https://rsf.org/en/country/qatar. See also Diop, Abdoulaye, Kien Trung Le, Trevor Johnston and Michael Ewers. "Citizens' attitudes towards migrant workers in Qatar." *Migration and Development* 6, no. 1 (2017): 144–60. https://doi.org/10.1080/21632324.2015.1112558. While Mohammad and Sidaway's study doesn't directly address media exposure, it sheds light on the socio-economic contexts and living conditions of migrant workers in Qatar, which may relate to their visibility and representation in the media: Mohammad, R. and J. Sidaway. "Shards and stages: migrant lives, power, and space viewed from Doha, Qatar." *Annals of the American Association of Geographers* 106 (2016), 1397–417. https://doi.org/10.1080/24694452.2016.1209402.

43 "Protests in Oman over economy, jobs continue for third day." Al Jazeera, May 25, 2021. https://www.aljazeera.com/news/2021/5/25/protest-in-oman-over-poor-economy-jobs-continue-for-third-day.

44 Selvik, Kjetil. "Elite rivalry in a semi-democracy: the Kuwaiti press scene." *Middle Eastern Studies* 47, no. 3 (2011): 477–96. https://doi.org/10.1080/00263206.2011.565143. This study argues that newspapers in Kuwait serve as political instruments in elite rivalries, despite liberalization, demonstrating their role in hybrid regimes.

45 Human Rights Watch. "Kuwait: Cybercrime Law a blow to free speech." July 22, 2015. https://www.hrw.org/news/2015/07/22/kuwait-cybercrime-law-blow-free-speech.

46 RSF, "Qatar."

47 Izzak, B. "Al-Watan daily's license canceled, case in court." Kuwait Times, January 21, 2015.

48 Zayani, Mohamed. "Transnational media, regional politics and state security: Saudi Arabia between tradition and modernity." *British Journal of Middle Eastern Studies* 39, no. 3 (2012): 307–27. https://doi.org/10.1080/13530194.2012.726486.
49 Freedom House. "Saudi Arabia: Freedom on the Net 2023 Country Report." https://freedomhouse.org/country/saudi-arabia/freedom-net/2023.
50 "All you need to know about Saudi Arabia's new social media influencer permit." Arab News, August 11, 2022. https://arab.news/8ph7n.
51 Human Rights Watch, "Kuwait: Cybercrime Law."
52 United States Department of State. "Oman." https://www.state.gov/reports/2022-country-reports-on-human-rights-practices/oman/.
53 "Exclusive: ex-NSA cyberspies reveal how they helped hack foes of UAE." Reuters, January 30, 2019. https://www.reuters.com/investigates/special-report/usa-spying-raven/.
54 Freedom House. "Qatar: Freedom in the World 2023 Country Report." https://freedomhouse.org/country/qatar/freedom-world/2023.
55 Gulf Centre for Human Rights. "Home." https://www.gc4hr.org/.
56 Freedom House. "United Arab Emirates: Freedom on the Net 2023 Country Report." https://freedomhouse.org/country/united-arab-emirates/freedom-net/2023. See "Limits on content" section.
57 Freedom House, "Saudi Arabia."
58 See, for example, this X (formerly Twitter) page discussing Bahrain–Israel relations – a few posts used pseudonyms: https://twitter.com/search?q=%D8%A7%D9%84%D8%A8%D8%AD%D8%B1%D9%8A%D9%86%20%D8%A5%D8%B3%D8%A4%D8%A7%D8%A6%D9%8A%D9%84%20&src=typed_query&f=top.
59 Freedom House. "Saudi Arabia case study: understanding transnational repression." https://freedomhouse.org/report/transnational-repression/saudi-arabia. Also see Gamawa, Yusuf Ibrahim. "United States, Turkey, Saudi Arabia and Middle East politics after Khashoggi's murder." *American International Journal of Humanities, Arts and Social Sciences* 1, no. 1 (2019): 1–3. https://doi.org/10.46545/aijhass.v1i1.42; "Qim 'abir lil-hudud" ithamat lil-Su'udiyyah bimulahaqat muwataniha bil-kharij wa 'al-safara' tard." https://www.alhurra.com/saudi-arabia/2022/11/02/%D9%82%D9%85%D8%B9-%D8%B9%D8%A7%D8%A8%D8%B1-%D9%84%D9%84%D8%AD%D8%AF%D9%88%D8%AF-%D8%A7%D8%AA%D9%87%D8%A7%D9%85%D8%A7%D8%AA-%D9%84%D9%84%D8%B3%D8%B9%D9%88%D8%AF%D9%8A%D8%A9-%D8%A8%D9%85%D9%84%D8%A7%D8%AD%D9%82%D8%A9-%D9%85%D9%88%D8%A7%D8%B7%D9%86%D9%8A%D9%87%D8%A7-%D8%A8%D8%A7%D9%84%D8%AE%D8%A7%D8%B1%D8%AC-%D9%88%D8%A7%D9%84%D8%B3%D9%81%D8%A7%D8%B1%D8%A9-%D8%AA%D8%B1%D8%AF.
60 El Taki, Karim, and Hind Al Ansri. "The Arab Gulf and Israel's war on Gaza." Carnegie Endowment for International Peace. https://carnegieendowment.org/sada/91002.
61 "Arrests reported in Bahrain, the UAE, and Saudi Arabia over pro-Gaza rallies." Euro-Med Human Rights Monitor. https://euromedmonitor.org/en/article/5976/Arrests-reported-in-Bahrain,-the-UAE,-and-Saudi-Arabia-over-pro-Gaza-rallies.
62 Human Rights Watch, "Bahrain: repression of Pro-Palestine protests."
63 Zayadin, Hiba. "The persecution of Ahmed Mansoor." Human Rights Watch, January 27, 2021. https://www.hrw.org/report/2021/01/27/persecution-ahmed-mansoor/how-united-arab-emirates-silenced-its-most-famous-human.
64 "Series of arrests in Saudi Arabia, Bahrain, UAE targeting pro-Palestinian gatherings." Shia Waves English. https://www.youtube.com/watch?v=Wx_4p7i2Px4.

65 Ibid.
66 "The Abraham Accords: unlocking sustainable and inclusive growth across the Middle East." UAE Embassy in Washington, DC. https://www.uae-embassy.org/abraham-accords-sustainable-inclusive-growth.
67 "Bahrain signed normalization agreement without learning details." Bahrain Mirror. http://bahrainmirror.com/en/en/news/58574.html.
68 Doha Institute. "Arab public opinion about the Israeli war on Gaza."
69 "24 organizations call on Bahrain gov't to expel 'Zionist Enemy's' ambassador, end normalization agreement." Bahrain Mirror, May 13. 2021. http://bahrainmirror.com/en/news/59636.html.
70 "Hashtag 'Khaleejiyun 'id tatbi'i' yatasaddar trend al-dawal al-'arabiyyah." Al Mayadeen News, August 15, 2020. https://www.youtube.com/watch?v=ghosJuWi3CA.
71 For an example of a Tweet using #Saudis_Against_Normalization from 2020, see https://twitter.com/5Jz13jg3oMQBTRS/status/1294224075217395713?ref_src=twsrc%5Etfw%7Ctwcamp%5Etweetembed%7Ctwterm%5E1294224075217395713%7Ctwgr%5E24c291e41c8080f6e5c1aa5c8e148d3ae6305f0d%7Ctwcon%5Es1_&ref_url=https%3A%2F%2Farabic.euronews.com%2F2020%2F08%2F14%2Fanti-normalization-hashtags-top-twitter-arab-world-gulf-countries-anti-erdogan-also.
72 Al-Jazeera. "'Qim 'abir lil-hudud.' itihamat lil-Su'udiyyah bimulaqat muwatiniha bil-kharij wa 'al-safara' tard." August 14, 2020. https://www.aljazeera.net/politics/2020/8/14/%d8%a8%d9%8a%d9%86-%d8%a5%d9%85%d9%84%d8%a7%d8%a1%d8%aa-%d8%a3%d9%85%d9%8a%d8%b1%d9%83%d9%8a%d8%a9-%d9%88%d8%b1%d8%ba%d8%a8%d8%a9-%d9%81%d9%8a%d9%84%d8%b3%d9%84%d8%a7%d9%85.
73 Sharp, Jeremy. "The United Arab Emirates (UAE): issues for US policy." Congressional Research Service, September 13, 2023.
74 Freedom House, "United Arab Emirates."
75 "Exclusive: ex-NSA cyberspies."
76 Freedom House, "United Arab Emirates."
77 "Bayan mushtarik min nashatat imaratiyyin 'id tatbi'iyya hakumat al-Imarat ma'a al-'adu al-Sahyooni." August 18, 2020. https://bdsmovement.net/ar/news/%D8%A8%D9%8A%D8%A7%D9%86-%D9%85%D8%B4%D8%AA%D8%B1%D9%83-%D9%85%D9%86-%D9%86%D8%B4%D8%B7%D8%A7%D8%A1-%D8%A5%D9%85%D8%A7%D8%B1%D8%A7%D8%AA%D9%8A%D9%8A%D9%86-%D8%B6%D8%AF-%D8%AA%D8%B7%D8%A8%D9%8A%D8%B9-%D8%AD%D9%83%D9%88%D9%85%D8%A9-%D8%A7%D9%84%D8%A5%D9%85%D8%A7%D8%B1%D8%A7%D8%AA-%D9%85%D8%B9-%D8%A7%D9%84%D8%B9%D8%AF%D9%88-%D8%A7%D9%84%D8%B5%D9%87%D9%8A%D9%88%D9%86%D9%8A
78 "Imaratiyun 'id tatbi'iyya." Al-Khaleej al-Jadid, August 26, 2020. https://www.youtube.com/watch?v=kigay1_1gB8
79 Ghubash, Rafia. https://twitter.com/drRafeah. X (formerly Twitter).
80 Abdullah, Abdulkhalek. https://twitter.com/Abdulkhaleq_UAE. X (formerly Twitter).
81 Landau, Noa. "Ninety percent of Arabic social media chatter about Israel–Gulf deals negative, report finds." Haaretz, October 12, 2020. https://www.haaretz.

com/israel-news/2020-10-12/ty-article/.premium/report-90-percent-of-arabic-social-media-chatter-about-israel-gulf-deals-negative/0000017f-efee-d223-a97f-efffd1850000.

82 al-Surub, Yughrid Kharij. "Mas'ul imarati yufjir al-ghadab wayubirr mani' al-Imarat litadhahurat da'm Ghazzah (Video)." Watan, October 30, 2023. https://www.watanserb.com/2023/10/30/%D9%85%D8%B3%D8%A4%D9%88%D9%84-%D8%A5%D9%85%D8%A7%D8%B1%D8%A7%D8%AA%D9%8A-%D9%8A%D8%A8%D8%B1%D8%B1-%D9%85%D9%86%D8%B9-%D8%A7%D9%84%D8%A5%D9%85%D8%A7%D8%B1%D8%A7%D8%AA-%D9%84%D8%AA%D8%B8%D8%A7%D9%87/

83 Goodman, Amy. "COP28 activists defy UAE protest restrictions to demand ceasefire in Gaza." Truthout, December 4, 2023. https://truthout.org/video/cop28-activists-defy-uae-protest-restrictions-to-demand-ceasefire-in-gaza/.

84 Human Rights Watch. "UAE: mass surveillance threatens rights, COP28 outcome." November 30, 2023. https://www.hrw.org/news/2023/11/30/uae-mass-surveillance-threatens-rights-cop28-outcome.

85 Landau, "Ninety percent of Arabic social media chatter."

86 Ibid.

87 Zalayat, Ilan, and Yoel Guzansky. "Three years to the Israel-Bahrain normalization: the forgotten peace." *INSS,* August 31, 2023. https://www.inss.org.il/publication/israel-bahrain-3/.

88 Human Rights Watch. "Bahrain: repression of pro-Palestine Protests."

89 "Grandson of Bahrain's top Shia cleric arrested over Gaza protest." Middle East Eye, November 3, 2023. https://www.middleeasteye.net/live-update/grandson-bahrains-top-shia-cleric-arrested-over-gaza-protest.

90 "Pro-Palestine Bahrainis arrested, UAE must release prisoners on COP28 eve." Voice of Bahrain (blog), November 29, 2023. https://vob.org/en/?p=11793.

91 Freedom House. "Bahrain: Freedom on the Net 2022 Country Report." https://freedomhouse.org/country/bahrain/freedom-net/2022.

92 Ibid.

93 According to a 2023 poll conducted in August 2023, even in the absence of a formal agreement, a significant minority of Saudi society is favorably disposed toward business ties with Israel. Around a third say that when it comes to "some initial steps short of official relations," they would approve of "cooperat[ing] with Israeli technology companies on things like climate change, cybersecurity, and water resource management." That proportion is slightly higher (33%) among Saudi adults under 30 than among their elders (28%). Overall, this represents a slight decline (possibly due to the current Israeli government's hard-right tilt) compared with responses to very similar questions over the past three years, where the level of acceptance of allowing "business ties" with Israel approached 40%. Pollock, David. "A third of Saudis want business with Israel now, even without formal ties; 'Muslim rights' top list of public's terms for full normalization." Fikra Forum, September 18, 2023. https://www.washingtoninstitute.org/policy-analysis/third-saudis-want-business-israel-now-even-without-formal-ties-muslim-rights-top.

94 Farouk, Yasmine. "What would happen if Israel and Saudi Arabia established official relations?" Carnegie Endowment for International Peace, October 15, 2020. https://carnegieendowment.org/2020/10/15/what-would-happen-if-israel-and-saudi-arabia-established-official-relations-pub-82964.

95   Felesteen. "#Sa'udiyun 'id tatbi'I … al-wajh al-'akhir lilsa'udiyin min (Isra'il)." November 29, 2017. https://felesteen.news/post/17941/; "Arab public opinion about the Israeli war on Gaza."
96   Felesteen, "#Sa'udiyun 'id tatbi'I."
97   Landau, "Ninety percent of Arabic social media chatter."
98   Aldohan, Majid. "How Saudis express their problems." Raseef22, October 4, 2016. https://raseef22.net/english/article/1067401-saudis-express-problems.
99   Younes, Ali. "Dozens of Palestinians face 'terrorism court' in Saudi Arabia." Al Jazeera, March 9, 2020. https://www.aljazeera.com/news/2020/3/9/dozens-of-palestinians-face-terrorism-court-in-saudi-arabia.
100 Human Rights Watch. "Saudi Arabia: abuses taint mass terrorism trial." April 17, 2020. https://www.hrw.org/news/2020/04/17/saudi-arabia-abuses-taint-mass-terrorism-trial.
101 Saudi Leaks. "Al-Su'udiyya tanfi waqf al-tatbi'i ma'a Isra'il ba'd harb Ghazzah." October 21, 2023. https://saudileaks.org/%D8%A8%D8%B9%D8%AF-%D8%AD%D8%B1%D8%A8-%D8%BA%D8%B2%D8%A9/
102 "Mashaikh al-Saudiyyah yarfa'una sha'ara la ara la asma' la atakallam fi al-harb 'ala Ghazzah." Zatmasr. https://www.youtube.com/watch?v=KJxrtSK02qY.
103 "Khutbat al-Jum'a fi al-Haramayn al-Shareefayn tudu'u li Ghazzah wa tandud bi 'Zulm al-Sahayinah'." https://www.aa.com.tr/ar/%D8%A7%D9%84%D8%AF%D9%88%D9%84-%D8%A7%D9%84%D8%B9%D8%B1%D8%A8%D9%8A%D8%A9/%D8%AE%D8%B7%D8%A8%D8%A9-%D8%A7%D9%84%D8%AC%D9%85%D8%B9%D8%A9-%D9%81%D9%8A-%D8%A7%D9%84%D8%AD%D8%B1%D9%85%D9%8A%D9%86-%D8%A7%D9%84%D8%B4%D8%B1%D9%8A%D9%81%D9%8A%D9%86-%D8%AA%D8%AF%D8%B9%D9%88-%D9%84%D8%BA%D8%B2%D8%A9-%D9%88%D8%AA%D9%86%D8%AF%D8%AF-%D8%A8%D9%80%D8%B8%D9%84%D9%85-%D8%A7%D9%84%D8%B5%D9%87%D8%A7%D9%8A%D9%86%D8%A9/3077349
104 Freedom House, "Saudi Arabia."
105 El Taki and Al Ansri, "Arab Gulf and Israel's war on Gaza."
106 "Qa'imah al-'aar.Xlsx." https://docs.google.com/spreadsheets/d/1QRVFKxv4pyl60__oiSI1z6Cqyptf-_m2/edit?pli=1&usp=embed_facebook.
107 al-Surub, Yughrid Kharij. "Ma al-sir wara'a an mu'adhamehum min al-Saudiyya? … 'Qa'imah al-'aar' bi asma' al-mutasahhineen al-'Arab." Watan. https://www.watanserb.com/2023/12/08/%D9%85%D8%A7-%D8%A7%D9%84%D8%B3%D8%B1-%D9%88%D8%B1%D8%A7%D8%A1-%D8%A3%D9%86-%D9%85%D8%B9%D8%B8%D9%85%D9%87%D9%85-%D9%85%D9%86-%D8%A7%D9%84%D8%B3%D8%B9%D9%88%D8%AF%D9%8A%D8%A9%D8%9F-%D9%82%D8%A7/
108 Safi, Khaled. https://twitter.com/KhaledSafi/status/1732619273330155594. X (formerly Twitter).
109 Faozi, Ahmed. https://twitter.com/AFYemeni/status/1733935237564952912. X (formerly Twitter).
110 Ala'nnani, Khalil. "Tafkeek 'Al-Sihyooniya Al-Arabiyya.'" Al Jazeera, November 26, 2023. https://www.aljazeera.net/opinions/2023/11/26/%D8%AA%D9%81%D9%83%D9%8A%D9%83-%D8%A7%D9%84%D8%B5%D9%87%D9%8A%D9%88%D9%86%D9%8A%D8%A9-%D8%A7%D9%84%D8%B9%D8%B1%D8%A8%D9%8A%D8%A9

111 "Israel's renewed affair with Oman." Jerusalem Post, November 8, 2018. https://www.jpost.com/opinion/israels-renewed-affair-with-oman-571410.
112 Arabi 21. "Tawasul intiqadat al-nashatat li-istiqbal Musqat li-Binyamin Netanyahu." October 27, 2018. https://arabi21.com/story/1132958/%D8%AA%D9%88%D8%A7%D8%B5%D9%84-%D8%A7%D9%86%D8%AA%D9%82%D8%A7%D8%AF%D8%A7%D8%AA-%D8%A7%D9%84%D9%86%D8%B4%D8%A7%D7%D8%A1-%D9%84%D8%A7%D8%B3%D8%AA%D9%82%D8%A8%D8%A7%D9%84-%D9%85%D8%B3%D9%82%D8%B7-%D9%84%D8%A8%D9%86%D9%8A%D8%A7%D9%85%D9%8A%D9%86-%D9%86%D8%AA%D9%86%D9%8A%D8%A7%D9%87%D9%88; Arab 48. "'Al-'Aar yamshi 'aari'an': tansil sha'abi 'umani min ziaraat Netanyahu." October 27, 2018. https://www.arab48.com/mediya/mediya/2018/10/27/-al-aar-yamshi-aari-an--tansil-sha-abi-umani-min-ziaraat-netanyahu.
113 "Israel's Netanyahu meets Sultan Qaboos in surprise Oman trip." Al Jazeera, October 26, 2018. http://www.aljazeera.com/news/2018/10/26/israels-netanyahu-meets-sultan-qaboos-in-surprise-oman-trip.
114 Freedom House. "Oman: Freedom in the World 2022 Country Report." https://freedomhouse.org/country/oman/freedom-world/2022.
115 IFEX. "Two Omani internet activists arrested due to their pro-Palestinian writings." November 8, 2018. https://ifex.org/two-omani-internet-activists-arrested-due-to-their-pro-palestinian-writings/.
116 "Badr Al-Busaidi: Nansaq ma'a Riyadh fi qadaya al-mintaqa wa lan nakun thalith dawlat khaleejia tatba' ma'a Isra'il." Aawsat. https://aawsat.com/node/307175.
117 Albusaidi, Badr. "The use of the veto at Security Council is a shameful insult to humanitarian norms …" X (formerly Twitter), December 9, 2023. https://twitter.com/badralbusaidi/status/1733374636513964348
118 Al Khalili, Ahmed. X (formerly Twitter). https://twitter.com/AhmedHAlKhalili.
119 Ibid.
120 Hamzawy, Amr. "Pay attention to the Arab public response to the Israel-Hamas war." Carnegie Endowment for International Peace, November 1, 2023. https://carnegieendowment.org/2023/11/01/pay-attention-to-arab-public-response-to-israel-hamas-war-pub-90893.

Conclusion: Rules, Dissent, and National Security

1 "Ford's 50th anniversary show was milestone of '50s culture." Palm Beach Daily News. December 26, 1993. https://www.newspapers.com/article/palm-beach-daily-news-fords-50th-annive/59934494/
2 Eisenhower, Dwight. "Address at the Columbia University National Bicentennial Dinner, New York City." May 31, 1954. The American Presidency Project. https://www.presidency.ucsb.edu/documents/address-the-columbia-university-national-bicentennial-dinner-new-york-city.
3 Hellyer, H.A. "How Joe Biden sabotaged the rules-based order." Foreign Policy, May 10, 2024. https://foreignpolicy.com/2024/05/10/biden-israel-gaza-arms-rules-based-order/.

4   Hall, Richard. "State Department sees unprecedented flood of internal dissent memos over Gaza war." Independent, April 8, 2024. https://www.independent.co.uk/news/world/americas/us-politics/state-department-gaza-blinken-protest-b2525345.html.
5   Wong, Edward, and Matina Stevis-Gridneff. "Over 800 officials in US and Europe sign letter protesting Israeli policies." New York Times, February 2, 2024. https://www.nytimes.com/2024/02/02/us/politics/protest-letter-israel-gaza.html.
6   Birnbaum, Michael, and John Hudson. "Blinken confronts State Dept. dissent over Biden's Gaza policy." Washington Post, November 13, 2023. https://www.washingtonpost.com/national-security/2023/11/13/dissent-cables-gaza-policy/.
7   Gramer, Robbie. "The storm of dissent brewing in the State Department." Foreign Policy, November 1, 2023. https://foreignpolicy.com/2023/11/01/israel-hamas-war-state-department-internal-dissent-biden-policy/.
8   Birnbaum and Hudson. "Blinken confronts State Dept. dissent."
9   Gramer, "Storm of dissent."
10 Lee, M.J. "US offers assurances to Israel this week in the event of full-blown war with Hezbollah." CNN, June 21, 2024. https://edition.cnn.com/2024/06/21/politics/us-israel-hezbollah-assurances?cid=ios_app.

Acknowledgements

1   Hassan, Zaha, Daniel Levy et al. "Breaking the Israel-Palestine status quo: a rights-based approach." Carnegie Europe. https://carnegieendowment.org/projects/breaking-the-israel-palestine-status-quo-a-rights-based-approach?lang=en&center=europe.
2   Human Rights Watch. "A threshold crossed: Israeli authorities and the crime of authority." April 27, 2021. https://www.hrw.org/report/2021/04/27/threshold-crossed/israeli-authorities-and-crimes-apartheid-and-persecution.

www.ingramcontent.com/pod-product-compliance
Lightning Source LLC
Chambersburg PA
CBHW051935290426
44110CB00015B/1983